Peace Psychology Book Series

Series editor
Daniel J. Christie

For further volumes:
http://www.springer.com/series/7298

Jay Rothman
Editor

From Identity-Based Conflict to Identity-Based Cooperation

The ARIA Approach in Theory and Practice

 Springer

Editor
Jay Rothman
Program on Conflict Resolution and Negotiation
Bar-Ilan University
Ramat Gan
Israel

ISBN 978-1-4614-3678-2 (Hardcover)   ISBN 978-1-4614-3679-9 (eBook)
ISBN 978-1-4939-0920-9 (Softcover)
DOI 10.1007/978-1-4614-3679-9
Springer New York Heidelberg Dordrecht London

Library of Congress Control Number: 2012947398

Springer is part of Springer Science+Business Media (www.springer.com)

Preface

Imagine a world in which everyone could take the perspective of everyone else. Of course agreeing with each other about everything is neither possible nor ideal. But being able to understand, at least to some extent, what each other thinks, feels, and believes about something, and why, is the foundation of a world without war. However, agreeing with each other about everything always is not the root of peace. Rather, learning to live with our differences, and deeply hear and understand them, is.

> A successful work of art is not one which resolves contradictions in a spurious harmony, but one which expresses the idea of harmony negatively by embodying the contradictions, pure and uncompromised, in its innermost structure.
>
> Theodore Adorno (1967, p. 32).

My expertise is in group-based cooperation (at home and abroad), which mines the passions of dissonance and resonance (in identities, priorities, goals, styles, etc...) as a resource for dynamism, learning, and excellence. I root my work in musical metaphors (producing an aria, engaging in solos, duets, conducting interventions, moving through dissonance and fostering resonance, etc.). In my book *Resolving Identity-Based Conflict* (1997), I describe my method with the aid of a story about a string quartet that moves, with the help of a coach, from Antagonism to Resonance and on into Invention and Action (i.e., A.R.I.A.).

I have made music and engaged with musicians all my life. My primary passion in life is creativity. It may seem paradoxical that the main focus of my chosen work, or the work that seems to have chosen me, is conflict. And yet, creativity emerges directly out of friction. So the paradox is actually only superficial. At the deepest level conflict and creativity are interdependent. Nothing is created without some kind of friction. Think of a bow over a stringed instrument. Think of conflict that leads to exploration, perspective taking, imagination, and new discovery. The underlying theme of this book is that conflicts can become a source of creativity.

Back to the dream then: a world in which people deeply understand the perspective of each other. As I was completing this book, a good friend, decision-making researcher Gary Klein, told me about a family tradition that summarizes this ideal of skillful perspective-taking. When his daughters were growing up they developed a discussion rule that when his family got into a vociferous argument at the dinner table anyone, the adversaries or the observers, could call "switch!" and each side would have to take the other side's argument until everyone was satisfied that they were heard and understood.

The argument could then pick up again as a dialogue for learning instead of a diatribe for convincing.

One of the organizing experiences of my career was like this. As part of my dissertation action-research project I convened small groups of Israeli Arabs and Jews to engage in dialogue about inter-communal conflict and creative problem solving (1988). During one workshop at the Tantur Institute, a beautiful retreat center located just between Jerusalem and Bethlehem owned by the Vatican, Mohammed arrived late and out of breath.

> "I almost didn't make it," he exclaimed. "In fact, I just about turned around and went home."
>
> "Why," I asked in a way both gentle and urgent which, as will be seen, is the core process this book describes enroute to a world of skillful perspective-takers.
>
> "Because as I was sitting on a bus, a little Jewish girl, not more than 8 years old, looked at me and from me to the horrible sign on the bus reminding passengers of the danger of package bombs, "beware of suspicious objects," and with widening eyes exclaimed as she jumped up to join her mother and little sister in a different seat, Aravi! Aravi! (Arab, Arab).

Mohammed paused. One of the Jewish participants was about to fill the silence; I stopped her (another core tool for allowing perspective-taking–blocking argumentation or point scoring, which I sensed she was about to do as was confirmed a few minutes later).

> "How did this make you feel, Mohammed?" I asked.
>
> "Like this seminar on conflict resolution is too little and too late. That it should be for 8-year-old children. It is impossible that if a child of eight already fears and hates me and views me as a suspicious object that peace could ever come to this land. So we are fooling ourselves. And worse, we are not focusing on what we need to do: strengthen our own cause against injustice."

Not able to contain herself anymore, and I not stopping her this time, Orit explodes:

> "This doesn't make any sense. Of course this is why we are here! Maybe we can't change all children whose parents have ugly views. Maybe we can't replace all fear with hope or make injustice go away. But maybe we can learn more about how to solve our problems with each other. And we are the future as much as that 8 year old is."
>
> "Mohammed looked at her, shook his head and angrily said, "You don't understand how it feels to be in my situation…"
>
> "No," said Orit derisively, "and I wouldn't want to. You have it all wrong. And it makes me wonder too if being here makes any sense…"

Despite this intense beginning, or perhaps, in part, at least due to it, the workshop unfolded with a dynamism and energy that inspired and motivated my work over the next quarter of a century with antagonists from hot-spots around the world locked in deep battles, who were at least initially unable to hear or understand each other's perspectives.

What I learned from this first moment is that stories of pain, blame, and antagonism can provide a creative friction. When guided carefully this antagonism focuses the mind and, like art, renders a kind of intensification of life to bring one's senses and intellect into a state of wakefulness. And yet, this energy is so often squandered as lines are drawn and creativity is used to resist or undermine, instead of to join and cooperate.

The story took another negative turn the next morning when upon arriving in our seminar room, we saw the following curse:

Zionists out of Falastin. If you do not leave we will kill you!

We were all speechless. My colleague Amal and I tried to make a joke, pointing to each other and claiming the other had written it. No one laughed. We called in the director of the institute, the world-famous Quaker peace-maker Landrum Bolling. He was very flustered and apologetic.

Orit, the girl who had rejected Mohammed's story as nonsense, had one of her own now.

"I don't think I can stay anymore." She exclaimed now herself wide-eyed and despairing. "If here in this 'protected environment' we are hated and hunted, then maybe Mohammed was right. Maybe it's futile and worse, foolish."

"Mohammed looked at her and said quietly", "Now I think you do really under-stand what I was saying…But please, Orit, stay."

She did. And there was more!

In the early afternoon we "tested" to see if perspective had been taken. We asked for volunteers from each side to switch and speak in first person as if they were the other side about the deep needs and values that conditioned the other side's perspective, hopes, and fears. Mohammed volunteered.

"As an Israeli Jew," he began, "I feel that…" and on he went. When he finished, the Jews stood up and applauded.

Orit said quietly, "Mohammed, will you be our Ambassador at the United Nations?"

This in its most simple and basic sense is what my work and this book are about: helping people locked in deep conflict take each other's perspective and then cooperate in designing ways to create new futures that will serve the needs and vitality of each of them individually and collectively.

This edited book gathers advances in efforts to understand and creatively engage identity-based conflict and forge cooperation out of it. Such conflict is the deepest and often most destructive form of conflict. Thus creative engagement of it is pressing. This book takes up this challenge by describing various approaches to identity conflict, which, while eclectic, share a com-mon conceptual and applied framework called ARIA.

This process for moving Antagonists into Resonance and from there into creative Invention and Action has been studied and applied by each author in this book. Some have been working on these ideas and practices for the past year as part of a graduate seminar, some for a few years (e.g., as part of an Israeli-Palestinian initiative called "Kumi"), some for as much as several decades. This wide range of experience is a strength of this book as the new directions and ideas shared provide guidance and invitation to those who will build even newer directions and adaptations to follow. This is the excitement of this project. It builds on a solid theoretical and applied foundation and with hope that others will take up the task of ownership and creativity as well.

Each chapter is organized around "peace stories" about the theories and efforts of the authors to creatively engage identity-based conflict at different levels of social organization (from interpersonal to international) and from many conflicts in regions around the world (from the Mideast to the Midwest), from Eastern Europe to Africa and South America). Each case study is presented within the context of cutting-edge theories and methods of conflict and collaboration within and between groups facing deep identity-based conflict around the globe. This volume weaves together existing and newer conceptual and applied tools for creative conflict engagement among individuals and groups facing deep identity-based divisions.

This book is for students and scholars of conflict theory *and* practice with a major goal of further helping to bridge this unhelpful divide. In addition to chapters on theory and applications of ARIA, this book also presents references for practical application for the interest and use of educators and practitioners.

Overview of the Purpose and Plan of the Book

Identity-based conflict is arguably the most important and challenging problem of our increasingly global world in which similarities and interdependencies across groups and nations compete against polarizing differences and antagonisms. It is a race between confrontation and cooperation (Rothman 1992, 2012). Which will prevail? Or more to the point, what are experiences and methods for transforming such antagonisms into shared purposes and joints efforts?

Building on its fullest rendering in *Resolving Identity-Based Conflict: In Nations, Organizations and Communities* (1997), ARIA has evolved in two directions. Its initial focus on identity-based conflict began with my dissertation work to adapt the problem solving workshop approach to International Conflict Resolution for engaging ethnic groups in reflexive dialogue about their conflicts and prospects for cooperation (Burton 1990; Azar 1990; Azar and Burton 1986; Kelman 1993; Rothman 1988, 1989, 1992, 2012). In this form, it has been used and adapted for dealing with deep identity-driven conflicts at every level of social organization from interpersonal to international in hundreds of settings around the world.

Identity-based conflicts are essentially past-oriented. They are rooted in personal traumas and collective indignities born of the past that are engines of current confrontations. ARIA gives the past its due – not seeking to wall it off or even get beyond it – while helping parties discover ways to build on its ruins and glories and foster more constructive futures together. While rooted in the past, identity-based conflicts are also much more than this. They occur when individuals' needs, often in a collective context, are threatened or frustrated. Such conflicts are passionate because they are about core concerns. The heart of the matter of identity-based conflict *is* the heart of the matter.

To deal more directly with building new futures, a second set of ARIA processes have evolved for collaborative visioning. This type of ARIA retains a focus on *resonance* – through participants' narratives about their goals and passions – but it is more action and future-oriented. Its focus is on visions and goals for the future, though it too can be rooted in the past, albeit a more ideal, often mythological past. As Anthony Smith writes in his theory of the "Myth of Origins and Descent," all national groups have a story that includes a golden past that has been lost and which groups aspire to regain (Smith 1981). When such aspiration is blocked, identity-based conflict often occurs. When it is sought or achieved, *identity-based cooperation* can be in play.

The main conceptual switch between the two frameworks is summarized in the first letter *A*. In the first, *Antagonism* about the past is safely surfaced and engaged. In the second, *Aspiration* for the future is articulated by individuals and their groups and, ideally, instituted in the systems they constitute.

Part One: Conflict Engagement

The major idea of this book shared in stories, illustrated in action, and boiled down to useful tools is that conflict is best engaged. Sometimes it should be avoided; sometimes it should be overcome. But most of the time it should be engaged as an opportunity for learning: about oneself, about others, and about the interrelationships between self and others. Simple in concept, this work is very difficult in deed. Few and far between are the schools that teach tots to engage in conflicts. Instead, they tell them more often than not to "stop, duck, and roll." In other words, be afraid of conflict, avoid it if possible, and dispense with it if necessary; but most of all view it with a wary and defensive eye. In short, biologically conditioned fight or flight responses to conflict are culturally perpetuated.

Conflict engagement as we describe, advocate and illustrate it is a prelude to a song. At its highest form, which we also illustrate in this book, it is also a song itself. The music of conflict is creativity, imagination, possibility, and learning. It is perhaps a cliché that the deepest learning takes place out of adversity. No doubt, conflict is a form of adversity. However, as we suggest, illustrate, and share in this book, well-engaged conflict can be fascinating. Benjamin Zander, a conductor who teaches life through music and music through life advises the following: when you are confronted with a dilemma that stops you in your tracks, lift your arms skywards and exclaim: "how fascinating!" (2006).

Indeed, the ability to view a conflict as a possibility, and a fascinating one at that, is the first step in creatively engaging and fulfilling that possibility. This is also a profound switch for most of us.

Part Two: Collaborative Planning

The second half of this book, growing quite literally out of the work presented in the first half, is about how *to help good people do good work together better.*

While this book originally was to be called "Handbook on Identity-Based Conflict," I rediscovered that most essentially this work is about what I am now calling "Identity-Based Cooperation." The reason I have made my career in the former, as I've mentioned already, is my passion for creativity: that out of the friction of difference, creativity can emerge. So too, out of identity-based conflict, identity-based cooperation can be born.

If the former is the deepest type of conflict, as we suggest in the first half of this book, requiring its own unique analyses and processes, then it would seem the same is true of this form of identity-based cooperation. It is the deepest and most complex kind of cooperation.

Individually, when I am able to be "resonant" about what I want (e.g., my needs, values, priorities, aspirations) and why these are so important to me, it is the start of my ability to connect with you. If you can do the same, our connection grows even deeper. But even if I have done this work alone and you have not, I can change the dynamics of our interactions. As will be discussed in the first section of this book, the deeper the conflict, the more people are called to be clear about why it is important to them: to move away from the blame-game, the attributions and projections and accept ownership and agency over their problems. What is this conflict for? Why has it shown up in my life? In an age when individuals are increasingly being challenged to cooperate and collaborate with others, the deeper the cooperation, or the more the need for it, the more people must encounter themselves enroute to the other.

Collectively, it is the same. When groups seek to cooperate with each other across their boundaries, to create a shared "nexus" that is bigger than each of them, going "inward" helps condition and deepen external linkages. As in conflict, the more each side does their "solo" work first – who are we as a group and what do we seek and why is it important to us? – the more they can join another group in deep cooperation. This separate step is often resisted. Many times people will say that since they have come to cooperate with the other group, they find the request to first work in their own side uncomfortable. Sometimes we give in. But when we insist and they agree, we find it was worth the effort. While our natural inclination is to seek to join others as soon as possible, and to get beyond the barriers and boundaries we find between ourselves and others, in reality, we must indeed and first of all do the best we can to "our own selves be true."

Groups that seek to cooperate with each other often fail. This is not due to intention, but rather to the reality that different groups bring with them different cultures, goals, priorities, and values. When these are articulated internally among members of a group and then brought forward to another group, resonance is often close at hand. When this step of developing internal alignment is skipped, all too often groups find themselves at loggerheads with each other. Think of the many experiences you have had in which groups that seem to share the same purposes, quickly found themselves disappointed and enmeshed in disagreements. No doubt, the craft of cooperation is as demanding as the art of conflict engagement (Ross and Rothman 1999). We offer this book to provide insight and tools for creatively improving the theory and practice of both.

References

Adorno, T. (1967). *Prisms*. London: Neville Spearman.
Azar, E. (1990). *The management of protracted social conflict: Theory and cases*. Vermont: Dartmouth.

Azar. E., & Burton, J. (Eds.) (1986). *International conflict resolution: Theory and practice*. Boulder: Lynne Reiner Pub.

Burton, J., (Ed.) (1990). *Conflict: Human needs theory*. New York: St. Martin's Press

Kelman, H. (1983). Coalitions across conflict lines: The interplay of conflicts within and between the Israeli and Palestinian communities. In S. Worchel, & J. Simpson (Eds.), *Conflict between people and groups*. Chicago: Nelson-Hall.

Ross, M., & Rothman, J. (1999). *Theory and practice in ethnic conflict management: Conceptualizing success and failure*. London: Macmillan Press.

Rothman, J. (republished 2012). *From confrontation to cooperation: Resolving ethnic and regional conflict, Yellow Springs*, Ohio: ARIA Publications/Kindle Books.

Rothman, J. (1992). *From confrontation to cooperation: Resolving ethnic and regional conflict*. Newbury Park: Sage.

Rothman, J.(1997). *Resolving identity-based conflict in nations, organizations and communities*, San Francisco: Jossey-Bass/Wiley.

Rothman, J. (1989). Supplementing tradition: A theoretical and practical typology for international conflict management. *Negotiation Journal*.

Rothman, J. (1988). Analyses and strategies for peace: A methodology for international conflict management training and evaluation (a case study with Arabs and Jews in Israel), Ph.D. dissertation, Ann Arbor; UMI.

Smith, A. (1981). *The ethnic revival in the modern world*. New York: Cambridge University Press.

Zander, B. (2002). *The art of possibility: Transforming personal and professional life*. New York: Penguin.

Acknowledgements and Dedication

I owe a debt of gratitude for the completion of this book to many people: first of all to Dean Lawrence Johnson of the College of Education, Criminal Justice and Human Services (CECH) at the University of Cincinnati. Dean Johnson hired me to help redesign CECH using the collaborative visioning process described in part two of this book, with the input and active participation of the entire college faculty and staff, and to teach about my work in identity-based conflict, as described in part one of this book. It was his suggestion that I turn the writing of this book into a collaborative project by inviting promising young scholars from throughout the University to participate in a six-month research and writing seminar.

I am also grateful for financial support from Nelson Vincent, then College VP, to hire Brandon Sipes to be the indefatigable project coordinator of the book seminar (as well as co-author of Chapter 5). I am grateful to the head of the School of Human Services, Janet Graden, who sponsored this seminar and to my colleagues in the Counseling Program- Michael Brubaker, Ellen Cook, Kerry Sabera, Mei Tang, Albert Watson, Bob Wilson, Geoffrey Yager - for their encouragement and support. The students in the advanced seminar in Identity-Based Conflict and Cooperation deserve much credit for their persistence, patience and good spirits. I also want to praise and thank each non-student author in this book, most of whom also participated in the seminar as guest speakers (usually virtually). As described in their chapters, they are each helping to pave pathways to peace in our deeply troubled and yearning world. I also want to thank the Series Editor Daniel Christie and the editorial staff at Springer for making this book possible: Anna Tobias, Welmoed Spahr, Brian Helm and Rekha Udaiyar. I am also grateful to Marjorie Loyacano and Karen Ivory for their earlier editorial assistance. In addition, many colleagues have encouraged me in bringing this book to fruition. I would like to specifically thank Tamra Pearson-d'Estree, Victor Friedman, Marc Gopin, Gary Klein, Bernard Mayer, Richard McGuigan, Alexander Redlich, Marc Ross, and Bill Withers.

I am, as always, deeply thankful to my wife, Randi Land Rothman, who supported me throughout and who undertook the complete final copy editing of this book. It would not have been complete without her, as is even truer for my life. Finally, I dedicate this book to my father, Philip Rothman, who taught me, by word and example, the core value that upholds this book: to try always to say what I mean and do what I say.

Contents

About the Contributors

Daniella Arieli is a social anthropologist and lecturer with a dual appointment to the Department of Nursing Science and the Department of Sociology and Anthropology at the Max Stern Yezreel Valley College, Israel. Dr. Arieli received a B.A. in Israel studies and education from Beit Berl College, an M.A.in sociology and anthropology from Tel Aviv University, and a Ph.D. in sociology and anthropology from Hebrew University. Her research focuses on the socio-cultural aspects of health and illness and action research concerning intercultural counters.

Ahmed Badawi is an academic researcher, political analyst, and group facilitator. Dr. Badawi is a research associate at the Zentrum Moderner Orient in Berlin, and is the co-founder and co-executive director of Transform: Centre for Conflict Analysis, Political Development and World Society Research.

Donna Chrobot-Mason is an associate professor and director of the Center for Organizational Leadership at the University of Cincinnati. Dr. Chrobot-Mason is an adjunct scholar and trainer at the Center for Creative Leadership and serves on the editorial review board for the *Journal of Management* and the *Journal of Business and Psychology*. In 2010, she co-authored *Boundary spanning leadership: Six practices for solving problems, driving innovation, and transforming organizations* published by McGraw-Hill Professional.

Beth Ciaravolo is a master's student in political geography at the University of Cincinnati. Her research focuses chiefly upon the politics of identity formation in Eastern Europe and Russia.

Vaughn Crandall is the deputy director of the Center for Crime Prevention and Control at John Jay College of Criminal Justice. Vaughn is an assistant adjunct professor of public policy at New York University's Wagner Graduate School of Public Service.

John Davies is co-director of Partners in Conflict and Partners in Peace Building and Senior Associate with the Center for International Development and Conflict Management at the University of Maryland. Dr. Davies has led or participated in conflict transformation and conflict prevention initiatives in over 30 countries around the world.

Victor J. Friedman is associate professor and co-chair of the Action Research Center for Social Justice at the Max Stern Yezreel Valley College, Israel. His life's work is helping individuals, organizations, and communities learn through "action science" – theory building and testing in everyday life. Professor Friedman holds a B.A. in Middle Eastern studies from Brandeis University (1974), an M.A. in psychology from Columbia University (1981) and an Ed.D. in organizational psychology from Harvard University (1986). He has published in numerous academic journals and serves as associate editor of the Action Research Journal.

Sarah Haney is a doctoral candidate in counseling at the University of Cincinnati. She has a master's degree in mental health counseling also from the University of Cincinnati. Her current research interests include the globalization of counseling in third world countries and using community-based participatory research to build child and adolescent identity and self-esteem.

Mariska Kappmeier is a psychologist and a practitioner in the field of conflict resolution. Dr. Kappmeier's main research focus is the preparation of conflict intervention measures and trust assessment between conflict parties. She has worked as a trainer and facilitator in numerous training and conflict settings around the world, including especially Moldova and Transdniestria.

Sharon Miller is associate director at Auburn Seminary's Center for the Study of Theological Education. Dr. Miller is a sociologist by training; she has been involved with evaluation of Face to Face/Faith to Faith since its inception in 2001.

Alexander Redlich has been a researcher, practitioner, and teacher since 1976 in the Department of Psychology in the University of Hamburg. Professor Redlich is trained as a psychologist, a teacher and a social education worker. His main research interests are focused on resource-based social work, team development, human communication, and conflict work. His text, *Conflict Moderation within Groups* (1997, 2009) is published in German, Hungarian, and Russian languages.

Edward Kaufman has been the Director of the Harry S. Truman Research Institute for the Advancement of Peace at the Hebrew University of Jerusalem and the Center for International Development and Conflict Management of the University of Maryland. Dr. Kaufman is currently a Senior Research Associate in the latter. He has facilitated conflict transformation workshops in four continents focusing mainly on Latin American and Middle Eastern countries.

Evgeniya (Gina) Knyazev received her M.S. in criminal justice from the University of Cincinnati. She has a background and special interest in conflict resolution as applied to situations involving LGBT rights and women's rights, and in the psychology behind conflict resolution.

Harita Patel holds a master's in political science from the University of Cincinnati in the fields of comparative politics and international relations. Currently she is a Ph.D. student at the University of Massachusetts, Amherst.

Her research is focused on social and political development, social movements, ethnic conflict, and identity politics with a particular focus on South Asia.

Jay Rothman is a scholar and a practitioner of conflict resolution. Dr. Rothman is trained in international relations and political psychology and focuses his theoretical and applied work on issues of intergroup and organizational identity-based conflict and participatory evaluation. He is associate professor in the program on conflict resolution and negotiation at Bar-Ilan University. He is also the president of the ARIA Group, Inc. (www.ariagroup.com). He has held a number of senior academic and administrative positions in five academic institutions in the USA and in Israel. He is the author of four books, including *Resolving Identity-Based Conflict: in Nations, Organizations, and Communities*. He leads workshops and gives keynote presentations at conferences and convocations around the world.

Brandon Sipes is the president of RE-Frame, LLC, senior consultant to The ARIA Group, and co-director of the Kumi Academy, a research and learning network supporting the work of practitioners utilizing the Kumi methodology of conflict transformation. His work as a group facilitator, trainer and mediator focuses on innovative approaches to social change in the midst of conflict. His research and practice has included work in the USA, Europe, and the Middle East.

Michael Sternberg is a conflict transformation practitioner and researcher. He serves as an associate to the UK-based Responding to Conflict; he founded and directs the Conflict Transformation and Management Center (CTMC) at Shatil, the New Israel Fund's training and empowerment center for social change. Michael is also co-director of the Kumi Academy, a research and learning network supporting the work of practitioners utilizing the Kumi methodology of conflict transformation.

Michael J. Urick is an instructor of management and operations at the Alex G. McKenna School of Business, Economics, and Government at St. Vincent College in Latrobe, PA. He holds an MBA in human resource management, an MS in leadership and business ethics and is currently completing his Ph.D. in management from the University of Cincinnati. He focuses his research on organizational identity issues as well as conflict and tension, especially as they relate to generational differences.

Bill Withers holds a master's in conflict resolution from Antioch University McGregor, and is an organizational development consultant. His research focus and experience include cross-cultural and large group planning and conflict engagement at the community, organizational and public policy levels. He is the co-author of *The Conflict and Communication Activity Book*, 1993, and author of *Resolving Conflicts on the Job*, 2007.

Identity-Based Conflict Engagement

Engaging the Painful Past and Forging a Promising Future

Jay Rothman

Helping people who are in conflict "switch" and understand the perspectives of others is the core of my work. I do this through a kind of choreography in which they move from *adversarial* framing to *reflexive* reframing. Here is a simple illustration: Imagine you are in a bitter conflict with some other individual or group. In your mind's eye point your index finger like a gun at the Other. Familiar isn't it? In many conflict situations we metaphorically point our finger at those who we feel to be wrong and wholly to blame. Indeed, this adversarial approach is one of two biologically conditioned responses we have to conflict situations – fight (and blame) or flight. Hit before being hit. Strike before being struck. Or if you sense in advance that you'll lose – get out of town!

On the other hand, return to the same conflict situation you just recalled in your mind's eye. Now, while still pointing your index finger outward, slow down your reactive response and look at the other three fingers folded back to your palm. Note that they point back to your own heart. If we ask- Why does this make me so upset? What is going on with me that I want to strike out? Have I contributed anything to this situation? - we are already well on the way to taking perspective. It may seem odd that one of the best ways to take perspective of another is to look to oneself first. And yet, when we rage, the source is often internal. When we reflect, we often find new ways to heal and make connections with others.

> ...to thine own self be true,
> And it must follow, as the night the day,
> Thou canst not then be false to any [other].
> Hamlet, Act I, Sc iii

This chapter provides an overview of two variations of ARIA. The first is designed for creatively engaging *identity-based conflicts*. The second evolved out of efforts to deepen and sustain cooperation and to foster lasting *identity-based cooperation*. ARIA-CE (Conflict Engagement) was developed for engaging deep identity-based conflicts in which the painful past is surfaced, reframed and addressed through cooperative planning and action. ARIA-AE (Action Evaluation) then evolved out of the conflict focus for helping identity-groups work with each other to cooperate in defining, promoting and assessing some shared future in which agreements to reduce destructive dynamics and promote cooperation is practically consolidated through creative action.

One: ARIA Conflict Engagement

When deep conflicts are engaged and the painful past is surfaced, the starting place in a conflict engagement process is bringing out the Antagonism either analytically (What problems

J. Rothman (✉)
Program on Conflict Resolution and Negotiation,
Bar-Ilan University, Ramat Gan, Israel
e-mail: jrothman@ariagroup.com

J. Rothman (ed.), *From Identity-Based Conflict to Identity-Based Cooperation: The ARIA Approach in Theory and Practice*, Peace Psychology Book Series, DOI 10.1007/978-1-4614-3679-9_1,
© Springer Science+Business Media New York 2012

3

do we have with each other?), or more dynamically (What problems with each other must be surfaced, re-enacted and decided upon?). This dialogical process begins with framing a negative relational dynamic in terms of Us versus Them, and in seeing the Other and their behavior, as inherently blameworthy.

Such framing reflects an attributional bias in which each side sees the Other's blameworthy actions as part of their nature (Jones 1972; Sillars 1981; Donahue and Kolt 1992). *They do what they do because they are by nature faulty persons. While our side may act aggressively towards them, we do this because the situation propels us to such behavior. They, on the other hand, act aggressively because that is their character.* This attributional bias can lead to cycle of aggressive responses: if *they* are viewed by the nature of their character to be evil and aggressive, they must be stopped.

Making the adversarial frame even more self-fulfilling and difficult to escape is the use of projection, one of the most complex psychological dynamics that reinforces the adversarial view in which one's own negative traits, or "shadow sides," are thrust onto the other side as a vehicle for splitting off those unpleasant attributes from one's own self and placing them upon the other. This adversarial dynamic of polarizing, blaming, attributing and projecting leads to an outcome of expressed, or at least felt, **Antagonism**.

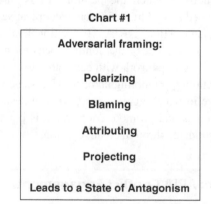

Chart #1

Adversarial framing:

Polarizing

Blaming

Attributing

Projecting

Leads to a State of Antagonism

But for peace to prevail, this adversarial and vicious cycle must be broken. To establish a new basis for cooperative action and a virtuous cycle, the next phase is a process of reflexive reframing (Stroh 2011; Rothman & Soderquist 2002). In reflexive reframing, disputants are asked to move

from an exterior focus on *them* and the blameworthy attributes of their adversaries, to an interior focus upon *oneself* and/or one's group. Disputants are invited to inquire into what is going on in a specific conflict that is so meaningful to them on a personal or group level. In other words, "Why do We/I care so much?"

Moving away from an external focus on the other and what they have done to me or us, parties are invited to explore why this situation has them so tangled and distressed. Why, we facilitators sometimes ask, are They "living rent-free in your head?" You go to bed with your anger about them and rise to its resurgence. At some point, disputants may be invited to inquire into their own *conflict agency.* That is, instead of being only victims of the other side, what have they themselves done or not done that may have contributed to the situation? This is a delicate frame change in which parties are *not* asked to shift their adversarial framing from the other side to themselves. Rather, they are invited to inquire about what conditions, memories, mistakes and so forth may have led them to do (or not do) things that could have contributed to the conflict dynamic. And just as eventually we ask them to consider the other side and their behavior with a sense of empathy, so too we suggest they be "easy" on themselves as well. If you behaved in a way that in hindsight was not the best, it is not that you are bad, rather there was something for you about the situation that led you to act that way. When adversaries begin gaining insight that this same dynamic may be at work with the other side, the switch begins.

A major goal for this reframing in terms of creative conflict engagement, is to enable parties to take a new view of themselves and eventually the other side as well through a lens of *analytic empathy* (Rothman 1997). This is a cognitive shift from attributions, blame and self-righteousness, to acceptance of universal human fallibility and situational constraints. Individuals and groups begin to understand their own actions (including inactions which, in conflict situations, are a form of action) in light of context and conditions. The point is not to provide excuses for misbehavior and adversarial attitudes. Rather, it is to expand and complexify thinking such that reductionism is replaced by a wider and deeper systems view of the situation

(Coleman 2011; Rothman & Soderquist 2002). Thus, in addition to beginning to ally with the Other, as in "we are in this together," parties can begin to think about ways that the situation, instead of the other side, may be changed. This sets the context for some joint thinking about the next stage of creative and cooperative Invention and Action planning. The reflexive reframing, taking the external situation as an opportunity to reflect internally, and taking one's internal situation as an opportunity to view the external situation differently, and more empathically, can lead disputants to begin transforming polarizing antagonism and cacophony into a sense of unifying resonance. How might parties begin to understand the negative cycle of the conflict situation that has been co-constructed and thus the possibility of co-constructing cooperation and a positive cycle? In short, how might they begin making a shift from Us versus Them to We?

Such reframing leads parties to stop blaming the other side and attributing character faults to them, and instead accept mutual responsibility and develop analytical empathy for situational experiences that both sides have had. In assisting disputants to accept that they too have acted in ugly and aggressive ways due to the situation and their experiences of loss, fear and hurt, they can begin to reduce their projective tendencies to make the other the repository of their own limitations. Once that is achieved, they can further develop the analytical empathy for the aggressive attitudes of the other ("I now understand that they attribute and project, just like I do") and accept that a period of trust building, shared planning and cooperative action must be unfolded to help deprogram such deep attitudes rooted in hurt, fear and mistrust.

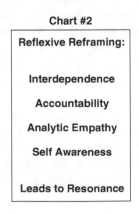

Chart #2

Reflexive Reframing:

Interdependence

Accountability

Analytic Empathy

Self Awareness

Leads to Resonance

Now the stage for creative Invention and Action has been set. This newly reflexive dynamic leads to a sequence of mutuality and interdependence, of joint accountability, self-awareness and analytical empathy. Together these building blocks shape a new resonance between adversaries and build foundations of joint action for peace.

Up to this point, this may appear to be a linear process. In practice, ARIA rarely goes in a straight line. Instead it is often quite iterative. Thus, before I complete the presentation of the full ARIA process (from *Antagonism* and *Resonance* to *Invention* and *Action*), let me take an important detour.

Movements and Variations

In a recent conversation with a group of graduate students who had been studying ARIA as part of their graduate seminar in conflict resolution, I found them surprised and relieved when I explained that ARIA is rarely practiced in a linear fashion. It is presented as such purely for ease of comprehension. Ideally, ARIA is flexible, malleable, imperfect and sometimes, frankly, even a barrier to encounter and improvisation, if taken strictly. Models are no more than reductions of reality into a language and set of images and concepts that can be shared and comprehended. The basic structure of ARIA is What (conflicts or goals), Why and How. It is enormously helpful when used to guide people to focus on the same things at the same time for common reasons in relatively the same ways. With models or frameworks or words, people can join each other as they engage and exchange in the Whats of things in commensurate ways (What is important here?), the Whys of them in compassionate ways (Why do we care?) and the Hows of things with a shared optimism for a joint future (How do we move forward together?). In the best applications, this all happens in alignment and – as much as is possible – in collaboration. However, it is important to remember that models and frameworks are no more reality than are words. They are merely a form of representation used to describe things, to help people understand each other, and to provide

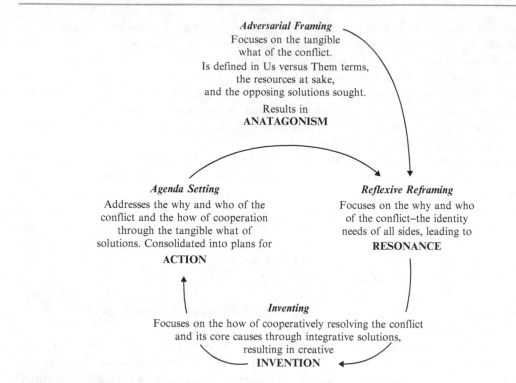

Fig. 1.1 The ARIA framework (From Rothman 1997, p. 19)

a bridge between some past and the future in a given present moment in time.

Mostly, ARIA is a cyclical and reiterative process (see Fig. 1.1) in which the simple What, Why, How pattern becomes shared as a common culture and the kind of underlying rhythm that culture provides (Cohen 1993) among a temporary or more permanent community of practice (Wenger 1998). Let me illustrate this with a current, emblematic example of identity-based conflict and how its adversarial framing could give way, iteratively, to reflexive reframing.

Antagonism and Resonance

On this morning's Hebrew news (during a summer in Jerusalem 2011), Israeli Prime Minister Netanyahu exclaimed in real or staged exasperation, " Tell Mr. Abbas it's just six words: 'Recognize Israel as a Jewish State.'" In retort, Palestinian Prime Minister Mahmoud Abbas responds, "No way!" At an identity-level, recogni-

tion would mean giving up on his Palestinian brethren who live in Israel – some 1.5 million of them. For him, a more acceptable formulation would be that Israel is "a State of All of Its Citizens" or possibly a newer formula "a State of all its National Communities." A common Israeli adversarial framing of this views Abbas' refusal to recognize Israel as a Jewish State as confirmation that he is "no partner for peace." I have heard Israeli Jews attribute, "It's simply a trick. First he gets back Yehudah and Shomron [the West Bank], what so many call an illegal occupation but which we won in a war of defense against annihilation, then East Jerusalem. Next, he and the fifth column within Israel who now call themselves 'Arab-Palestinian Citizens of Israel,' will take back the rest of what they call their 'illegally occupied homeland.' It is like a salami, slice by slice until Israel is eaten up."

An equally adversarial frame from the Palestinian side would view Netanyahu's demand as a ruse. First of all, it removes a major negotiation tool on the Palestinian side. If nothing else, *shuk* [marketplace] bargaining requires one not to give up any goods before real negotiation begins. But more importantly, at an identity level, just as the Palestinians demand that their refugees be allowed to return to their homes from which they were exiled by the establishment of the State of Israel, so they view the notion of a Jewish State as racist, exclusionary and continuing a policy of divide and conquer.

So far this adversarial framing is tit for tat and quite unidirectional: Us against Them. The artistry of ARIA is knowing when to invite the "switch" as partially described in the preface. The switch described there was about perspective: from mine to yours to ours. This switch is about frames: from Adversarial to Reflexive. At some point in an ARIA conflict engagement process the facilitator will ask in feigned innocence, "So, how are we doing? How are you feeling?" It will have been after some explosion or an air of intransigence or futility has prevailed. The common answer, shared in a chorus, will commonly be: "Horrible. This is worse than it was before we came here. Why are you doing this to us?" The response: "You are doing this to yourselves as you have been for years, decades, maybe millennia." Pause. "Want to do something different?" Again in one voice, "Yes, please, anything!"

We offer a new way forward, inviting participants to try a new way, a reflexive way of talking about themselves and their own needs and fears and hopes, in front of the Other and in the context of their shared conflict situation. We also offer a warning, "But you will fail. You have lived and framed your relationships in adversarial ways not just for the last few hours in this interaction, but for the last many years or decades or more. Switching won't be easy. In fact, you won't be able to sustain it." They demur, assuring us that they will. We persist. "Therefore, we want to invite you to ask us to maintain process control: to stop you when you go back to Antagonism." And they do.

Now the stage is set and we have already let them know that it will not be linear. We invite them to talk about themselves, "Jewish identity means to me…" and "Forging unity among our dispossessed Palestinian family means…" Yet, they will quickly point their fingers and begin

drawing on their wellspring of antagonism. We stop them with the reminder that they have agreed to try something different: a reflexive approach that is personal and relational. We ask them to share their own narratives, their own "why do I care so much?," to talk about themselves and their own needs and values in ways that may both clash and diverge as well as mesh and merge with the other. If they can do this without reverting to blame, or attribution, or polarization or projection, then we can keep moving forward.

If, despite our efforts to move them on, they cannot work together in this new way, then we may bring things to a halt and suggest that we have not finished with the adversarial stage and we may then move discussions back to Antagonism.

Here is a case in point. Several years ago I was leading a workshop for a group of Israeli and Palestinian peacemakers. After seeking and failing to discover common goals, we decided to set aside a morning to surface and engage differences and antagonism. After a few hours engaged in this difficult process of attribution, blame and polarization, the group said "enough!" I checked with each participant asking them if they wanted to move on in the fashion described above. Everyone exclaimed "Yes!" except for one Palestinian woman, who I will call "Raida." She said that she hadn't yet expressed the full depth of her hurt and anger. I invited her to say more. She did. Then the group as a whole was asked again if they were ready to move on to a discussion of their respective *resonance*. Again the group said yes, and very eagerly, as they were weary and wary about further antagonism, but Raida stood her ground. "No," she said, "I am still not really finished. However, to not block the group, I am willing to try to move in the direction you recommend." Asked if she was sure, she nodded, but with some continued reticence.

After a break, as the participants shared in narrative form their deeper concerns and inquired of each other about their respective stories, Raida continued to frame her narrative in terms of what the Israelis had done to her instead of why it so deeply mattered to her, as most of the others had been able to do. Asked if they needed to respond in kind, the Israelis said they did not. We took another break, and Raida was asked privately if she felt finished with the blaming phase now and was ready to move on to a more internal narrative discourse that could set a stage for a future-oriented discussion. She said yes firmly, and when we reconvened, she was fully in step with the rest of the group. At this point, the group moved deeply and together into resonance.[1] It doesn't mean that all was solved and that everyone agreed with each other. Rather, there was a spirit of "agonism" (Mouffe 2005), in which differences were viewed as natural, speaking about them was viewed as necessary and non-antagonistic, and moving on with them was viewed as possible and necessary.

The Power of Why

We call this process of dialogue for expressing and listening to people's deeper concerns "The Power of Why" (Friedman et al. 2006; and Chapter 2 in this volume). It can be one of the gifts of engaging conflict. This process is one in which people are asked to share in narrative form Why they care about a certain conflict; the deeper the conflict, usually the more they care. For this reason, this Why dialogue is particularly effective in identity-conflicts. It is the key question in the entire ARIA process – whether used for engaging conflict or for sustaining cooperation. In the conflict work, "Why" stories are often about pain and hurt. In visioning work they often are rooted in hope and a sense of possibility.

Ultimately story telling is about agency. What did we choose to do or not do in a certain situation? Why did we do it? Howard Ganz, in an elegant essay on Public Narrative (2008) as a transformational activity, says that narrative ultimately is about the question Why: "When we consider purposeful action, we ask ourselves two questions: why and how. Analysis helps answer the 'how question' - how do we use resources efficiently to detect opportunities, compare costs,

etc. But to answer the 'why' question – why does this matter, why do we care, why do we value one goal over another – we turn to narrative." (p. 3).

He goes on to describe the narrative process as moving through three steps. The first is the story of I. The next is the story of Us. The third is the story of Now and the actions we ought to take together.

> A story of why I have been called, a story of self; a story of why we have been called, a story of us; and a story of the urgent challenge on which we are called to act, a story of now. (p. 1)

The reflexive process at the core of the Power of Why is one in which I am linked to You (i.e. "us") by some context inviting action (i.e. "now"). Thus, when Raida insisted on sharing her Antagonism she was holding fast and true to her I. When the group resisted and sought to move on, their Us was incomplete because it excluded her. As she shared her pain and angst and anger and moved through them to some extent, she rejoined the group and they became more whole with her. Now the stage was set for them to design joint efforts to move into and foster a new future together, now. And so they did.

Narrative is also an act of integration. Neurobiologist Daniel Siegel presents a unique theory of integration that coincides perfectly with the move from Antagonism to Resonance and on to (integrative) Invention (2010). He suggests, somewhat counter-intuitively, or paradoxically, that integration is made of two parts: differentiation and linkage. Differentiation in which my I is set apart from your I. In conflict, I am mad at You. In development of identity, I am distinctive from You. And yet if group or individual identity are only formed and maintained in opposition to that of others, it is only a partial, underdeveloped identity as humans are social beings and require what Siegal calls "linkage" with each other. He says this is how the brain works in its own pursuit of integration across its own diverse parts (like left and right hemispheres). Along with healthy differentiation, we, and our brains, also require linkage in which I and You are linked through our humanity, our needs, and our stories. This approach is similar to the way in which ARIA suggests that in peacemaking conflict needs to be

---

[1] This narrative is abstracted from a fuller version published in Zartman et al. 2012.

first raised and engaged before common ground is pursued and forged.

Invention and Action

Once conflicts have been reframed and resonance is nurtured within parties and between them through narratives of Why, and linkage has begun to be found and formulated, a forward movement towards creative and integrative inventions becomes both possible and necessary. It is not enough to begin to think differently, though this is the necessary first step. For peace to prevail, for conflicts to be creatively engaged, we need to begin to act differently as well. However, not so fast.

Recall the story of the tortoise and the hare? Here's an ancient Middle Eastern rendition:

> Two people at the edge of the desert have to get to the other side. As the sun arose one pointed straight ahead and exclaimed, "If we are to make it, we must go now, we must go fast and we must go that away!" The other said, "Not so fast my friend. If we are to make it, we must consider our route carefully. I believe we must go first to the left and find an oasis to rest within. Then we will veer off in another direction where other oases have been known to be found. Eventually, we will make it."
> The first went on alone and perished in the desert. It was the "short-long" way. The other made it by going the "long-short" way. In other words, "going slow to go fast."
> (adapted from Talmud, Eruvin 53b)

Not only does a careful process of inventing take time, it also needs to continue to keep a frame change as the core focus. While much conflict resolution seeks to help people to find common ground across previously unbridgeable positions, ARIA doesn't advocate so much for that. Instead, it suggests that, in many cases, unbridgeable antagonism may remain unbridgeable. The focus of invention will be on ways to increase, enhance, and realize the resonance that has been articulated. This might include ways for each side to feel a greater sense of dignity than ever before, or more acceptance from the other, or safety, or a clearer picture about a better future. These relatively intangible needs and aspirations that have been narrated during the Resonance phase must now be converted into concrete ideas, symbolic

actions, co-designed projects and so forth. After inventions have been developed, they are assessed through a cost-benefit-analysis, or with a Lewinian force-field analysis of what will drive or restrain inventions in their movement forward (Lewin 1948). Finally, selections of inventions or some rank ordering of them will occur and parties will design a very detailed plan regarding who will do what, when, why and how.[2]

After a complete cycle of surfacing Antagonism, reframing to Resonance, fostering Inventions and planning Action has occurred, there is a kind of spiral dynamic with reiterations of Resonance (and sometimes regression back to Antagonism) and on to deeper and more complex Inventions and Actions (see Fig. 1.1). In fact, to increase the odds that the demon "GIBI" won't stop by – that is the common problem of "good ideas, bad implementation" – the second ARIA framework mentioned above was created to enhance the likelihood of good ideas and good implementation (and monitoring). This will be described shortly.

Advances in Theory and Practice

The original focus of ARIA on creatively engaging identity-based conflicts required at least in part that identity-based conflict be distinguished from other types of more "routine" conflicts. As it evolved in part to differentiate and operationalize identity-based conflict and conflict intervention, ARIA has become a broader contingency model with the type of intervention suggested dependent upon the analysis of the nature and depth of the conflict. International conflict theorist John Burton distinguished *Disputes* from *Conflicts* (1993), and I extend that distinction here by further operationalizing those terms (though somewhat differently than did Burton) and by adding a third category of *Problems*. Therefore, while ARIA's primary concern is still creatively *engaging* Identity-based *conflicts*, as a kind of byproduct of that focus, it also seeks ways to foster cooperative *management* of Goal-based *problems* and *settlement* of Resource *disputes*.

---

[2] For some more detailed and prescriptive ways to do Invention and Action Planning, see Rothman 1997 Chaps. 4 and 5.

I call this an ROI analysis (Rothman 2012). As with much of ARIA, there is a playful metaphor at work here. Just like ARIA suggests in its very name (music, song) that creativity is available within conflict, so too when we do a full analysis of conflict, understanding when conflicts are primarily about *R*esources, when they are more fully about *O*bjectives, or when most deeply they are rooted in *I*dentities, we get a "return on our investment." In short, we learn to make peace pay. Let us now look at these three levels of conflict. Envisioned as an iceberg, how do we use ARIA from the bottom up to engage conflicts over identity, goals/objectives and resources?

Identity-Based Conflicts

Identity-based conflicts, are the most emotionally-laden and difficult to engage and convert into opportunities. However, when handled effectively the creative rewards can be great. When mishandled, deeply destructive outcomes are common. One party may believe, "I deserve the corner office in recognition of my accomplishments and value to the company." The other may respond, "But I've been here twice as long as you. I've paid my dues and deserve, finally, to receive respect and appreciation for all that I have contributed." One or both may believe, rightly or not, that they are being judged by their age, sex, race, social standing, or other factors. In any case, creative inventions that go beyond the original point of contention may be needed to address the conflict in a manner that doesn't result in "winners" and "losers." Identity-based conflicts are often far beneath the surface, they can't be understood or seen empirically. In short, identity-based conflicts are about existential needs and values of individuals or groups that are threatened, frustrated or competitively pursued. The needs approach to identity-based conflict suggests that the main cause of such conflict and the reason they are often unresponsive to conventional negotiation, and even to interest based bargaining, is because they are rooted in the threat and frustration to non-negotiable basic human needs and their fulfillment. Such needs are defined differently by various negotiation, peace and conflict theorists. John Burton (1979) articulated them as irreducible collective human needs for security, predictability,

recognition, distributive justice, meaning and control. Edward Azar described them as a byproduct of political exclusion and underdevelopment (1990). Negotiation theorists Dean Pruitt and Jeffrey Rubin (1986) defined them as needs for security, identity, social approval, happiness, clarity about one's world, and physical well-being. Peace studies pioneer Johan Galtung (2004) articulated them as needs for security, freedom, welfare and identity. Anstey and Zartman define them as needs for protection, participation, power, privilege, and purpose (2012). Legal expert of minority affairs Yousef Jabareen (2008) summarized needs in to one main category, "participatory equality."

Regardless of the definition, when a conflict is primarily about Identity, Antagonism must first be surfaced so that people can bring the deep and dark conflicts they have with each other into the light so that a choice about how best to engage them can be made. Otherwise, such conflicts "work on us," and usually in detrimental ways. They often "live in our heads, rent free." We bring them to light, not so much to "vent" them out, but so that they can be analytically scrutinized and choices can be made about whether and how such conflicts can be constructively engaged. While the field calls this conflict resolution, with John Burton insisting that when needs are at stake, it is a resolution, not management process that is required, I think this is a major linguistic error that has hurt the field since its inception. In a private conversation I had with one of the fields' founders, Kenneth Boulding, I recall him ruing the day that he helped name the first journal in the field "The Journal of Conflict Resolution." He said this set up the field for a fall. In my visits to many hot-spots around the world, I have experienced many skeptics in my work who have said, "Conflict Resolution? You must be joking. Impossible!" and I have agreed with them. I do not believe the kind of deep identity-based conflicts this book addresses will ever be "resolved," that is, as long as we use the conventional meaning of "resolved" as concluded, ended, at peace, with no more antagonism but with prevailing resonance.

In the first sentence of a brilliant book, conflict theorist Peter Coleman has become enmeshed in this linguistic trap when he writes, perhaps a bit tongue in cheek though also quite seriously, that his book strives to answer the question "Why are some conflicts impossible to solve and what can we do to resolve them?" (2011). Clearly, if they are impossible to solve, we cannot do anything to resolve them! Along these lines, I recall a time when I was asked to consult to a major foundation that had invested millions of dollars in promoting conflict resolution in the Former Soviet Union after its breakup in the late 1980s. I received an urgent invitation from the program officer to convince his board that their investments had achieved a great deal. I asked him to send me descriptions and analyses of the work of a dozen of his funded projects. After reading the project reports, I told him the bad news: I fully understood his board's confusion. These projects had promised "conflict resolution" and yet the conflicts in the Former Soviet Union were on the rise. It didn't appear that any had been "resolved." And indeed the program was ended and the program officer lost his job.

I have proposed, to some effect, that this work of dealing with deep conflicts be termed "conflict engagement" and that it be modified by the adjective "creative." I say to 'some effect' since from the time I proposed this language shift in my 1997 book, the term has caught on and a number of theorists, practitioners and programs now use the term (Mayer 2009). Maybe now we can begin to recapture the skeptics (including unfortunately many in the funding community who -like the foundation mentioned above- have stopped funding the development of the "conflict resolution" field). Even more importantly the term helps us determine the focus and parameters of our work. To repeat: when we are dealing with deep conflicts, ones Coleman and others unfortunately call "Intractable" (which I believe has the opposite effect of using the term "Resolution"), but which I and others call "Intransigent" (See Ross & Rothman 1999), our job is not to resolve them. Rather it is to help disputants, leaders, policymakers, even the media find ways to help reduce the destructiveness and violence of conflict. Conflict *engagement* seeks to enhance creativity and imagination by viewing such conflicts as

opportunities for greater self-awareness and "analytical empathy" among disputants for needed social change, structural adjustment and – in many situations – increased participatory democracy.

Goal/Objective Problems

When Problems occur that are primarily about Goals or Objectives, an analysis of the reasons people care about their goals – or their Resonance – should launch the intervention process. The sources of goal problems are not as deeply rooted as identity-conflicts, but they still may require some digging to determine what they are really about. Is our example of two executives fighting for the same office space just a question of preference, or do one or both parties have some underlying reason for wanting the office? When an intervener asks the right questions to uncover these reasons, and does so proactively, differences over objectives can become a source of clarification and joint problem solving. "I want the corner office so that I can meet with clients in an aesthetically pleasing and quiet environment – and I need the space to keep my files and books at my fingertips." Or, "I want the corner office because natural light affects how well I am able to work; I get headaches from the fluorescents in my current work space." Perhaps other solutions can be found to meet those objectives, aside from the ultimate claim on the office. Objectives-based problems are commonly about contending priorities or poor communication over them. Goals, in their most elemental form, are those things we seek to accomplish or attain. Problems, most essentially, are those things that keep us from fulfilling our goals. In a widely quoted operational definition of conflict, Hocker and Wilmot (1985), suggest that *conflict is the interaction of interdependent people who perceive incompatible goals and interference from each other in achieving those goals* (see also Folger et al. 2005). Like the part of the iceberg that lies beneath the water, they cannot be seen. You can't quite see the goals of the other side and often even one's own goals are ill-defined or too complex to articulate simply. When engaged proactively and in an environment of good listening, problem solving and effective communication, problems over goals and objectives need not be as troubling or difficult to manage successfully as are identity based conflicts. Goal-based problems without a great deal of emotional content can often be managed dispassionately, rationally and effectively with or without third party assistance.

Resource Disputes

When disputes arise mainly over *Resources* – competition over them, or scarcity of them and their distribution – the previous phases can be skipped and interventions can begin with creative invention. These conflicts are tangible and observable. If each party wants the corner office simply because it is large and comfortable, this is clearly about the resource itself. Such conflicts are fairly routine and relatively easy to "fix," perhaps with a decision based on a tangible measure such as relative number of years with the company. Conflicts occur frequently over competition for scarce resources and who will get them when and how. Resource conflicts can be settled and mutual gains achieved for all parties with effective and timely interest-based negotiation and problem solving.

Putting It All Together: The ARIA Conflict Contingency Approach

While the focus of ARIA was originally on creatively engaging identity-based conflicts with the idea that the deeper the conflict the more need and potential for creativity, ARIA has evolved in to a more comprehensive approach that builds upon and synthesizes other approaches, with the type of intervention dependent upon the analysis of the nature and depth of the conflict.[3]

---

[3] Much of this section is adapted from my article in the *Encyclopedia of Peace Psychology* (2012).

Step One: Conflict Analysis

ARIA begins with a detailed process of conflict analysis asking disputants to determine separately and interactively: What is this conflict about? Why does it matter to you? How deep does it run? What is functional about it? What is destructive about it? For whom, when and why? What might be done to mine its creative potential and reduce its destructiveness? Diagnosis is a form of creative conflict engagement in itself that sometimes requires nothing additional afterward since clarity and insight can themselves often heal wounds derived from misunderstanding and misperception. Often, however, analysis leads to concrete plans and strategies for intervention of one form or another (e.g. from mediation to dialogue and many methods in between).

The first step in effective conflict engagement is the analytical art of "going slow to go fast," that is, taking the time required to get the definition and dynamics of a conflict conceptually right. This in turn can propel and even expedite practical efforts to creatively address it later. Given that most people tend to have a natural and conditioned aversion to conflict, interveners commonly push quickly toward a solution which they think could overcome resistance and lessen the divide. The problem arises when there is a rush to solutions before achieving adequate understanding of the parameters and causes of the conflicts. The deeper the problem, the more likely that this premature solution-seeking will result in solving the wrong problems (Doyle and Straus 1976). For example, it may lead to attempts at settling resource disputes when goal problems need attention, or addressing goal problems with "interest-based" solutions when engagement of identity issues should precede. Additionally, when conflicts are about identity they may be resistant to "solutions" and thus the effort to "solve" them may lead to deeper intransigence. Instead, other types of creative and insight-oriented advances may be necessary. While it may be relatively impossible to "solve" identity conflicts, it is possible to gain insight about them and reach agreement about their dynamics.

ARIA addresses this issue by introducing disputants and interveners to its contingency approach to conflict analysis and intervention as one way to effectively engage conflicts instead of fleeing from them, fighting them or seeking to prematurely solve them.

What's the Issue?

Picture conflict as an iceberg, with identity-conflicts at the murky bottom. Goal conflicts rise above identity-based conflicts and reside just beneath the water's surface. Resource conflicts are above the water and are in plain sight, the most empirical and tangible of the three.

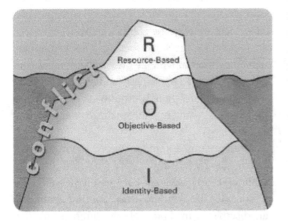

Another way of differentiating these conflict levels is by the simple questions "What?" "What for?" and "Why?" At the top of the iceberg are the tangible "Whats" of a conflict. For example, "I want that house. I understand you do too." Going down one level are the slightly less tangible "What fors" of a conflict. "I want that house because it fits my family perfectly. How about you?" Finally, the deepest level of "Whys" are repositories of identities such as "I want that house because it is in a neighborhood where I have close friends and family members. Why would you want that house?"

This "levels of analysis" approach visually suggests an important feature of identity-based conflict that distinguishes it from the other two. Identity-based conflict contains within it the other two levels of conflict as well. Conceptually moving up the

iceberg, a conflict for example over *home* and one's access to and control over it (the root of many community and international identity-based conflicts), will also be about goals (e.g. to accomplish sovereignty and territorial integrity) and resources (e.g. economic and military strength). On the other hand goal conflicts will be primarily about goals and resources (e.g. to establish an independent state in order to be able to gain and control of economic and military resources). Resource conflicts, while also having seeds of goal disputes and even identity-issues if they are poorly handled, are fundamentally about the who, when, and how of the control of tangible resources (e.g. gaining access to and control over scarce resources).

With a "levels of analysis" approach, the next step before focusing on solution seeking – in the form of dialogue, negotiation or some problem solving process that seeks to foster collaboration and coordination between conflict parties and reduce destruction and violence – is determining the right kind of approach for which type of issue: a conflict over identities, problems over goals or disputes over resources. In their classic article, Sander and Goldberg describe the importance of "fitting the forum to the fuss" making the obvious but essential point that one size cannot fit all in conflict work (1994). Fisher and Keashley were among the first to describe the need for and outlines of a contingency approach to conflict analysis and resolution (1991). In my work it is not so much the scale of conflict (i.e. international versus community) but rather the type (i.e. conflicts, problems or disputes). In review, here are two examples, domestic and international for applying the ARIA contingency approach:

Suppose a window office becomes available in a certain department and there are two people with the same job classification who qualify for the office. How do you decide who gets it? Is this a resource-, objective- or identity-based conflict? On the surface, this type of conflict seems like a resource-based conflict: two employees are fighting over the office. However, the conflict could also be about deeper conflicting objectives among office personnel. Perhaps one person sees the window office as providing necessary space for doing his or her job better. Or, is it rooted even deeper in people's sense of self-worth (e.g., "I didn't get an office window because the boss doesn't think I'm as valuable to the company as others"). ARIA suggests that interveners seek to help conflict parties start at the highest level that seems plausible to them, in this case viewing the problem as simply one of resource scarcity, and then inductively discover whether it is necessary to move down to lower levels if parties are unsatisfied or if problems worsen from the intervention.

Or at the international level, imagine Israelis and Palestinians all seeking an end to the conflict and agreeing in principle about the need for a two-state solution. Next steps might be easy right? Not at all unless it is clear at what level they are operating. Is it about negotiating final status agreements over who gets what resource, when and how (i.e. the nature of a political settlement)? Is it about the nature and purposes of that two-state solution (i.e. is it to be demilitarized? Are Palestinian refugees able to resettle in their old homes within Israel as part of that agreement or not)? Or is it about the values and needs of each community (i.e. for identity, dignity, control over destiny and so forth and ways that state will fulfill or further frustrate such existential needs and values)?

Why Is It Happening?

Having diagnosed the predominant level at which the conflict resides in a certain context of time and place, interveners and disputants then analyze the causes of the conflict. By asking the appropriate questions (why does this problem matter to you so much? what do you think some of its causes have been?), and utilizing the resulting self diagnosis of conflict, interveners design, or better yet, elicit from the disputants themselves, an approach to address the conflict.

This previously described "Power of Why" process is one in which people are asked to share their personal narrative about Why they care about the situation (see Chap. 2). The deeper the situation, usually the more they care. The process is particularly effective in identity and goal based issues. It can also be useful, however, in a more mechanical way in determining whether concrete issues are at stake.

Step Two: How Should the Issues Be Addressed?

A hallmark of ARIA is the way it encourages everyone engaged in a specific conflict issue to deal with the same things, in mostly the same way, for largely the same reasons. This is no small task, and perhaps due to the complexity of this effort, it is all too rare. Commonly in conflicts, people are talking about different things, in different ways, for different reasons. So conflicts often protract and worsen as they are surfaced, and the conventional fight-flight response is further encouraged. People involved in the ARIA process develop a single score for all to read from together by getting everyone to share an analysis of the core features or main presenting issues of the conflict and its history. Next, by suggesting different types of intervention strategies and lining them up with the conflict analysis, everyone can start off on the same footing. This is a largely analytic process in which we study the type of situation that emerged in the past – a dispute, a problem or a conflict – and then determine the best path forward to constructively settle, manage or engage it in the future.

Paraphrasing a famous quote from philosopher Soren Kirkegaard, "Life [or Conflict] is to be understood backward but lived forward."

Consider the window office conflict again. We can discover why both persons might think that they should get the window office. If viewed simply as a resource, the office designation might be based purely on seniority. In other words, parties should be proactive and figure out the best and fairest ways to divide up or allocate this resource. If it is viewed as objectives or goals-based, then after probing more deeply to understand what function the office might serve, we must find ways to have that function addressed (with or without the office). For example, the desire for the window office might be based on health concerns, like someone who may get headaches from artificial lighting, or the need for a larger space for holding meetings. If it is seen primarily as an identity issue, the concerns might be based on the feeling of not being valued by the company, and thus these deeper problems must be surfaced and eventually addressed in a more comprehensive way.

The ARIA Acronym

In addition to being a metaphor for creativity (i.e. ARIA is the Italian word for "song"), ARIA is also an acronym for four categories of conflict intervention that align with different conflict types: Antagonism, Resonance, Invention and Action (Rothman 1997).

  A – Surfacing of Antagonism: mostly rooted in the past and most clearly in evidence in identity-based conflicts. Some of the conflict intervention processes used in this phase are dialogue, empowerment mediation, confrontation, and facilitation.

  R – Narrative excursion in to the Resonance of peoples' hopes, fears, needs and values, is often the starting point for goal-based conflicts. Some of the conflict intervention processes used in this phase are narrative mediation, storytelling, and transformative processes.

  I – Invention process of seeking creative ways to foster and promote greater resonance through concrete fulfillment of needs, values and goals. Some of the conflict invention processes used in this phase include interest based bargaining, collaborative visioning, goal setting, and action research.

  A – Action planning process of concretely designing and implementing ways to sustain and further creative inventions. Some of the conflict intervention processes used in this phase are negotiation, action planning and techniques drawn from organizational development.

The ARIA Contingency Approach

If the conflict is rooted in identity issues, then intervention processes that safely surface the hurts and indignities of the past – or antagonisms – are often necessary. If the conflict presents mainly at the goal level, then understanding and engaging each side's needs and values, their "resonance," is the suggested starting point. If the conflict is mainly about resources, then proactive processes for inventing mutual gains outcomes, or settling differences amicably, are suggested. The intervention processes suggested by this model move up the iceberg along with the levels of analysis. For example, when starting at the Identity-level, begin with Antagonism and then move upwards to Resonance, then Invention, then Action and so forth.

Conflicts, Problems or Disputes often present clearly at one level – the window office is quite concrete and resource-based while the Israeli-Palestinian conflict is deeply existential and clearly identity-based – but shift up or down depending on if or how they are handled.

In the case of the window office, or territorial settlement in the Israeli-Palestinian conflict depending upon how it is analyzed at a given time and place, a concrete solution, or at least a way to concretely address the concerns, is most useful. In such cases, inventive and proactive interest-based bargaining, collaborative goal setting and negotiation strategies are often useful to begin with.

If the conflict has to do with the goals or purposes a window office or a two state solution will serve those seeking it, then a sustained effort to clarify separate and overlapping goals, objectives and values of each party is essential. We label this "Resonance" to connote internal clarity about an issue, which when expressed well often forges mutual understanding of where such concerns overlap and can begin to "vibrate" together harmoniously. Fostering this clarity of goals and purposes through internal and interactive goal clarification and collaborative planning is a useful way forward.

If the issue has more to do with individuals or groups who feel that their needs and values are threatened or frustrated, then a dialogical approach may be most useful. The antagonisms of the past can be safely surfaced and recognized as a first step to moving into a new future. Given that such conflicts, rooted as they are in past hurts and indignities, are often deeply antagonistic, we start this type of dialogical intervention with what we call "Antagonism."

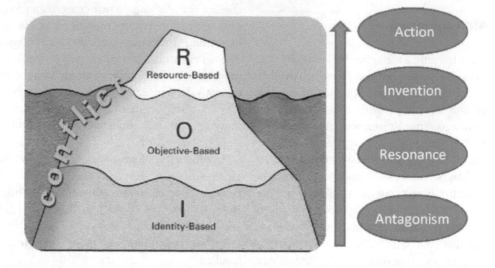

A closing caveat and invitation: The ARIA framework helps organize reality. It is obviously not reality. Disputes over resources are rarely "pure." Nor are problems over goals. They both contain elements of the deepest conflicts – identity – either expressed or latent, and can "move down the iceberg" fairly easily. That is why proactive conflict engagement, beginning with a contingency analysis, can be so important. If we know what we are dealing with, we might be able to proactively address issues at "higher levels" and keep them from sinking into the more difficult, deeper and darker conflicts at the bottom of the iceberg. On the other hand, all identity conflicts contain problems over goals and competition over resources. And so too, goal conflicts hold within them the "higher level" disputes over resources. In short: be proactive!

Two: Identity-Based Cooperation: Predicting the Future by Creating It

"Oh my!" I exclaimed as I watched President Bill Clinton pull together the reluctant warrior-turned-peace-maker Prime Minister Yitzhak Rabin and the Chairman of the Palestinian Liberation Organization and President of the Palestinian Authority, Yasser Arafat. The two then shook hands. Of course this handshake soon turned into an arm-wrestle but at that moment I, and most of the audience in the Rose Garden on that sunny October day in 1993, cried (though I noted that Henry Kissinger who was two rows ahead of me was stony-faced and dry-eyed). Mine were tears of joy and frustration. This was so easy and obvious. This was so necessary. Why did it take so long!?

"Enough of blood and tears," then said Rabin, who was later shot down by an assassin of peace, "The time for peace has come."

In the next morning's Philadelphia Inquirer, I wrote an op-ed piece, "Unofficial Talks Yield Middle East Peace" (Philadelphia Inquirer, Sept. 14, 1993). I suggested that the secret Oslo talks were neither a fluke nor a moment when the stars finally lined up to shine a light on the troubled Middle East. Rather, the foundation for these talks, which at the time pointed toward a pathway for peace, was laid by decades of careful, painstaking work in what is called "track two" diplomacy (see Chapter 6).

This foundation was built on many hundreds of "academic" meetings held in the US, in Europe, and in the heart of Jerusalem. I was one of many conveners who held dialogue meetings in Jerusalem between political, community and student leaders from both communities. Eventually, these meetings contributed, if indirectly, to a legitimization of dialogue and helped shift the negotiation agenda. Despite what would eventually become the woeful fate of those peace accords, the agenda had shifted. It moved Middle East peace negotiations from purely positional bargaining (or, "war by other means"), or interest-based bargaining (of the Camp David variety that contributed to the Israeli-Egyptian accords), to a more identity-based and existentially-focused agenda.

Participants in these track two meetings voiced their hopes and fears and about their communities' needs and values. Participants – academics, business elite, policymakers, media people, community leaders, analysts and artists – pointed to new ways for adversaries to become allies. In short, as I wrote in 1993, conflict resolution had made a contribution to setting the stage for the handshake at the White House.

In response to this piece, I got a phone call that changed the course of my work from a focus on engaging identity-based conflicts to a new emphasis on forging identity-based cooperation. That call was from the program officer at a major foundation. He challenged me to share with his increasingly dubious board, why conflict resolution matters and made a difference in this most "intransigent" of conflicts. In addition to giving him the bad news that there was no deep theory of success in the proposals we reviewed and thus short of "resolving" conflicts, his board's skepticism may have been well founded, I had the audacity to ask for a grant to study success and failure in international conflict engagement, and I got it.

Prior to being able to answer whether complex conflict resolution initiatives had succeeded or not, it would be essential to develop compelling visions and nuanced *criteria* of success for the field as a whole through a disciplined focus on goals, values and action strategies for specific initiatives. My colleague Marc Ross and I studied dozens of initiatives around the world to determine what kinds of criteria of success they were using in their work. This led to our book called *Theory and Practice in Ethnic Conflict Management: Conceptualizing Success and Failure* (Ross & Rothman 1999), in which the most consistent feature in the search for criteria of success in these initiatives was a focus, more or less disciplined, on setting and pursuing goals. Over the next two decades our efforts to address this lack of systematic definitions of success in the field, led to the development of ARIA-Action Evaluation, a computer assisted social technology for helping key stakeholders in conflict resolution and community development initiatives work individually, in groups and across the groups as a community of practice to define, promote and assess success. While this methodology will be fully described and illustrated in the second half of this book (with a full overview of the process in Chap. 7), here I want to present the philosophy behind it as it operationalizes the notion of "Identity-based Cooperation" quite well. I will do so through highlighting some excerpts of cases to be presented later in this book.

This second, newer form of ARIA, instead of beginning with Antagonism and a backward gaze, begins with a look to the future and generates Aspiration. Individuals are invited to share their visions for some future (answering a web-based survey that feeds into a complex database system for organizing and analyzing qualitative data – see Chap. 7) in terms of What goals, Why values, and How actions. The second type of ARIA is used when the parties have not been particularly engaged in deep conflict, but are dealing with complex and either ill-defined goals or goal problems. Unlike in the first variant, in this one they do not have to work through the lens of the past before envisioning a new future. Or at least so it seems on initial analysis.

From Conflicts to Cooperation

ARIA-Action Evaluation(AE) is applied either when a goal and future focus is already possible, or after an identity-based conflict has been well and fully engaged such that the "switch" has been made sufficiently and the parties are on the same side of the table and have the will to work together for some better future. Where identity based conflict is rooted in a look to the past and adversarial framing, identity-based cooperation is promoted by looking to the future and reflexive reframing. Identity-based Cooperation, when emerging out of conflict situations, is the flow from one state of mind and relationship to another:

FROM--------------->TO:

Polarizing------------> **Interdependence**
Blaming------------------> **Accountability**
Attributing------------------> **Analytic Empathy**
Projecting------------------------> **Self-Awareness**

While this flow suggests again a kind of linearity, it is often a much more iterative process. For example, in 2001 I was invited to help the police and the African American community in Cincinnati, Ohio to improve their relationships after a series of incidents and accusations of racial profiling (see Chap. 11). Federal Judge Susan Dlott, a former domestic relations attorney, determined that a court was not the best place to deal with such fraught relationships, and asked me to propose an alternative to a protracted and bitter court case. While I suggested to the parties, consisting of leaders from the local Black United Front, the ACLU, the police leadership, police union leaders, and representatives of the City, that we would need to do an ARIA beginning with directly surfacing and engaging Antagonism about the past, the police leadership resolutely refused. Either we do something different or we go to court. They said, "we didn't do anything wrong, and we can prove it."

In pre-negotiation with the sides and the Judge, I had already determined that this was a conflict that clearly presented at the identity level with both sides feeling deep hurt and mistrust about the other, and holding radically different interpretations about the reality they each experienced with the "other" (See Ross 1993). Thus Antagonism would need to be surfaced and engaged and at least a clear and shared definition of "racial profiling" would need to be developed in which parties would agree on a common problem that is beyond Us versus Them but is still conditioned by adversarial attitudes (for example, "I am deeply afraid of you," and "so am I" – see Chap. 3). So it was either let it go back to court to fight it out there or hold them at the table with some other proposal. Sweating while the parties were beginning to pack their bags, I suggested that we

could do a future-focused agenda setting process to improve police-community relations. The police were satisfied and sat down again, "Of course, this is what we are about so if you can assist us with this we are willing to try." The city leadership was relieved, "If this will keep us out of court, let's go for it!" The police union was willing. The ACLU and Black United Front were skeptical but sat down again as they expressed willingness on condition that the outcomes have teeth, insisting that "the Judge ensure that any agreement we reach be monitored by the Court." Thus, we began our plans for an ARIA-AE process about the visions of the community as a whole for an improved future in police-community relations.

The process limped along. My success in knitting together these leaders with their radically different views of the situations and goals for our process was limited at best. Moreover, there was deep antipathy and mistrust bubbling just beneath the surface. We met for several weeks as I tried to build them into a well-functioning "design team" who had previously been sharpening their swords to fight it out, in court if possible but on the streets if necessary. Things were barely civil, and few decisions were being made. In the midst of these efforts, just six weeks after we began, riots broke out in the city after an unarmed African American male was shot and killed by a rookie police officer.

Antagonism was unleashed. Polarization, blaming, attributions and projections ran rampant. Now we could begin a transitional process to foster resonance – why are we so hurt and scared? Why do we care so much? We launched a very successful process of collaborative visioning rooted in dialogue over "Why we care?" and "What we Want for the Future" and "How can we Get There?" that led to 3,500 participants from various stakeholding communities (police, African Americans, youth, business, etc.) who together set a new agenda that ten years of court monitoring later is known as a model of police-community relations and is being copied elsewhere (for a full description of this process and outcomes see Chap. 11).

In this case, we moved away from an attempt to engage conflict when my proposal to directly address the accusations of racial profiling was rejected, to a limping effort to envision the future (ARIA-AE). It was given real impetus after the riots, an expressed form of Antagonistic Conflict Engagement, before initiating successful Collaborative Visioning. In another case in this book, things moved in exactly the opposite way (see Chap. 8). When a mixed class of Arab and Jewish nursing students in a college in Northern Israel decided to engage conflict, the decision was nixed by the administration as "too risky." The fear was that surfacing conflicts in a proactive way would "arouse sleeping dogs" and someone was sure to be bitten. So after a lecture and discussion about their conflicts, which served as a form of analytical antagonism such that the past wasn't fully ignored or "walled off," the students engaged in a very constructive ARIA-AE process to envision their future together."

The case about the Medical School (Chap. 9) moved through yet a different journey in the balance and relationship between engaging conflicts from the past and collaboratively envisioning the future. This project began as a "simple" strategic visioning and planning process, but soon got mired in what turned out to be some deep and hidden identity-conflicts. Thus the visioning process was put on hold as we engaged the conflict issues effectively. After the conflicts over the identity of the school had been safely surfaced (even if not "solved") we then returned to the visioning process with renewed vigor and focus.

ARIA-AE can gain quicker traction when a future focus is unimpeded by significant identity-conflicts, and some organization, initiative or community of practice determines that they want to enhance their cooperation to solve shared problems or deepen already existing cooperation.

The case about the intercultural youth camp (Chap. 10) is one example of a "pure" ARIA-AE process in which visioning is neither preceded nor interrupted by any need for direct conflict engagement. It began and concluded at the level of articulating goals and actions.

Conclusion

Ships are lost in the Bermuda Triangle and never found again. Identity-based conflict often eats its young. They grow up in war and hatred and they

die with or by them. And yet, as described in this chapter and in the rest of this book, identity-based conflict can also be a source of deep insight about self, other and situation and an opportunity for creative transformation and cooperation. Amin Maalouf describes the complexity of identity as its promise for progress (2003). Cobb in her work on Narratives and Conflict talks about the difference between "thin" and "thick" narratives with the former being polarizing and reductionist and the later being multi-dimensional with room for intersection across differences (1993). When identity is one-dimensional and exclusive, it is by definition defensive, ethnocentric and more often than not aggressive in its self-preservation and aggrandizement. However, when identity is multi-dimensional and reflexive in its understanding and expression – as summarized in the South African notion of Ubuntu: "I am because You are" – it becomes a bridge that spans the globe. Maalouf describes identity as both vertical and horizontal. The first is the sum total of one's heritage and ancient history – ancestors, place, language, culture and heritage. The second derives from one's situation in current life and relationships.

As Maalouf (1993) writes in the introduction to in his book about "violence and the need to belong":

…Identity would then be seen as the sum of all our allegiances, and, within it, allegiance to the human community itself would become increasingly important, until one day it would become the chief allegiance, though without destroying our many individual affiliations.

References

Azar, E. (1990). *The management of protracted social conflict: Theory and cases.* Aldershot: Dartmouth.
Burton, J. D. (1979). *Terrorism and war.* Suffolk: Martin Robertson.
Burton, J. (1993). Conflict Resolution as a Political Philosophy. In D. Sandole and H. van der Merwe, (eds.) *Conflict resolution theory and practice: Integration and application.* Manchester and New York: Manchester University Press.
Coleman, P. (2011). *The five percent: Finding solutions to seemingly impossible conflicts.* New York: PublicAffairs Books.
Cobb, S. (1993). Empowerment and mediation: A narrative perspective. *Negotiation Journal, 9*(3), 245–259.

Cohen, R. (1993). International negotiation: Does culture make a difference? An advocates view. In J. Rubin & G. Faure (Eds.), *Culture and negotiation* (pp. 22–38). Newbury Park: Sage.

Donohue, W., & Kolt, R. (1992). *Managing interpersonal conflict*. Newbury Park: Sage.

Doyle M., & Strauss, D. (1976). *How to make meetings work*. New York: Berkley.

Fisher, R., & Keashly, L. (1991). The potential complementarity of mediation and consultation within a contingency model of third party consultation. *Journal of Peace Research, 28*(1), 29–42.

Folger, J., Poole, M., & Stutman, R. (2005). *Working through conflict: strategies for relationships, groups and organizations* (5th Edition). Boston: Pearson/Allyn and Bacon.

Friedman, V., Rothman, J. & Withers, B. (2006). The power of why: Engaging the goal paradox in program evaluation. *American Journal of Evaluation, 27*(2), 1–18.

Galtung, J. (1990). Cultural Violence. *Journal of Peace Research, 27*(3), 291–305.

Galtung, J. (2004). *An introduction to conflict work (peace by peaceful means)*. London: Pluto Press.

Ganz, M. (2008). What is public narrative? Online article at http://grassrootsfund.org/docs/WhatIsPublicNarrative08.pdf. Accessed on 2 Mar 2012.

Hocker, J. and Wilmot, W. (1985). Interpersonal Conflict (2nd Ed.). Dubuque, IA.: Brown Communications.

Jabareen, Y. (2008). Toward participatory equality: Protecting minority rights under international law. *Israel Law Review, 41*, 635.

Jones, E. (1972). *Attribution: Perceiving the causes of behavior*. Morristown: General Learning Press.

Lewin, K. (1948). *Resolving social conflicts*. New York: Harpers.

Mayer, B. (2009). *Staying with conflict: A strategic approach to conflict*. San Francisco: Jossey-Bass.

Maalouf, A. (2003). *In the name of identity*. New York: Penguin Books.

Mouffe, C. (2005). *On the political: Thinking in action*. New York: Routledge.

Pruitt, D., & Rubin, J. (1986). *Social conflict: Escalation, settlement and stalemate*. New York: Random House.

Ross, M., & Rothman, J. (Eds.). (1999). *Theory and practice in ethnic conflict management: Conceptualizing success and failure*. London: Macmillan.

Ross, M. (1993). *The culture of conflict: Interpretations and interests in comparative perspective*. New Haven: Yale University Press.

Rothman, J. (2012a). Identity-based conflicts, the ARIA contingency approach. In D. Christie (Ed.), *Encyclopedia of peace psychology*. New York: Blackwell.

Rothman, J., & Soderquist, C. (2002). From riots to resolution: Engaging conflict for reconciliation. *The Systems Thinker, 13*(8), 2–6.

Rothman, J. (1997). *Resolving identity-based conflict in nations, organizations and communities*. San Francisco: Jossey-Bass.

Rothman, J. (1999). Articulating Goals and Monitoring Progress in a Cyprus Conflict Resolution Training Workshop. In M. Ross and J. Rothman (eds.) (1999). *Theory and practice in ethnic conflict management: Conceptualizing success and failure*, (pp. 176–194). London: Macmillan Press.

Sander, F., & Goldberg, S. (1994). Fitting the forum to the fuss: A user-friendly guide to selecting an ADR procedure. *Negotiation Journal, 10*, 49–67.

Siegal, D. (2010). *Mindsight*. New York: Random House.

Sillars, A. (1981). Attributions and interpersonal conflict resolution. In J. Harvey, W. Ickes, & R. Kidd (Eds.), *New directions in attribution research* (Vol. 3). Hillsdale: Erlbaum.

Stroh, D. (2011). The system dynamics of identity-based conflict. In D. Korppen, N. Ropers, & H. J. Giessman (Eds.), *The non-linearity of peace processes* (pp. 167–182). Farmington Hills: Barbara Budrich.

Wenger, E. (1998). *Communities of practice: Learning meaning and identity*. New York: Cambridge University Press.

Zartman, I.W., Antsey, M., & Meertz, P., (eds). (2012). *The slippery slope: Negotiating identity to Genocide: Reducing identity conflicts and preventing mass murder*. New York: Oxford University Press.

The Power of Why

Victor J. Friedman, Jay Rothman, and Bill Withers

Introduction

This chapter focuses on the question "why?" – a question that lies at the heart of ARIA. It is the process by which resonance is found or fostered. In ARIA this question is asked to uncover the existential needs and narratives that live in the depths of conflict and provide foundations for visions of a better future. The why question is the key that unlocks the door between Antagonism and Resonance (in conflict work) or between Aspiration and Resonance (in visioning), enabling people to give expression to what drives the intense emotion and makes compromise difficult or a better future necessary. Asking the "why" question aims at stimulating a process of resonance among people that leads to a fundamental change in relationship and opens the way to cooperation. The "why dialogue" seeks to elicit the values and *passions* that motivate people to conflict and potentially to cooperate. Ultimately, the question "why" is also key to the articulation and the construction of identity.

In the 25 years we been developing ARIA, we have repeatedly experienced the "power of why"

in enabling stakeholders with different, even contradictory, interests and identities to agree on common goals to which they are truly committed. The question "why" and what it elicits among people helps lay the foundation for the deep and collaborative work of building a new future together. The goal of this chapter, then, is to delve more deeply into the "power of why" as the operational vehicle for fostering resonance, in order to provide a clearer understanding of *what* this means, *why* it is important to participants in and facilitators of ARIA processes, and *how* it is carried out in practice. This provides a necessary building block for all the chapters that follow.

What Is the "Why Dialogue"?

When we bring stakeholders together to deliberate on their conflicts or goals, "why?" is the main, if not always the first, question we ask. Asking people why they feel passionate about their goals or conflicts is not asking for explanations, justifications, or rationalizations. Rather it is an invitation to reflect on themselves, and the source of their conflicts or commitment to the goals they have chosen. On the one hand, the "why" question is so simple that it almost goes without saying. On the other hand, asking this question in the right way, at the right time, and for the right reason often takes people aback – precisely because it is so rarely asked, or asked well. As they respond, people are often surprised by what emerges.

V.J. Friedman • B. Withers
e-mail: victorf@yvc.ac.il; wwithers@rocketmail.com

J. Rothman (✉)
Program on Conflict Resolution and Negotiation,
Bar-Ilan University, Ramat Gan, Israel
e-mail: jrothman@ariagroup.com

J. Rothman (ed.), *From Identity-Based Conflict to Identity-Based Cooperation: The ARIA Approach in Theory and Practice*, Peace Psychology Book Series, DOI 10.1007/978-1-4614-3679-9_2,
© Springer Science+Business Media New York 2012

In our conflict engagement work, the interactive why process between disputants is often proceeded by a "solo" process (see Chap. 3) by individuals or within identity-groups, in which they become clear about what motivates and animates the intensity of their conflict. Once individuals are brought together to engage in an interactive ARIA, after concerns are framed (Antagonism), reasons and resonance are explored. (For a full explication of this process at the intragroup and intergroup level see Chap. 5.) In Action Evaluation, the "why" dialogue usually involves groups of no more than ten people sitting in a circle with a facilitator and a "scribe" who records what is said. The facilitator begins by asking the participants, one by one, to share their "whys" (more detailed description of the AE facilitation process is given below and in Chap. 7). Each participant is then given space, with no interruptions except gentle probing from the facilitator, to think aloud and to tell their stories.

The following why excerpts are from a program that brings together young people from regions of conflict around the world to work on interfaith relations at a summer camp (see Chap. 8). The participants were asked to try to sum up their "why" in a single world (a "passion point") and to tell a story that would illustrate it for their listeners (the italics in some of the quotations that follow indicate the probing from the facilitator):

> **"COMMUNITY"** – Last Ramadan when the fast was broken at Iftar, I was taking part in setting up the arrangements for the celebrations and was expecting a large turnout from the local Muslim community. But I was not expecting the large turnout of all different religions and races from my area in Ohio. This gave me a great sense of different communities coming together as one which made me think about the work carried out at (the program) and how there are some tangible results to this. Especially as there is a growing Somalian community in Ohio which is mainly Muslim and has been made to feel very welcome, which also shows a great sense of community.

> **"FORGIVENESS"** – Three years ago I had a very close friend, but we had stopped talking. I was supposed to be in a Christian camp together with that friend, and one day before camp started I said I don't want to go. Then I decided to go so I can get to know new people and have other friends. Saturday night we were praying and this girl that

used to be my friend was standing alone by herself. She looked so sad and lonely then I moved to stand next to her and we both started to cry and I hugged her. I sensed then that we were friends again stronger than before.

> **"FREEDOM"** – One day my family decided to go to Jerusalem to visit my grandmother. There was a check-point along the way, and we were stopped there for three hours. Just one kilometer later, there was another check-point. We passed through it and continued on, eventually coming to the Old City where my grandmother lives. There were many soldiers there, and they said that only those who live in the Old City [i.e. who have an Old City address on their ID card] could enter. So after the long journey, only my father could visit her. *Could you explain more how this story represents freedom for you?* Everything I want to do is closed for me because of the Occupation. If I had freedom, I would be happy and be able to do what I want.

> **"MEETING"** – I was brought up in a very liberal house, and I was always taught not to have prejudice, to be open for everyone. I was 4–5 years old, and I was playing with dolls when my mom came and gave me a black doll. I didn't play with it, and she asked me why I wasn't playing with the black doll. I saw her eyes and the way she looked at me, and I knew I did something wrong, but I really didn't want to play with the black doll. She was angry, and I started crying. I knew I really upset her, but I just didn't want to play with it. I was raised in an environment where I had to be accepting, but I just couldn't meet people from other races or backgrounds. You can't be open to something if you don't meet it. So here I am, I'm here to meet.

These excerpts are particularly poignant, but not atypical, examples of the power of why. This power awakens something in both the speaker and the listeners. The speakers explore and share parts of themselves and their experience which they rarely, if ever, openly expressed or even have been fully aware of. It is a moment of rich self discovery and sharing.

Here are some more complex examples of whys that were articulated during conflict engagement. The first two come from an interpersonal, gender and race-based ARIA mediation (see Chap. 3):

> **"FEAR"** – Black Man – "I have lived all my life in my skin and size. It hasn't been easy, not because I am not proud of myself, but rather I'm always, 24/7, aware of others' fears and perceptions. It's

exhausting. This event, at work – where I had felt that finally who I am and what I do are valued – has really set me back. It hurts; our exchanges have hurt; my hopes are hurt."

"FEAR" – White Woman – "Milt, you don't know how long and hard I thought about filing that complaint before I did. I know this exchange of ours is stereotypical. But that's not why it happened. Simply, you frightened me and afterward you never were willing to sit down and talk about what happened and why. I could never express my concerns to you, so they grew. Now, I think I have some sense of why that happened before and why the gulf between us grew into a chasm."

The following came from an Israeli-Palestinian conflict engagement workshop (see Chap. 5):

"COMMONALITY" – Palestinian Man – "When the meeting ended yesterday, I was very stressed. Then there was an initiative from the Israeli side to sit and talk on our own. It was difficult for me at first because I have issues about socializing with Israelis, whether rightly or wrongly. It took a real effort at first. However, once we started talking and drinking, I was amazed to see that there was so much in common. It is possible to live as neighboring countries. As time passed, all the ice was breaking and we started talking about songs and music and all sorts of common interests."

"MEETING" – Jewish Israeli Woman – "I was so scared on my first day because of him [pointing to the Palestinian participant quoted above who, by now, was looking more relaxed]. When he was talking, I saw a very tough guy, and I said to myself, why did I come here? This person does not want peace. He wants war, look at his body – when he talked to me, it was as if he said, 'go, I don't want to see you.' He looked like my enemy, like what I'm afraid of all the time. And I thought, why did he come here? In the second night, I couldn't sleep. After two days, we passed by each other and he asked me something, then we talked, and after that I understood the he has a family, a dream, lots of things that I also have. Now I am very happy we had a chance to meet."

One can hardly listen to these expressions of profound personal reality without being touched by them. They move something deep inside of us and stimulate empathy, even if we come from a very different reality or opposite sides of a conflict or are gathering to envision a future that will take collaboration. This response is what we call "resonance" – a kind of invisible, living connection created when one person's fundamentally human,

existential need touches something deeply human in another. Resonance creates openings for people to come together, despite differences, to create something new.

As these excepts illustrate, "whys" can be profoundly affirmative or deeply painful expressions of experience, but either way they provide a window into each other's experience. Although the "whys" sometimes carry content that might be threatening to others, they are spoken in a way that encourages listening on all sides. Participants in a "why" dialogue are not expected to respond directly to or discuss each other's "whys". Indeed, critical and judgmental comments are discouraged. There is no need for agreement, which is reserved for the discussion of goals or inventions. Instead, people are guided to speak and listen for understanding.

When people express their authentic "whys," it creates a moment of profound self-awareness and presence with others – something Rothman calls "interactive introspection" (1997). People who are engaging each other across a conflict divide or may have worked together for years in joint efforts, experience each other in an often open-hearted way when they engage in a why dialogue. It is not magic, but it is not infrequently magical. Rather than minimize or obscure differences, this approach aims at making commonalities and differences at all levels as visible as possible so they can be seriously engaged before a program actually takes shape. Indeed, this process creates conditions under which stakeholders discover commonalities and appreciate differences. It stimulates people to move out of entrenched positions, to take the others' needs into consideration, and to think seriously about goals to which all sides are truly committed. It also enables people to question their own goals, reframe them, and to discover new ones.

Why in Identity-Based Conflict and Cooperation

The "why" question originated in the theory and practice of addressing "identity" conflicts (Rothman 1992, 1997), such as the struggle between Israel and the Palestinians or the friction between the Black community and the police in Cincinnati that erupted into violence for several days in 2001(Rothman and Land 2004). Identity conflicts may present themselves as competition over resources, interests or goals, but they are rooted deeply in people's individual and collective purposes, sense of meaning, and definitions of self. They are particularly intransigent because they involve threats to, or the frustration of, fundamental human needs, such as dignity, recognition, safety, control, purpose, and efficacy (Azar 1990; Burton 1990).

Dealing with identity conflict requires deeper interventions than the typical bargaining for settlements through zero-sum, power-politics models of negotiation (Banks 1984) or even through "interest-based" models that aim for cooperative solutions (e.g. Fisher and Ury 1981; Tjosvold 1991). When progress toward the creative engagement of a deep identity conflict is stalled, our approach is to carefully ask the people on both sides of the conflict *why* they feel the need to hold on to their positions and *why* they feel so passionate about them (Rothman 1992, 1997; Rothman and Friedman 2003). Each party to a conflict is asked to tell its "story" in the presence of its adversaries. With the probing of a skilled mediator, all parties to a conflict reflect upon and clarify the needs and values that are driving them. Conducting this inquiry process in an open and structured way enables each side to hear the other side – often for the first time. This approach enables each side to understand, though not necessarily agree with, the other side's viewpoint.

At the core of this process is the fact that many individuals and groups define their identity as much as by what they are not as by what they are: being an Israeli means that I am not a Palestinian Arab, being a woman means that I am not a man, being a worker means that I am not a manager, etc. The question "why" makes this process of self-definition explicit and positive. It asks people to reflect on and express the experiences and values that drive their commitments to particular positions or strategies of action. Most importantly, it takes us where we need to be to work together to consciously define who "we" are even if it is oppositional. When parties are ready to

move to a more positive reframing (i.e. Resonance), the stories begin to be less focused on the self that is not the other and more on the core of the self that has positive needs and values. Ultimately, as the process progresses towards collaborative Invention, these stories and the values they contain help to shape *what kind of relationship we want to have and who we are or need to become to have it*. Indeed, it begins to forge a broader and more inclusive notion of identity in which each side needs the other in order to be itself and be able to forge a foundation for reaching what both sides need – viable and sustainable cooperation. (Mayer 2004; Lederach 1995; Rothman 1997; Rupesinghe 1995).

Once this relationship is articulated, the final stages of the ARIA process call for the "Invention" of specific ways of envisioning that relationship and "Action" to put that vision into actual practice. However, early on we discovered that the Action stage is extremely problematic to implement without some kind of concrete framework. The exhilarating experience of Resonance and Invention often seduces people into believing that they have worked their way through the conflict to a new future. Participants leave the negotiating process with hope and good intentions, but only vague plans for action. The problem that presents itself is that transformed relationships are rarely sustainable if they are not consistently reinforced by new patterns of behavior – what we call a "relational infrastructure." As a result, the gains of successful conflict resolution often dissipate once the parties return to their respective communities and former routines.

As a way to strengthen the sustainability of ARIA conflict engagement work, with an emphasis on practical outcomes, Action Evaluation was developed as a method for facilitating the transition from Invention to sustainable Action. AE shifts the focus from the past to the future and to the different reality that parties wish to create for themselves. It attempts to ensure the sustainability of transformed relationships by giving them concrete expression in programs, projects, or other forms of organized action.

Translating intentions into concrete programs, however, raised a new set of issues to be addressed.

For example, in their study of conflict resolution programs, Rothman and Ross (1999) found that different stakeholders (e.g. funders, administrators, professionals, participants) often have very different definitions of "success" for the very same program. Effective programs and effective evaluation require a process for forging common goals that engage different stakeholders' definitions of success.

In practice, the desire to get a program up and running creates strong incentives for stakeholders to charge ahead without really taking seriously the differences in their goals (Weiss 1993). In the start-up phase of a program, when parties are full of enthusiasm and hope for the future, it is quite natural for them to ignore or smooth over differences so as to get things off the ground. Program designers frequently set multiple objectives and obscure inconsistencies with vague and inspirational language, allowing stakeholders to interpret both ends and means in significantly different ways (Friedman 2001; Wholely et al. 1971). As a result, different stakeholders hold different, and often conflicting, expectations from the same program. During implementation, these differences inevitably resurface as tensions and conflicts among stakeholders (Friedman 2001a). It then becomes more difficult to resolve these conflicts or even to discuss them openly because people have invested time, funding, and political capital into the program. The avoidance strategies and defensive routines (Argyris and Schon 1996) that prevented differences from being dealt with in the first place become even more dominant so that the conflicts become "undiscussable," leading to dysfunction within the program or even to an eventual explosion.

Action Evaluation emerged as an attempt to engage the issue of goal conflict by systematically applying principles of identity conflict resolution to program design. As the method developed, it was applied to programs – indeed to almost any kind of sustained action – in a wide range of fields. As Michael Patton (1997) framed it, program goal-setting is rooted in the tension between rationality and values. Thus, goal clarification is a bit like standing on the edge of an abyss of "irrationality". Rather than stepping back from the abyss, we advocate leaping into it by encouraging stakeholders not only to make their goals explicit but also to give full voice to the *passions* – their Whys – underlying them. Action Evaluation does not suggest that every program is defined by deep identity conflict, but rather that many initiatives themselves are, or at least should be, an expression of the identities of their stakeholders (certainly this is true of inventions derived from a conflict engagement process). This focus on identity also means that the key to success for programs is defining goals to which all stakeholders feel *passionately* committed (Hirschhorn 2003). The challenge of AE was finding a way to enable stakeholders at the individual, group, and intergroup level to have their passionately held goals incorporated into program planning and design. Giving voice to these passions in a controlled, structured way creates openness for consensus building in program goal-setting and deepens stakeholders' internal commitment to the goals themselves.

What happens if stakeholders do not feel passionate about the project goals that they have defined? On this issue we take a frankly normative stance that reflects Max Weber's statement that "nothing is worthy of man as man unless he can pursue it with passionate devotion" (1918a, cited in Gerth and Mills 1946, p. 135). Good program goals are ones that stakeholders feel passionate about. People should not invest their time, talent, money, or authority into programs they do not care that much about. Passion, as Weber pointed out, is not simply the expression of strong emotion and need not be dampened in order to ensure productive work and relationships. Passion can be rational, in the sense that it helps people carry out difficult, mundane or sometimes even distasteful action steps because, as Weber understood it, it is linked to responsibility.

Of course, this standard only applies when stakeholders come to the table with some positive investment in the program even if they might hold divergent program goals. If people are stakeholders in a program with which they disagree in a fundamental way, it most likely is because they have not been involved in its design, or have been involved only nominally, withholding genuine participation. If the "why" dialogue is carried out after a program has begun and some of the stakeholders have felt uninvolved or coerced, then we are at least initially in a conflict engagement process. It is important to note the difference between the "why" question in conflict engagement and its use in goal-setting. The former inquires into needs that are threatened or violated whereas the latter inquires into the needs and purposes that drive commitment.

To sum up, the importance of "why" in program goal-setting and design (including Invention and Action at the tail end of an ARIA conflict engagement process) can be understood by thinking of a program as a tree. The "whats," or program goals, are the fruit that we want to pick. The "hows", or the means for achieving these goals, are the trunk and branches that produce the fruit. The "whys", or the underlying values and motivations, are the roots that nourish the tree and hold it steady in the face of factors that threaten to stunt, topple, or destroy it.

There are two significant features to this metaphor. The first feature is that a failure to tend to the roots of the tree, or a program, can be fatal. Fruits, like goals, may be picked, destroyed or even changed from year to year without permanently affecting the tree. Branches may be pruned, cut, or damaged, but the tree will still grow. If the roots die, however, the tree cannot survive. The second feature of the metaphor is that a tree's roots, like a person's values and motivations, are invisible and, hence, easily ignored. By focusing first on the "whys" and making them an integral part of the ARIA processes, we place a conscious emphasis on tending and nourishing healthy roots at a program's outset.

Program roots need tending especially when there is little substantive disagreement on the face of things, but much emotional turmoil under the surface. Under these conditions, stakeholders suspect each other's motives, fear that their interests are threatened, and are wary of domination by others. When conflict is avoided, these fears cannot be tested openly and remain beneath the surface where they silently poison trust and open communication. When substantive conflict does surface, people tend to unilaterally define their positions and defend their interests. Either way, these dynamics retard healthy program develop-

ment and create conditions under which little on-going learning can take place.

A "why" dialogue can be powerful not just at the beginning but at later stages in a group's life as well. One of the authors of this chapter (Withers) had the following experience which he shared as a Why story when we authors were planning this chapter and sharing our stories about why we do the work we do and care about sharing it in this chapter:

> I was working with the medical staff at an inner-city AIDS clinic. These people were under great stress. It was the mid-'90s and we were just beginning to see a high number of infected infants. People were sniping at one another. The administrator hired me and a grief counselor to run some workshops and to "fix" the team. This was a group with a clear, established, and proven set of goals and procedures. They were even achieving much of what they had agreed to. Though this was decades before we "invented" our systematic process of asking Whys, I somewhat naively asked two simple why questions in one-on-one interviews: "Why did you become a nurse?" and "Why on earth did you choose a field of practice where every one of your patients dies?" The responses were powerful. In a feedback session, I read the "why" responses without names back to the group. The responses were not identical, but a couple of weeks had passed since the interviews, and most people could not identify their specific response. It was an emotional dialogue as people piggy-backed on what had been said. In the follow-up, some tried and true "whats" and "hows" ended up being changed and some were re-embraced driven by the resonance of shared "whys".

As this vignette illustrates, a "why" dialogue can help a group that is experiencing distress by reaching down and reconnecting with its collective roots. Doing so not only stabilizes and strengthens a group, but also provides a basis for effecting change and maintaining continuity at the same time. The Why process, we each discovered in our own way, *helps good people do good work better.*

Why 'Why' Is So Powerful

What accounts for the power of "why"? Argyris and Schön (1996) argued that under conditions of value conflict, people can engage in a kind of inquiry (i.e. "double-loop learning") that "gets underneath the members' initial commitments" and in which participants "ask why they hold the positions they do and what the positions mean" (p. 21). To be effective, however, this kind of inquiry needs to be guided by a set of higher-level values: ·valid information, free and informed choice, and internal commitment to choice and constant monitoring of its implementation (Argyris and Schon 1996, p. 118). An effective "why" dialogue promotes all three of these higher-level values. It generates valid information by making stakeholders' underlying motivations public and observable. Rather than suppressing or advocating what they think, people display their thinking – literally holding it up as if suspended before them – so that they and others can see and understand it (Isaacs 1999).

The extent to which participants are open and honest, of course, determines the degree of validity of this information. This approach to goal inquiry helps participants understand and make sense of their own and others' values. It does not mean accepting, rejecting, or judging values as right or wrong. This feature of the "why" dialogue is closely related to "appreciative inquiry" that gets "beyond superficial appearances to deeper levels of the life-generating essentials and potentials of social existence…to affirm, and thereby illuminate, the factors and forces involved in organizing that serve to nourish the human spirit" (Cooperrider and Srivastva 1987, p. 131).

The essence of the "why" dialogue is in the illumination of a person's choice to participate in a particular program or process. This illumination often occurs to the speaker him or herself, along with listeners, when answering "why it matters to me" questions and follow up inquiries. It asks people to take that choice very seriously and to consider why their participation is truly important to them. In this way it informs choice – often from a place closest to them and yet one about which is rarely actually inquired. This process helps make peoples' own needs, values, and desires conscious and explicit first to themselves, so that they can be explored, questioned, and subject to choice. Thus the eventual choice of goals draws on a wider base of information than is usually readily available. The choice is now informed

by a new understanding of one's own motivations and the motivations of others. As one participant put it, "When I thought about 'why' it made me change my 'what'." Participants in a "why" dialogue come to appreciate their differences in ways that lead them to seek common ground.

Passion is under-explored in the literature, perhaps because it is so out of step with the dominant espoused values of rationality in organizational life (Boverie and Kroth 2001; Hirschhorn 2003). Maybe passion is the ultimate stretch into discomfort that all learners need to take. It may be that we avoid engaging passion because it has been mistakenly associated with the irrational – a loss of self-control and the heated emotions that sweep people up and lead to tragic consequences. Weber made a distinction between passion "in the sense of *matter-of-factness* of passionate devotion to a 'cause,'" and passion as a "sterile excitation… devoid of all feeling of objective responsibility" (Weber 1919, cited in Gerth and Mills 1946 p. 115). Passions are not an obstacle to productive work and relationships. Our observation is that passion which is at the root of people's authentic "whys," when linked to responsibility, is essential to good work for both program stakeholders and evaluators alike.

Finally, we believe that the power of "why" stems, at least in part, from a fundamental change it encourages about the way one thinks about oneself and about one's relationship with others – that is, identity. The essence of the "why" dialogue is articulating and sharing one's passionate devotion to a goal, a program or a cause in the presence of others, moving participants far outside the norm of a typical planning session. Asking "why" sets into motion a process of "reflexive" dialogue in which the experience of the other touches and resonates with something in ourselves. This process yields a kind of "analytical empathy" (Rothman 1997, p. 45) in which both sides discover similarities and commonalities at the level of their deeper, existential needs.

Martin Buber claimed that an individual's most basic "I" (needs, values, desires) is articulated through an encounter with a "Thou" (Buber 1970). Buber suggested that in such encounters people "respond" rather than "react" to each other:

In our life and experience we are addressed; by thought and speech and action, by producing and by influencing we are able to answer. For the most part we do not listen to the address, or we break into it with chatter. But if the word comes to us and the answer proceeds from us then human life exists, though brokenly, in the world. The kindling of the response in that "spark" of the soul, the blazing up of the response, which occurs time and again, to the unexpectedly approaching speech, we term responsibility (Buber 1966, p. 19).

This kind of response and the emergent feelings of responsibility that accompany it is what we see time and again during the "why" dialogues that we facilitate. It is not about creating in-group intimacy (though that can often occur as a side-benefit). It is the experience of coming together in order to accomplish purposes valued by the stakeholders in a wider environment (Hirschhorn 1990). Paradoxically, the "why" dialogue enables people to focus on their joint tasks and objectives, moving them beyond the interpersonal and political, by making these values very personal. We believe that the "why" dialogue that always precedes the work of Invention in conflict engagement and collaborative goal setting in Action Evaluation, is the key to our success. This has been demonstrated in hundreds of meetings with thousands of participants in more than a dozen countries while supporting groups to come up with consensus goals about an initiative they are about to launch.

How to Facilitate a "Why" Dialogue in Action Evaluation

Over the past 15 years we have facilitated hundreds of "why" dialogues and trained others to do so as well.[1] One of the reasons that we have been so impressed by the "power of why" is that we have each independently experienced similar patterns in our work. We have all seen groups suddenly shift into a dialogue that moves them to a different level of awareness and commitment. Each new "why" dialogue presents a unique context and set of challenges, and each of the authors tends to approach facilitation differently based on our personal styles and backgrounds. We have experimented with different facilitation approaches from completely open dialogue to a highly structured process.

Participants' initial responses to the "why" question on a questionnaire we distribute prior to collaborative goal setting (see Chap. 7) are usually of a descriptive, explanatory nature and often quite superficial. And not every "why" dialogue generates the kind of resonance described above. In fact, the psychotherapy and counseling literature warns that the question "why?" elicits reason or intellectualizing (Cormier and Cormier 1991) and is often experienced as intrusive or offensive, creating defensiveness in the client (Ivey et al. 1980; Pedersen and Ivey 1993). Thus, careful framing, guidance and participants' choice about their level of involvement are all required to achieve the kind of resonance we have so often experienced as both participants and facilitators in Why dialogues. In each case, the challenge in facilitating the "why" dialogue is moving the discourse from explanations to passions.

On the basis of our collective experience so far, however, we can suggest one among several methods that we have particularly found helpful for facilitating a "why" dialogue that leads to resonance (see Table 2.1: "Why" Dialogue Facilitation Checklist). As pointed out above, we conduct the "why" dialogue *prior* to the discussion of goals and explicitly ask participants *not* to connect their "whys" to their "whats". We say, "Don't tell us the about the 'What' goal from

---

[1] The Power of Why process is our key way of making manifest the Resonance we speak about in the two ARIA processes – those focused on conflict engagement and those focused on collaborative planning and evaluation. It is done differently in the two processes, but the core is the same. It is easier to present, and conduct, the Why process within the ARIA visioning sessions than in the conflict engagement efforts. Thus, we will first present a full step-by-step way to foster a why dialogue in Action Evaluation. We then summarize how to do it in Conflict Engagement.

Table 2.1 "Why" Dialogue Facilitation Checklist

Steps	Directions for facilitator
1. Introduce the workshop	Welcome participants
	Introduce them to the power of why process
2. Introduce group dialogue	Explain roles of facilitator and scribe
	Orient participants
	Make a 30-second round of introductions
	Explain that the recorder will be capturing the stories
	Explain Do's and Don'ts (see Table 2.2)
3. Begin dialogue	Explain and model the process
	Model use of keywords and narrative presentations
	Allow participants to share their "Whys"
	Guide "Why" dialogue and keep time

Table 2.2 The "Why" dialogue: Do's and Don'ts

Do

Ask questions to better understand where the person is coming from

Respond to the person if or when something is said that you can deeply relate to

Try to deeply understand where the person is coming from

Encourage group members to effectively probe as well – this contributes to a good group dynamic

Don't

Judge or evaluate another person's "why"

Question the legitimacy of the person's "why" – this is not a debate. Ask questions to better understand where the person is coming from

Be disrespectful or confrontational to any participant in this activity, nor allow any disrespect between participants

which you generated your 'Why' response. Just tell us Why it matters to you." Participants are sometimes taken aback by this approach, which seems counterintuitive, but it has significant advantages. First, it frees people from having to express "why" in defense of "what" (fixed positions) or in opposition to someone else's "what." The fact that there is no need for debate, agreement, or decision-making is extremely liberating. It relieves people of the burden of having to defend themselves or persuade others. The very strangeness of "why" without "what" often shakes participants out of their resistance to goal-setting and gets them thinking in non-conventional ways.

The first step in the "why" dialogue is creating the group and the setting. As a rule of thumb, a "why" dialogue should last between 60 and 90 min and involve no more than ten participants in order to provide everyone with the space they need to fully express their "whys" (in about 7–10 minutes) without the process becoming tedious for those listening. In practice, we have conducted "why" dialogues with as many as 20 people and as few as two people. However, when there are very large stakeholder groups, it is advisable to divide them up into smaller groups and hold multiple "why" dialogues with them so that all who want to can participate. In addition to the participants, there should be a facilitator and, if possible, a "scribe," whose role is to faithfully record the dialogue as

closely to verbatim as possible. Participants should be seated in a circle, preferably in an open circle of chairs rather than around a table.

The facilitator opens the session with a short introduction to orient participants and to explain her or his role as facilitator. For example, we might say to the group:

> We are now going to talk about why these issues are so important to us, personally. This should help all of you to think about why this matters to you, as well as to get a sense of why it is important to the other people in your group. We find this is an essential and often missed step in building a vision for a future that the people who will live there really want.

We then make a very quick round of introductions that are limited to name and perhaps one other simple identifier (e.g. profession or favorite bird) as an ice-breaker. We explain that the scribe will be trying to capture the stories while being spoken so that we have them in the future. We also let them know that the scribe may slow them down or ask them to repeat an important narrative if they haven't been able to capture it accurately.

It is extremely important for the facilitator to be absolutely clear about the ground rules of the "why" dialogue before it begins (See Table 2.2: The "Why" Dialogue: Do's and Don'ts). For example, the facilitator might say: "The purpose of this dialogue is for everyone to understand where each person is coming from and why they care. Nothing anyone says is open for debate, but it is open for clarification."

We are careful among ourselves to refer to this step in the process as a "dialogue" rather than as a "discussion" because it is much closer to what Isaacs (1999) calls "dialogue" in which people "think together…exploring the nature of choice…evoking insight… reordering knowledge, particularly the taken-for-granted assumptions that people bring to the table" (p. 45). Dialogue improves the quality of talk by "helping to create an atmosphere in which we can perceive what really matters most to us, and to one another" (p. 47). We differentiate between "dialogue" and "discussion" as does Isaacs (1999) who explains that "discussion" is about "making a decision…which seeks closure and completion" (p. 45).

The most important ground rule in the "why" dialogue is providing all the participants with ample uninterrupted space to express themselves. The easiest way of doing this is to invite a volunteer to start by sharing his or her "why" and then to go around the circle from there. People should be given a two-minute warning before their time is up. If participants are not ready yet to share their "whys", they should be allowed to pass and returned to after the initial round has been completed. It rarely happens that participants choose not to openly express their "whys", but no one should feel coerced into doing so. Silence is honored as a legitimate form of participation rather than as a sign of resistance.

To launch a process we usually collect and analyze participants' What, Why and How goals in advance (see Chap. 7). We generally give participants their individual data and a few minutes to silently review them and to think more deeply about their "why" responses:

> You will have 7–10 minutes to share some of your Why responses with one another. I will guide this through having each of you discover and discuss what we call "passion points," or one-word summaries of why you care and personal stories that help you illustrate to your colleagues here why this word is so meaningful to you.

We have found it useful to ask participants to think of one word (a "passion-point" or keyword) that summarizes one or more of their "why" responses and to think of a short story or anecdote that illustrates their "why". It helps if facilitators model this process by introducing themselves through the use of a passion point and a story that makes it come alive. For example (from Friedman):

> My passion point is "potential". I began my career as a teacher of English as Foreign Language in Arab villages in Israel. One of my students was a kid that everyone called "the donkey" because they thought he was stupid. And, like many of the students in that school at that time, English seemed to him to be completely beyond his reach. But we took an immediate liking to each other and that ignited a liking in him for English. I didn't think he was stupid and believed in his potential. He sensed that as well and really applied himself. I paid attention to him and encouraged him and his love for English. Eventually he became an English teacher. As long as I live, I don't think anything could have given me more satisfaction than that.

One important guideline regarding passion points is that they should always be positive even if the stories behind them have negative content. The first few minutes of a "why" dialogue are often uncomfortable. Getting to passions requires gentle probing – "Yes, and why do you care so much about that?" or "Why do you feel *passionately* about that issue?" Once participants realize that they are not being asked for descriptions but rather to reflect on deeper motivations, and to illustrate them as best as they can, it can also be discomfiting because they are simply not accustomed to being asked to think about *why* they hold the values that they hold. If necessary, facilitators may ask participants to share more, go deeper, or clarify what they have said. They may also reflect back the core values expressed in the participant's stories or dialogue in order to help the participant gain clarity and for the scribes's benefit. A facilitator may want to gently "guide" the speaker's words – lifting them with their hands as it were from him or her (often the speaker will respond by looking at and talking to the facilitator) to the other participants.

The facilitator may even quietly say, "Tell *them*." Other participants are encouraged to join into this inquiry process in the same way. They can deepen or test their understanding of the speaker by asking their own why questions. This process continues until the facilitator begins to experience resonance, other group members do as well, the speaker indicates that he or she is finished, or the time is up.

Another important guideline is that each participant should treat others respectfully no matter what arises in the dialogue. Neither the facilitator nor any of the other participants should comment on, judge, or analyze another participant's "why." The goal is resonance and understanding, not argument or agreement. It is also important to prevent others from interrupting the time and space allowed for each participant. In the method suggested here, at least, the focus should stay on the one person and not shift to others even if they feel that they have experiences to share that are relevant. Each individual has her or his space and that needs to be guarded and respected. A "why" dialogue is not a game of "ping-pong" in which participants shoot comments back and forth to each other. Rather it develops as a kind of spiral, as each person's "why" resonates with others, elicits deep response, and generates new meaning which often contributes to how the following speakers frame and share their "why" narratives.

The most important facilitation tool for the "why" dialogue facilitator is the reflexive self – that is the self in context and relationship. See Friedman's example above in which he as young teacher, the context of the school and his relationship with the student were mutually formative of that student's eventual purpose and professional success. It also shows Friedman's sense of purpose, and success, as well. Facilitators model the process as they guide it. Their level of confidence, enthusiasm, and engagement will be reflected in the participants. Because the "why" dialogue is about people's hopes, passions, values, and stories, facilitators need to be very reflexive in the way that they guide and invite participants into the process.

Facilitating Why in ARIA Conflict Engagement

In the Antagonism sessions that precede Resonance work, participants engaged in either an analytical or adversarial dialogue about their antagonism toward each other (see Chaps. 3 and 5).[2] The group is now likely in a frustrated place (emotionally and/or conceptually), having spent the last three hours (or more) focusing on their conflicts and inability to move forward.

However, they should also be ready to "choose" another mode of operation, another way of engaging each other. That is where this session begins, with the turn from Antagonism (framing our conflict in terms of the Adversary) to Resonance (framing our conflict reflexively by looking at our own place in it). The participants will now begin the process of reframing the conflict and goals in terms of each sides' own needs, values and narratives rather than antagonism about and against the other side.

By the end of the session, the participants will have reset their agenda based on needs (which are articulated by their passion words) and moved onto resonance framing, thus building a new way of interacting with the other conflict party. In order to do this, participants are asked to begin exploring *why* the issues they articulated in the Antagonism sessions are so important to them, and *why* the issues continue to be a barrier to moving through their conflict.

The participants have now been prepared to share with each other the narratives that illuminate their basic human needs that have been frustrated, restricted, or denied in the conflict. Previously, all their focus was on the other. In fact, there is typically such a fixation on the other that conflict disputants rarely are able to analyze what has been at stake for themselves.

During the session just previous to this, the participants began changing their focus from their antagonisms toward the evil and aggressive "*other*" to themselves and their own needs and

[2] Refer to http://www.ariagroup.com/?page_id=3 for a fuller step-by-step presentation of this process.

values. They should have been able to reframe their Antagonistic statements into statements that articulate the needs underlying their blame, etc.

The goal for this Why session is to have the participants articulate and understand each other's reframed, resonant agenda (i.e. what "vibrates" or mirrors as most essential for each side and both together). By the end of the session, the participants should have an understanding of the *others'* resonant agenda and have achieved some level of analytic empathy. Additionally, participants will have affirmed that this type of dialogue and framing is more constructive for successful and meaningful work together.

This exercise is designed to have participants clearly tell the other parties what is at stake for them in this contradiction or conflict and why they care so deeply about it at the personal and collective level. The facilitators encourage participants to focus on their own needs/values as they speak, and on the needs/values of the other as the other speaks. Participants are invited to reframe their perspective of the conflict around these needs.

Facilitators encourage participants to tell narratives rather descriptions. As participants begin to tell why their values and needs are at stake, they are encouraged share a specific story and provide a rich illustration about why these needs and values were so important to them. At this point facilitators need to be very vigilant to protect the group from moving back to Antagonism. They have agreed to have this new conversation. Some will be wanting to have it, but may not be strong enough to maintain their desire to stay with it. Some will want to revert to antagonism. Thus, the facilitators:

1. Remind participants that they agreed to try this new way.
2. Remind them of the frustration of Antagonistic discussion.
3. Encourage them to listen to the stories of the others and see if their perspective can shift.
4. Keep participants from challenging the narratives of the others. They are invited to ask, in the first person, questions for clarity, they can support, they can affirm, but not to challenge the subjective reality the participant is expressing.

5. If it seems some participants still need to express further antagonism, take a break and have a conversation with them. Find out what they would need to continue this conversation. If they are still wanting to engage antagonism, facilitators then bring it to the group and see what they would like to do.
6. When all participants who would like to speak are finished, provide some space and silence to ensure that all have said what they need and are ready to move ahead.

Depending on where participants are in their process together, the "next steps" will be very different. The key to wrapping up the Antagonism to Resonance session is to ensure that all participants feel like they have spoken and been heard and that there is enough understanding and commitment to each other to move forward into Invention and Action stages.

References

Argyris, C., & Schon, D. A. (1996). *Organizational-learning II: Theory, method, and practice*. Reading: Addison Wesley.

Azar, E. (1990). *The management of protracted social conflict: Theory and cases*. Aldershot: Dartmouth.

Banks, M. (Ed.). (1984). *Conflict in world Society: A new perspective on international relations*. Sussex: Wheatsheaf Books.

Boverie, P. E., & Kroth, M. (2001). *Transforming work: The five keys to achieving trust, commitment, and passion in the workplace*. Cambridge: Perseus.

Buber, M. (1966). *The way of response*. New York: Schocken.

Buber, M. (1970). *I and Thou*. New York: Scribner. originally published, 1950.

Burton, J. (Ed.). (1990). *Conflict: Human needs theory*. New York: St. Martin's Press.

Cooperrider, D., & Srivastva, S. (1987). Appreciative inquiry in organizational life. In W. Passmore & R. W. Woodman (Eds.), *Research in organizational change and development* (Vol. 1, pp. 129–169). Greenwich: JAI Press.

Cormier and Cormier. (1991). *Interviewing strategies for helpers*. Pacific Grove: Brooks Cole.

Fisher, R., & Ury, W. (1981). *Getting to yes: Negotiating agreement without giving in*. Boston: Houghton Mifflin.

Friedman, V., & Rothman, J. (2001). Action evaluation for knowledge production in social-educational programs. In S. Shankaran, B. Dick, R. Passfield, & P. Swepson (Eds.), *Effective change management through action research and action learning: Frameworks, processes and applications* (pp. 57–65). Lismore, Australia: Southern Cross University.

Friedman, V. (2001a). Action science: creating communities of inquiry in communities of practice. In P. Reason & H. Bradbury (Eds.), *The handbook of action research* (pp. 159–170). London: Sage.

Friedman, V. (2001b). Designed blindness: An action science approach to program theory evaluation. *American Journal of Evaluation, 22*(2), 161–181.

Friedman, V., & Rothman, J. (2001). Action evaluation for knowledge production in social-educational programs. In S. Shankaran, B. Dick, R. Passfield, & P. Swepson (Eds.), *Effective change management through action research and action learning: Frameworks, processes and applications* (pp. 57–65). Lismore: Southern Cross University.

Gerth, H. H., & Mills, C. W. (1946). *From Max Weber: Essays in sociology.* New York: Oxford University Press.

Hirschhorn, L. (1990). *The workplace within: Psychodynamics of organizational life.* Cambridge: MIT Press.

Hirschhorn, L. (2003). *Passion and group life.* Philadelphia: Center for Applied Research (CFAR). www.cfar.com.

Isaacs, W. (1999). *Dialogue and the art of thinking together.* New York: Doubleday Currency.

Ivey, A., Ivey, M., & Simek-Downing, L. (1980). *Counseling and psychotherapy: Skills, theory, and practice.* Englewood Cliffs: Prentice-Hall.

Lederach, J. P. (1995). *Preparing for peace: Conflict transformation across cultures.* Syracuse: Syracuse University Press.

Mayer, B. (2004). *Beyond neutrality: Confronting the crisis in conflict resolution.* San Francisco: Jossey-Bass.

Patton, M. (1997). *Utilization-focused evaluation* (3rd ed.). Thousand Oaks: Sage.

Pedersen, P., & Ivey, A. (1993). *Culture-centered counseling and interviewing skills: A practical guide.* Westport: Praeger.

Rothman, J. (1992). *From confrontation to cooperation: Resolving ethnic and regional conflict.* Newbury Park: Sage.

Rothman, J. (1997). *Resolving identity-based conflict: In nations, organizations and communities.* San Francisco: Jossey-Bass.

Rothman, J., & Friedman, V. (2003). Action evaluation for conflict management in organizations and projects. In J. Davies & E. Kaufman (Eds.), *Second track/citizens' diplomacy: Concepts and techniques for conflict transformation* (pp. 285–298). Lanham: Rowman & Littlefield.

Rothman, J., & Land, R. (2004). The Cincinnati police-community relations collaborative. *Criminal Justice, 18*(4), 34–42.

Rothman, J., & Ross, M. (1999). *Theory and practice in ethnic conflict resolution: Conceptualizing success and failure.* London: Macmillan.

Rupesinghe, K. (Ed.). (1995). *Conflict transformation.* New York: St. Martin's Press.

Tjosvold, D. (1991). *The conflict-positive organization: Stimulate diversity and create unity.* Reading: Addison-Wesley.

Weber, M. (1919a). Politics as a vocation. In H. H. Gerth & C. W. Mills (Eds.), *From Max Weber: Essays in sociology* (pp. 77–128). New York: Oxford University Press.

Weber, M. (1919b). Science as a vocation. In H. H. Gerth, C. W. Mills, H. H. Gerth, & C. W. Mills (Eds.), *From Max Weber: Essays in sociology* (pp. 129–156). New York: Oxford University Press.

Weiss, C. (1993). Where politics and evaluation research meet. *Evaluation Practice, 14*(1), 93–106.

Wholely, J., Scanlon, J., Duffy, H., Fukumoto, J., & Vogt, L. (1971). *Federal evaluation policy: Analyzing the effects of public programs.* Washington, DC: The Urban Institute.

Intrapersonal and Interpersonal ARIA Process

Jay Rothman and Donna Chrobot-Mason

Before turning to more complex applications of ARIA in identity-based conflicts in the US, Israel, Palestine, Moldova, South America and elsewhere in the following chapters of this book, we will explore an interpersonal mediation to illustrate the theory of ARIA in a fairly straight-forward and step-by-step fashion. ARIA begins with the "solo" process of engaging each party separately to articulate their conflict, why it's important to them and what they think could be done about it (i.e. What, Why and How), as well as to ask them to begin to take the perspective of the other side (see for a detailed description of the solo process and its mechanics). After this first step, if parties in their own and the mediator's judgment seem ready to engage each other in at least the first two steps of ARIA – Antagonism and Resonance – they will be invited to engage in a "duet" with the third party serving as "conductor."

We use this terminology both to build on our musical metaphor extending the notion that conflict can be a source of creativity and imagi-nation, and also to distinguish ARIA conflict engagement from most forms of conventional mediation. In conventional mediation solving problems is the primary goal. While alternative forms have evolved in recent years, most notably Empowerment Mediation (Bush and Folger 1994) and Narrative Mediation (Winslade and Monk 2000), the dominant approach is still problem solving focused mediation (Fisher and Ury 1991, Susskind & Field 1996). The conductor is one who simply supports musicians as they make their own music. The score already exists. The musicians bring it to life. The conductor helps them do that. He or she is more of a facilitator, an enabler, an ally in the musicians' creative expres-sion of given music rather than an engineer of new forms or outcomes. Thus the conductor met-aphor also fits especially well with identity-based conflict in which discovery of each sides' deepest concerns, values, hopes and fears is the main pur-pose for which expert guidance is needed. Solution seeking itself must remain in, or revert to, the hands of the involved parties when conflicts are deeply rooted. Otherwise, the chance that the parties will have the sense of ownership or com-mitment to new approaches to their problems is slight at best and may in fact lead to negative reactions instead.

To further illustrate this process, we shall use the metaphor of a musical ensemble as that con-text highlights the importance of solo and duet work as well as the critical role a conductor plays in weaving both together within a larger whole to create a beautiful musical masterpiece. Consider the creation of music. When you attend a concert,

J. Rothman (✉)
Program on Conflict Resolution and Negotiation,
Bar-Ilan University, Ramat Gan, Israel
e-mail: jrothman@ariagroup.com

D. Chrobot-Mason
The ARIA Group, Inc.,
Yellow Springs, OH, USA
e-mail: robod@UCMAIL.UC.EDU

J. Rothman (ed.), *From Identity-Based Conflict to Identity-Based Cooperation: The ARIA Approach in Theory and Practice*, Peace Psychology Book Series, DOI 10.1007/978-1-4614-3679-9_3,
© Springer Science+Business Media New York 2012

you likely think little about the hours of practice each musician has undergone in preparation or the countless hours the percussion section spent working together to achieve precise timing and synergy. Instead, you simply enjoy the music as the conductor raises his or her baton to signal the first downbeat and the sounds of a variety of instruments and musical notes wash over you.

In creating music, notes come together in synergy to create a melody and various instruments play their unique melody or accompaniment that is woven together within a larger whole to create what you experience as music. In some ways, the ARIA approach is similar in that the process involves engaging conflict as a means of bringing out or creating the "music" within and between people by combining their respective parts within the whole score – the individual in a relationship, the group in context, and the community with its constituents. In this chapter we present two case studies to illustrate the application of ARIA conflict performances as Solos, Duets and Conducted interventions. In doing so, we seek to highlight the important role of solo work, duet or relational work, and the important role of the conductor (i.e., a facilitator) in weaving this work together within a larger context to create a new approach to dealing with the conflict at hand.

Conflict as a Source of Understanding: Solo Work

The whole problem of conflict, writes philosopher Martin Buber, is that people don't say what they mean or do what they say (Buber 1950). This isn't because people are hypocrites by nature. Rather, it's because most of us are unclear about what we mean, particularly in situations of stress. Paradoxically, conflict can reveal a great deal about ourselves to ourselves if we will mine it for such lessons. This chapter will show just how to do that, providing tools and examples at each practical step. The ARIA method grew out of years of Jay's professional experience as a theorist and intervener in many conflicts around the world. Yet, it is also something we have used to help us understand and

creatively engage in our own personal conflicts and, as such, we begin with a personal example. Later, we provide an example of how a third party, in the role of a conflict-coach, can use the solo process to help disputants make sense of their conflict situation and get clearer about their own goals, values and alternatives. This process of guiding disputants through the solo process, may or may not then lead to an interaction – a duet – with another. Yet, as we highlight in this chapter, solo work is critical to creative conflict engagement and thus an important first step that must not be overlooked. In this chapter, the solo process does lead to systematic application of ARIA to facilitate a successful dialogue between professional colleagues whose relationship became mired in deep misunderstandings due significantly to gender and racial differences.

The Solo Process: An Illustration of the Core of ARIA

The conceptual foundations of ARIA are based in the human needs theory of international conflict and conflict resolution first developed by John Burton and his colleagues in England in the 1950's (see Fisher 1997). As described in Chap. 1, Burton has suggested that all deep conflicts are rooted in the threats to and frustration of *individual* basic human needs. While a number of these needs as he views them are collective – like the need for valued relations – they begin in the individual human heart. Building on this conceptual framework, ARIA also starts with a focus on individual needs and values whether we are addressing interpersonal, intergroup, organizational or international conflict. Thus, the variable in ARIA as described in Chap. 1, is not the unit of analysis but rather the type of conflict. If a diagnosis of the conflict situation determines that it is primarily about identity, then ARIA theory suggests that the first step is internal work – whether individual or intragroup (Rothman 2011). Thus, the ARIA solo was born as the building block for larger systems efforts. And yet, those of us who have used it have found it to be a very powerful tool in and of itself. All too often conflicts between people do not lead to necessary and promising self-awareness because of a natural tendency to avoid responsibility and to attribute blame. In developmental, spiritual and very practical terms, this tendency is often a source of conflict escalation and distress. The consequence is that most people view conflict as a negative experience to be avoided as much as possible. Instead, if people in conflict – and third parties who accept the burden and blessing of helping others creatively engage their conflicts – would see that the starting point for any type of deep conflict engagement must be the self, the *potential of conflict* as a source of self-awareness and improved relationships with others would more often be realized.

One of the most important and delicate parts of the ARIA process is surfacing Antagonism in a safe way. To do this often requires a well-trained and experienced third party. How then is it possible, let alone useful, for an individual to surface their antagonism and negative feelings toward someone else, alone? This important question contains the answer: given that it is *their* antagonism it is therefore up to each party in a conflict to become clear about its nature (source, dynamics, components, etc.) and meaning for themselves. Thus, the solo process leads one to ask when in a conflict with a family member, for example, Why am I so upset about this? How is this conflict rooted in my own reality such as my family of origin and how as a child I experienced something similar? And furthermore, in what ways might it help me better understand myself and my relationship with my child or spouse such that I am able to make more informed and hopefully more effective choices in the future that will either enable us to avoid a repeat of the negative interaction or at least know how to engage this type of issue and each other more constructively? In this sense then, solo work can be the foundation for the entire conflict engagement process. Gaining clarity about one's own identity (values, priorities, experiences, etc.) is a necessary yet insufficient step toward transforming identity-based conflicts from destructive to creative. Ideally, after people have been introduced and guided in the use of the solo process, they will

have developed the capacity to use it on their own in the future. We like to say, "A solo a day will keep the mediator away."[1]

Elements of Solo Work

The next chapter will illustrate the "collective solo" process (i.e. intragroup pre-negotiation). However, in this chapter, we will share the conceptual and practical building blocks of the solo

---

[1] **ARIA Solo – See http://www.ariagroup.com/?page_id=3 for worksheets and more instruction on the solo process.**

Using ARIA personally as a solo process allows one to calmly view one's own conflict "performance" from a distance, and then step back into one's own conflict – to analyze and reflect upon its origin, meaning, and steps for resolution.

ROI – First, diagnose the conflict for yourself and the other party to determine the level(s) of conflict present in the situation (see Chap. 1).

Antagonism – Find a quiet and private space, where you can take a few moments to vent. There you can engage in an expression of Antagonism alone, allowing yourself to express your frustrations and "let it all out." To begin, point your index finger outward as if you are blaming the other. As you point the blaming finger, mentally or out loud verbalize all the frustrations and anger involved in the conflict.

Resonance – Now, regaining some composure, notice the next finger pointing back at yourself as you engaged in Antagonism. Use this finger to gently ask yourself, "Why do I care so much about this situation?" Take a few moments to analyze why this issue is so important to you. Be careful not to slip back into the blaming of Antagonism (neither the other side nor yourself!) – concentrate on what the conflict, issue, or relationship means to you personally from the inside – why it matters to you.

Invention – Move to the next finger pointing back at yourself, and ask, "What ideas do I have to improve the situation?" This may be designing a way of engaging the other party to help you constructively address the conflict. It may also be deciding to do something entirely on your own, like changing your own behaviors, learning to deal with the other party differently, or even removing yourself from the conflict situation. Be creative about all the ways you might deal with the conflict.

Action – Viewing the final finger pointing back to yourself, ask "How will I implement my solution?" Select one of your Inventions, and plan your actions specifically. Prepare meeting times and places, ways to monitor your new behaviors, or any other arrangements necessary to implement your solution. What steps will you take, when and in what ways?

process in and of itself (by oneself and for one-self) in preparation for an interpersonal and conducted ARIA duet (i.e. a mediation).

Perhaps the most important two principles of the solo are "know thyself" and try to "take perspective" of another with whom you are in conflict. As discussed already, conflict is paradoxically one of the richest sources of self-awareness. It is a paradox because most of the time people flee or fight conflicts with someone else – trying to avoid them at all costs or putting the onus on the other side and trying to defeat them – meaning they don't engage conflicts as a resource for inner-learning. In that case, conflicts more commonly become barriers to self-awareness as people use all sorts of routines such as attribution of the evil nature of the other side, projection of one's own shadow on to that evil other, polarization of the good us from the bad them, and blaming all ills on the other side, to avoid what Buber calls the decisive but often reviled "inner turning."

He writes that "At first, a man (sic) should himself realize that conflict-situations between himself and others are nothing but the effects of conflict-situations in his own soul [that is – his whole being]; then he should try to overcome this inner conflict, so that afterwards he may go out to his fellow-men and enter into new, transformed relationships with them." He goes on to describe how such an acceptance of internal responsibility, even agency, is "extremely repugnant" to us given the normal appeal to the "fact that every conflict involves two parties and that, if he is expected to turn his attention from the external to his own internal conflict, his opponent should be expected to do the same." And here is where Buber's teaching is at the core of the Solo process: "But just this perspective, in which a man sees himself only as an individual contrasted with other individuals, and not as a genuine person, whose transformation helps towards the transformation of world, contains the fundamental error…The essential thing is to begin with oneself, and at this moment man has nothing in the world to care about than this beginning" (Buber 1950, p. 28).

Many scholars have argued that at the heart of long-lasting conflict lies identity differences (Ernst and Chrobot-Mason 2010; Putnam and Wondolleck 2003). The most significant barrier to collaboration involves our divergent values, priorities, experiences, and opinions which often lead to intransigent conflict. The ARIA process suggests that to get to the core issues of a particular conflict, we must engage in solo or individual work focused first on our own identity.

Individuals have both a personal and a social identity (Pelham and Hetts 1999) and because each has psychosocial and emotional significance for us, they both contribute to our self-concept (Tajfel and Turner 1986; Turner and Giles 1981). While our identity serves an important function because it helps meet a basic and important fundamental human need to experience belonging and uniqueness (Brewer 2001), it also creates divisions and potential sources of conflict as we categorize others as "like us" or "not like us." Individuals tend to categorize themselves and others in ways that distinguish "in-group" members from "out-group" members (Ashforth and Mael 1989) and this categorization process often results in polarization and strong emphasis on differences which can result in greater conflict (Northrup 1989).

Attribution theory has been both theoretically (Jones and others 1972) and experimentally (Sillars 1981) developed primarily in social psychology. It has been frequently applied to conflict theory and resolution (see Coleman and Deutsch 2000). In his book on interpersonal conflict resolution Donahue focuses a great deal on attributions and how to overcome them (Donahue and Kolt 1992). Attributional bias in conflict leads disputants to generalize what they view as negative behavior of their adversaries as dispositional (i.e. "their nature") but see their own hostile or aggressive actions toward the other as rooted in situational constraints (i.e. the environment). In other words, when we have a disagreement with our spouse that leads to a negative dialogue in which both of us speak in a disparaging way toward the other, we are much more likely to attribute our spouse's comments as reflective of his/her pessimistic disposition but our own negative comments as due to a situation like having had a poor night's sleep. Thus, when each side sees the other as negative by nature, effective negotiation is very difficult because it reduces the will to mutual accommodation. If the other side is by definition negative, then it is not very rational to accommodate them as it might simply provide the "evil other" with more opportunity for hostile action.

Recently, some scholars have suggested that parties involved in identity-based conflict seeking resolution must engage in a multi-phase process which begins with a focus on positive distinctiveness (Fiol et al. 2009) and identity clarity (Ernst and Chrobot-Mason 2010). Identity work (Ferdman 1995, 2003) involves clarifying who we are, what is important to us, what experiences have shaped our values, and how our identity impacts the way we interact with others. Clarifying our identity and in particular, the aspects of our identity that are threatened in a given conflict situation, is important work that must be done before a mutually positive solution can be determined to resolve the conflict. Ferdman (2007) suggests, "when I can understand who I am and what that means to me, I can also be clearer with other people about what I want and need as it relates to my identities, without wanting or expecting them to read my mind or to make decisions on my behalf" (pp. 13 and 14). Thus, identity work is an important part of the solo work done as part of the ARIA process. By starting with a clarification of our own identity and how this helps shape our experience of the conflict situation, we are better able to gain a wider and more thorough view of not only the conflict itself, but also possible actions that may lead us down a different and better path.

Thus the process of ARIA begins with the solo process. First one expresses *What* bothers oneself about the other person and the conflict with him or her. The instructions invite the soloist to calmly view one's own conflict "performance" from a distance, and then step back into one's own conflict – to analyze and reflect upon its origin, meaning, and steps for creative engagement with or without the other side as if one is "on the balcony" viewing one's own situation as an interested but dispassionate observer might (See Ury 2000).

The following case study, which begins with the solo phase of the ARIA process, illustrates the importance of recognizing and exploring our own identity as it relates to a particular conflict situation. During times of conflict, when differences in opinions and perspectives emerge, identity often becomes more salient. Individuals experience a sense of threat when their identity salience is heightened and they perceive that they are being devalued (Crocker et al. 1998; Murphy et al. 2007). Research findings suggest that even some minor events may "trigger" social identity threat which lead to conflict (Chrobot-Mason et al. 2009). People tend to have very strong visceral reactions when they perceive their identity is being devalued. In the case that follows, Donna describes a conflict situation with a colleague and the solo process she engaged in to help her determine how best to handle it.

We had recently formed a hiring committee comprised of myself and three senior male colleagues. The committee had narrowed the pool of candidates to three (two men and one woman) and invited each for an on-site interview. Following the set of interviews, the committee met to discuss perceptions and to rank order the three candidates and identify our top choice to whom we would extend a job offer.

My three male colleagues chose one of the male candidates as their top choice while I chose the female candidate. Given that majority opinion ruled, the committee extended a job offer to male candidate one. Two days later, I received an email from a disgruntled student with what seemed to be very legitimate complaints about male candidate two who had not received a job offer but was still considered a front-runner until male candidate one either accepted or rejected our offer. Thus, I forwarded this email to each of the hiring committee members and expressed my concern over such comments.

The next day, one of the male colleagues on this committee and also my department head (Jack) asked if I had seen the email that Larry, one of the committee members, sent. He showed me the email that was sent to the other male committee members but not to me. It read: "Hell hath no fury…"

I thanked Jack for showing this to me and typed these words into my computer. What came up of course was that this common phrase or expression often attributed to Shakespeare is meant to suggest that there is nothing as furious as an angry woman.

That evening at home, I grew more and more angry as I pondered the meaning and intent of the email. As a junior faculty member seeking the support of these senior male colleagues for my tenure decision, I knew it was risky to respond at all. However, as a woman, I knew I had to respond professionally and wisely. Thus, I engaged in the ARIA process to consider an appropriate response to this conflict situation.

i. Antagonism. I asked myself a series of questions to uncover the negative feelings and thoughts I was having about Larry – what I blamed him for and my perception of his role in the conflict situation. I clarified for myself that I blamed him for being dismissive of me and my input when all I did was attempt to provide necessary information to the hiring committee. I thought his actions were sexist and that he decided to have a "joke" with his male colleagues at my expense.

ii. Resonance. After surfacing my anger toward Larry, I moved to the resonance phase of the process by asking myself why I was so upset by Larry's actions and why this was so important to me. I realized after doing some journaling that the situation was painful for me because I felt devalued and that my ideas were not being taken seriously. I also felt torn. I wasn't sure I should report the incident because it could impact my ability to get tenure in the future. Yet, I did not ethically feel that I could just let this treatment of women go undeterred. I felt I had an obligation as a diversity scholar and a female to speak out against such sexist behavior. After becoming more aware of my own feelings, I began to ask what I might have done to contribute to this negative situation. This took a bit more time to uncover and actually required coming back to thinking about the conflict situation again the next day after sleeping on it and letting some emotions cool a bit. What I then realized was that I might have come across in my e-mail as overly negative toward the male candidate and that I was perhaps overly sensitive toward gender issues as a female and a diversity scholar in a male dominated profession.

iii. Invention. Once I had considered my own feelings and how I was contributing to the conflict situation, I was able to brainstorm ideas for improving the situation. I was able to come up with a list of possible actions that included things such as confronting Larry and letting him know that I found his email offensive as well as writing a letter to Larry to document what happened and why this was hurtful to me, but then not sending the letter. I also began to consider how this conflict might become an opportunity to discuss the issue of gender in our department not only with Larry, but will all my male colleagues.

iv. Action. I then considered my options one more time and began to think about how Larry might respond to each of the ideas I listed as well as possible consequences for each. The solo work that began with uncovering my own negative thoughts and feelings led to a deeper understanding of why and how the situation was affecting me and my perception of Larry. Through this process I was able to clarify for myself the fact that my identity as a diversity scholar and a woman felt threatened. Knowledge of this perception ultimately allowed me to engage in a well-thought out plan of action.

The next case you will read exemplifies the important role of self-examination in conflict engagement and how an investment in this internal, private solo work may facilitate a healthier outcome: learning. Davidson and James (2007) describe a process for developing positive relationships across difference in which they describe core skills needed to transform conflict into learning. They argue that individuals must gain awareness of and process the emotions associated with conflict through reflection, "self-talk", writing about their experience, and mindfulness (Davidson and James 2007, p. 149). Solo work is often a necessary pre-cursor to successful interaction between two divergent parties. Such pre-work can facilitate shifting the focus of the conflict from entrenched positions to a better understanding and appreciation of one another. In the next case study, we illustrate both the solo and duet work involved in a conflict situation involving a black man and white woman and illustrate how Jay worked with both parties separately and then together in an attempt to engage the conflict more effectively.

Conflict and Creativity: From Solo Work to a Conducted ARIA Duet

The following case involved two mid-level managers at "Acme, Inc." who worked closely with each other in a marketing and development office.

"Carrie," a petite white woman in her late 40's, planned to file a sexual harassment complaint with her human resources manager about "Milt," a very large African-American coworker in his early 50's. After drinks at a staff retreat six months earlier, Milt had said something that upset and frightened Carrie; the encounter had

since snowballed into an increasingly caustic relationship. Simmering tensions and antagonistic interactions between them spiraled into overt hostility that made working together virtually impossible; their hostility spilled over into the workplace, causing problems for other coworkers as well.

The departmental supervisor persuaded Carrie to wait and pursue mediation before filing a complaint. She tentatively agreed, but Milt was skeptical about the usefulness of a mediation process. Further, he saw race as an underlying factor in Carrie's accusation and was threatening to resign or perhaps to file a lawsuit for defamation of character. "If I weren't so Goddamned furious at her," he told their supervisor, "I would quit. But I'm not going anywhere until my good name is restored. Besides, if anyone should leave it's her, not me."

Milt and Carrie's situation was a toxic mix of race and gender, anger, and seemingly irreconcilable differences – making the possibility of conflict "resolution" almost unimaginable. Yet use of the ARIA Framework as a process for conflict engagement has helped people like Milt and Carrie, and thousands of others over the past three decades who found themselves in "impossible" situations in businesses, communities, nonprofit organizations, and public institutions; at home between family members; and in political hotspots around the world.

A major focus of ARIA is its disciplined approach to *conflict as opportunity;* that is, its practitioners seek to transform the negative dynamics of conflict into positive opportunities for learning and constructive change. With music – the "aria" – as an organizing metaphor, ARIA represents four complementary phases in conflict intervention: Antagonism, Resonance, Invention, and Action. Together, these four make up the "aria," the creative process that enables antagonists like Carrie and Milt to find a way through the rancor and to start building a productive way forward.

Another central characteristic of ARIA is that *how* it is applied in a given conflict is contingent up on the circumstances specific to that situation. That is, before conflicting parties, with or without a mediator, begin any of the phases of the ARIA, they first diagnose the level or type of conflict they're facing. Only when the nature of a specific conflict is understood can mediators and disputants begin to formulate the most creative and effective ways to engage it.

The dispute between Milt and Carrie was unquestionably an identity-level conflict. Like most such conflicts, however, it also manifested certain characteristics of less complex conflicts. It included, for example, an element of objectives-level conflict: both parties wanted to pursue an action (harassment complaint or lawsuit) in order to achieve a particular goal (cessation of harassment or restoration of reputation). Without a doubt, however, the heart of the conflict went deeper, to the disputants' very sense of identity and personal security. For Carrie as a petite woman, feeling like she was viewed as an object of sexual advances, whether in jest or not, was deeply disturbing to her. It was also not unfamiliar, which made the insult all the more injurious. For Milt, a large black man, being seen as a threat simply because of his size and skin color was all too familiar. And infuriating. Moreover, the image of black men being lynched for little more and often less than simply "looking at a white woman" made this issue volatile.

The Self-directed ARIA as Solo or Duet

Although an ARIA usually refers to a piece for a solo voice, as noted we stretch the musical metaphor by asserting that ARIA can be effective as a "solo" or a "duet" when used to address conflicts between individuals. That is, one person can work through all or part of the process independently and then engage the other party to work through, perhaps, the last two phases (Invention and Action) together. Or, depending on the specifics of the situation and its particular antagonists, the parties might work through the entire process (Antagonism, Resonance, Invention, Action) in tandem.

Either of these approaches, in which the solo and duet are self-facilitated, are often appropriate for resource-based conflicts (which may not require the parties to engage in the Antagonism phase at all). Complex identity-level disputes, however, almost always require a third-party to intervene and facilitate the ARIA. It is difficult to imagine Milt and Carrie, for example, working through their conflicts without assistance. In this case, the antagonism was too deep and too raw to be handled without the support of a third party. The organizational leader called Jay in to serve as a mediator.

A Call for Mediation

The president of Acme, Inc., who I had known socially for some time, called to tell me that I would soon be hearing from the manager of his marketing department (Tom) who was at his wits end about two direct reports who were at war with one another. When Tom called he told me that Carrie, a white woman, had planned to file a Sexual Discrimination Complaint with the human resource manager about Milt, a black man in his department. Tom said he had convinced Carrie to wait and instead pursue mediation. Carrie agreed pending meeting the mediator and reviewing this option fully. The problem was Milt. He was so steamed up about the whole thing, he was threatening to quit. Tom told me that Milt was very skeptical about the usefulness of mediation and was considering filing a lawsuit for defamation of character. However, he agreed, on the president's urging, to talk with me. Was I willing to take this on?

I told him I would certainly be willing to meet with each of them separately and conduct a solo interview. After that I would let each of them and Tom know if I thought mediation might help and if I was willing to conduct it.

My phone call with Milt was painful, but he agreed, reluctantly, to meet with me. "Milt," I assured him, "you really do have a choice about this. If you don't want to do this you don't have to."

"Oh really? Even though the president has said I should, I can just walk away, huh?"

"You have a point. Anyway, let's meet and if after we meet you don't want to do this, I will support your choice to the president if that will be of any help. In fact, I will be willing to tell him I think it's a bad idea."

The conversation with Carrie, on the other hand, was different. She expressed great relief that we might be able to set up a mediation. "I only threatened to file the harassment complaint, because he wouldn't discuss anything with me. Both Tom and I had previously suggested mediation and

he refused. I know this comes from the top, but hey, anything to get us talking effectively together is worth it."

My solo interviews with each of them left no doubt in my mind that this was an identity conflict for both of them and that the ARIA process might be able to make a difference. But I was by no means confident that it would. That, of course, would depend on the party's will. My job therefore would be to help them lay bare their respective feelings and understand fully the negative consequences of continued antagonism and stalemate. On the one hand the mutual threats to take legal action was making the dynamic war-like. On the other hand, this "fallback" position, could lead to a clear "win" if they could find a way forward together. Meanwhile, their antipathy was as thick as molasses. They used the word "hate" and "despise" in speaking about each other. They had avoided direct communication for the past two months even though they attended staff meetings and worked side by side almost daily in their small 10-person department. Each told me the situation was unbearable.

Pre-mediation: The Solo Interviews

I begin with Carrie. She is enthusiastic and relieved. She tells me again that the only reason she filed the complaint was so Milt would take her seriously. In fact, she felt he objectified her and this was the source of her antagonism. She feels unseen, unheard and disregarded by Milt. She understands his own antagonism and the very difficult position this put him in – symbolically and practically. A white woman charging sexual harassment by a black man was, to say the least, politically incorrect for both of them. Moreover, if he was angry at her before for what he called a "misunderstanding" he was furious with her now for her perceived willful aggression. She also had significant analytic empathy – even while she felt hurt, offended and angry at him – about what her accusation might do to his own sense of face and dignity. Nonetheless, she felt he left her with no alternative but to pursue an aggressive course, until and unless he was seriously willing to engage in dialogue and some form of problem-solving with her.

As I walked her through the solo interview process, she was clearly engaged and mostly eager for next steps: meeting together with him. However, she also expressed skepticism and even fear. "I don't imagine he will be willing to go through with this. And worse, she said, he may agree only so he can tell me what a dumb *@#! I am. And a racist one at that…" as she began to tear up. "I don't want to hurt him. But he sure hurt me. I don't know what else to do. I sure hope you can help, Jay." She ultimately viewed herself as a victim and would either get some kind of acknowledgement from him that he had violated her, even if unwittingly, or would have her "day in court" to restore her sense of honor.

Milt felt he had done no wrong and that Carrie was being malicious and racist. She was just the latest in a long line of white oppressors. Victimizers. He also felt furious at the situation with me. "I am not mad at you, but at the role you are playing and have further put me in. I can't say no to you or I "prove" my own guilt. If I am not willing to try an alternative to the more formal dispute resolution process coming out of the company's office of personnel, at best I'll be blamed for wanting a fight. Well, actually, I do. But don't blame me! She has splattered my good name and I'll have my day in court if necessary against her. But I can't really say no to you can I or I'll be seen as the aggressor I am accused to be."

Clearly he is in a dilemma and seeking to fulfill the adage of "doing no harm," I assure him that he can say no and not be hurt by this; in fact, I say, unless he is internally motivated to do this, I want him to say no. He looks hopeful and skeptical at once. I explain that I had told his president that my only commitment was to do an assessment of whether this situation was "mediation-appropriate." I can easily tell him that after an assessment I find that I can't help. I can do this in a clearly no-fault way by saying some conflicts, perhaps like this one, have reached a stage of no return in which a binding third-party process is the only way to go. Milt visibly relaxes and says he will trust me and will go ahead on the condition that either of us can say no and no blame will accrue to him. I agree as long as this "no" comes before we start. I explain to him how the ARIA process (which he too has read about in summary form before meeting with me), requires a commitment to the first two steps of the process. I explain again that if parties leave in the middle of the first step, surfacing Antagonism, and certainly before we move through the second step, Resonance, it is quite probable that things will get worse than they already are. He says he fully understands and accepts this. In fact, he says he is grateful for what seems to be a very structured and rational process given how irrational everything seems. He now goes on to tell me how Carrie completely misunderstood and blew out of proportion what was simply some friendly bantering between them

at a company picnic. And yet as, he goes on, he recalls that when he was hired she seemed to be against him from the start. "Actually," he says, "I believe this complaint is simply a ruse to get rid of me. For whatever reason she feels threatened by me professionally and she has turned this into a lynching…"

After these initial discussions I ask each of them to go through the solo questions (in interview form) and gain a clearer picture of the deeply identity-based and volatile conflict confronting them both. The mediation is set for one week from now.

In Milt and Carrie's case, there was never any question of a self-facilitated ARIA. When their supervisor enlisted me as a third-party mediator, an ROI analysis (see Chap. 1) readily revealed that both were reacting not only to their own perception of each other's actions in a particular situation, but also to profound and tangled emotions that sprang from their respective life experiences as a white woman and as a physically large small black man.

In the following pages we summarize the ARIA process through which Jay guided Milt and Carrie. The actual process took more than 10 hours over the course of four meetings (two separate and two together).

The Duet: Facilitating the ARIA Process

My initial solo interviews with each of them left no doubt in my mind that their antipathy for each other was extreme: each used the word "hate" in speaking about the other. They told me they had avoided direct communication for the previous two months. For both of them, this was clearly a very deep and destructive identity conflict, but I believed the ARIA process might be able to make a difference. And so, through the course of conducted solos, I helped each to begin to surface their antagonism and to draw up a summary list of issues each hoped to raise when they came together for a duet.

Preparing for the ARIA

At the opening of our duet session, Carrie asked why they couldn't just skip to the second phase of the process: "We both know the Antagonism parts of this conflict all too well. You already heard them in our solos." This is a frequent question from parties in identity-based conflict. Yet, as I explained to Carrie, skipping the Antagonism phase and trying to move prematurely to Resonance almost assures failure for two basic reasons. The first is that antagonism normally is unbounded and undisciplined. In the ARIA process, we guide it, even choreograph it so we can steer its passion, ultimately, in creative ways. If we don't walk through the morass of antagonism purposefully in identity-based conflicts, it will assuredly hit us in the back of the head when we're not looking. Secondly, unless both disputants decide to let go of the way they have been viewing the conflict and the way they have been engaging in it, any fix will be temporary at best. The decision to move to more constructive ways of dealing with the past and future, comes from a present experience that intensifies the negative reality antagonists have been living with and leads them to say, "Enough! No more!"

After getting Milt and Carrie's agreement to move ahead and to stay the course as the process unfolded, I asked them to articulate some outcomes they would like to see from the process.

Carrie: "That we can communicate with each other and not get angry, or a stomach ache, during the process."

Milt: "Communicate would be good. Before that, however, my goal is that we can stand to be in the same room with each other."

Carrie: "That we can do our work together efficiently as professionals."

Milt: "And that our colleagues aren't watching us wondering when the next explosion will happen."

Antagonism

To begin the Antagonism phase of the ARIA, sometimes I need to stoke the fires a bit to get disputants to state their antagonism and overcome a kind of polite but artificial posturing with statements like "I wish things weren't so bad between us." Such stoking was not necessary with these two. I asked, "Okay, who wants to start? That is, who will describe a conflict issue you want to raise?"

Milt: "I'll start. I detest that woman."

Carrie: "He picked the wrong woman to harass!"

I tried again: "Could either of you give me one substantive issue that is at stake here, besides your mutual distain?"

Milt: "That she will withdraw her false account of harassment."

Carrie: "Only if he truly apologizes for harassing me!"

I reminded them, "I want you to be able to share your issues in ways that the other side can hear – not necessarily as accurate – but not as a direct attack either."

Milt: "Okay, I can modulate my anger. But... I want to understand why she has attacked me and wanted me out of the company, even before I was hired."

Carrie: "What in the hell are you talking about? I...."

Jumping in once again, I told Carrie to hold on, that we were still trying to put together our agenda for the day's discussion. They would have the chance to discuss issues soon and to question one another about their respective issues.

The ARIA facilitator, who has explained the process as fully as possible to participants before they agree to engage in it, nonetheless has to jump in frequently and quite forcefully at times, cutting people off mid-sentence, if it is clear that their trajectory is off course for the current stage and purpose of discussion, as in the case above. And so Carrie and Milt made another attempt to list their conflict issues:

Carrie: "His profanity and intimidation tactics."

Milt: "The way she needs to be in control over everything. And, to summarize, the mistrust between us."

Carrie: "The things he said to me during our staff retreat six months ago."

Milt: "The way this whole issue has been handled."

Carrie: "His whole attitude regarding this effort, and previous attempts to get past our problems, has been one of resistance and disinterest."

Milt: "Your lies. You have wanted me out and used a bit of truth to hide a pack of lies."

Carrie: "You see yourself as a victim, since I was going to file a complaint against you (and still will if this doesn't succeed!). I don't see it that way."

The next step for me, once Milt and Carrie's issues were on the table, was to encourage them to ask each other questions about any of the issues they had raised.

Carrie: "Yes, if it's OK now, I'd like to understand your perspective about why in the world you think I have had it in for you? I supported your candidacy for this job and worked hard to work with you. You undermined it all, not me."

Milt: "We see things very differently. My analysis is that either you have a black man/white woman complex or for some other reason you are threatened by me. I know I'm big. I know I'm black. I have been all my life. And I've scared white people. So, I'm careful. But you know, it's your problem. I'm tired of it. I don't accept it as my problem. You just need to deal with it. I didn't want to engage this issue with you, essentially because I didn't

*want to legitimize your delegitimization of me. I'm
f******fed up with it!"*

*Carrie: "That's a bunch of nonsense. You're so
full of yourself, you're so filled with your own self-
pity, you project all sorts of evil on to me. You are
the one who behaved badly. You are the one who
drank too much and lost control, and yes, you made
me scared. Not because you are black. But because
you are a man. And yes, because you are big. And,
because you got drunk and out of control. And
because you have never apologized, never accepted
your behavior, I'm afraid of you."*

*Milt: "You are a liar. You lie to yourself. You lie
to get sympathy. You are still angling to get me out
of this job. I may have left on my own before, but by
God until you are revealed for the liar you are and
my good name is restored, I'm not budging. This is,
as I feared, going nowhere fast."*

*Carrie: "Look, I came here to try to talk things
through reasonably. You know exactly what I will
do if this breaks down. I will renew my sexual
harassment complaint."*

*Milt: "And I will hire a lawyer.... In fact, one is
only waiting for my signal and you'll see all hell
break out. You and the damn company as well!"*

*And so it went for two painful and volatile
hours, after which both parties felt drained and,
in fact, they both said, worse than they had
expected to. Neither was optimistic about the next
scheduled meeting, but I reminded them that they
had agreed to follow through with the entire
process.*

Why were things so heated? How can two
people see a situation so very differently? Again,
identity is likely at the heart of the matter. Our
identity differences shape divergent views of various situations and events and can cause individuals to consider a conflict-laden interaction
(particularly one in which an identity threat is
perceived) from the naturally biased lens of their
own values, priorities, needs, and background. In
the relationship between Milt and Carrie, we see
identity threat as the cause of some very strong
visceral reactions from both sides of the conflict.

Research and theory on "faultlines" by Lau
and Murnighan (1998, 2005) suggest that identity differences are similar to geological faults in
the Earth in that they are always present but may
remain dormant until some external force or pressure causes the faultlines to break apart. Their
research shows how faultlines may become acti-
vated in the workplace as some event serves to
polarize and illuminate identity differences which

often results in conflict. In the example of Milt
and Carrie, we see the faultlines of gender and
race break apart and see how with each interaction, the divide seems to grow wider and wider.
Northrup's (1989) work suggests that identity
threat plays a significant role in the conflict process. Initially, she says, an event occurs that is
perceived as invalidating a group or group members' identity. This often leads to a distorted view
of the situation from the perspective of both parties, followed by increasing levels of polarization
and exaggerated differences.

However, in this case we illustrate how the
ARIA process serves to safely surface the conflict
between Milt and Carrie. In the next section,
notice how the conductor (Jay) is able to guide
the musicians (Milt and Carrie) toward greater
understanding and appreciation of their identity
differences.

Resonance

*At the outset of our second session together, I
reminded Milt and Carrie that although so far they
had focused on blaming each other, at this session
they were both to focus on themselves, their own
narratives, and their own experience of the conflict.
"My goal," I told them, "is to assist each of you in
hearing the other's narrative as genuine. It may be
partial; from your perspective it may even be all
wrong. But in order to plan a future different from
your past, it will be very important for you to recognize that the other's narrative is, at least to them,
valid. This will inevitably challenge some conclusions you may have reached about the other side
and the situation itself. I ask for you to suspend at
least some disbelief that a new analysis is
possible."*

*Carrie: "This sounds all well and good, theo-
retically. But in fact, I'm mad as hell and the last
session didn't soothe my spirit one bit."*

*Milt: "Indeed. I am more sure she's the bitch I
knew she was...."*

*No matter how many conflicting parties I guide
through the ARIA process, I will almost inevitably
come to a point when I think to myself, "Maybe it's
hopeless. Maybe these two are simply and utterly
incapable of behaving civilly toward one another."
But even with Milt and Carrie's reflexive return to
hostility, I wasn't ready to give up. So I reminded
them that they had both agreed to do things differently this time. Acknowledging that they would
occasionally move back to the blaming mode – out*

of habit or in defense – I also reminded them that they had agreed to let me guide the process and redirect them to a mode of speaking so the other can listen, and listening so the other can speak.

"The main underlying concerns that I heard you speak last time, and in your solos," I told them, "were a sense of mutual threat and vulnerability, feelings of disrespect and wounded dignity." I invited them to share their own stories about this conflict, based on those threatened or frustrated needs, or on other issues around which they could explain their experience of the conflict.

Milt: "I think I know what you want, but why should I? She has done this to me. I'm struggling to keep myself standing, so why should I give her any more ammunition to hurt me with?"

Carrie: "Exactly. I don't want to be any more vulnerable than I already am."

Again, a reminder from me: "I need you each to stop blaming the other and talk about yourself, your own experiences, fears, and hopes."

What followed was the "magic" I'd been hoping for, as Milt and Carrie slowly, reluctantly, painfully, began to find resonance between their feelings, concerns, and fears:

Milt: "Okay...." He paused, pulled himself together and said quietly to Carrie, "You scare me to death." His voice choked and he said, "whether you meant it or not, I have experienced what you say about me as challenging me as an individual. I can't help but recall experiences of my people being lynched for looking at white women...."

Carrie: Visibly moved, her voice, too, choked as she said, "But Milt, I'm scared of you … and I deeply do not want to be."

This is where it happened – an almost imperceptible "look," in which Milt and Carrie saw one another, as if for the first time. Before that moment each saw only a preconceived image of the other, images that were, ironically, distorted by Milt and Carrie's own complex perceptions of self. What happened with that exchange was profound. Clearly, it marked a turning point as Milt and Carrie began to see the relationship from each other's perspective.

Such turning points can drain people's emotional and even physical energy, and so I suggested a break. Carrie walked out, looking more relaxed than I'd seen her. Milt, however, didn't move; he clearly wanted to talk. When he asked what I thought had just happened, I told him I wasn't sure but that it seemed authentic. He asked where we might be heading, and I told him again that I wasn't sure, but that if indeed a crack had appeared in their self-sealing interpretations of each other's nefarious motives and character, perhaps we could think about next steps.

When Carrie returned, I shared what I had just said to Milt. Both agreed, and began talking with each other – really for the first time. The quality of their discussion had changed perceptibly. I was able to relax, and with just a few gentle interventions to keep them in dialogue, watch as a marvelous performance of resonance and reason unfolded:

Milt: "I have lived all my life in my skin and size. It hasn't been easy, not because I am not proud of myself, but rather I'm always, 24/7, aware of others' fears and perceptions. It's exhausting. This event, at work – where I had felt that finally who I am and what I do are valued – has really set me back. It hurts; our exchanges have hurt; my hopes are hurt."

Carrie: "Milt, you don't know how long and hard I thought about filing that complaint before I did. I know this exchange of ours is stereotypical. But that's not why it happened. Simply, you frightened me and afterward you never were willing to sit down and talk about what happened and why. I could never express my concerns to you, so they grew. Now, I think I have some sense of why that happened before and why the gulf between us grew into a chasm."

Clearly, Carrie and Milt had cleared a hurdle, and it would have been tempting to bask in the good feelings and send them on their way. But knowing we had more work to do, I began to lay the groundwork for our next meeting: "I believe we can invent some careful and new ways for you two to interact and work more effectively together," I told them. We agreed to meet again in a week to take stock and begin designing concrete ways to renew their relationship and build safety and structure into how they would interact. I expected that a level of civility and generosity would prevail through the week, but told them they should not yet expect the gains reached in the past hour to be sturdy. We would need to consolidate it with concrete agreements about behavioral expectations.

Invention

It was a good sign when Carrie arrived early to the following session and began telling me how different things had felt at the office that week, but I suggested she wait to share those reflections when Milt arrived. He came in late, explaining that he'd been unable to get off the phone with a client who had called to vent about a problem. Another good sign: Milt was sharing professional angst, and Carrie was sympathizing.

The three of us then chatted comfortably and informally for several minutes, until I opened the session by acknowledging the "tough stuff' of the previous week and the eventual breakthrough to a sense of authentic connection. I then asked Milt and Carrie to share with one another their feelings about the previous week at work. Both said they felt they'd made progress toward building the safer and more effective workplace relationship they sought.

I then proposed a "proof-test" to see if Milt and Carrie had authentically gained resonance and built a firm foundation on which to invent creative next steps. I asked each to express the other's core concerns or values, to demonstrate that real perspective-taking had occurred. This would serve not only as evidence of resonance, but would also establish criteria to insure that the ensuing inventions met the underlying concerns at the core of this dispute.

Milt was quick to resist, declaring he didn't see why they needed to spend more effort trying to understand or articulate each others' motives. "I think," he began, "it's actually rather simple, and Carrie and I both agree. Respect is the bottom line. We need to move on to the mechanics of figuring out next steps for the business of the business." He added, somewhat apologetically, that he didn't mean to undermine or disrespect the process I'd been guiding them through.

In fact Milt had begun to do exactly what I was looking for, as he articulated what he saw as a core value or concern for himself – and for Carrie. I pointed that out to him, and asked if he saw anything else as essential from Carrie's perspective. He didn't have any other suggestions, so Carrie added that "clear boundaries" were important to her. For Milt, she felt "professional autonomy" was important.

After discussing and clarifying these values, we attempted to add more to the list, but that effort soon felt contrived and unnecessary. So having established, or re-emphasized, core concerns, we were ready to move to a more functional, forward-looking dialogue.

We reviewed, for example, what they'd learned about listening – really listening – without immediately engaging the urge to respond. Similarly, we reviewed the notion of inquiring, rather than making assumptions. It seems they had fairly well disabled the assumptions with which each had come to the earlier meeting.

Moving to the meat of the Invention phase, Milt and Carrie assembled a list of ways to promote continued resonance by meeting their mutual needs, values, and goals.

First, they would not, at least in the near future, have private meetings. If they needed to talk to each other, one could come and stand at the other's office door.

Secondly, they would not make assumptions by trying to "read" each other's facial expressions; rather, they would inquire about what they perceived as negative reactions. Further, if the atmosphere between them became overly intense,

both should discipline themselves to walk away and come back later. In other words, in their interactions with each other, Milt and Carrie would modulate their usual tendency to be direct and confrontational in relationships.

Action and Postscript

This mediation, which was one of the most powerful interpersonal interventions of my career, "magical" as Carrie exclaimed during final evaluations, was also one of eventual failure. I made a major strategic mistake that I have never repeated since. While I had told them things might well regress and they should call me when they did, neither they nor I paid much attention to those too prophetic (if in hindsight rather obvious) words. Indeed, they regressed only months later. Things got volatile again, and as he promised he would, Milt left the company and the relationship died. Now whenever I contract to conduct an ARIA, we schedule a four to six week "check up." Would our meeting again have made the difference? Obviously, I can't say so with any assurance, but I certainly wish we had had the chance. Conflict resolution is one of those strange processes in which we only know for sure, when it has failed. And of course, even then, we don't know what other factors may have actually been responsible. Moreover, and perhaps most importantly, failure is not an objective dynamic. What seems at one moment to be "failure" may later unfold to be more "successful." Much has to do with timing and context. Surely, if learning has occurred, then whether or not this or another "solved" conflict has flared up again doesn't by definition mean failure. Indeed, learning itself may in many situations be the main marker of success, and the deeper the more so. Bob Dylan croons in "Love Minus Zero/No Limit" that "There's no success like failure" but then as if to admonish one not to rest on that reassurance concludes, "and failure's no success at all."

Conclusion

Conflicts involving identity are both complex and deeply rooted. Resolving such types of conflict involves reducing the perceived intensity of identity threat. As this chapter illustrates, conflict engagement and the ARIA process begins with a focus on one's own identity first to uncover why we feel that our identity is threatened and thus why we are having such a strong negative response to someone or something. Rather than focusing on minimizing or battling over our differences, the goal is to understand and appreciate them. In the same way a conductor appreciates and integrates the unique contribution of each instrument to the overall concert piece, so too must individual identity differences be appreciated and valued for their contribution to the overall goal. This is true whether the goal is to co-exist peacefully and cooperate with a colleague at work or the goal is to achieve lasting peace between two warring countries. Learning from conflict requires effort; the rewards, both immediate and long-term, can be enormous.

Recent work on boundary spanning by Ernst and Chrobot-Mason (2011) suggests that we must first clarify and identify our differences so that we may understand and value the identity of the other rather than feel threatened by our differences. Although paradoxical and counterintuitive to our general nature which is to focus on similarities and minimize differences, boundary spanning is a process that begins with a deep understanding of the boundary or differences that divide us. To achieve the full potential that exists when individuals and groups collaborate effectively with one another, they must be able to first understand and then leverage both their similarities and differences.

The ARIA solo and duet process shows us how to engage in this important foundational work necessary to reduce the negative impact of identity-based conflict and instead, engage in learning that spans across our identity differences. Indeed, as we both reflected upon our own personal conflict experiences in writing this chapter we began to see with greater clarity the importance of framing conflict engagement as an opportunity for learning. If success is defined narrowly as resolution of conflict, then most of us are likely to go to great lengths to avoid conflict with others and "smooth things over" as quickly as possible, knowing that conflicts are rarely if ever "resolved" completely. This response to conflict, though natural and quite common, is not actually in our best interest. Because conflicts are always embedded within a larger context that inevitably involves dysfunction, failure, and change, we wish to argue that the real goal of conflict engagement is not resolution but rather learning about oneself and others.

Ideally, we may begin to view conflict engagement as a process of learning, growth, and personal development such that we become increasingly competent in creatively engaging our own conflicts with ourselves, for ourselves by ourselves (though stimulated by some conflict encounter with another). Regardless of whether the relationship ends, future encounters are restricted, or the deeper issues fail to get "resolved", we still may receive the *gift of conflict*, which is empathy and insight.

Working in conflict is largely an unsung labor. It is, ultimately, a hopeful expression about the human enterprise. Bach said of music that its purpose is to refresh the soul or celebrate the Creator. Assisting enemies to become allies, helping to shed light where there are shadows, helping people's hurts find rational expression are also forms of refreshment and celebration of creativity.

References

Ashforth, B. E., & Mael, F. A. (1989). Social identity theory and the organization. *Academy of Management Review, 14*, 20–39.
Brewer, M. B. (2001). The social self: On being the same and different at the same time. In M. A. Hogg & D. Abrams (Eds.), *Intergroup relations: Essential readings* (Vol. 2, pp. 45–253). New York: Psychology Press.
Buber, M. (1950). *The way of man, according to the teachings of Hasidism*. London: Routledge & Paul.
Bush, R., & Folger, J. (1994). *The promise of mediation: Responding to conflict through empowerment and recognition*. San Francisco: Jossey-Bass.
Chrobot-Mason, D., Ruderman, M. R., Weber, T., & Ernst, C. (2009). The challenge of leading on unstable ground: Triggers that activate social identity faultlines. *Human Relations, 62*(11), 1763–1794.
Crocker, J., Major, B., & Steele, C. (1998). Social stigma. In D. T. Gilbert, S. T. Fiske, & G. Lindzey (Eds.), *The handbook of social psychology* (4th ed., Vol. 2, pp. 504–553). New York: McGraw Hill.
Davidson, M. N., & James, E. H. (2007). The engines of positive relationships across difference: Conflict and learning. In J. Dutton & B. R. Ragins (Eds.), *Exploring positive relationships at work: Building a theoretical*

and research foundation (pp. 137–158). Hillsdale: Lawrence Erlbaum.

Deutsch, M., Coleman, P.T., & Marcus, E.C. (Eds.). (2000). *The handbook of conflict resolution: Theory and practice*. San Francisco: Jossey-Bass Publishers, 2006.

Donahue, W., & Kolt, R. (1992). *Managing interpersonal conflict*. Newbury Park: Sage.

Ernst, C. & Chrobot-Mason, D. (2011). Boundary spanning leadership: Six practices for solving problems, driving innovation, and transforming organizations. New York: McGraw-Hill Professional.

Ferdman, B. M. (1995). Cultural identity and diversity in organizations: Bridging the gap between group differences and individual uniqueness. In M. M. Chemers, S. Oskamp, & M. A. Costanzo (Eds.), *Diversity in organizations: New perspectives for a changing workplace* (pp. 37–61). Thousand Oaks: Sage.

Ferdman, B. M. (2003). Learning about our and others' selves: Multiple identities and their sources. In N. Boyacigiller, R. Goodman, & M. Phillips (Eds.), *Crossing cultures: Insights from master teachers* (pp. 49–61). London: Routledge.

Ferdman, B. M. (2007). Self-knowledge and inclusive interactions. *San Diego Psychologist, 22*(5), 25–26.

Fiol, C. M., Pratt, M. G., & O'Connor, E. J. (2009). Managing intractable identity conflicts. *Academy of Management Review, 34*, 32–55.

Fisher, R. J. (1997). *Interactive conflict resolution*. Syracuse: Syracuse University Press.

Fisher, R., & Ury, W. (1991). *Getting to yes: Negotiating agreement without giving in*. Boston: Houghton Mifflin.

Jones, E., et al. (1972). *Attribution: Perceiving the causes of behavior*. Morristown: General Learning Press.

Lau, D. C., & Murnighan, J. K. (1998). Demographic diversity and faultlines: The compositional dynamics of organizational groups. *Academy of Management Review, 23*, 325–340.

Lau, D. C., & Murnighan, J. K. (2005). Interactions within groups and subgroups: The effects of demographic faultlines. *Academy of Management Journal, 48*, 645–659.

Murphy, M. C., Steele, C. M., & Gross, J. J. (2007). Signaling threat: How situational cues affect women in math, science, and engineering settings. *Psychological Science, 18*, 879–885.

Northrup, T. A. (1989). The dynamic of identity in personal and social conflict. In L. Kriesberg, T. A. Northrup, & S. J. Thorson (Eds.), *Intractable conflicts and their transformation* (pp. 55–82). Syracuse: Syracuse University Press.

Pelham, B. W., & Hetts, J. J. (1999). Implicit and explicit personal and social identity: Toward a more complete understanding of the social self. In T. R. Tyler, R. M. Kramer, & O. P. John (Eds.), *The psychology of the social self*. Mahwah: Lawrence Erlbaum.

Putnam, L. L., & Wondolleck, J. (2003). Intractability: Definitions, dimensions, and distinctions. In R. J. Lewicki, B. Gray & M. Elliott (Eds.), *Making sense of intractable environmental conflicts*. Washington, DC: Island Press

Rothman, J. (2011). The insides of identity and intragroup conflict. In W. Zartman, M. Anstey, & P. Meerts (Eds.), *The slippery slope to genocide reducing identity conflicts and preventing mass murder* (pp. 154–172). New York: Oxford University Press.

Sillars, A. (1981). Attributions and interpersonal conflict resolution. In J. Harvey, W. Ickes, & R. Kidd (Eds.), *New directions in attribution research* (Vol. 3). Hillsdale: Erlbaum.

Susskind, L., & Field, P. (1996). *Dealing with an angry public: The mutual gains approach to resolving disputes*. New York: Free Press.

Tajfel, H., & Turner, J. C. (1986). The social identity theory of inter-group behavior. In S. Worchel & L. W. Austin (Eds.), *Psychology of intergroup relations*. Chicago: Nelson-Hall.

Turner, J. C., & Giles, H. (1981). *Intergroup behavior*. Oxford: Blackwell.

Ury, W. (2000). *The third side: Why we fight and how we can stop*. New York: Penguin.

Winslade, J., & Monk, J. (2000). *Narrative mediation: A new approach to conflict resolution*. San Francisco: Jossey-Bass.

Experimenting with ARIA Globally: Best Practices and Lessons Learned

Edward Kaufman, John Davies, and Harita Patel

Overview

This chapter provides an overview of the ways in which the Center for International Development and Conflict Management (CIDCM) at the University of Maryland, College Park, has made wide use of ARIA in many countries, in transforming conflict both across and within borders. For roughly two decades of experimentation, and in more than 100 workshops, CIDCM has included ARIA as a technique for building consensus on how to transform conflict at every level from local village communities, to societal to inter-state. While focusing more in Latin America and the Middle East, CIDCM has also facilitated many ARIA workshops in Africa, South Caucasus, South, Central and Southeast Asia, Eastern Europe and North America. Most have involved participants from opposing parties in dyadic conflicts, which were often ethnopolitical and strongly identity driven. CIDCM has also conducted many training workshops both around the world and at least twice yearly at the University of Maryland, the latter typically including several international participants.

Participants in our ARIA workshops are usually referred to as Partners in Conflict, or at a later stage, as Partners in Peacebuilding, or in short, as

Partners, a term that we use to stress that while the participants are coming from contending sides, they are nevertheless selected because they share a common denominator across the divide. Typically they are selected as civil society opinion leaders, informally representing the parties ("second track" process) where official ("first track") leaders have become entrenched in their positions and resistant to negotiation. The common linkage between groups may be as fellow "influentials" in specific categories, such as, policy advisors, university rectors or professors, newspaper editors or journalists, religious or traditional leaders, environmental specialists, leaders in human rights, business, and civil society organizations, or leaders among women or youth.

Often we have found it is better to take a bottom-up, multi-track approach, working initially with Partners at a local level in several locations, creating models of success that then lead to opportunities to move toward the center, engaging influentials (second track, or lower level officials) at higher levels until the political leaders (first track) are directly involved. For example, in one case presented here (Lesotho), we began working with local chiefs and council members, and then with police, District Administrators, Ministry of Local Government officials, Principal Chiefs, and finally the leaders and deputy leaders of all political parties represented in parliament, including the Prime Minister, who were able to reach consensus among themselves and with the Principal Chiefs

E. Kaufman • J. Davies • H. Patel
e-mail: ekaufman@cidcm.umd.edu;
JDAVIES@cidcm.umd.edu; hapatel@polsci.umass.edu

J. Rothman (ed.), *From Identity-Based Conflict to Identity-Based Cooperation: The ARIA Approach in Theory and Practice*, Peace Psychology Book Series, DOI 10.1007/978-1-4614-3679-9_4,
© Springer Science+Business Media New York 2012

on how best to transition to democratic forms of local government.

There have been a wide variety of issues dividing the Partners in these workshops. For example, in the Israeli/Palestinian conflict alone (e.g., Kaufman et al. 2006) issues included: finding a new paradigm for prisoner exchange/release (documented as one of the case studies in this chapter); refugees; the status of Jerusalem; allocating water rights; the "separation barrier/security fence/apartheid wall;" a democratic Israel for Jews or for all citizens (Arabs and Jews). Other examples include: opening borders (Armenia/Turkey, India/Pakistan, Egypt/Gaza); post-war peace building (Peru/Ecuador, Argentina/United Kingdom: e.g., Kaufman and Sosnowski 2005); environmental damage (Uruguay/Argentina); balancing land rights with ecological and indigenous protection (Indonesia, Canada); balancing long-term fishing rights with ecological protection (Galapagos, Ecuador); inter-religious and ethnic violence (Banaras, Gujarat, West Bengal, and Assam in India, Kalimantan, Maluku, Bali, Aceh, and West Papua in Indonesia, Mindanao in Philippines, Bulgaria); transition to elected local government (Lesotho, Indonesia: Davies et al. 2009); allocating water rights (Egypt/Sudan, Israel/Palestine, India/ Pakistan, Lesotho: e.g., Beach et al. 2000); introducing changes in the school system (Paraguay, Egypt); principles for autonomy or independence (Nagorno-Karabakh/Azerbaijan/Armenia; Abkhazia/Georgia; South Ossetia/Georgia; Aceh/ Indonesia); bilingual high school education (Kazakhstan); political violence at universities (Venezuela); normalization in bilateral relations (Cuba/United States); and revocation of an amnesty law (El Salvador).

The chapter is divided into five sections: (1) Background on our involvement with ARIA; (2 and 3) Innovation and adaptation of ARIA methodology in our approach to conflict transformation using Innovative Problem Solving Workshops (IPSW); (4) Three case studies discussing our experimentation with ARIA in macropolitical contexts; and (5) Conclusion – some lessons learned.

Background and Relationship with ARIA

Edy Kaufman's long tenure as Executive Director of the Harry S. Truman Institute for the Advancement of Peace at the Hebrew University of Jerusalem coincided with Jay Rothman's initial applications of ARIA in the Holy Land in a search for common ground between Arabs and Jews as part of his dissertation research there in the late 1980s.[1] Rothman was a doctoral student and Junior Fellow of Professor Edward Azar, founder and director of the Center for International Development and Conflict Management at the University of Maryland. Azar and his close colleagues John Burton, Christopher Mitchell and others were at that time testing and developing the international Problem Solving Workshop approach (PSW) to conflict resolution (see Chap. 1, this volume, Azar and Burton 1986; Fisher 2005; Kelman 2003; Mitchell 1981; Volkan 1988; Montville and Davidson 1981). As a close colleague of Azar's, Kaufman hosted Rothman at the Harry S. Truman Institute for International Peace as Rothman undertook his dissertation research to adapt the PSW to inter-ethnic relations between Jews and Arabs in Israel (Rothman 1988, 1989, 1992, 1997). As Rothman piloted ARIA as a way to operationalize, test and develop the PSW approach, Kaufman saw the potential of ARIA to meet the need for a structured process for addressing identity-driven conflicts, through transforming an adversarial stance between groups into an integrative search for common ground.

The concept of "dialogue" is often perceived, especially by the "underdog" in an asymmetric conflict, as an easy out, a way for the "top dog" to postpone or avoid action to address injustices (Kuttab and Kaufman 1998). So moving from the concept of dialogue into a "problem solving" approach was a realistic proposition for mediating the conflict, especially after the first *intifada*

---

[1] We use this term "Holy Land" as a neutral term acceptable to both parties covering territories claimed by both.

(Palestinian uprising) at the end of 1987 (Kelman 2003, pp. 81–106). The sense of empowerment among Palestinians resulting from this uprising – predominantly without using lethal weapons – gave them confidence to engage with Israelis through second track diplomacy to generate realistic propositions for how to implement the newly accepted concept of a "two-state solution." These academically facilitated second-track processes became popular, with one of them maturing into the multi-track Oslo process, which went a long way toward demonstrating the feasibility of a two-state solution. In the transition from reactive flows of aggression to mutual understanding and finally to constructive action, new avenues for the search for common ground were opened on the "final status issues" such as Jerusalem, refugees, borders and security, settlements and water. In projects co-facilitated in the Truman Institute, the ARIA framework became increasingly popular.

Particularly appealing was the way in which ARIA facilitated the parties to go deeper to understand the roots of a conflict, not limiting the process to adversarial dialogue but rather exploring the underlying human needs motivating the parties. The understanding of the conflict required a framework that included not only the tangible interests of the parties (land, water, a viable economy, rule of law, access to holy sites etc.) but also the underlying human motivations (fears and needs such as those for security, justice, respect and recognition) – the intangibles behind these concrete demands.

The untimely illness and death in 1991 of Dr. Edward Azar, the founder of CIDCM, resulted in Kaufman's appointment to replace him as Director of the Center. John Davies had joined the Center in 1988, initially focusing more on conflict analysis, early warning and prevention, and later (from the early 1990s) beginning a continuing partnership with Kaufman as co-directors of the Center's Partners in Conflict and Partners in Peacebuilding program. Kaufman began experimenting with the ARIA approach, and in time it became a primary tool of practice at CIDCM, beginning with Rothman's facilitation, at Kaufman's invitation in 1993, of an ARIA-based workshop with Palestinian and Israeli students leaders at College Park on the issue of Jerusalem.

The most striking recollection from this first workshop was when, in the reflexive or resonance stage of ARIA (see Chap. 2), he asked the students a question they'd never been asked before: *why* do you need Jerusalem? After some mumbling, protest and confusion ("I live in Jerusalem", "I am part of it", "I am a Jerusalemite"), a young Palestinian woman tried: "Jerusalem is like the heart of a body; you can go without a hand or a leg, but without the heart there is no life." When Jay went on funneling deeper, asking: "What do you mean when you say Jerusalem is the heart?" then she was able to articulate a new concern we had never heard before: "There is no other city on which we ourselves can agree to be our capital. If Gaza City, the West Bankers will oppose; if Nablus, or Ramallah, the Gazans and Hebronites will oppose, and so on. Jerusalem is the only place we can all agree on." In further discussion it became clear that Palestinians needed Al Quds (Jerusalem's name as the sacred city in Arabic) since it was uniquely central to their shared identity as Palestinians. Once it was clear that shared identity was the primary need (rather than the specific territory which supported it), it also became clear that their Al Quds did not have to overlap much with the Jewish Yerushalaim (the Hebrew word for Jerusalem), regarded by Israeli Jews as their eternal capital.

After the workshop was over, when participants were lunching at the nearby Naval Academy in Annapolis, a young submarine officer misunderstood and thought that his neighbor was from Pakistan and not Palestine. This infuriated the student, who told us: "Why do *we need* Jerusalem? Everybody knows about the Holy City, but not about Palestine. Jerusalem gives us recognition." This anecdote demonstrates how looking for the *why* behind the official discourse in terms of human needs (in this case identity or recognition), can shift the parties from polarization and deadlock to a joint effort to address the needs of both parties. Over time, it became a common illustration when training new participants to understand the relevance of the reflexive or resonance stage (the "R" of ARIA).

This observation brings us to some explanation of why this chapter utilizes the former naming system of the four stages of ARIA (adversarial, reflexive, integrative and action (see Rothman 1992)) rather than the newer naming that Rothman has adopted building on the metaphor of musical harmony (antagonism, resonance, invention and action (see Rothman 1997)). It wasn't until preparing this chapter that we understood *why* we reverted to the older naming system. At one level it may have been a matter of inertia, when our books, documents and instructional materials were already using the original naming. On another level, for us the original terms were more consistent with our process. The adjective *adversarial* meant more of an active attitude or approach, a strategic option that people adopt in the early stages of a dispute, particularly when the expectation is that the "other" will push back, or escalate. Antagonism as a noun seems more of a passive description than a matter of choice. *Reflexive* (or reflective) in our application recognizes the direct implication and value of both reflecting on their own deeper motivations, and also of reflecting back the voice of the other in a joint exploration of the needs behind their positions.[2]

The newer term for the third stage, *invention*, seems to capture well its main purpose as required in the search for solutions. However, keeping the original term *integrative* serves us well, since it highlights a strategic shift, where the parties now choose to work cooperatively to address the needs identified in the second stage. The strategy to build common ground in this stage requires movement through three steps in which the parties are progressively more integrated in their work together: (a) creative thinking in the brain-storming process requires letting go of blame and of exclusive ownership of any specific ideas; (b)

critical thinking in the evaluating and formulating process, requires closer collaboration among topic experts across conflict lines; and finally (c) the process of consensus building among all participants requires communicating and understanding the principles behind any objection and an effort to integrate those principles into a joint resolution. The *action* stage is well named in that it deals with the many obstacles and opportunities in moving from consensus ideas to practical implementation and long-tem follow through. As explained in the next section, this action stage (the term is retained in the newer ARIA terminology) has also become a multi-step process.[3]

We acknowledge that the new naming system may be just as reflective of the deductive and theoretical utility of ARIA, and we by no means are averse to utilizing it. Instead, we see this choice in how ARIA is applied and utilized within our own work as a manifestation of its flexibility and applicability in diverse situations. The new naming system has taken us towards a deeper understanding of ARIA, one that Rothman hopes to share with all those who utilize ARIA and make it their own. In the following sections we discuss the use of ARIA as we have adapted it in the context of our Innovative Problem Solving Workshops (IPSW – see Davies and Kaufman 2003).

ARIA in Innovative Problem-Solving Workshops: Adversarial and Reflexive Stages

IPSWs consist of four parts: trust building, skills building, consensus building and peace building. The first two stages we have found to be essential in preparing the ground for success with ARIA as a method for building consensus and crafting action plans for sustainable peace building. *Trust building*, both before and during the first days of the workshop, includes familiarizing

---

[2] As Rothman writes in his 1997 book, disputants may be able to explain the external attributes of their conflict and the suffering it has caused them, but they are often hard pressed to verbalize the conflict's inner meaning. As he writes, it is uncommon for disputants to try to do so since other forms of explanation are simpler, and blame is likely more familiar, rhetorically appealing and, in the short term, psychologically comforting. ARIA helps make this deeper discussion possible.

[3] As can be seen in the ARIA diagram in Chap. 1 of this volume, Rothman's original terminology inductively describes the dynamic input of an ARIA process (e.g., Adversarial framing) while the newer terminology deductively suggests its dynamic output (e.g., Antagonism).

the Partners with the process, agreeing on location, ground rules and issues to be addressed, and getting to know each other better. *Skills building* then gives the Partners confidence that they have what they need to ensure that the process will work to their benefit. Skills may include listening to understand, non-violent and cross-cultural communication, reducing prejudice, negotiation and mediation techniques, creative thinking and consent-based decision-making. When there has been enough progress with these skills, Partners will want to shift the focus to working on their own conflict, and we make the transition to ARIA.

The Adversarial (Antagonism) Stage

In this stage, it is important to provide some time for each party to first prepare to make their case persuasively, since often this is the first chance they have had to articulate what is important to them directly to the enemy – the "other" in relation to whom their primary identity may have been built – as well as to respected third parties. Authentic communication is most likely when parties are allowed to speak from the adversarial perspective that has been most familiar to them in the course of the conflict. On the one hand, participants in each party work together to accumulate sufficient arguments for all team members to play a part in articulating them. On the other hand, they strategize how to be persuasive, preparing the lines of argument, and ways to articulate them firmly and clearly.

This stage will serve several functions: it will firstly make clear what issues are currently in dispute (since these tend to shift as the conflict evolves). It will also establish the credibility of the participants as knowledgeable and effective spokespersons for their communities, who might therefore also be effective in persuading their own communities to consider any new perspectives that may emerge from the consensus-building process for resolving the conflict. And it makes clear that neither party can be persuaded to concede on the key issues, showing where they will stand firm, demonstrating the limits of a purely adversarial approach.

There is rarely any need to spend much time training the participants, since adversarial discourse has been the norm in many societies, particularly those with protracted conflicts. The setting we use for this phase is commonly a fishbowl, with two chairs per team facing each other in the center of the room and the rest of each team sitting behind. These four chairs serve to focus the debate, the ground rules requiring that only those sitting in them may speak, and that they yield their seat as others from their team come forward to replace them. All are encouraged to take a turn, and anyone may return to speak again. We call the lead speakers for each team the 'pilot' and 'co-pilot,' normally selected in the preparatory phase of this stage, from those who are more knowledgeable or articulate.

It should be remembered, however, that confrontational discourse is not a universal concept: some Japanese, Burmese and Thai participants we have worked with found it very difficult to articulate arguments in an adversarial manner. In such cases, some training in culturally appropriate advocacy skills (which may not need to be overtly antagonistic), may be beneficial for the Partners; and it will be important to emphasize that the aim of this stage is to clarify the positions of the parties, not to determine who is right or wrong.

We have found it highly beneficial in this stage to include a second round of discussion, with each team being invited to play the role of the other party. Often, there is resistance to representing the views of the other, but since the rules of the game have been clarified and agreed in advance, the Partners almost always are able to overcome this natural aversion and proceed to energetically defend their opponents' arguments. Several interesting patterns should be readily apparent. More often than not, they voice the more extreme positions of the other, either because they were less alert to the more moderate arguments or because politically and psychologically it may be more expedient to portray their rival as extremist and resistant to compromise. In the reverse role playing, the presenters tend to raise their voices more, show more aggressive body language and/or become more pointed and critical of each other. This session can be tense, but it occasionally provokes laughter or a smile at the ability of one side to represent so accurately at least the more extreme views of the other, and there is generally a softening of the tensions manifested in the first round of this stage (it is interesting to compare this to Rothman's use of reverse role playing in the Reflexive stage – see Rothman's preface to this volume). The facilitators should be vigilant, however, in upholding the ground rules throughout the simulation, to keep the discussion focused within the four speaking chairs, and if possible to engage all the Partners, while ensuring the process is stopped for debriefing before tensions are allowed to escalate to levels unacceptable to participants. The debriefing and evaluation that follows the role reversal should review the strategies used, including body language, and what was accomplished, before moving rapidly into an analysis of the value and limitations of the adversarial stage.

To a large extent, this stage is "a dialogue of the deaf" and, as such, only excites each side against the other. People are inclined to cease listening, becoming aggressive and verbose. Each listens only to find flaws in the arguments of his/ her antagonist and to counter the arguments. This form of discourse tends to affirm the participants' preconceived points of view, and to preserve or promote a prematurely closed-minded attitude, with a digging in to previously held positions. On the other hand, this stage fulfills important functions, such as helping to develop the ability to frame official positions in a powerful way, perhaps helping the opposing party to realize that both parties do have good points, after all. It also allows each side to feel pride that there is a platform from which to deliver what is normally not demagoguery but merely strongly-felt principles that might be accepted by both sides as truthful and just, and to recognize that their counterparts are also effective representatives of their community and, as such, potentially influential Partners.

Further, there is a catharsis in the process, as it allows the Partners to speak what is in their hearts, expressing their negative feelings over injustices suffered at the hands of the other, that if covered over, could later erupt or otherwise undermine the capacity of the Partners to under-

take the integrative work required to reach common ground. In other words, people may not be able to fully hear and understand their adversaries without first having been able to verbalize their own strongly held convictions in front of them. Many of the grievances brought out are genuine and profound, and there is a need to air these emotions in public before it is possible to consider different pathways to peace.

Before ending the day, it is a good idea to find a way to explain the nature of the reflexive stage, since it may be difficult for some Partners steeped in the adversarial attitudes of societal conflict to get a good grasp of it and participate in it without prior practice or awareness of its power. Often, conflict situations arise or are made worse by lack of communication and knowledge of what is important to the other. An extra effort is called for the next day, to reflect on one's motivations, values or needs, to express difficult feelings, and to listen with attention, respect and empathy to better understand Partners on the other side. To an extent, the reverse role-playing has opened the way for putting ourselves in the shoes of the other, which is a key part of the exercise to follow.

The Reflexive (Resonance) Stage

The reverse role-playing in the previous stage already provides a transition from the aggressive, polarizing tone of the adversarial stage to the capacity to argue the position of the other with passion and some empathy. Now the challenge is to move fully out from the dialogue of the deaf to an active listening mode (what Rothman calls "Resonance listening"). The reflexive stage is essential in reframing the conflict, so it is understood not just in terms of opposing positions, but at a deeper level, in terms of the underlying human needs motivating each party involved. It also significantly de-escalates the antagonism that was allowed to surface the previous day.

The transition from the adversarial stage implies shifting to a deeper level of empathy, for both sides. The facilitators should generate an intellectual comprehension of the concept of "needs" through serious discussion (see Chap. 5).

It should be explained to the Partners that when one seeks to understand what drives people and nations to the extreme of sacrificing their own lives and well being for a cause, we find that as human beings there are strong inner forces that drive us. We use the drawing of an iceberg to illustrate that what we can see through the adversarial perspective is only the top which is above water. But in order to avoid escalation or stalemate we need to explore the much bigger mass that is hidden under water (this use of the iceberg metaphor is similar but not identical to Rothman's use of it – see Chap. 1).

Human needs such as physical security, freedom from oppression and discrimination, economic well-being, group identity recognition, dignity and respect, access to political and economic participation – these are some of the human necessities which are most commonly expressed in societal conflict situations, and which appear to be universal across cultures (Azar 1990). Unlike demands or interests, which may be understood as strategies for addressing needs, human needs themselves can be seen as non-negotiable (Azar 2003), so that a settlement which does not address those which are primary for each party is unlikely to hold.

It is here that understanding the psychology of conflict, stress, motivation, and behavior becomes useful. A "dual concern" model to promote such understanding defines continuums of behavior varying with awareness or concern in two different dimensions (e.g., Pruitt and Kim 2004, Chap. 3). One represents a range of concern for self, from low (leading to yielding or avoidance) to high (leading to confrontation or collaboration); the second dimension delineates a range of concern for others, from low (leading to confrontation or avoidance) to high (leading to yielding or collaboration). Too often in complex conflicts, it is assumed that these two concerns, defined in terms of competing demands or even interests, are inherently incompatible, representing opposite poles on a one-dimensional model, with choices limited to confrontation, yielding, avoidance or possibly a zero-sum compromise. However, by recognizing that there are two distinct dimensions of concern, for self and for other,

that on the level of human needs, are not incompatible, one can discern a third continuum, from low concern for both (leading to avoidance or inaction) through moderate concern (allowing compromise), to high concern for both, which motivates collaborative effort to find a win-win or positive-sum outcome (Fig. 4.1).

This latter spectrum, representing equal concern for both parties, lies between the former two, and opens a way to move beyond them. On conflicts over issues (needs) of high concern to both parties, only full collaboration creates a stable solution satisfying both parties; any of the other options leaves one or both parties partially or completely unsatisfied, and thus represents an unstable settlement of the conflict.

There are a variety of ways to help improve the participants' talking and listening skills, and hence their ability to engage in the reflexive stage, since it is the most personal and therefore the most threatening stage for many people. Like the adversarial stage, this can be particularly difficult in some non-Western cultural systems. In America, self-examination in public is part of the popular culture, and when carefully guided in a safe setting, many Americans feel free to discuss psychological or personal problems with others, sometimes even including strangers. When dealing with Partners across cultures and nations, more often than not it is necessary to spend a good deal of time in preparing, to make participants comfortable with this more intimate and introspective session. In general, we have found it best to work in small groups of three, or four at most, and only at a second stage to share with the rest of the group in more general terms the "whys," the underlying needs that were disclosed during the active listening exercises in small groups.

In the preparatory skills building stage, Partners will have received training in active listening. In addition to giving undivided attention and respect, listening skills we have found useful include: (1) *Paraphrasing* to reflect back with empathy what the listener hears as the key statements of the other. These may include what the speaker has observed relating to their issues of concern, how the speaker feels about them, or what is behind those feelings – in other words,

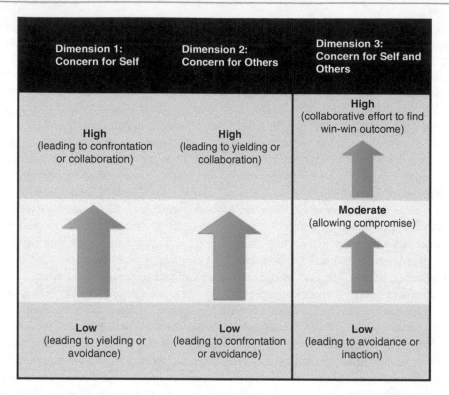

Fig. 4.1 "Dual concern" model

what it is they need. Any statements of blame, judgments, assumptions or interpretations going beyond observations, are left aside without comment. Empathy is promoted to foster understanding about what the other is experiencing and what they need as a human being, without judging them as right or wrong and without sympathizing, colluding or palliating. (2) *Summarizing* to clarify the implicit logic or structure in what the speaker is saying, which otherwise may be hidden in the flow of emotions and spontaneity. (3) *Eliciting*, in which the speaker is encouraged to say more regarding the most pressing issues, until related events, feelings and needs are clear. For Partners in conflict, some funneling may be needed to open and explore painful issues more deeply, with empathetic appreciation of the fears, motivations, values, concerns and human needs which may surface.

The tone is significantly different from the previous antagonistic stage. For example, the participants are encouraged to use "I" statements, rather than the incriminating "you" from the pre-

vious stage, to talk of their own experiences, and to be honest about their feelings. It is important to remind everyone that they should provide only as much information as they feel comfortable sharing with others, while at the same time emphasizing that opening up is not a sign of weakness. Facilitators should validate the willingness of participants to share experiences and concerns. Their concerns are often deep and personal, and therefore an empathetic and sensitive atmosphere should be constructed. This can be best achieved working in small groups.

What we originally conceived as "one to one" conversations with Partners rotating between being the speaker and the listener, evolved into groups of three, in which the third person becomes a facilitator and note taker, so that the needs of each party are recorded. Of course, the third person will also be from either one party or the other, so the note-taker job rotates between the two participants that represent the same party in each group.

The needs are best recorded on a flip chart divided into two columns, one for each party (say

Palestinians and Israelis). If we are working with 18 participants, for example, we create six groups, and over a couple of hours, facilitators generate six posters with many items on each side. When groups return back to the plenary, we post them all in order to compare and integrate the lists to reflect the overall pattern of needs motivating each party. For instance, we may start with Palestinian needs, asking the original facilitator of group six to read aloud their list, with facilitators of the other groups confirming where similar needs emerged in their respective groups. The facilitator of group six adds the number of con-curring groups for each need (if unanimous it could be a maximum of six – indicating a need of major concern for Palestinians and so for Israelis as well), and the other group facilitators delete each need from their lists as it is counted. Then the facilitator of group five goes through a similar process with the remaining needs on their list, and eventually to group one, where any remaining need would get only one vote (indicating a need not broadly shared or central to the conflict). We can then reverse the process and ask the group one facilitator to start reading their Israeli needs, mov-ing through to group six. We may also edit specific concerns or needs for clarity and consistency.

Over the evening, we rank the needs accord-ing to frequency (between one and six) to high-light the major needs for each party, noting also where similar needs are expressed by each side. This summary is circulated via internet and dis-played the next morning in preparation for the third stage of ARIA, the integrative stage, where the plenary group will start focusing on how to address the prevailing needs.

In de-briefing this stage, the effectiveness of such listening and reflective techniques is dis-cussed, and perhaps recognized as life skills that could be used also for de-escalating disputes within the family or community. Partners are asked to evaluate what they have learned, and how they might improve their listening skills in future potential conflict situations. Their percep-tion of the relevance and validity of the specific exercises can be assessed, along with their evalu-ation of the extent to which knowing the "why" behind the Partners' positions may help in mov-ing the negotiation process along. The discovery of the unexpressed reasons motivating the par-ticipants gives valuable insight both for those speaking and for the listeners.

It should now be clearer how much misper-ceptions have distorted the messages of both sides, and inclined each party to expect the worst behaviors and conspiracies of the other. The Partners are now more aware that different indi-viduals and nations tend to express their needs only indirectly, that they have universally recog-nizable human needs, and that different needs will be more salient to different groups. For example, Israelis are overwhelmingly concerned with security, at the national level as well as at the personal level of daily existence; at the same time, Palestinians most strongly feel the need to be master over their own destiny and not con-trolled by others. Once both needs are clearly understood, it becomes clear there are ways in which both can be met, generating potentially complementary and mutually beneficial out-comes. It is the search for such common ground, based on an evolving understanding of shared or complementary needs, which motivates the par-ties to make the transition from personal issues to group problem solving during the next day.

No doubt, it is the inclusion of the reflexive stage, translating the needs-based approach into part of the process, transitioning the participants from an adversarial to an integrative perspective, that is Rothman's major contribution to the field. In traditional diplomacy, participants too often attempt to move from a declaratory/antagonistic stage straight into a search for solutions. Without a reflexive stage the real issues are likely to remain hidden behind the rhetoric of official statements and positions.

Agenda Setting: The Integrative and Action Stages of ARIA

The Integrative (Invention) Stage

Now that we have a sense of the primary needs to be addressed, the search for common ground shifts into more concrete terms. During most of this and the following stage, the participants should be sitting together in one circle or semi-circle as a single group rather than in distinct groups as for most of the previous two stages. In light of the primary needs, the specific agenda or concrete focus for the next day's brainstorming session can be set in one of several ways: (1) By getting feedback from official first-track negotiations, either of impasses that have emerged, or of points of discord that have been avoided thus far but still require addressing before a final agreement. (2) By looking to the best and worst plausible future scenarios emerging from an earlier "shared vision" exercise (recommended as part of building both trust and skills in consensus decision making) and then "back casting" from the preferred future (say, 20 years ahead) back to the immediate issues that would need to be addressed if the vision is to be achieved. (3) By requesting the participants themselves to suggest the most viable and important issues they think should be addressed.

It may help to split the participants into small groups, with each identifying the specific problems that they would like to address, and then reporting back their collective preferences to the plenary, where a consensus can be built on the priority issues. Criteria for selection can be suggested, such as: salience, gravity (degree of violence or suffering), relevance of the participants' knowledge, simplicity, relevance for a majority of the people in both parties, and possibilities for early warning and preventive action.

It is advisable to appoint from among the Partners a small preparatory committee that will meet with the facilitators a day or two prior to the brainstorming session to discuss not only potential topics, but also practical issues that might arise while addressing them. For example, in one case dealing with the Palestinian/Israeli conflict during the second intifada, we looked into ideas for countering the negative effects of potential acts of terrorism or mass violence by either side, considering what might be done in response to events that may impact private (family) or public domains. The subject/s for the integrative phase should be presented to all the Partners during the previous day's session so they can have time to

think about the issue and sleep on it, before the integrative stage starts.

We are careful to distinguish several separate phases within this integrative stage. The *first phase* is brainstorming options for addressing the priority issues, engaging *creative thinking skills* through whole-brain thinking, supporting Partners in moving from reliance on the more linear-thinking left hemisphere typically dominant in high-stress situations, to include the more holistic right-hemisphere of the brain (e.g., de Bono 2009). Doing this requires balancing techniques that are logical and sequential, with those that are open and freewheeling. The *second phase* is classification, re-formulation and evaluation, engaging *critical thinking skills*, whereby Partners organize the ideas generated in terms of their priorities and re-draft them, to make the language more accessible to people outside the workshop, avoiding rough or potentially offensive "hot button" wording in thinking about creative ways forward.

As a first step in this evaluation phase, the ideas generated in the brainstorming phase are posted around the room, and each of the "partners in conflict" is asked to individually assess each idea in terms of its relevance and likelihood of being accepted by his/her own group (at home), marking with ++ the most positive down to – for the most negative assessment. Once this is done, the ideas are divided into several baskets according to sub-themes, such as economic, social, cultural, political, security, and humanitarian concerns. Small groups of 3–5 participants are formed to focus on each theme or basket, including representatives from each party, selected according to expertise or interest relevant to each theme.

Each group takes it upon themselves to refine, reword and make presentable the ideas arising from the brainstorming that needed further development. Each group should evaluate at this time only those ideas within their specific area. We may suggest a quick procedure where each group member rates each idea from 1 to 5, so with five participants, the maximum points could be 25. This is not a vote, but along with the positive and negative ratings from the plenary group, it helps the group identify which ideas are popular, which may need more refinement to attract consensus,

Table 4.1 Levels of consensus

1. "I agree wholeheartedly with the decision. I am satisfied that this decision was accepted by the whole group"
2. "I find the decision to be acceptable"
3. "I can live with the decision"
4. "I do not totally agree, but I will not block the decision, I will support it"
5. "I do not agree with the decision and wish to block the decision being accepted" (a reasoned and paramount objection, but ready to explore alternatives)
6. "I believe there is no unity in this group. We have not reached consensus"

and which are unlikely to make it. High scoring ideas are normally those we call "apple pie" – all like them, but there is not much new "out of the box" thinking behind them. Paradoxically, the more innovative ideas typically come with many pluses but also minuses, so there is an important opportunity for the small group to re-evaluate and develop in their own way these more creative, if perhaps unconventional, ideas.

Getting each small group to rate the suggestions in their own way, while also noting the marking by all participants, allows them to take ownership of their work in refining the ideas as needed to find consensus in the small group on the ideas to be presented in the next phase to the plenary. Ideas which are then presented enthusiastically to the plenary, let's assume by an Israeli and Palestinian member of the small group, have a much higher chance of acceptance. Parties attach different values to gains (and losses) in each of the baskets, and even if one basket seems to have the most important issues at stake, the introduction of many groups (sometimes more than ten) makes both sides alert to the potential trade-offs, which they may benefit from only if they are willing to be flexible on the more difficult and important issues. This small group process continues as facilitators and participants begin to understand and prioritize what is of concern for both parties, and lays the ground for the *third phase* of the integrative stage, which is a search for common ground.

During this phase *(applying consensus building skills)* it is made clear that a consensus is not achieved through majority vote or avoidance of anyone's objections. Everyone should have his or her concerns brought before the entire group, and only when that participant is comfortable with relinquishing an idea or an objection should the group let it drop. True consensus finding requires that people actively listen to each other and seek ways to satisfy the important concerns of everyone. This takes longer than majority voting, but the resulting buy-in is critical to avoiding anyone sabotaging the project at a later time. If participants feel unduly pressured, they will have a hard time implementing any ideas they are not happy with, particularly in the context of ongoing complex societal conflicts. Transforming such conflicts to where sustainable peace building is possible requires building genuine consensus on ways to address the concerns of all parties.

In the consensus building process we have used a "jigsaw puzzle" strategy, moving first on the acceptance of individual ideas before integrating them into a comprehensive consensus agreement. We differentiate several levels of consensus (as below) and seek agreement on using the fourth as a modest and achievable goal. This ladder illustrates what different degrees of consensus may sound like, moving from the clearest level of consensus to that showing most concern. #4 represents a minimum level for consensus; #5 and #6 may lead to majority vote, but no consensus (Table 4.1).

In cases where one or more participants express a reservation (fifth level), and can explain the principles or concerns behind their objection, we can take a few minutes to discuss it and look for friendly amendments that address the concerns both behind the idea and the objection. But if unsuccessful, then using the jigsaw puzzle strategy, we first frame a consensus document with the easier pieces or ideas, leaving for the end the most difficult ones. Once we have the borders of the puzzle completed it then becomes easier to place the remaining pieces as needed to close the gaps, and the desire to complete the picture is higher.

At times we may not be able to reach consensus, even on a second round, on some pieces that could be the most out of the box and creative options. Ideas that are still controversial even for "partners in conflict" who have the benefit of our socialization, trust and skills building processes, clearly would be out of reach for the officials of both sides, but need not necessarily be abandoned. One option is that the participants agree to include them in an agenda for further treatment at a later stage, making it clear that this waiting list does not imply any prior agreement. It merely confirms that such ideas were brought up, did not reach consensus, and yet may deserve revisiting by the same group or by others in the future, when circumstances change. Alternatively, it may be agreed, if time permits, to reconvene the next day and consider an action testing process for some of the more powerful and innovative ideas that have remained controversial. The Partners would seek agreement on what short or long-term outcomes in this testing process would be sufficient to convince opponents of the idea to drop their objection.

Action Stage

Too often in peace making, coming to agreement between the parties is considered to be the primary goal, and is celebrated as the achievement of peace, rather than the beginning of an extended peace building process. So it is not surprising that almost half the official peace agreements that are negotiated for societal conflicts, fail within the first eight weeks (Hewitt et al. 2011). In second track work, the agreement itself is unofficial, and has value only to the extent that it generates action to create the conditions for sustainable peace. Stage four of ARIA focuses on action planning and preparation for re-entry by the Partners back into their home communities, giving them the support needed to engage in action for conflict transformation in the real world (see also discussion of re-entry in Chap. 8). Without this post-consensus focus on planning and support for implementation, peacemaking workshops become isolated events. This is not only economically unsound, but can be counter-productive, by raising hopes and then producing an anti-climax that can feed cynicism and despair, with Partners feeling isolated, lost or confused after re-entry.

The re-entry process has been described as a culture shock both for the separation from those who had undergone a shared experience, and for the exposure to some sort of inquisition from others in a still hostile environment when they attempt to share new insights. Without adequate preparation and support, participants who wish to share new and moderate ideas from the workshop may be regarded by some in their home community as fools, naive, or worse, as victims of brainwashing or even as traitors.

Training for re-entry requires anticipating likely challenges such as this and preparing to meet them. For example, to avoid being perceived as proselytizing or preaching, Partners are guided to speak modestly of their lessons learned, and to actively seek and receive feedback on new perspectives before seeking to promote them. In order to stimulate team-building, it is suggested that Partners prepare themselves for joint presentations to officials or other local or mixed audiences, to write an op-ed together, or to explore other forms for joint expression. At College Park we have arranged for young Partners in small groups to jointly visit schools where peer mediation takes place, and to have them talk about their conflict and current experiences in addressing ways to resolve them. If they are academics or professionals, the Partners can be asked to share the podium at a university, a relevant embassy or elsewhere in a safe environment before considering what might be possible in their home country.

While speaking jointly in public, new Partners must take care to minimize the potential for ending the presentation in an adversarial manner. One way of doing so is to include at least two rounds of presentations. In the first round the Partners speak introspectively and responsibly about their own side of the conflict, looking only at the performance of their own government and society. In the second round, they can comment on the performance of the other party and, if necessary, note any possible biases in the presentation by the other presenter. The order of speakers is reversed in this round. This two-staged approach encourages self-responsibility, alleviates the uncertainty of going first, and avoids the temptation to attack immediately as a pre-emptive measure.

In general, workshop organizers should plan to provide follow-up opportunities in at least one or two minimal ways in the same location, to keep building on the momentum of the workshop, as well as longer term in their respective communities after they have returned. Giving Partners opportunities for shared outdoor activities or excursions that require some investment of energy and human resources can also promote team building in more informal ways.

In particular, the Partners should be supported to jointly design and develop action plans and collaborative projects, with timelines and detailed strategic planning for activities designed to implement or promote the ideas agreed on. This is a good time to familiarize the participants with potential sources of funding, fundraising issues, and the possible involvement of the hosting institution in future plans. The current funders for the project may also be invited for a conversation with the Partners, along with other project development specialists. The types of projects that can be developed are nearly limitless, but must take into account practical constraints imposed by budgetary considerations. There are many training resources for action planning, each often copywriting their own product. We have used different organizing frameworks, mostly based on systematic common sense, dealing with short-term objectives and long-term goals (what?), motivation (why?), division of labor (who?), timeline (when?), activities (how?) and, obviously, budget (how much?). Partners should be supported to ensure planned action commitments are set out in actionable and verifiable terms, to recruit appropriate involvement from other participants, and to organize follow-up meetings to evaluate and adjust ongoing action strategies to unfolding realities on the ground.

It is useful to sow seeds as needed for developing a shared mechanism or institution to sustain these projects. A loyalty can develop to a transnational joint enterprise or epistemic community that may transcend the original loyalty to separate groups. Such institutions may take on a life

of their own and promote problem solving through the generation of shared values. For example, Kaufman's team-teaching and collaborative initiatives with a Palestinian colleague for several years has not only afforded him a good understanding of his Partner's perspectives (each could probably lecture in the other's place) but both Partners' views have become closer and more integrative. The recurrent practice of pedagogic or other joint activities tends to unite Partners, especially when facing a hostile environment in their own societies.

Case Studies

Experimenting with ARIA in different cultural and political contexts has brought home to us the adaptability of the methodology and the diversity of outcomes that can be achieved. We review three cases here which exemplify this flexibility and diversity.

Israeli/Palestinian Prisoner Release/ Exchange

The Israeli-Palestinian conflict is frequently framed as a resource-based conflict over territory (i.e. "who gets what, when and how"), however this conflict is, we believe, a quintessentially identity-based conflict; what Edward Azar framed as a "Protracted Social Conflict." Azar defines protracted social conflict as one whose focus is on "religious, cultural or ethnic communal identity, which in turn is dependent upon the satisfaction of basic needs such as those for security, communal recognition and distributive justice" (Azar 1990).

We had three opportunities to experiment with this issue in the 1990s, within our broader ongoing work with the deeply protracted identity-based Israeli-Palestinian conflict: first, a simulation at the University of Maryland, with the participation of at least one Israeli and one Palestinian serving to anchor other participants supporting each side; second, working with a group of Palestinian ex-prisoners and mainstream

Israeli NGO professionals; and third, working with the Palestinian and Israeli students enrolled in the MA program at Gotheberg University, that took place in the Holy Land in the mid-1990s .

Their most important contribution was a paradigm shift from referring to the crimes committed in the *past* (e.g., the prevailing Israeli objections to the release of those who have had "blood on their hands") to a future-oriented perspective (e.g., prioritizing the objective of making sure that there will be no recidivism). So regardless of past behavior, the Partners were able to focus on how to best ensure that violence will not be used by the released prisoners, thereby collaboratively addressing the primary needs of the parties for security and justice. The consensus document was brought to the attention of the Israeli Minister of Justice at that time, and his Director General went through the recommendations one by one; even after a change of Cabinet, the new Director General took an interest as well.

The issue of prisoner release later was replaced by the issue of prisoner exchange, when an Israeli soldier was captured and held by the Hamas organization ruling in Gaza. There have also been efforts to get agreement between groups of relatives of victims killed by acts of war or terror (one, a peace-oriented Israeli-Palestinian NGO professional supporting prisoner release/exchange, the second a Jewish-only NGO professional objecting to any release/exchange). While these talks did not directly bear fruit, they have contributed to an environment that has allowed for a major prisoner exchange to proceed with broad public acceptance (e.g., Baskin 2011). More work is needed to set an agreed basis for future releases or exchanges, which could help to strengthen a moderate Palestinian Authority based in the West Bank, and progress toward a two-state solution.

This case demonstrates the ability of Partners to move beyond past behavior on sensitive subjects, exemplifying the transformation of antagonism through the Adversarial, Reflexive and Integrative stages in ARIA, with the internalized understanding found in the Reflexive stage allowing for more stability when moving to the Integrative and Action stages. One of the challenges in identity-based conflicts in particular,

which ARIA helps to meet, is in the need to help partners come to terms with their own framing of the 'other,' so that they can move beyond the desire for retribution or violence, and constructively engage in a peaceful discussion for cooperation for mutual benefit.

Peru/Ecuador: Second Track Diplomacy and the Role of Civil Society in Peacemaking

The peace treaty signed by Ecuador and Peru in October 1998, following their most recent war in 1995, appears to have brought to an end the longest-standing border conflict on the continent. An initial treaty had been contested by the Peruvian government, arguing that they felt a level of coercion when signing, due to Ecuador's upper hand in this war. Tensions, mainly over disputed territory and borders, had led to a process of alienation over time that had erupted into three separate wars. It had seeped into many aspects of each society to the point that shared stereotypes and assumptions of enmity became normalized in everyday life and education. However, it became apparent to us early on that attitudes toward the border disputes were less antagonistic among civil society representatives, as compared to governmental and military, who were more concerned with elections and legitimacy in the post-Cold War era.

Second track negotiations between civil society leaders therefore provided a way to move beyond this new first-track stalemate, while engaging local communities directly involved in the border conflict also helped to build public trust and a culture of peace. A total of four workshops were conducted over the course of four years, beginning in August of 1997 in College Park, Maryland, a neutral location with a tradition of peace building initiatives that was acceptable to both parties. "Grupo Maryland," the title that the group eventually gave themselves, was an expression of their commitment to their goals for a collaborative approach to conflict resolution (Kaufman and Sosnowski 2005).

In this first workshop, there were ten participants from each country, including opinion leaders from the capital cities. Given that the violence had already ceased, ice-breaker and skills-building exercises served to quickly and efficiently build relationships of trust. In then preparing for the ARIA process, the parties engaged in a frank and rather confrontational review of historic relations between the two countries.

On the second day, the adversarial stage began, with the participants arguing and defending the official positions of their respective nations. In the second adversarial round, roles were reversed and participants argued the position of the opposite side, allowing each to experience the perspective of their opponents. This process helped make clear how differences in the language used to communicate their interpretations of the same protocol made it seem as if they were referring to two completely different versions of the same document. These differences were then addressed through an active listening process in small groups during the ARIA reflexive stage, making participants on each side aware of the foundations of their perceptions in discovering the different human needs moving them.

For the integrative stage, a working group was selected to prepare the specific issues on which to focus the brainstorming meetings for the entire group. In this stage the first goal is to find as many innovative options for addressing needs as possible. The participants drafted a list of proposals during the brainstorming session, and these proposals were then evaluated by five parallel working groups and refined to create a final set that were approved by consensus. Most of these ideas were directed towards tasks for the civil societies in Ecuador and Peru, while others focused on the ongoing first-track process in Brasilia. Specifically, the working groups focused respectively on: environmental problems in the conflict region; the role of the press and mass media in impacting public opinion; the role of education in developing mutual understanding; and the role of businessmen in local economic development. The fifth group focused on possible contributions of civil society to first-track diplomacy, emphasizing the need for the governments to reiterate their commitment to maintaining peaceful channels for conflict resolution and dis-

carding the use of force. Most conflicts at this level are multifaceted, and require not just one solution but many. Having multiple working groups is efficient in helping Partners to focus on what's at stake, and to assure that needs on both sides are addressed so that more mutually acceptable solutions can be developed.

In the final ARIA stage of action planning, the participants agreed to join forces as a "Research Group for Ecuadorian-Peruvian Peace and Cooperation" (the name was later shortened to "Grupo Maryland") to draft a series of proposals contemplating reciprocal concessions, and generating mutually beneficial options to promote peace.

By the end of the deliberations in a concluding action planning workshop, many practical proposals emerged, that were shared in a visit to the Peruvian chancellery and ambassador. Four of the original Partners in the Maryland group were later brought into the first track negotiation process, three as advisers to the Ecuadorian side and one to the Peruvian. In this action planning workshop, particular attention was paid to the effective implementation of ideas generated within the previous workshop. In the reflexive phase, participants explored the underlying reasons why sovereignty was being seen in zero-sum terms, preparing the ground for the possibility of establishing a "bi-national" or "transnational" definition of sovereignty to be applied in the critical geographic areas in dispute.

The first track negotiations then resumed in El Pueblo, Peru in March 1999, when both chancelleries had reached a consensus regarding nearly all the issues under dispute, including those related to the Commerce and Navigation Treaty. However, this was not the case with regard to drawing a common border. This turned out to be the most sensitive issue not only in terms of the relations between the two countries, but also those between each president and his society. In response, the wording "bi-national" was proposed, and following intense negotiations, it was decided to include it in the final formula, creating a demilitarized environmental reserve in the zone where the most recent conflict took place. The agreement recognized the symbolic value in Ecuador of this small territory of one square kilometer, Tiwintza, by awarding the status of public domain (permanent property rights for Ecuador), while allowing Peru to retain sovereignty.

As part of a strategy of sustained follow-up from the original ARIA workshop in Maryland, particular attention was also given to the concrete actions that Partners, as citizen leaders, could take given their respective professional and personal positions.

A few months after the signing of the official peace agreement, the Ecuadorian government requested that we involve the officer in charge of the implementation of the accords and bi-national ventures in our process. The facilitators approached the Peruvian government which also expressed a similar interest. Hence, the "Grupo Maryland" became what is known as a track "one and a half" process, at this stage dwelling mostly on ensuring maximal implementation and fulfillment of the official signed document (Nan, 2005, Nan et al., 2009).

The fourth and final workshop took place in Cuenca, Ecuador in August 2000. Now the objective was the consolidation of peace, 11 months after the treaty was signed. The workshop centered on collaboratively developing a scope of work, reviewing what had been accomplished to date and laying down a foundation for promoting a culture of peace between the two countries. The main practical challenge now was securing the funds needed for the border region's economic development. One significant action step was to expand the capacity of the Ecuadorian and Peruvian Partners to meet their longer-term objectives by training a group of rectors from the universities in the border region (northern Peru and southern Ecuador) to work with them in the peace building process, with the training taking place in Cuenca following the Grupo Maryland workshop.

In conclusion, this case demonstrates the value of a multi-track process in engaging different levels of stakeholders in a societal conflict. While on a military level (and to some extent also the political level) the conflict was real and deeply entrenched through institutional interests, in terms of the broader civil society the discord was milder. This contributed to the success of a second track process in restoring the momentum for peace when the first track had stalled, and made clear the value of keeping both tracks engaged in the longer-term implementation process.

Lesotho: A Comprehensive University of Maryland/National University of Lesotho Program for Conflict Transformation and Democratic Transition

We were invited to work in Lesotho in the wake of rioting and violence in 1998 in reaction to national elections where, in spite of support from about half the population, the opposition parties had failed to get more than a single seat in the parliament. The invitation came initially from the Lesotho Ambassador to the U.S, who had participated in our training in multi-track diplomacy at the University of Maryland, who facilitated a working partnership between ourselves and the National University of Lesotho (NUL).

On arriving in the country and conducting an initial capacity and needs assessment, it became clear to us that work to reform the electoral system following the violence was well under way, but that too little attention was being paid to widespread local unrest and resistance to early moves toward transitioning local governance from the traditional chiefs to elected local councils. This resistance seemed rooted in tribal sensitivities and identity-based concerns. We thus made a strategic decision to proceed via a bottom-up approach, working first at the local level in villages around the country, to bring together supporters of both the chiefs and the transitional councils to use ARIA techniques to collaboratively address local conflict situations, and working up to engage leadership and address issues at the district and national levels as we may be invited based on successes at the local level.

Thirty-three ARIA-informed workshops were conducted in a little over two years, engaging more than 700 national and community leaders, about a third of them women (well over the proportion of women currently in leadership positions), and including leaders of all political parties represented in parliament (including the Prime Minister), principal and local chiefs, senior police, senior Ministry of Local Government (MLG) officials, heads of all ten district administrations, Independent Electoral Commission (IEC) representatives, community council members, and CSO professionals. Of these, nine brought together chiefs, councilors and others at the local or district level, covering eight of the ten districts; three were national trainings, two for chiefs from all districts, another for senior police at both national level and the ten districts; eight brought together party leaders, principal chiefs, district administrators, senior MLG ministry officials and others at the national level; and ten were follow-up workshops (Davies et al. 2009).

The local and district level workshops brought together interim community councils and chiefs and other critical stakeholders directly involved in day-to-day political and social conflict situations. They were able to find consensus positions on a range of contentious issues, while strengthening the new community councils and helping traditional leaders (chiefs) adapt and professionalize their continuing roles as community mediators and peace builders ("peace officers"). Issues addressed included such themes as conflicting land allocations by chiefs and councils, grazing rights on common lands, cattle theft, access to water sources and power grids, contested jurisdictional boundaries, and division of responsibilities among chiefs and councils, or between principal chiefs and district administrators.

The success of these ARIA-informed workshops, adapted to build on traditional methods of peacemaking, created a greater demand to bring the underlying issues of transitioning from traditional to elected leadership to the national level, engaging party leaders, members of parliament, principal chiefs, police and district administrators in better preparing the ground for a nonviolent transition to elected local government. Three national workshops addressed this theme, generating consensus agreements on topics such as: clarifying roles of, and relationships among, principal and local chiefs, district administrators, councilors and MLG (Ministry of Local Government), codes of conduct, terms of appointment, election and retirement of chiefs, training and mechanisms for conflict management, clarifying council and chieftaincy boundaries, consultation with local stakeholders and voter education prior to local elections. A separate extended follow-up workshop for senior MLG officials and representatives of the IEC (Independent Electoral Commission) translated these agreements into systematic action planning and implementation in preparing for local government elections.

In harmony with work conducted by other NGOs and agencies, our Partners were able to make the following meaningful contributions (Table 4.2):

Conclusion: Some Lessons Learned

A goal of this chapter was to review some representative cases in which ARIA was applied in workshops conducted by CIDCM. Our experience in applied work across types of societal conflict (identity based and territorial, interstate and intrastate) is that ARIA is a flexible methodology for fostering a more productive second- or multi-track discourse between groups or nations.

More particularly, our experience is that the first ARIA stage (Adversarial), when undertaken following appropriate trust- and skills – building, can be a powerful and effective way to engage the parties in a direct exchange that feels authentic, clarifying the issues and allowing a cathartic expression of often long-simmering feelings while also demonstrating the limits of adversarial positioning. The baring of highly polarized and entrenched attitudes in this stage increases tensions, but these can be eased through reverse role playing, which also prepares the ground for a transition to the second (Reflexive) stage, enabling Partners to reflect more deeply on underlying feelings and needs, and awakening the empathy needed for compassionate listening and the understanding and human connection required for building sustainable partnership.

Rothman has been able to translate into more practical terms the insights of his mentor, Edward Azar, regarding the necessity of exploring the deeper human needs hiding below surface positions – as in the case of an iceberg under cold water. The simple switch from "WHAT?" to "WHY?", if systematically carried out, leads to uncovering the universal human needs which are the root motivations of the parties, and which unlike their positions and specific interests, are not only understandable across cultures, but by

Table 4.2 Lesotho workshops – contributions, outcomes and grounding actions

Contribution area	Outcome	Due to the following action(s)
(a) Prevention of electoral violence	No violence took place and for the first time since independence the opposition parties broadly accepted the results of the elections	Several workshops being focused on inter-and intra-party tensions to help a broad-base effort to prevent recurrent violence following national elections
(b) Inter-party relations	Political parties began to communicate more amicably; joint planning of workshops, press conferences; established a coordinating office; agreed to jointly monitor the first local elections	The project brought together political parties to creatively address, among other things, inter-party conflicts
(c) High-level political support from local and national level authorities and actors	Attracted both bottom-up and top-down support. This translated into extensive cooperation from both the Ministries of Local Government and of Home Affairs, as well as from the chieftaincy and political party leaders, including the office of the Prime Minister	Emerged from the fact that we began by engaging the main stakeholders and responded to the needs they identified, and from the respect for NUL as a politically neutral academic institution
(d) National training for senior police hosted by Ministry of Home Affairs	Outcomes from this were exemplified in significant reductions in violent crime and in repeated successes in resolving deadly conflicts through police mediation	Decision by the Ministry to cover the cost of training its senior police officers speaks to the impact of the training on those police who attended the project workshops; teams from head office and all districts completed detailed action plans for integrating the new skills into their work
(e) National training for chiefs	Consequent active collaboration from chiefs in supporting the transition to elected councils, appears to give greater respect for the key role that chiefs continue to play as peace officers in their communities, and an enhanced capacity for chiefs to deal effectively with local conflicts while reducing the number of referrals to a chronically overloaded court system	A high level of cooperation from the chieftaincy as needed to mount this training was again evidence of the impact of earlier trainings for both local and principal chiefs
(f) Involvement of senior officers at the Ministry for Local Government	Action planning workshop for officers at the Ministry for local Government. Held at the initiative of the Minister and engaged the Ministry's senior officials in translating into action the agreements, which emerged from project workshops on preparing for the first nationwide local government elections	Several of the ideas in these agreements that required legislative action were raised during parliamentary debate and resulted in amendments made to the Local Government Act and related legislation. The Minister and others commented particularly on the constructive nature of these debates and on their value in contributing to needed reforms
(g) Success of the transition to elected local government	This allowed for a more systematic voter education campaign, clarification of roles and responsibilities in part through legislative reforms, and time to adequately resolve many local conflicts	Following these workshops, the time allowed for preparing the ground for the first nation-wide local government elections was substantially extended

nature intangible and so not zero-sum. This in turn opens the door for an innovative search for positive-sum options for addressing the needs of both sides in the integrative stage.

Through the persistent use of this framework we seem to have mastered the ARI part of the equation; we have not found it difficult to bring the parties to consensus on how to settle and transform complex conflicts. However it seems the greater challenge comes in adequate planning and sustained action for implementation – the final A (as we understand, Rothman's related methodology of Action Evaluation was specifically developed to address this limitation, see part two of this book). Action plans often were not accomplished, for one or both of two reasons – because of lack of financial or human volunteer resources, or because the obstacles to translating action commitments back to the realities of complex societal conflicts were not adequately anticipated and prepared for. For example, in the case of the Peru-Ecuador conflict, the fourth workshop was largely dedicated to securing funds to help foster economic development within the border region. But it failed in its attempt to involve civil society organizations both in monitoring implementation, and in securing funds from international NGOs for the development of this neglected region. The attitude of both the governments and potential funders was like saying thanks Grupo Maryland for the good services in getting the peace agreement completed and now it's time for governments to take over.

Among the lessons learnt we should mention the need for flexibility in the use of ARIA, given the need to adapt it to different cultural contexts and to build on existing cultural and individual strengths. While starting two decades ago with a rather rigid approach to the conduct of the four stages, we have now highlighted the spirit of each stage, not necessarily regimented by the use of particular techniques. For example, in the Lesotho case, we found that finding reconciliation and forgiveness were often as much or more highly prized than more practical agreements on how to address specific needs and resolve competing demands. Where the sense of shared identity between or among parties in conflict is strong, reconciliation can set the ground for renewed commitment and energy for the community to work together in addressing a broad range of issues and needs in a sustained manner without formal agreements being required. In this context, ARIA can be modified so that in the reflexive phase we support the Partners in reflecting together in one group, so that each can acknowledge to all their (or their group's) contribution to the problem – in hindsight recognizing what they may have said or done differently, or avoided saying or doing, that may have helped create a better outcome. Once all have stepped from blame into self-responsibility in this way, and then (through the integrative stage) have found consensus on how to resolve the issues, the Partners can be asked if they are willing to forgive the mistakes that have been acknowledged and open a new, forward-looking chapter for their

shared community, This is generally given and can be celebrated according to local tradition.

A further lesson learned relates to the importance of two preliminary stages to ARIA: trust and skills building. As much as we are tempted to proceed straight into problem solving, we need to have the right atmosphere and some tools to maximize the chances of consensus building on as many innovative options for addressing the issues as possible, and to build a foundation for transforming the relationship between the parties from polarization and blame to mutual understanding and long-term partnership with the capacity to address future disputes without violence or outside support for finding common ground

Another issue we have confronted is that, while in the way it was originally designed, ARIA works best in dyadic conflicts, in more and more of the intra-state conflicts, we are facing multi-sectoral concerns, such as conflicts related to common-pool resources and environmental degradation. How do we adapt, for instance, the adversarial stage to more than two Partners? We confronted a situation like that in the Galapagos Islands, where the original Partners in Conflict were defined as the environmentalists and the fishermen. And yet we found among the participants the tourist guides and the National Park Guards. We divided them each into two groups, who joined the original two. Simulating being fishermen or environmentalists was not a difficult undertaking for them, and the process benefitted from the perspectives they brought to the process. And yet, this "out of the box" arrangement is not necessarily the best in all multi-party situations, and more research for conflicts with multiple actors is required.

Another adaptation we have used in dealing with multiple parties, is to conduct the adversarial phase as a round, where each party in turn speaks their mind on what has been happening in the conflict situation and what is behind it, allowing all perspectives to be expressed but without actual debate. This has worked best in situations where (as in the Lesotho case) the underlying sense of shared identity is still strong. Another successful alternative is where the multiple parties are the result of fracturing within each of two major parties, as has happened in working between Palestinians and Israelis, for example. In this case, we can bring together the factions of one party first, using the ARIA process to help them find common ground, so that there is a foundation for them to work together in choosing and legitimizing representatives of their shared community to engage the other party in ways that can be accepted by both factions.

We continue to work with ARIA, as recently in preparing the ground for nonviolent democratic transition in Egypt through the Arab Spring, or as currently used in the first steps of a Cuba/USA academic diplomacy process in which experts on each other's' country – including former ambassadors and national security officers now in academia – are building up consensus on the issues that separate their respective governments. With more experimentation, our expectation is that ARIA will continue to be refined and adapted to meet the requirements for conflict transformation across an increasing diversity of changing environmental, cultural and political contexts.

References

Azar, E. (1990). *The management of protracted social conflict: Theory and cases*. Aldershot: Dartmouth.

Azar, E. (2003). Protracted social conflicts and second track diplomacy. In J. Davies & E. Kaufman (Eds.), *Second track/citizens diplomacy: Concepts and techniques for conflict transformation*. Lanham: Rowman & Littlefield.

Azar, E., & Burton, J. (Eds.). (1986). *International conflict resolution: Theory and practice: Lebanon a case example*. Boulder: Lynne Rienner.

Baskin, G. (2011, October 19). My part in the prisoner exchange deal. *Jerusalem Post*.

Beach, H., Hamner, J., Hewitt, J., Kaufman, E., Kurki, A., Oppenheimer, J., & Wolf, A. (2000). *Transboundary freshwater dispute resolution: Theory, practice and annotated references*. New York: United Nations University Press.

Davies, J., & Kaufman, E. (Eds.). (2003). *Second track/citizens' diplomacy: Concepts and techniques for conflict transformation*. Lanham: Rowman & Littlefield.

Davies, J., Fekade, W., Hoohlo, M., Kaufman, E., & Shale, M. (2009). Partners in peacebuilding in Lesotho.

In C. Zelizer and R. Rubinstein (Eds.) *Peacebuilding in practice: Reflections from the field*. Sterling: Kumarian.

De Bono, E. (2009). *Lateral thinking*. New York: Viking.

Fisher, R. (2005). *Paving the way: Contributions of interactive conflict resolution to peacemaking*. Boston: Lexington.

Hewitt, J., Wilkenfeld, J., Gurr, T. R., & Heldt, B. (Eds.). (2011). *Peace and conflict 2012*. Boulder: Paradigm Publishers.

Kaufman, E., & Sosnowski, S. (2005). The Peru-Ecuador peace process: The contribution of track-two diplomacy. In R. J. Fisher (Ed.), *Paving the way: Contributions of interactive conflict resolution to peacemaking*. Oxford: Lexington.

Kaufman, E., Salem, W., & Verhoeven, J. (Eds.). (2006). *Bridging the divide: Peacebuilding in the Israeli-Palestinian conflict*. Boulder: Lynne Rienner.

Kelman, H. (2003). Interactive solving problem as a tool for second track diplomacy. In J. Davies & E. Kaufman (Eds.), *Second track/citizens' diplomacy: Concepts and techniques for conflict transformation* (pp. 81–106). Lanham: Rowman and Littlefield.

Kuttab, J., & Kaufman, E. (1998). An exchange on dialogue. *Journal of Palestine Studies, 17*(2).

Mitchell, C. (1981). *Peacemaking and the consultant's role*. New York: Nichols.

Montville, J., & Davidson, W. (1981). Foreign policy according to Freud. *Foreign Policy, 45*, 145–157.

Nan, S. A. (2005). Track one-and-a-half diplomacy: Contributions to Georgian-South Ossetian peacemaking. In R. J. Fisher (Ed.), *Paving the way: Contributions of interactive conflict resolution to peacemaking*. Lanham: Lexington.

Nan, S. A., Druckman, D., & El Horr, J. (2009). Unofficial international conflict resolution: Is there a track 1 ½? Are there best practices? *Conflict Resolution Quarterly, 27*(1), 65–82.

Pruitt, D., & Kim, S. H. (2004). *Social conflict: Escalation, stalemate, and settlement* (3rd ed.). New York: McGraw Hill.

Rothman, J. (1988). *A guide to Arab-Jewish peacemaking organizations in Israel*. Jerusalem: New Israel Fund.

Rothman, J. (1989). Supplementing tradition: A theoretical and practical typology for international conflict management. *Negotiation Journal, 5*, 265–277.

Rothman, J. (1992). *From confrontation to cooperation: Resolving ethnic and regional conflict*. Newbury Park: Sage.

Rothman, J. (1997). *Resolving identity-based conflict in nations, organizations, and communities*. San Francisco: Jossey-Bass.

Volkan, V. (1988). *The need to have enemies and allies: From clinical practice to international relationships*. Northvale: Jason Aronson.

From Antagonism to Resonance: Some Methodological Insights and Dilemmas

Ahmed Badawi, Brandon Sipes,
and Michael Sternberg

Introduction

Ofra (not her real name) spoke in a high-pitched voice. She was responding to a question from a Palestinian woman about why young Israelis were so keen to join the army, serve at checkpoints and cause so much hardship for Palestinians. She said that the Palestinians had created a reality in which Israelis feared them and saw them as irrationally violent. She argued that their behavior (Palestinians in general not necessarily those gathered in the room) had often proven them to be an aggressive people and that Israelis were only reacting to that aggression.

She went on to talk about her mother who, over the course of her life, grew increasingly afraid of the possibility of being attacked by Palestinians or some other menacing, unknown assailant. Whether they were walking through the streets of Jerusalem or travelling abroad, her mother always felt the same fear for her life:

> This summer I was with my mother in Europe, not a place someone should be scared. We got to the hotel, on the first day, around 9 or 10 in the evening. I took out a five Euro note from my wallet and my mother freaked out as if someone was threatening her with a gun. "What are you doing?! If they see that we have money they're going to do something to us." I opened the window and there were empty buildings across from us. I said "No one is there." She replied, "You never know who is there."

Ofra initially shared this to explain to the Palestinians in the room how Israelis experienced the fear of living in a conflict zone: the constant possibility of bombings, rockets and suicide attacks. She wanted the Palestinian participants to get the message: she squarely blamed them for that reality.

As the workshop progressed, however, her narrative changed. Instead of pointing the finger of blame toward others, she began to look inwards and describe *why* she and her mother felt afraid:

> I grew up with the fear of being exterminated. This big sentence is repeated in Israel at every ceremony: "Remember, don't forget. If you forget for a minute, it will happen again." We convince ourselves in stories, textbooks and the media that we are good, moral – it's a mechanism that I don't understand but I know that it exists. We, as soldiers, believe that what we're doing is moral, even at checkpoints. It is possible to kill someone and to think it is moral. In order to fight, to be a soldier, you have to lose something – an innocent child [inside of you] must be killed.

She began to shift her focus from blaming the Palestinians in the room for their perceived aggression and violence, to the fact that she and her mother were afraid and why this was so. This is the shift that we hope participants can make: away from focusing on the adversary to looking inward and discovering what is at stake for them in the conflict and expressing that reality to others.

A. Badawi • B. Sipes • M. Sternberg
e-mail: ahbadawi@yahoo.com;
bsipes@ariagroup.com; michaels@shatil.nif.org.il

J. Rothman (ed.), *From Identity-Based Conflict to Identity-Based Cooperation: The ARIA Approach in Theory and Practice*, Peace Psychology Book Series, DOI 10.1007/978-1-4614-3679-9_5,
© Springer Science+Business Media New York 2012

In engaging identity conflicts, how well a participant is able to be *reflexive* will ultimately determine the success of the intervention. That is, we hope participants can move beyond simple reflection: "this is what happened and how I reacted" to reflexive practice: "this is what happened and I am examining why I reacted in that way." In the case of Ofra, she eventually began to describe the effect her mother's behavior, and the wider social context in Israel, has had on her, how it made her afraid and programmed her to react out of fear and suspicion. She then started to recognize throughout the remainder of the workshop when she was falling back on that habit with knee jerk reactions rather than careful, thoughtful responses.

Moving from adversarial frames and perspectives into a reflexive approach is a dramatic shift. In the process of articulating antagonistic positions, the focus is on the other, on *them*, with a strong outward view. Disputants say, "You're the problem; you're the aggressive one." Reflexivity, on the other hand, is interactive. It begins from the self and gradually shifts focus to the interchange between *us* and *them* (Rothman 1997).

This is a central movement when attempting to resolve conflicts that are identity-based: disputants are guided to speak with each other about their essential concerns, and then ideally resonance is fostered between them. Adversaries gain insight into what is truly at stake in the conflict for each of them and why it matters to them so much. While adversarial framing continues to escalate the conflict, reflexive reframing can provide an interruption in the violent discourse in which participants engage and provide an opening for a new and cooperative way forward.

The hope is that in this space former adversaries engage in a deeply interactive reframing process, and may experience an underlying resonance emanating from the core of the conflict – namely, why and how this conflict threatens and frustrates their identities. The conflict sits between them. The potential of this space is that it is filled by both *us* and *them*: We. By transforming the frame of their conflict from an adversarial perspective to a reflexive one, parties in conflict become more able to look *within* themselves and focus on the relationship *between* each other.

The last few decades have witnessed a growing appreciation by scholars and practitioners of the role that identity plays in sustaining conflicts and making them intractable and difficult to resolve. The pioneering work of John Burton (1990a, b), Johan Galtung (1969, 1975, 1976), Herbert Kelman (1965, 1987, 1997) and others has demonstrated that there is more to conflict than meets the eye. They showed that the polite language of diplomacy and its efforts at reaching compromise between various conflict parties are insufficient to produce sustainable results. Beneath interests, there is identity and its reflection in the mostly unspoken fears, dilemmas, and prejudices, as well as in the contradictory visions of the future held by adversaries. The work of Jay Rothman is an extension of these early efforts and represents an attempt to engage deeper levels of conflict and transform them into resources for resolution and conciliation (Rothman 1992, 1997).

Rothman's method for engaging identity-based conflict, ARIA, is the focus of this chapter. We present two case studies from the Israeli-Palestinian conflict and use them to describe and reflect on the two key components of ARIA: surfacing Antagonism and achieving Resonance. We believe from our experience over the past half-dozen years that peace workers ought to understand and learn how to engage these powerful mechanisms of antagonism (adversarial framing) and resonance (reflexive reframing). If successfully done, this may help to challenge the destructive dynamics of identity conflict and to foster its creative potential. It helps conflict parties traverse the often treacherous journeys between despair and hope; fear and the willingness to trust; exclusivity and inclusivity; *us* as the victims and *them* as the transgressors. Engaging and effectively guiding conflict parties from Antagonism into Resonance helps them transform their adversarial frames of each other into reflexive ones, thus creating possibilities for new hope and a common future that satisfies their respective basic human needs.

The rest of this chapter will explore this movement from antagonism to resonance. Each of the two case studies relates to a workshop facilitated by one or more of our chapter authors. These workshops were part of a multi-year[1] project funded mainly by the European Commission's Partnership for Peace program. As we will see, the results from these two sessions were mixed. The first, while we were still in our early stages of learning how to help parties move from Antagonism to Resonance, was not successful. However, we learned a great deal from it and applied this knowledge to a much more successful second case (as defined by helping participants effectively move through Antagonism and then on to Resonance).

While neither of these experiences should be considered normative, they do offer an opportunity to explore some lingering questions regarding the practice of moving from adversarial framing to reflexive reframing. In the concluding section, we will briefly share some of the insights and dilemmas that preoccupied us as a result of our facilitation experience. We will not provide definitive answers, simply because we do not have them. Instead, we invite readers to join us in our process of reflexive learning that is part of our ongoing engagement with the Israeli-Palestinian conflict.

Before proceeding, a word of caution is warranted. Although the turn to identity in the field of conflict engagement has been a welcome development, it must be remembered that social conflict and violent cross-border disputes are complex phenomena that should not be reduced to any single factor. The identification of a causal factor that was missing from mainstream debate, such as the role of identity in both enabling and managing conflict, should not be taken to mean that only identity matters. Consequently, we suggest that conflict workers remain continuously ready to update their methods of intervention and attempt to keep expanding their strategies and approaches in order to be able to cope with an ever-increasing number of factors that need to be addressed in work on conflict. This must include the willingness on the part of conflict workers to discard ready-made blueprints for conflict resolution and instead deeply examine the conflict with which they are dealing to determine the exact role identity and other factors (such as interests or a skewed balance of power) play in its dynamics. Only then they would be in a position to identify and apply the appropriate tools for intervention.

In addition, this chapter has set for itself a narrow technical focus, which should not be taken to mean that what happens inside a single workshop, or even in a series of workshops, is in itself sufficient to bring peace or transform conflicts within and between communities. There are larger challenges involved, both theoretical and practical. In fact, countervailing political, economic and cultural factors, both domestic and international, that are mostly responsible for sustaining conflicts and making them intractable could be mystified, camouflaged, obscured and hidden from view by what could be described as the "workshop model" of conflict engagement and an exclusive focus only on identity. We will briefly discuss some of these complex facets of the reality of social conflict in the concluding section, but a deeper engagement with them falls beyond the scope of this chapter.

The Kumi Method

Kumi, meaning 'rise up' in both Arabic and Hebrew, is a tool for organizing in situations of conflict. It is a process within which individuals and groups who are working for social and political change are able to reflect upon the root causes of the conflicts in which they are involved and collectively mobilize towards creative alternative solutions. Combining research and experience from the fields of conflict resolution and grassroots organizing, Kumi offers a method for transforming the contexts in which conflict arises. The method is used in workshops that are facilitated by Kumi practitioners, all of whom work with the groups over an extended period of time. Through a process that involves careful preparation and follow-up, the aim is to provide a tool that can be used for collective social action.

---

[1] After completing the chapter, the authors shared it with other facilitators who took part in the case studies discussed in it. Anat Reisman-Levy, Ruham Nimri and Shiri Bar provided helpful comments that were duly incorporated in the text.

The Kumi Method has been developed within a larger approach to engaging conflict, an approach which we refer to as "Social Transformation in Conflict." This approach is guided by the idea that conflicts exist within broader contexts in which deeply rooted identities are bound together with entrenched social structures. It is characteristic of conflict that attention is much focused on identities, while the larger social structures, which contribute to the establishment and perpetuation of group identities, are perceived often in a limited or oblique way. Becoming conscious of the interrelation between identity and social structures and the way in which conflict is an expression of that interrelation enables individuals and groups to look for non-violent, transcending solutions that fulfill the basic human needs of all parties to the conflict. This allows them to challenge those larger forces, thereby creating the possibility for a change in the conflict itself. Put simply, the approach holds that meaningful change in situations of protracted and deep-seated conflict is tied together with larger social change, so that sustainable conflict resolution involves social transformation.

The Kumi Method borrows from ARIA the components of Antagonism and Resonance and combines them with components from two other approaches. The first is an approach to conflict analysis and transformation based on a critical reframing of Transcendence, developed initially by Johan Galtung. This approach was codified by Wilfried Graf and Gudrun Kramer, with contributions from Edgar Morin and Herb Kelman, among others (Galtung 1969, 1975, 1976, 1996, 2004; Graf et al. 2008, 2010). The second methodological approach is the Institute of Cultural Affairs' Technology of Participation (ToP), with its focus on consensus-based participatory strategic planning for collective action (Stanfield 2002; Bergdall 1993). ARIA's place within Kumi, its signature contribution, rests on its relevance and capacity to assist participants in engaging the deepest dimensions of the conflict they are experiencing. In the case studies, the antagonism of the participants and the difficulty and benefits of engaging it while moving toward resonance are made clear. Each of these case studies are examples of ARIA's place within the Kumi process and can therefore be seen as examples of how the components of ARIA can be adapted and incorporated with components of other methods in order to enhance the scope of planned interventions.[2]

Case Study A

In November 2009, a group of participants from two organizations: one Israeli and one Palestinian, came together for a Kumi workshop. The two organizations had been working together over the past few years but were having trouble sustaining their cooperation. They had jointly organized a series of dialogue encounters between young Israelis and Palestinians together with Europeans. Many of the Israeli participants perceived such encounters as helpful in that they allowed them to get to know Palestinians better and to learn about their grievances and hopes for the future. But for the Palestinians, the encounters fell far short of their key expectation, namely to engage the Israelis in meaningful activities, both inside Israel and across the conflict lines, aimed at ending the occupation. The objective of the Kumi workshop was to identify the problems that were blocking these two organizations from continuing to work together and facilitate them into transcending these problems.

The workshop took place at a time when the Kumi Method was in a relatively rudimentary stage of development, most notably before ARIA's Antagonism and Resonance components had been adequately integrated, and the facilitation team was still preoccupied by the diverse challenges inherent to the integration of the three methods that make up Kumi.

As mentioned above, this workshop brought together two organizations that had previously cooperated. Unfortunately for the workshop, many of the actual participants who arrived had

---

[2] As Kaufman, Davies and Patel rightly argue in Chap. 4 in this volume, discarding the two other components of Intervention and Action from ARIA is not appropriate. However, in Kumi, the Transcend approach and ICA's ToP have invention and action planning components that adequately compensate for the loss.

either not been active within the organizations for several years, or they were only loosely related to them. They were, therefore, not particularly representative of the actual organizations, but were rather two collections of individuals with loose affiliations to each organization. This caused some difficulties in the process throughout much of the workshop, some of which presented itself while the participants were attempting to negotiate the challenging transition from antagonism to resonance.

Setting the Stage: Participants' Conflicting Expectations About the Workshop

At the outset of the workshop, the participants identified ground rules for the dialogue ahead. The majority of these ground rules were directly related to communication: respect people, one speaker at a time, respect each others' feelings, no hard feelings, confidentiality, and ask for clarification before disagreeing with another person.

These rules could be seen to represent the participants' understanding that they were about to enter "difficult" ground. They highlight some of the assumptions held by the participants about the difficulty of raising conflict-related issues in a manner that would not be experienced as offensive and lacking respect to each other. In the terminology of ARIA, there appeared to be a sense that antagonistic discourse was to be expected and that participants were preoccupied by the challenge of how to allow for open discussions without experiencing destructive discourse among themselves. In other words, from the outset, participants were aware that the dialogue and learning process ahead would be deeply influenced by adversarial positions and perceptions between the conflict sides involved.

It must be noted here that some of these ground rules, for example the one about "no hard feelings", may not be appropriate for interactive antagonism work. This is why we emphasize that these rules are applicable for interaction during the whole Kumi workshop, which includes many components. When the time comes to take the participants through the antagonism/resonance components, the facilitators introduce an alternative set of rules to allow for an authentic expression of both antagonism and resonance.

After this introductory evening of setting some "operating principles" and exploring the trends presenting themselves in the conflict (what we call the Context Check), the next morning provided the participants the opportunity to set their goals for the workshop. What did they hope to achieve during their time together? This process immediately uncovered much of the conflict and tension between the participants in the room. The session began with each organization (and therefore each identity group: Israelis and Palestinians) separately defining their goals for the workshop before they met together to try to gain a shared agreement about their goals for the next few days.

This initial intragroup goal-setting step went easily on the Palestinian side, with participants interacting well together during breaks, and without a great deal of turmoil. On the Israeli side, however, there was tension between those who wanted to define the goal of the workshop to be focused on dialogue and understanding of the other side, and those who wanted the goal to be an exploration of possibilities for carrying out joint activities aimed at challenging the status quo. When the Israeli and Palestinian groups came together to reach agreement on their intergroup goals, difficulties emerged. The session was supposed to be completed in the morning. But the participants found themselves struggling to reach agreement and progress with each other about their goals for this workshop as the day wound into the afternoon and early evening. Most of the Israeli participants focused their workshop goals mainly on theoretical exercises: evaluation of past work together and gaining understanding of the other participants. The Palestinians, on the other hand, wanted to engage the core issues of the conflict in order to mobilize activists and produce some activity on the ground aimed at ending the occupation. This disagreement on goals was a typical problem encountered by the two organizations in their previous cooperation, as mentioned above: Israelis usually consider their participation in dialogue workshops as a form of activism while Palestinians come to these workshops in order to promote change on the ground.

Antagonism soon began to find its way into their language. Sometimes this was disguised as "terminological conversations," like the one here from a Palestinian participant: "We have different concepts, for example, the fence and the wall. The settlements; some people call it villages. We should define the meaning or the titling of the names and their interpretation and discuss the interpretation to arrive at a common meaning of each expression related to the core of the concept....It is, at the very beginning, a pre-step towards moving forward."[3]

Not long after this, as the participants struggled to categorize and define their goals, the exchanges became more direct:

> Palestinian (P) (trying to categorize a group goal of the Palestinians into a goal category shared between Israelis and Palestinians): "I would like to place the Palestinian goal 'to mobilize the minorities on both communities to end the occupation' under the category 'exploring new ways of action'."
> Israeli (I): "I think that mobilizing minorities applies. The second part, ending the occupation, would need to be changed in order to apply to minorities in Israel. 'Ending the occupation' restricts the mobilization of minorities."
> (P): "We are not able to mobilize the minorities without the corollary [of ending the occupation]."
> (I): "'End the occupation' doesn't speak to the [entire] Israeli side."

Clearly, the group was already beginning to muddle the goals of the workshop with the goals of the groups and individuals in the wider conflict context, largely because their adversarial frames naturally moved them in that direction. The participants were already latently experiencing antagonism. It was affecting their ability to reach shared goals. In retrospect, this is very clear. During the workshop, however, while the facilitators quickly understood that antagonism was surfacing, they did not react quickly enough to begin shaping it into productive dialogue and

encourage the participants to make healthy decisions about how to engage it. In many cases, individuals and groups can quickly, and without much angst, reach agreements on how to move forward together and where they are heading. However, in cases like the Israeli-Palestinian conflict, the identity components often muddle the water and end up determining the participants' ability to reach such agreements.

Much effort was needed to move through the conflicting perspectives and expectations between Israelis and Palestinians in order to identify goals both sides could agree to. As with most encounters between Israelis and Palestinians in the course of the Kumi workshops, the conflicting perspectives and positions raised were reflective of the asymmetry inherent in the conflict. For example, Israeli participants favored goals related to learning about each other's points of view, understanding the conflict, identifying opportunities for building a better future. Palestinian participants, on the other hand, favored goals related directly to dealing in a more focused manner with the core issues of the conflict, such as settlements, refugees, Jerusalem, and foremost how to advance the end of occupation. Israelis tended to view the dialogue ahead as an opportunity for exploring the sides' conflict perceptions whereas for Palestinians the major motivation appeared to be the task of identifying ways to create opportunities for achieving progress towards ending occupation and all it implies to those who experience the hardship and injustice of life under foreign military rule.

In this workshop the conflict sides clearly expressed their conflicting perceptions and positions, indicating that underlying antagonistic assumptions were present. In terms of facilitation, there were ample challenges about how to cope with the antagonism already present close to the surface of the discourse that developed in the group even though the workshop was still in its early stages.

This raises the question of the "opportune time" to intervene with an engagement of that antagonism. How and when do facilitators know the right time to dig into the adversarial frames that create antagonism and that block forward progress between groups? The facilitators in this

---

[3] In the Israeli Palestinian conflict both societies created concepts of clearly political nature, such as the "fence" vs. the" wall". In Israeli discourse, fence implies a needed and minimal defense mechanism to prevent terrorist attacks within Israel. In Palestinian discourse, wall implies separation of territory and people, a violent obstacle to freedom of movement and, in general, deliberate infringement by Israel on Palestinians' property and human rights.

instance did not immediately recognize the intensity with which the participants were experiencing their antagonism. In fact, there was an effort to restrain the participants from fully engaging it so that the groups could move forward according to the process. The assumption was that there will always be levels of antagonism in groups so profoundly wrapped up in conflict. Allowing the space to engage this safely is a gift we can offer them, but only if conditions are right for safety and for a full engagement of the issues.

At this point in the workshop, the facilitators did not feel the participants were ready to do so, and that the conditions were not right for a fruitful engagement. While this may have been true, in retrospect it may have caused the group to now distrust each other *and* the facilitators. Part of the problem was the facilitators' own differing views on antagonism and how best to engage it: avoiding it themselves and encouraging the participants to engage in non-violent, non-antagonistic communication, or confronting it head-on and allowing the participants to do the same. The facilitators were divided on which approach to follow. Due to lack of agreement among the facilitators, they tended to avoid direct engagement with antagonism at this early stage of the workshop and, paradoxically, that may have enabled it to fester unproductively and take hold of the participants. That is, they may have unwittingly stepped into the mine-field that ARIA seeks to avoid by addressing Antagonism in conscious and forthright ways so that it doesn't hit people in the back of their heads when they are not looking. Or more concretely, the anger and mistrust that antagonism generates can be modulated and redirected through careful engagement and facilitation, not by avoidance.

Ultimately, late in the afternoon, after much pulling and pushing, the group managed to reach agreement on two major goals on which to focus during the workshop:

1. Gain a deep and mutual understanding about the conflict and its core issues (Jerusalem, settlements, refugees, land)
2. Explore new ways of action and new solutions to old problems, work towards an end to occupation and a just and peaceful resolution of the conflict

The first goal they identified as foundational for success of the second goal. That is, in order to explore new ways of action, they would have to deeply explore their understanding of the conflict and its core issues. Given their difficulty during the morning and afternoon, the participants were eager to move into these discussions.

Looking at Core Issues and Expressing Conflict

Based on the participants' first goal, the facilitators then guided them through a deep analysis of the core conflict issues. The session began with a theoretical discussion on the definition of conflict. Participants were encouraged to share their understanding of conflict in general and different forms of conflict and their representations within the specific Israeli-Palestinian context.

The facilitators then invited the participants to break into three groups to address core conflict issues that had been suggested by the group: one working on the issue of Jerusalem, another working on refugees and a third on settlements. Each of these groups were bi-national and were tasked with developing a timeline that included both society's perspectives on the issue they had selected. They would work on the same large page, but would define the timelines according to each of their identity group's narrative.

When it was time for the groups to present their work, the Jerusalem group took a great deal of time to discuss their product, and it led to a very deep discussion that again began to tilt toward antagonistic discourse:

(P): "To add something related to Jerusalem… there is a big difficulty for people to live in Jerusalem…they are not allowed to build on their own land…in some places they are not allowed to change the exterior of the houses…so it's not only having Jerusalem or not, but how we live once we have it."

(I): "Do you think about how Israelis view East Jerusalem, or do you just see the Palestinian point of view?"

(P): "I'm just discussing the current realities of East Jerusalem."

(I): "From what you are saying, just to express my feelings, I'm not sure if there is openness to the Israeli view towards Jerusalem."

(I): "For example Jerusalem is mentioned in every Jewish marriage ceremony. It's part of the basic Jewish identity. You have to try to understand what it means in order for discussion to be possible."

(P): "But Israelis must understand the importance of Muslims being able to reach Jerusalem. Why is it always that we are blaming? Because we feel that we are the weakest part."

(I): "It bothers me, your tendency to generalize things towards always and ever…it's not true and blocks the dialogue."

This session came at an unfortunate time, and highlighted another organizational difficulty of the workshop. The participants were now reaching the end of their first of two weekends and were beginning to seriously engage their antagonism toward each other. As facilitators, we felt it was a bad idea to end a day on antagonism, even if participants were returning the next morning. Now we were in a worse situation, as we would leave an entire week in between meetings. We deemed this irresponsible: to allow the participants to get in an emotional and adversarial mood and simply send them back to their communities to stew over it.

When the participants returned from lunch, we instead decided to try to help them already begin the Resonance process (see Chaps. 1, 2 and 3), even if it could not fully be achieved in the short two hours we had until the end of this session. Participants gathered in small mixed groups and shared personal narratives about the topics they had addressed in the morning. Why were these issues so important to each of them, why did the discussion earlier become so difficult for many of them?

The feedback from these conversations was very positive, and when the facilitators pushed the participants to discover what they might be taking away from the first weekend, the responses were energizing:

(I): "I feel the conflict outside is much worse. I feel that here we were able to reach some beginning of understanding. Both sides showed a willingness to listen to the other side, and that is not something that you'd find outside of this room."

(P): "Indeed for me I feel I have a deeper understanding of the Israelis. I appreciated the question I was asked today as to whether I had thought about the question of Jerusalem from the Israeli perspective. I'm not sure I had ever thought of it that way."

(I): "I think what I learned is that I also share the feeling of having gained a deeper understanding, of learning different things. I learned today when people say things, what reaction it causes in different people. Certain words block people that don't want to hear it – what takes away that block – what things can people say that push my button and causes my walls to go up."

(P): "In yesterday's session I thought we were stuck, we were blocked, there was no way out. Today in the discussion we found many things in common, where we agreed."

While this was a positive end to the weekend, and participants had real and formative encounters with the *other* and ample opportunities to challenge themselves, the facilitators recognized that the latent antagonism still had not been fully engaged in a way that would allow the participants to continue moving forward. As mentioned, given time constraints and our concerns about ending our first weekend in antagonism, we cut it short and moved participants somewhat prematurely to resonance. Based on the ARIA perspective, we may assume that since in this case the facilitators did not allow for an in-depth expression and acknowledgement of antagonistic views and emotions, the group was not yet ready to move fully towards resonance. In fact, we predicted their expressions of resonant thinking noted above would likely not remain in place on their return the next weekend. The power of antagonism was weakened and its immediacy delayed. Had we made the switch self-consciously as described in Rothman's preface and first chapter of this book, resonance could more easily be re-asserted the next time the adversarial discourse began to re-emerge: "remember," we could assert with their prior permission, "that you wanted us to keep you from reverting to antagonism? Well, we're doing that now."

As a result of this, the facilitators felt the group did not achieve the goals that were set out for that stage, which were to build on their own experience of conflict in the here and now as they seek to deepen understanding of the conflict issues in general (as opposed to only beginning to voice and experience them), understand the relationship between the conflict in the room and conflict outside, and create a new understanding of the conflict and our place in it. While the participants began to both experience and analyze the conflict issues, the facilitators should have realized that the temporary suspension of antagonistic discourse was deceiving and that there were no shortcuts in engaging identity based conflict. This was carefully considered later, as the facilitators reflected on the weekend's experience and began to plan for the following weekend's sessions.

Revisiting Contradictions and Creating the Space for Surfacing Antagonism

The participants returned the following week for the second half of the workshop, when the facilitation team decided to cope with the difficulties and lack of progress identified so far by revisiting the conflict issues they had discussed and facilitating a shortened version of the antagonism session. Feeling like the group still needed to deeply engage each other on these issues, the facilitators invited the participants to move into single identity groups and to list their antagonism towards the other group (this is akin to the first step in a kind of "collective solo" process – see Chap. 3). Each group of Israelis and Palestinians was to focus on the issues discussed and clearly articulate their blame regarding the *other* and how *they* contribute to the escalation and maintenance of these conflict issues.

After each identity group listed their antagonisms, they presented them to the other group so that they could see and hear what the other side blamed them for. Each group was given the opportunity to ask clarifying questions about the antagonisms presented toward them, but not much more. In a fuller, engaged, ARIA process, the participants would then continue in deep discussions about these issues. But we were still faced with time shortages for doing the entire process, as well as some continued resistance by some of the facilitators to really let the antagonism genie out of the bottle, and thus chose to circumscribe the process to be analytical and not so much emotional or interactive. Moreover, most of the facilitators felt that given the time constraints as well as the reality that the participants

had already begun *some* resonance work, this analytic viewing of their antagonisms (e.g. what does each side blame the other for?) would provide sufficient space and voice to the respective adversarial frames each side holds about the other, and that they could then continue moving forward in their process.

Representatives from each identity group sat across from each other, with the rest of their groups sitting behind them. Each group presented their antagonisms toward the other, and fielded questions of clarity:

Israeli list	Palestinian list
• You escalate this conflict by explaining everything solely because of the occupation	• I blame you because you thought of your need for an Israeli state and you ignored the existence of other citizens that already were living there (whom you killed)
• I blame you for missing historical opportunities	• You take one-sided decisions of destroying Jerusalem houses, take land of Palestinian people, expanding the Jerusalem municipality to include also settlements, massacres and wars in the West Bank and all the violence you practice on us although you use the previous experience of violence in Europe as an excuse to need a land
• I blame you for escalating this conflict by choosing and legitimizing armed struggle against civilians	• You escalate this conflict because you believe in being the chosen people by God and the holy land is all your promised land and the other nations exist only to serve you, where you changed the historical facts to serve your existence as a blue-blood nation
• You escalate this conflict by institutionalizing the refugee problem and status	• You make it us vs. them because you separate the two parties of the conflict by creating new situations in the excuse of security (checkpoints, wall, detention, separate roads) which make matters even worse

These lists caused a lot of conversation, and indeed the participants wanted to engage them, asking how they could discuss these issues. In particular, a short discussion about the Palestinian use of the idea of the Holocaust as an "excuse" for Israeli aggression drew particular ire from some of the Israeli participants. Despite the facilitator's intentions, the process was being pulled into deeply emotional and engaged antagonism. So the facilitators pulled it back in an attempt to move the process, prematurely as it turned out, forward to resonance.

When some of parties objected that they were just getting to the heart of the matter, the facilitators attempted to explain why the process was done this way (e.g. time constraints, a sense that resonance had begun and more space could be made for it through analyzing each side's antagonism but not really engaging it, etc.), and why they would now attempt to move ahead instead of opening up this conversation fully. Participants in conflict are often comfortable with this kind of rhetoric, and want to stay there. However, the facilitators wanted to return the group to where they ended last week, but now, hopefully, with recognition by the parties of the danger of reverting to antagonism, and seeing each other only as the adversary and not as partners.

From a purely analytic perspective participants accepted the guidance of the facilitators and dealt with the task set for them. But it was clear during the following session that from an emotional point of view, the antagonism experienced and expressed, and in particular the way it was prematurely concluded, did not yet create readiness to move towards effective communication and interaction based on the principles of resonance. In fact, participants began to deeply question the process and its ability to meet the goals they had defined for the workshop. In short, they began to project the repressed antagonism they had towards each other onto the facilitators throughout the entire Kumi process:

(P): "I feel like a lab rat testing this Kumi thing."[4]
(P): "I feel this only benefits you."
(I): "The thing is, it feels a bit like too much talk about things on a theoretical level, to get deep, it feels a bit fake. I feel like you're observing our reactions as big brother. It's like we're all in an apartment and everyone is looking at what we're doing. I don't understand the process at all, even where I'm going."
(P): "In the aims it says deepen the understanding. We haven't discussed things."

A small part of this was the actual structural makeup of the previous few sessions, where participants were given tasks in small groups and then reported back to the large group. This led to an overall feeling of sending the participants out for research and hearing their findings when they returned.

More importantly, however, the relatively haphazard way in which antagonism was engaged produced first mistrust among the participants, then with the method and finally to some extent with the facilitators. Tension between the participants remained high; there was a clear gap between the analytic dimensions of the process (the analysis of conflict issues), on the one hand, and the emotional dimension of the process which aimed at transforming antagonism between participants into resonance, on the other hand.

The facilitators attempted again later to introduce a conversation about basic human needs as a way to understand the conflict issues they had identified and were attempting to address within the room. While some valuable discussion occurred, the group again found itself at the end of the exercise questioning its impact on them and their progress because of the failure to address the antagonism:

(I): "I feel we cannot move on because we do not have a platform to move on. I think we didn't succeed in this exercise because the other platform, the one we did before [the analytical ARIA process attempted earlier], was not finished."
(I): "I disagree with the way you understand my position. What I think you misunderstood is that it is not my interest to yell at Palestinians but to understand how they view Israelis and what they think. What we did earlier is that we surfaced the antagonism but didn't have a chance to understand what was going on."

Engaging Antagonism: One More Time

The facilitators recognized the need to cope with the gap between content-related work that was planned for the remaining workshop sessions

---

[4] This feeling was probably accentuated by the fact that sometimes there were as many as eight Kumi practitioners in the room: two facilitating and the others documenting and observing.

(conflict analysis leading to action planning on how to engage with conflict) and the emotion-related work regarding how to deal with antagonism still present between participants. The assumption was that without a transformation of communicative patterns and relationships between the conflict sides the group would not be able to engage in action planning, since that element of the workshop raised questions about how to cooperate in order to address the conflict reality in a strategic and practical manner. The facilitation team assumed that without transforming perceptions and relationships within the workshop, participants would not be ready to cooperate in order to create substantive and sustainable outcomes in terms of shared strategic directions for action.

The facilitators sought a way that would help participants move from a largely attributional discourse to a more reflective one. Even though the group went through the stages of listing and expressing antagonistic statements, the participants did not seem ready to move beyond, or at least set aside, their blame towards the other side and were not expressing analytic empathy. The ability to jointly explore how each side experienced the conflict and how to identify creative new ways for change in that conflict had not yet been reached.

During the closing moments of the last session, as participants were expressing their desire to return to the issues and to confront each other, several of them felt that they got off track directly after their lists of antagonisms were formed, shared, but then not fully engaged. They wanted to return to this place in the conversation. Additionally, because of their growing suspicion about the method, they suggested an alternative format: for the Israelis to take the list of blames created by the Palestinians (and vice versa) and look deeply at them to consider how they might have contributed to the blame put upon them by the *other*. What could our contribution be to this? What could we as an identity group have done to develop such a response in others?

The participants returned to their single identity groups with the opposing lists in order to engage these questions. When they returned, the power asymmetry in the room and in the conflict became a major stumbling block to the efficacy of the exercise. Palestinians found it very difficult to accept any role in the blame the Israelis had put on them:

> (P): "I think it will be very hard to understand each other because on our side we don't blame ourselves. There is a powerful country and a weak one."
>
> (I): "For me it was choosing from what the other side says which blame I take."
>
> (I): "I was expecting you guys to engage in some introspection because I think you made some bad decisions as well."
>
> (P): "When there is a strong part and a weak part then it's hard to say we have blame on ourselves and so should you."
>
> (I): "I personally think that the decision of blowing up buses is something you should think about. It's simply not true that we have done everything and you have done nothing."

In this way, the participants finally and openly engaged their antagonisms. This seems paradoxical at first but, as with many paradoxes, it has a certain logic to it. It took them taking on the antagonisms attributed to them before they really unleashed their antagonism toward the other side.[5] The facilitators mainly stepped out of the conversation and allowed the participants to engage each other. This went on for some time, with participants exhibiting the type of Antagonistic discussion listed just above, and floating back and forth between this and a more reflective discourse. The group reached a place where a long break was needed. Afterwards, the facilitators checked in with them to see how they were doing. The participants expressed a desire to continue to engage the issues, but in a "strategic way." In other words, the participants wanted now to test their commitment to action (and the depth of their engagement with each other) by attempting to create solutions to some of their conflicts and possibly develop actions out of them. While participants were sincere in this desire, the conditions were simply not sufficiently set for their success.

The facilitators obliged, nevertheless. Retrospectively, that was not particularly wise.

---

[5]In fact, Rothman (2012) has been experimenting with what he calls a "reverse attributional process" which these participants intuitively invented.

Before moving on to action planning, the facilitators would need to test whether the participants understood (not necessarily agreed with) each others' narrative of self, what was deeply important to them and why. If so, then action planning could follow. Rothman calls this testing for "analytical empathy" (see Chap. 3). If not, even more resonance building (including unfortunately maybe even further regression into antagonism) would be necessary.

As should have been expected, participants up until the end of the workshop retained a sense that the "other side" was not open to the perspectives and needs expressed by "us," and that there was too little ground for creating a shared space of mutually shared insights, values and objectives. Even though the participants went through the motions of fulfilling their tasks, the workshop ended with a sense of creating little headway for new types of cooperation on strategic action in relation to conflict reality.

This is not to say that the workshop had no positive impact or that there was no significance for the participants. One of the great difficulties of the conflict field is its "efficacy" and how we measure success. Many of the participants expressed gratitude for their time together and real engagement with the other side that they had never before experienced, and some of them did create ideas and action plans that they followed through on (separately) after the workshop.

However, in hindsight, a major shortcoming of our time together that November was in not engaging antagonism properly. We can boil down the causes of this to a few things:

1. Not recognizing early enough the desire of participants to engage each other in this way.
2. Once antagonism was surfaced, not allowing participants to fully engage each other until they were "satisfied."
3. Going back and forth between antagonism and resonance, a process we normally try to restrain participants from doing themselves. A significant part of this may have come from ambivalence, and perhaps even fear, about facilitating a structured Antagonism session by some of the facilitators.

This workshop clearly indicates the costs of not allowing the participants to more fully express and process antagonism in order to move towards resonance. As can be discerned from this workshop, as long as participants remain preoccupied by their need to express and confront antagonistic positions and attitudes, they are not ready to engage in a significant manner with tasks that demand a reflexive state of mind. Even though participants were invited to employ analytic concepts and tools relevant to the tasks of conflict analysis and reassessing their involvement in the conflict processes within the room and societal reality outside of the room, it appears that their capacity to deal with these tasks was seriously impeded by their emotional preoccupation with antagonism. But one of the aims of the workshop was to precisely engage and transform such a preoccupation, an aim that could not be achieved due to workshop conditions and the relative inexperience of, and disagreements among, the facilitators in engaging antagonism directly and self-consciously.

Since the workshop structure at that point of the Kumi pilot phase did not yet clearly articulate a systematic engagement of the challenge of transforming the tunnel vision of antagonistic and non-reflexive perceptions, the workshop process was probably, in the final analysis, a mostly frustrating experience for participants as well as facilitators. The workshop functioned largely as an accumulation of significant elements of conflict engagement, but this did not lead to a process in which participants experienced the opportunity to fully engage in the challenge and opportunity to transform antagonistic positions, attitudes and emotions towards each other. Without that process, participants could not gain significant new insights about their involvement in the ongoing conflict reality and cooperate in the search for new and relevant strategies towards transforming it.

Case Study B

In April 2010, a group of seven Israelis, seven Palestinians and four Europeans participated in a five-day Kumi workshop that took place at a conference center just outside Berlin, Germany. The Israeli and Palestinian participants were young politicians and political activists, though none came in an official capacity as representatives of their parties, but rather as individuals. The Israeli participants represented a significant spectrum of Israeli political parties, and all held positions of middle rank influence within their parties as either district organizers or advisers to ministers and members of the Israeli Knesset. The Palestinian participants were less diverse politically, but nonetheless held equivalent positions of influence. The four European participants were older and some of them had many years of experience in engaging with the Israeli Palestinian conflict. The workshop was facilitated and documented by an international team made up of two Israelis, an Israeli Palestinian, an Egyptian, an Englishman, and two U.S. Americans based in Europe. The workshop took place after substantial changes were made to Kumi since the workshop described in Case Study A. The flow was, by now, seen as a more logical one, and the antagonism and resonance components were more fully integrated. Mainly because of this, and a number of other factors explored below and in the following section, the dynamics of the workshop and its outcome diverged greatly from those of the other workshop described above. In short, it was far more successful and satisfying for participants and facilitators alike.

The Protagonists Get Ready to Engage

At the start of the workshop, two contradictory trends became immediately obvious. On the one hand, the participants showed a readiness to engage in antagonistic discourse. On the other hand, and as would be expected, they proceeded with caution and apparent civility as if they were testing the water and sizing up their opponents. The facilitators started by asking the participants to articulate their expectations for the workshop. The participants saw this as an invitation to skirmish. There was a long discussion about whether the participants should dwell on the past or not.

The participants expressed their expectations as demands: We *should/should not* talk about the past, we *must* find solutions, we *want* to know what the others think, etc. Eventually, the participants agreed on a set of ground rules to guide the remainder of the workshop: respect; listen effectively; one voice in the room; accept and understand the other despite differences; accept disagreements; stick to timetable and switch off phones. Some of these behavioural expectations assisted greatly in the smooth operation of a workshop and yet ran counter to what is often required for an authentic engagement of Antagonism. Typically, in a pure ARIA process, the only ground rules are: keep your seats, don't leave until we have moved from Antagonism into Resonance, mind the process. While some of the guidelines this group set up are not in direct contradiction to an Antagonism to Resonance process, once the Antagonism process is reached participants may experience a disconnect if their expectation is to respectfully focus on the future and seek only agreement.

Once the participants reached agreement on the ground rules, the facilitators laid out the plan for the days ahead, which was a summary of the new Kumi flow: context check, identification of goals, surfacing contradictions of goals, engaging antagonism, achieving resonance, analyzing the conflict, finding transcending solutions and action planning. The facilitators were aware that going as far as action planning might not happen, given the sharply opposing views of the participants. It was placed there as an aspiration for the end of the workshop. At the end of the workshop, though, both the facilitators and the participants were surprised by how much further they felt they could have gone, despite their own expectations, if only time had permitted.

A brief look at the biographies and the behaviour of the participants outside the workshop room reveals some of the underlying dynamics of this and other similar encounters. Underneath the polite and careful language of the first few hours, one could feel the tension already building up. The fiancé of one female Palestinian participant was killed a few years ago by an Israeli soldier, perhaps of the same age and background as some of the Israeli participants, almost of all whom served in the Israeli army. This was the first time she ever sat in an encounter with Israelis. An Israeli female participant, also sitting with Palestinians for the first time, approached one of the facilitators on the first evening in a sort of a panic, asking whether she could spend the night in the facilitator's room because she was scared that the Palestinians might use the opportunity to attack her.

Overall, there was a sense of both curiosity and pessimism in the room at the early stage of the workshop. This came across while doing the environment check, an early stage in the Kumi process where participants share their understanding of the larger environment of the conflict. They had similar perspectives about the evolution of the conflict and the regional and global trends that are shaping it, mostly negative, while there was some degree of hope about the future. The tension in the room escalated about the choice of certain words, such as terrorist, to describe the leaders from respective sides. This prompted the facilitators to contain the tension and the underlying antagonism while inviting the participants to remain attuned to the immediate task of setting the scene for the work to come over the next days. In other words, the natural inclination at this point of the participants to be antagonistic had to be slightly suppressed for now, and this had to be done while ensuring that trust was being built among them and the facilitators. It was a delicate balancing act in which the facilitators demonstrated their control, but also didn't shut down the beginning of the participants' emotional expressions of anger, fear, hurt and loss.

Tensions continued to build while the participants were asked to agree on a focus question to serve as an anchor for the workshop. In the invitation letter sent to the participants and in the preparatory meetings held with them on a uni-national level by the facilitators and the organizers, the objective of the workshop was presented as a discussion about the right to self-determination and the role of Europe in the Israeli-Palestinian conflict. They oscillated between choosing a more factual focus for the conversation, for example, how does one define self-determination, and a more subjective expression of contradictory and antagonistic positions. In the words of one Palestinian participant addressing himself to the Israelis in the room:

> "We agree on the notion of self-determination in general, but when you get it, you deny it to others. You fought for your country but you deny the Palestinians the right to fight for theirs. Europeans fought to win their right to self-determination but now they are supporting those Israelis who are denying the same right for the Palestinians."

Tensions mounted, with Palestinians demanding a clear definition of "terrorism" from the Israelis, with the Israelis chastising the Palestinians for their corrupt leadership, violence and ingratitude. As one Israeli participant put it, "you should be grateful that we provide you with water and electricity. We could switch off the taps tomorrow and you would not be able to do anything about it. You lost your territory in a war that was not of our own making and now you have neither right nor power to demand this territory back. Instead of making peace, you resort to violence and terrorism which would not get you anywhere."

With tension increasing, and participants eager to engage in antagonistic discourse, the facilitators invited them to articulate their goals. In a workshop in which participants are reluctant to engage in conflict this is the stage in which it could be surfaced. In this specific workshop, however, the conflicting sides involved were in a rather different position. Personal antagonism was clearly high from the outset, and the challenge rather was how to create a more substantive focus on the parties' conflicting needs, interests and positions in order to allow, at a later stage, a facilitation of focused and constructive conflict engagement.

What started to emerge throughout the day became well established by the end of it. Israeli and Palestinian participants were eager to engage in conflict, their communication swiftly moving into adversarial framing. Conflicting narratives were forcefully expressed and the Europeans in the room found themselves in a kind of "back-seat" position, at times trying to lessen the tension by introducing more factual and non-judgmental voices, but to little avail.

The past kept coming up. Here is an example from an Israeli participant:

> "Let something be clear. I am looking to the facts. In 1948, you had an opportunity to build your country. Instead of building your country, you attacked us. In 1965, you established a movement called Fatah, two years before 1967. In 1967, you attacked us again, from the south, from the north. How many opportunities do you think we will give you to establish your own country? Instead of seeking peace, you always attack us. Now you have to understand that we have strategic territories that we cannot move from, because if we move from them you will attack us again. Just because we have a strong army, we took from you the land to protect ourselves. Our side does not want these wars."

This went on until the end of the day. The facilitators had to deal with the challenge of how to assist participants to disengage sufficiently in order to allow for closure before breaking up for the evening.

Israelis and Palestinians were eager to express blaming, to challenge each other's positions, to express their narratives, points of views, emotions. The challenge for the facilitators was to contain these expressions and ensure that these energies were funneled into the framework of the day's major task: setting the stage for a more in-depth exploration of the conflict between the sides at a later stage of the workshop.

The Kumi workshop flow that was established in the months before this workshop now began to assert its value. It allowed the participants to engage authentically from early on in the workshop, and at the same time allowed for the evolution of a framework that would guide participants toward a more focused and structured conflict engagement at the upcoming stages of the workshop. The antagonism that the participants brought with them into the encounter with the "other" was allowed for; its presence was acknowledged from the outset. At the same time, the day's structure and the focused facilitation created containment of the rising tension among

participants until the appropriate moment later on in the process when the antagonism could be released in a more structured and constructive manner.

We Can Behave as Political Adversaries and Relate to Each Other as Human Beings, but Not at the Same Time

The Kumi process used in this workshop was a five-day, 24 hours a day experience. Participants pointed out that there were already two major modes of communication present. One was the antagonistic one in which the sides expressed their contradictory positions in a language of blame and accusation. The other was communication based on the recognition of basic similarity of needs as human beings. The Palestinian female participant who lost her lover at the hands of an Israeli soldier made it clear on the first day that she was not willing to talk to Israelis outside the workshop room. This would be "normalization," in her view. However, this is what she said at the morning of the second day of the workshop:

> "When the meeting ended yesterday, I was very stressed. Then there was an initiative from the Israeli side to sit and talk on our own [without the facilitators]. It was difficult for me at first because I have issues about socializing with Israelis, whether rightly or wrongly. It took a real effort at first. However, once we started talking and drinking, I was amazed to see that there was so much in common. It is possible to live as neighboring countries. As time passed, all the ice was breaking and we started talking about songs and music and all sorts of common interests."

The group expressed awareness that there were two possible modes of communication, which appeared to be mutually exclusive. The solution for them was to create a split: antagonism would be dominant within the workshop sessions, more reflective and empathetic dimensions were reserved for the informal parts of the day. This also indicated the potential of moving between those different modes of relating to each other. As one of the facilitators put it, "What I'm hearing is this duality. We have a strong conflict in the room but also recognition that we could relate to each other as human beings."

The facilitators had to be careful not to fall into the trap of thinking that all was suddenly well in the relationships between the participants. They invited the participants to focus further on the conflict in the room by introducing the definition of conflict (at this preliminary stage, defined as a contradiction in goals) and the relationship between contradicting goals and the experience of conflict. The focus on the participants' goals and where they were in contradiction caused the early Antagonism to return quickly to the room. One Palestinian participant went as far as saying: "For a long time I have been working for peace, but yesterday was a revelation for me. This is not acceptable. I have always been in favor for a two-state solution. But now, I tell you, I need the whole of Palestine back."

Time was now ripe for the full release of antagonism. The emotional energy of the Israeli and Palestinian participants was driving them to speak out against each other, and little energy was available for empathy and reflection. At this same moment, the Europeans in the room expressed their apprehension towards the growing antagonism and attempted to introduce some hope for other types of communication between the sides. They often felt as though their role in the workshop (as is sometimes the case in the conflict) was that of a mediator or moderator. While they understood the need to deeply engage the issues, the Europeans were very keen to avoid the type of direct and often aggressive language on which the Antagonism process relies. As one European participant put it:

> "I would like to say something. I do not consider what happened yesterday evening as a fight because for me it was the opposite. I think the engagement, being together, spending time together, communicating – both groups discovered so many similarities. I think this was a great achievement because only if you spend time together and learn who is on the other side can you move a step further. I see this as a window to come closer to a solution. Because if you bring these people together and they engage in dialogue and learn about each other

then they will not perceive each other as this huge enemy and will maybe put their weapons aside."

The Israelis and Palestinians were quick to brush this aside and express readiness to enter direct antagonism with each other.

Engaging Antagonism, Differently

In single identity groups, the Israeli and Palestinian facilitators assisted their respective groups to list their Antagonisms toward the other side. However, as became apparent in the plenary session later on, each facilitator dealt with Antagonism from a different premise. Whereas the Palestinian facilitator instructed the Palestinian group *not to mince words* about the others, the Israeli facilitator instructed the group to present a list of adversarial frames *in a diplomatic way, without using overly offensive language*. This difference in instructions created a challenging dynamic when the groups faced off again: an emotional response from the Israelis of feeling unjustly framed by the Palestinians and a sense of empowerment on the Palestinian side, who felt that they somehow prevailed over the Israelis.

On the surface of it, this difference in instructions could be seen as a "technical" issue, due to lack of coordination between the facilitators. But if we look at the specific dynamic that evolved as a result, this might also be analyzed as a kind of coping mechanism related to power asymmetry between the sides, an issue that also the Israeli and Palestinian *facilitators* experienced themselves. Throughout the workshop, Israelis and Palestinians clearly acknowledged the power asymmetry between the sides. For the first time in this workshop, Israelis felt on the defensive, while the Palestinians in the room had some kind of rhetorical victory by surprising the Israelis with the harshness of their attributions. In a sense, both sides seemed shocked and confused by this sudden and unexpected reconfiguration of their power relationship.

Palestinian list:	Israeli list:
• Expansionists	• Lack of Education for peace
• Survive on conflict	• Lack of leadership
• Dwell on the idea of victimhood	• Image of the weak
• Obsessed with security	• Disrespect for agreements
• Racists	• Little value for human life
• War criminals, blood thirsty, brutal and children killers	
• Cheap and arrogant	
• Brainwashing society through education and media	
• You claim that we are terrorists but you are the ones who inflict terror upon innocent civilians	
• Thieves of culture, history and heritage	

The difference in the language used by each side points to the different levels of engagement by the Israeli and Palestinian facilitators in the workshop and in the wider conflict. The behavior of the facilitators in a workshop is also a reflection of the conflict and its dynamics. It is sometimes difficult for facilitators to disconnect from the reality of the conflict and observe rules of impartiality. They, consciously or not, act according to who they are, as part of one of the conflict parties. In our case, the Israeli facilitators were not able to assist the Israeli participants in listing their antagonistic blaming towards the Palestinians. In fact when some Israeli participants tried to do this, and did mention some very antagonistic, honest and painful blaming, one of the Israeli facilitators asked the participants to do it in a more diplomatic way. One explanation for this is that the Israeli facilitators, themselves dovish in their political attitudes, could not accept an Israeli being so aggressive towards the Palestinians. It was against the facilitators' own beliefs about how Israelis should relate to Palestinians (including perhaps feeling of guilt and self-doubt). This was further complicated by the fact that the Israeli facilitators in this case were ideologically far removed from today's mainstream

Israeli society. Their own political views were not similar to the views of the Israeli groups they were facilitating. So they were facing a situation in which they were facilitating a group of Israeli participants representing the Israeli mainstream, and at the same time they felt ideologically much closer to the other group in the room, i.e. the Palestinians.

The Palestinian facilitators, on the other hand, did not face such a difficulty. They were ideologically situated in the middle of the Palestinian mainstream, and this made it much easier for them to facilitate a group representing the Palestinian mainstream. For them, being part of the conflict as the weaker party, the occupied, it was a chance to empower themselves and the Palestinian participants. It was an opportunity to bring the Palestinians back to the room as fully equal with the Israelis. As a result (and as can be seen above), the power asymmetry of the conflict outside the room was not reflected in the room, and they, both Palestinian facilitators and participants, managed to use this situation in order to say whatever they wanted to say to the Israelis without fear of reprisal. In fact, if we look back at the two lists, we could see that the Palestinians did "the best" they could do, in trying to list the most antagonistic blaming, and the Israelis, prompted by their facilitators, modulated their antagonism in a diplomatic way.

At this stage of the workshop, both sides encountered some of the underlying animosity that is part of the conflict discourse on both sides. The Israeli side had to confront the reality of the moral cost of military and political superiority, which included the difficulty of justifying violence by simply pointing to the violence perpetuated by the other side. The Palestinians experienced the opportunity of "being strong" in presenting their positions, but also the futility of a "rhetorical victory" because that in itself did not create a breakthrough on the substantial issues of concern. All in the room strongly experienced the dead-end of blaming since it involved a never-ending and ultimately vicious cycle of arguments and counter arguments without achieving any sense of progress in reaching a shared understanding of conflict dynamics and means of how to engage it.

Thus, though not in a linear way, the Antagonism process was well conducted and served its major purpose: both sides' viewed this type of dialogue as ultimately counter-productive. Thus, "room" was made emotionally and analytically for a new way forward: Resonance.

At this point in the workshop a particularly dramatic event occurred. Here it is narrated by Ruham Nimri, who was one of the Palestinian facilitators:

> The reaction of the Israeli participants was severe. They were wondering, was it the Palestinian facilitator who did not follow "the rules" since the Israeli facilitators asked them clearly to list their blaming in a diplomatic way, or was it the Israeli facilitators who "betrayed" them and prevented them from expressing themselves in as forceful a manner as possible? One Israeli participant began crying when she saw what the Palestinians came up with, and said she never thought this was how the Palestinians saw the Israelis. Another Israeli participant stood up, started shouting at the facilitators, opened the door, left the room and slammed the door shut. The facilitators asked the participants to stay in the room and not leave. I (who am a Palestinian citizen of Israel) went out after the participant. I found the Israeli participant outside taking a walk in the woods, joined him and had a long conversation with him. We then went back to the room to finish the process.

> It is very interesting how I as a Palestinian facilitator managed to bring back an Israeli participant to the room in such an extreme emotional experience. I used this situation to talk with the Israeli participant about my own feelings towards Israeli Jews and what I have experienced in this relationship on a daily basis. I also helped the Israeli participant to share his feelings about Palestinians in general and specifically about Palestinian Israelis in his own town (a mixed town in the north of Israel). The participant then began talking about feelings of fear, weariness and exhaustion. At the same time, I invited him to bring out his fears and listened to him very carefully. We reached a point where the Jewish Israeli participant realized that he and I, the Palestinian Israeli facilitator were experiencing the same feelings towards each other. Eventually, we found some kind of resonance between us that allowed him to go back in the room and continue the process. It was a powerful and unique experience for both of us.

We were highly engaged in an emotional conversation, a conversation that managed to keep us both from being excluded by ourselves or others from the rest of the workshop.[6] It also managed to create a special relationship between us. From this point on, we spent more and more time together outside the workshop room, and we have met after the workshop and are still in a good relationship until today.

Towards the end of the day, Israelis and Palestinians were ready to move back into single identity groups in order to reflect on the antagonism session and to be prepared to move into resonance. The Israeli group had a general feeling of frustration. However, one of the Israeli participants managed to push the others to move from feelings of hurt to a more pragmatic orientation. He reflected on the price of relying on military power only, a theme that was previously expressed by the Palestinian group. He made a strong plea to find ways of engaging in a search for solutions that would release Israel from the need to keep on investing in "power over" the Palestinians, and open up possibilities for alternative types of security. This perspective encouraged the other Israeli participants to look for a way to transform the antagonistic discourse dominant so far in the workshop sessions. On the other hand, the Palestinians in their single identity group realized that now that they had their rhetorical victory, they needed to shift gear and engage in a more constructive search for solutions. Both sides were now ready to continue their journey and attempt to engage in reflexive reframing.

---

[6] I as a Palestinian Israeli facilitator, was viewed with suspicion by the Israelis in the room, and I became self-consciously troubled by this. At one point, I spoke to the Israeli participants in Hebrew. They immediately responded, tongue in cheek, by saying, "So, you're one of us." I did not know how to respond, and until this encounter with the Israeli participant outside the workshop room I had doubts about how to relate to the Israeli Jews and whether I had the capacity to continue in my role as a facilitator.

Achieving Resonance: Are We actually Ready for Non-antagonistic Conversations?

After pointing the finger of blame at each other, the Israeli and Palestinian participants were invited by the facilitators to look inward and explain to the other their innermost needs. The participants welcomed the opportunity to be more introspective. Needs were expressed and clarified, and a new level of awareness was reached by everyone in the room. It became analytically clear that antagonism was a perspective, a choice of how to frame the other, and so was resonance. Here again, facilitators could not let themselves be lulled into a false confidence that the conflict in the room was being resolved. Rather, reaching resonance provided a new opportunity to deepen the inquiry and press for a deeper understanding of the conflict dynamics – together.

At this stage, the facilitators introduced the notion of basic human needs and the participants were quick to get a core concept at the core of Kumi: deep conflict grows out of contradictory goals that are conditioned by the threat to or frustration of basic human needs. Resonance paves the way for a common search for ways to transcend the contradictory goals that were identified earlier on in the process. As participants discover the needs they share across their conflict, they begin to focus not on the *other* or even solely on their own needs, but rather on how they can move forward together and fulfill *all* their needs. On the way through this process, the participants resorted again to antagonistic discourse. But it was of a different type. It was not just a general lashing out at the other. It was more a soul searching attempt to learn from the mistakes of the past and come up with some original thoughts about how to make the future a better one for all. This was clearly shown in the breakout work-groups discussing specific issues such as Jerusalem and settlements. In the group working on settlements, for example, some of the Palestinian participants kept falling back on a position which rejected allowing any settlers to continue living in the West Bank following Israeli withdrawal. But when such views came

up, other Palestinians emphasized the learning that all basic human needs must be respected. They argued that with certain conditions, such as respecting Palestinian sovereignty and providing adequate compensation for those Palestinians whose lands were confiscated in order to build this or that settlement, whoever wishes to reside in lands considered by them to be holy should be allowed to do so. The facilitators had to keep reminding the participants about the new things they had just learned, about basic human needs and the fact that they were on the same side in their search for a reality where the conflict between them loses its destructive power.

During the following few days, the participants kept wavering between antagonistic and non-antagonistic discourse. But there was now a different spirit in the room. The movement from antagonism to resonance, and the introduction of the notion of basic human needs worked well for the participants. The antagonism expressed was deeply related to the emotional impact of violence. Since the Israelis and Palestinians are deeply affected by the violent character of the ongoing conflict, their "natural" response was to recreate it in the dialogue itself. This was natural because the conflict had become deeply, even inextricably intertwined with their identities. It was hard to perceive themselves as normal human beings without perceiving the other as an adversary.

Challenging this frame surprised the participants and disoriented them. They found it hard to believe that they could relate to the other not as an enemy but as a partner in searching for a way out of the vicious conflict cycle. The conflict was not a detached, political concept for these Israelis and Palestinians. It is who they are, and it is much easier for both to hide behind well-rehearsed positions rather than tampering with the core of their identity, shaped by the conflict. They came to encounters driven by curiosity and the need to break out of the trap of violence. But in their communication, they managed to recreate exactly the same violent patterns that they wished to break out of. Facilitators play a key role in inviting the participants to reflect upon and find ways to deal with this and other types of paradoxes that characterize their relationship.

My Way, Your Way, No Way?

Where to go next? According to plan, now was the time to deepen understanding about conflict dynamics, to engage in conflict analysis in order to pave the way for reaching transcending solutions to the contradictory goals. But some of the participants had other opinions on how to proceed. There was a revolt against the facilitators. It was a welcome sign that, in fact, should be encouraged by the facilitators. Coming from the Israelis, however, it was rejected by the Palestinians, who insisted on completing the workshop as planned. Now there was engagement in a different order of conflict, about the process itself.

One of the Israeli participants wanted to stop the normal workshop process, eschew conflict analysis and go straight to have a free conversation with the Palestinians. He was convinced that with sufficient will, and in the right atmosphere, all problems could be solved. He was worried that the process was taking too long, and that there was a risk that they would go home empty handed, without reaching any agreements. On a deeper process level, this participant was reflecting the communication split pointed out above. Within the boundaries of the workshop sessions, the major discourse was a largely antagonistic one, participants "stayed in role" and became voices of their societal/political positions. There was a need to release the group from the strictures of antagonistic discourse, to allow communication between actual and authentic individuals, as opposed to negotiation between "spokespersons" who need to adhere to prescribed positions.

The whole group then entered a conversation about how to move forward, about the trust in the process, about the trust between themselves, about their concerns about failure and success of the workshop. The facilitators decided on the spot to use the conflict in the room as an opportunity for the introduction of tools for conflict mapping and to engage the energy generated by the "here and now" conflict for the task of learning and creating progress.

In terms of the ongoing and reiterated transition from antagonism to resonance, the group at this stage coped with the challenge of creating a new balance between concurrent facets of conflict discourse – "protection" and "openness", safety in a structured process and progress in a free-floating conversation. These were not dichotomous either/or facets but complementary both/and dimensions of the conflict discourse inside the workshop. The facilitation at this stage served to assist the group in searching for a way that would allow transcendence. The facilitators invited the group to look for a solution about how to proceed that was attuned to *both* protection *and* openness: protection in terms of clear boundaries for the group's task, openness in terms of allowing participants to enter a more open mode of conversation between individuals within small groups.

In this conflict over process, a pattern emerged whereby the Israelis wanted to impose their way on the Palestinians while the Palestinians wanted the facilitators to protect them and reject the proposal of the Israelis. The facilitators, on the other hand, used this opportunity to demonstrate to the participants that they could reach a solution that was acceptable to them all, one that met their respective needs. Eventually, the facilitators and the participants found such a solution. The workshop was to proceed as planned, but mostly in small, self-selected groups. The task remained the same, namely transcending the contradictory goals – over Jerusalem, refugees, settlements, etc. – that the participants identified at the start of the workshop.

We Can Agree on Disagreements and Disagree on Solutions. Most of all We Can Acknowledge Our Mutual Needs

The outcomes of the afternoon work in small groups were exciting. In the plenary, the group at large experienced that new ground was covered. For some, it was an opportunity to engage in needs-based conversations. For the two dominant political leaders in the group, it was an opportunity to design needs-based solutions to crucial issues on the ground. For all, the major breakthrough achieved inside the breakout groups, as expressed by one Israeli participant, "was that Israelis could look at things through Palestinian eyes and Palestinians could look at things through Israeli eyes."

By the end of the day, the group and the facilitators experienced a deep sense of accomplishment. At this stage, the group proved the value and the capacity to engage in the conflict on the premise of respect for each other's needs and concerns. The group recognized that it achieved the capacity to engage in a discourse of resonance.

The last day of the workshop was about reflection and acknowledging the outcomes of the shared workshop experience. Many of the statements by the participants specifically related to the personal change and relationships that occurred. It seems that the experience of moving from antagonistic discourse to a discourse of resonance was the major experiential outcome. For example, the Israeli participant who expressed her fear to one of the facilitators on the first day said:

> "I was so scared on my first day because of him, [pointing to a Palestinian participant]. When he was talking, I saw a very tough guy, and I said to myself, why did I come here? This person does not want peace. He wants war, look at his body – when he talked to me, it was as if he said, 'go, I don't want to see you.' He looked like my enemy, like what I'm afraid of all the time. And I thought, why did he come here? In the second night, I couldn't sleep. After two days, we passed by each other and he asked me something, then we talked, and after that I understood that he has a family, a dream, lots of things that I also have. Now I am very happy we had a chance to meet."

Looking at the results, the group emphasized by the end of the workshop that a transformation had occurred: of feelings, thoughts and relationships. And for some, transformative solutions to the key conflict issues could begin to be discerned. The concepts of antagonism and resonance capture well this experience of transformation, especially if we add the concept of needs. Participants experienced transformation when they recognized that needs-based discourse is the basis of their conversation and perspective-taking of each other, what Rothman calls "the switch" (see preface).

The major factor is the group's and facilitators' insistence on discovering ways for transforming the defensive quality of antagonistic discourse in order to allow an authentic needs-based dialogue to develop within the group. Antagonistic discourse is well present when sides meet in the context of violent conflict; it is intrinsic to the conflict experience. The dialogue in the room appears to be an ongoing and never-ending search for how to introduce the opportunities for the identification and acknowledgement of needs as a basis for conflict transformation – among participants involved in the dialogue and as an element of the reality on the ground outside the workshop room.

Insights and Dilemmas

The journey from antagonism to resonance is neither linear nor tidy. It can suffer from setbacks, detours, emotional outbursts and a great deal of frustration. If successful, it can become a profound and life changing experience. If not, it has the potential to cause harm: loss of faith in the humanity of the other, reliving traumatic experiences and entrenching prejudices and destructive stereotypes, to name but a few of the problems that well-meaning but ill-equipped facilitators could encounter. And sometimes, it is a combination of both deep insight and revisiting of trauma. In short, engaging Antagonism, especially if it is not done skilfully and judiciously, can be dangerous. If unwary, facilitators may be entrapped by intractable dilemmas that can overwhelm them, as was somewhat illustrated in the first case. Facilitators can unwittingly lock participants in exactly the same emotional and analytical zone of conflict from which they were supposed to break free.

Starting from the discursive level, the first dilemma to be discussed here involves language. Participants come to the workshop from a traumatic reality of conflict. They have a need to express their feelings, perceptions and to blame the other for their misfortunes, usually without mincing words. Must the facilitator make a choice? He or she could either ask the participants to fully vent their anger and express their antagonism toward the other in the strongest possible language, or ask them to choose their words carefully and to avoid the use of abusive language. Choosing the former option, there is the danger of creating in a careless manner the experience of escalation. Choosing the latter option, there is the danger of creating superficial harmony and the risk that the participants perceive the facilitator as too soft, biased or conflict averse. As can be seen in the examples above, the facilitators attempted (with varying degrees of success) to be clear about and committed to the principles of dialogue that were developed with the participants. While a facilitator in pure form is just the one guiding the content of the participants, there is also the reality that facilitators interject methods, tools and forms of discourse they feel, based on their professional judgements, are appropriate for the group to move forward. In each of the workshops above, regardless of the overall principles of dialogue, the facilitators could have benefitted from a more explicit agreement among themselves about what is required in authentically engaging Antagonism, even if not in a formalized way.

There is a delicate balance here. We want participants to express in an authentic manner what they have in their minds and their hearts, and we should not encourage them to be violent in their speech. We may appeal to their sense of civility, remind them that the other side is also made up of human beings with feelings and sensitivities, and suggest that the choice of language will influence the capacity of the others to relate to what is raised against them. Yet we cannot press this too far at the phase where participants are surfacing their antagonism. After all, our work is based on the assumption that the capacity for empathy will gradually evolve in the transition from the stage of antagonism to the stage of resonance. This then is the answer to this dilemma: we do not engage Antagonism to "vent" the feelings of the participants, but rather because we believe doing so will open up the possibility of a new dialogue and a new way of seeing the other (see Chap. 2). Ultimately, we

cannot and should not control the participants and we must accept that due to their strong emotional involvement their language might at times be abusive. But we can, and if we are taking on antagonism we must, control the process. The key thing here is to establish clear rules of engagement applicable to all participants, and facilitators. These rules will ultimately contribute to the group's capacity to contain and process the emotional upheavals that are intrinsic to such a process.

A major problem could arise if the facilitators who are assisting single identity groups to voice their antagonism provide participants with contradictory instructions, as we have seen in Case Study B. Indeed, "a major purpose of facilitation is to ensure that everyone is on the same page, talking about generally the same things, in mostly the same way, for primarily the same reasons in the same ways" (see Chap. 3). And thus, facilitators are themselves the first ones that must reach deep agreement about their purposes and methods. It can be hazardous to the health of the participants or the process if one facilitator chooses to encourage one group of participants to mind their language while the other does the opposite. The outcome could be, as in the case described above, frustration and sense of betrayal by one side and a sense of an initially satisfying but fleeting rhetorical victory by the other side. This, however, raises a difficult question. In the case of a conflict characterized by clear power asymmetries between the conflict parties, perhaps engineering such a rhetorical victory may be a positive thing, from the perspective of the weaker party. But doing so would be tantamount to crossing the thin line that separates facilitation from manipulation. This aside, what is of paramount importance is the capacity of the facilitators to be clear on their choices, be aware of their own biases and preconceptions when working within the context of emotionally tense processes, and to be very highly coordinated in terms of the instructions they provide to the participants.

Surfacing antagonism and directing blame towards the other conflict party is familiar territory for the participants. Confusion sets in, followed by a new awareness, when the reality of the other pervades their being, perhaps for the first time. This could be a profoundly transformative experience; when disputants see the light of resonance, this is what allows the reflexive process to take root in individuals and makes possible the shift from heaping blame on the other to taking responsibility for one's own role and contribution in sustaining the conflict. The facilitator's job here is twofold and contradictory: on the one hand, to ensure free listening and authentic speaking and, on the other hand, to intervene as quickly as possible if necessary in relation to the session's goals and ground rules. For the aim of a significant learning conversation to take place it is essential that the facilitator allows space for individuals to speak to each other and engage with each other without much intervention. But if disputants become too antagonistic and create traps of emotional turmoil that only reinforce given preconceptions and mutual suspicion, the facilitator should intervene, quickly and frequently as necessary. As individuals begin sharing deep concerns and values, the facilitator must protect those moments, allowing them the time, space and the intentional, active listening they deserve. But how does the facilitator know the right balance? It is mostly intuitive and depends a great deal on the tacit knowledge of the facilitator. These moments are so tender, and so pregnant with the possibility of hope *and* failure, the facilitator must be quick to assure safety for each individual. If a disputant starts to argue or become antagonistic during the other's sincere moment of resonance, it is possible that such a moment could derail the entire process. If a disputant interrupts, even innocently, the facilitator must quietly suggest that the original speaker pause and firmly remind the others of agreed-upon rules for discourse including, for example, that when someone is telling their story, we listen for understanding instead of interrupting to make a counterpoint or even to agree. It is when a disputant is at his or her most vulnerable that they are the most authentically resonant, requiring the attention and care of all who are present, in a manner that is carefully orchestrated, or guarded, by the facilitator.

For the facilitator of a resonance session there should be – and needs to be – an intentional decision to move the disputants from antagonism to resonance. He or she should ask the participants if they are ready to try another method of dialogue, of engaging the conflict (see Chap. 3). At this point, the facilitator should have earned the process power and the trust of the group to begin that shift. Make no mistake: this is a big power move. The facilitator is asking individuals to change their frame of perception toward the conflict just after they have been at their most heightened state of anxiety, anger and duress. By this point, the facilitator should have developed "power" in the session by enforcing the shared rules of the dialogue and ensuring that the process is held true. He or she should have by now developed trust by creating safety for the disputants and stepping in to defend them when things become too intense. Another purpose of asking for permission to move on is that the facilitator can use this permission when disputants begin to slip back into antagonism, which almost universally happens. It is at that moment that the facilitator can remind them of the frustrations they felt with the antagonistic approach and of their commitment to do things differently.

It is not the task of the facilitator to make a mental checklist and ensure that individuals are "hitting all the bases." That is, the movement from blame to responsibility should not be floating in our heads, waiting to be checked off on our way from "Us vs. Them" to "We." We are aware of these transitions in a general sense, but what we should be most aware of is the disputants' sense of hearing each other and of being heard. This breakthrough, where the participants feel they are clearly being heard and understood, and are discovering shared concerns and values, is a dynamic one in which facilitators can mostly "lose themselves" and gently guide the conversation not so much with their minds but more with their gut feeling. After the fact, in analyzing what exactly happened, we can see the movement fairly clearly, as was described above in the experience of our participants. In the midst of the process the facilitator needs to rely on intuition that is informed by the experience of engaging with the intense emotional impact of conflict.

One difficulty the facilitator will encounter is the disputants' movement back into antagonism once they have made a decision to try to reflexively reframe their conversations. It happens very naturally in a conflict situation, as these individuals are not only used to a history of antagonistic behavior toward each other, but have come to define their identity in relation to each other in this way (i.e. I am I because I am not you: you *are* aggressive which is why I *act* aggressively). The facilitator will need to strike a balance between letting this occur and stepping in to remind the participants of their commitments. Too light a hand, and the disputants will slip fully back into antagonism and lose their trust in the facilitator and the process. Too heavy a hand and the disputants will never realize how quickly and easily they can revert to adversarial frames and again will lose trust in the facilitator and process. Whatever he or she does, the facilitator needs to provide the mirror in which the participants can reflect on their behavior and, through it, can learn to catch themselves whenever they unwittingly revert to destructive discourse.

If, however, they continue reverting to antagonism, it is likely there are some issues that have not been surfaced fully and they may actually need to step back in the process in order to surface and engage them. There is the possibility of course that disputants may simply not be able to engage in resonance dialogue. They may be interested only in proving their positions and not changing and therefore not be fully committed to changing the conflict dynamic. Or it may be the case that the perception of oppression by one side is so great and is backed up by objective oppressive practices by the other identity group that resonance may not be possible or even advisable. Or they may be so stuck on one particular antagonistic issue that they are unable to see beyond it to other areas of concern and possibility. In such cases, it is up to the facilitator to determine whether this group is ready for this process, or if this process is appropriate to this situation. It is

partly an intuitive and subjective judgment on the part of the facilitator that must be made in order to protect all parties.[7] In this case, it might be a simple solution to ask permission to set the antagonistic issue aside and focus on the other less controversial topics, such as goals for the workshop. If the participants are unable to do so, again, the facilitator may need to decide whether the process is useful and possible at that point, and should not hesitate to conclude it, after doing the necessary check out exercises.

Here it must be remembered that when we deal in the specific context of violence, the movement from antagonism to resonance is not a one-time event. It is a process that is reiterative and progressive, but never final. It can be prepared for and tested, but it is fragile, as are human emotions. Nonetheless, the move from Antagonism to Resonance can be somewhat "captured" by making progress in the full ARIA process that includes the concrete and cooperative work of Invention and Action (or in the KUMI language, Participatory Strategic Planning). By making concrete decisions about their future together – decisions made possible by their newfound perspective on themselves and the other – participants make "real" their experiences. But this does not mean that by fulfilling it, feelings of antagonisms are no longer there. They are likely to always be there and they relate to the experiences of threats and grievances that continue to exist outside the workshop room within the ongoing conflict reality, and its violent past and inevitably aggressive future. The duration of a single workshop is part of a much longer process that needs to take place. Reducing active grievances and ameliorating suspicions is a long-term, complex intervention (in fact, in many cases, it can only be incremental and partial at best). In terms of facilitation and workshop design, we must keep in mind that there will be elements of blaming that would linger on even after the successful conclusion of the

---

[7] On the other hand, Rothman makes the case in Chap. 1 that a contingency approach to determining which type of intervention is best in which type of conflict can be analytically determined.

workshop. We need the structured model to guide antagonism forward and capture resonance as we can, but we need to keep in mind that reverting to blame will occur and we need to create space for it. Similarly, resonance is sometimes only fleeting and it needs to be captured through concrete practical or symbolic action.

No matter what the "end" structure of the workshop or engagement looks like, we need to create ways to reaffirm with the participants that what we are doing is not engaging antagonism to get rid of it so we can move forward. What we need to reaffirm is that we are illuminating and demonstrating our normal ways of dealing with issues that raise antagonism so that we can learn how, now and in the future, to deal with the issues in more constructive ways. It is part of a continuous process of creating the needed trust on an interpersonal and intergroup level so that all can participate in the challenges of exploring in a constructive manner the conflict issues and possible ways of resolving them as well as challenges related to the task of creating solutions that fully relate to the needs of the sides involved. In order to create the possibility of transforming conflict issues we need to create the possibility for a transformation of conflict relationships between those involved in the conflict dialogue. Especially in the context of prolonged violent conflict, it is only over an extended time frame with repeated exposure to each other, in carefully choreographed encounters, that we can hope to reduce the virulence and prevalence of antagonism and move from a largely destructive dynamic into a creative partnership.

In Case Study A we tried to use shortcuts. We tried to create a shortened version of antagonism to resonance because of the logistics of the workshop. There was not sufficient time to do the whole process. This is common in this work. We might find ourselves with too little time to go through the whole process. What do we do? If we take into account that antagonism needs to be addressed in order to move into resonance and create the necessary preconditions for constructive work on the more analytical level, then we need to keep in mind that we must be generous with time. If there is a lot of antagonism and little

time to confront and process it, this means that we may need to redefine the objectives of the workshop and to reduce our expectations. Perhaps then we begin looking more broadly at objectives not for a single workshop but for a series of workshops. In this way, we may initially ask participants to define what it is they hope to accomplish together before moving to actual work on the concrete conflict issues and related emotional dimensions. This might also mean that in the case of complex conflict situations, as is the case of prolonged violence, it might be necessary to work in an open-ended time frame and in a participatory manner to develop the work process without defining in advance how many meetings the process as a whole will take.

The guiding principle shifts from defining time frames to defining goals and objectives that evolve in the course of the dialogue process. The key problem here is the availability of the participants, and their capacity to commit to a continuous and open-ended process. Ideally, the facilitators could invite participants to let the structure of the engagement evolve in the course of the process that develops. But this creates great challenges due to the various other commitments of the participants; and not less important, there usually will be funding constraints since sponsors and donors might resist the idea of contributing to processes that by definition are non-linear and open-ended in terms of goals and outcomes.

This means we will almost always be limited in terms of time in relation to the immediate process ahead. It is fine sometimes to go slow, to do less. And if time is just too limited, then perhaps the whole intervention should be postponed or even cancelled. The mistake is in trying to achieve too much in terms of content; we should not try to push the group to create outcomes that are not proportional to the emotional work that needs to be done before. The issue here is the balance of emotional work that needs to be done and the analytic work that leads to concrete outcomes, such as conflict analysis, reaching transcendent solutions or designing action planning. If we push too much, the quality of the outcome will be low or the group will not be able to follow through and commit to what has been achieved. Or the group may rebel and decide not to continue because of their sense of distrust among each other and the process as such. Or the group may act as if all is good when this is not really so. There are no shortcuts.

There are also no easy solutions for the gap that inevitably exists between what takes place inside the workshop room, on the one hand, and the reality of conflict outside, on the other hand. In intractable social conflict, there are structures of oppression and real-life politics outside the room. We should be careful not to create a sense of false symmetry inside the workshop room. But that leads to a most profound dilemma. A sense of false symmetry is ultimately created if the intervention has been successful – resonance is reached inside the workshop room, participants develop what Rothman calls "analytic empathy" (1997, pp. 44–47), and learn to see each other as equally worthy human beings sharing similar values, concerns, hopes and dreams – and then they go back to their communities separated by the conflict line, and the harshness of reality – with its injustices and violent practices – hits them in the face. The sense of frustration may cause a relapse and a loss of belief in the efficacy and possibility of working together to make peace. At the end of each workshop, participants face this challenge of re-entry, which creates the challenge of containing a kind of dual reality (see Chap. 10 for more on this dilemma of re-entry and some possible solutions).

On the one hand participants transform patterns of animosity and experience the value and benefit of partnership based on trust and cooperation in searching for new ways in how to deal with the shared conflict experience. On the other hand the harsh conflict reality continues to challenge participants on an emotional and practical level. Part of such a process is coping with the challenge of how to sustain hope among participants that their shared process will prove of value in terms of creating impact on the conflict reality outside the workshop and create the capacity to contain these contradicting realities.

The assumption is that the emotional and analytical work that allows participants to reach resonance and cope with their recurrent antagonistic feelings creates trust, which becomes the basis for cooperation towards transforming the environment through effective collective action across the conflict lines. But what if the environment is not yet ripe for the breakthroughs in understanding that might develop between participants and the kind of behavior that we expect them to adopt as a result? This is particularly relevant when working on the grass-roots level, where the participants are not in positions of influence capable of shaping policy. There is no clear answer to this dilemma. There needs to be a balance between the depth of emotional work and the trust building that occurs and the analytical, strategic and organizational levels of work. The participants need to come up with solutions that are based on a robust understanding of the conflict issues, which is only possible once they have cleared a path through the antagonistic foliage that envelops their being. But, having done that, they then need to find relevant strategies for how to work on creating a different reality outside the workshop room, and develop sound organizational structures to enable them to do so. To the best of our knowledge, no one has yet managed to meet this challenge in Israel and Palestine in any convincing manner.

Concluding Remarks

Each of the chapter authors and workshop facilitators who worked on this project have experienced the depth, and the difficulty, of engaging Antagonism as an integral part of our work in conflict transformation. Our experiences detailed in the workshops above show both the promise of this kind of deep work, as well as the difficulty facilitators and participants experience in truly and effectively engaging their Antagonism.

Our hope is that this chapter will be seen as a reflexive, learning document. We do not assume that we have unearthed all the dilemmas and insights, or that we have provided case studies that so illuminate the Antagonism to Resonance process that you may walk away with the complete knowledge needed to unerringly facilitate the process. What we do assume is that these case studies and our reflections on them will add to a growing volume of work suggesting that there is much value in addressing these elements during a conflict engagement process.

We encourage you then to take what we are learning and test it. Help us more deeply reflect upon these and other case studies. Adopt or adapt our methods and send us the reports. Ask the questions we are asking and test the assumptions underneath our approach to engaging these issues. We want our work to be a part of the larger community of practice, to both share with and learn from that community.

Engaging identity conflicts, as seen above, takes skilled facilitation, an artistic and intuitive approach to working with participants, and a wealth of theoretical and practical knowledge. It is exactly the complexity of the issues addressed that requires this broad mix of skills, abilities, and approaches. Additionally, it is the complexity of identity that almost ensures that no two engagements will be the same. These traits of identity-based conflict can seem daunting to the mediator.

However, the promise of this work is that in mining the deepest dimensions of our experiences *with each other*, we might more authentically move toward peace *together.* When conflicts rage in violent spikes, or sustain interminably over time, we can be assured that there are some basic human needs at stake and that the participants are experiencing the conflict at a very deep level fundamental to their identity. Only by asking participants to explore this reality deeply and authentically can we effectively provide the type of process that can encourage and enable them to become partners in lasting peace and cooperation.

References

Bergdall, T. D. (1993). *Methods for active participation.* Nairobi: Oxford University Press.

Burton, J. (1990a). *Conflict: Resolution and prevention.* New York: St Martin's Press.

Burton, J. W. (Ed.). (1990b). *Conflict: Human needs theory.* London: Macmillan. New York: St. Martin's Press.

Galtung, J. (1969). Violence, peace and peace research. *Journal of Peace Research, VI*(3), 167–191.

Galtung, J. (1975). *Scarcity, conflict and identity* (Human identity in nature science and society, pp. 69–79). Bossey: Ecumenical Institute.

Galtung, J. (1976). *Peace, war and defense.* Copenhagen: Christian Ejlers.

Galtung, J. (1996). *Peace by peaceful means: Peace, conflict, development and civilization.* London, UK: Sage.

Galtung, J. (2004). *Transcend and transform.* London: Pluto Press.

Graf, W., Kramer, G., Nicolescou, A. (2008). The art of conflict transformation through dialogue. http://www.iicp.at/communications/publications/papers/WP0804_ConflictTransformationDialogue.pdf

Graf, W., Kramer, G., Nicolescou, A. (2010). Complexity thinking as a meta-framework for conflict transformation, in Search of a paradigm and a methodology for a transformative culture of peace. In: W. Wintersteiner, V. Ratkovic, (Eds.). *Culture of peace* (pp. 58–81). Klagenfurt: Drava.

Kelman, H. C. (1965). Social-psychological approaches to the study of international relations: Definition of scope. In H. C. Kelman (Ed.), *International behavior* (pp. 3–39). New York: Holt, Rinehart and Winston.

Kelman, H. C. (1987). The political psychology of the Israeli-Palestinian conflict: How can we overcome the barriers to a negotiated solution? *Political Psychology, 8*(3), 347–363.

Kelman, H. C. (1997). Negotiating national identity and self-determination in ethnic conflicts: The choice between pluralism and ethnic cleansing. *Negotiation Journal, 13*(4), 327–340.

Rothman, J. (1992). *From confrontation to cooperation: Resolving ethnic and regional conflict.* Newbury Park: Sage.

Rothman, J. (1997). *Resolving identity based conflict in nations, organizations and communities.* San Francisco: Jossey Bass.

Rothman, J. (2012). The insides of identity and intragroup conflict. In I.W. Zartman, et. al. (eds.) *The slippery slope: Negotiating identity to Genocide: Reducing identity conflicts and preventing mass murder.* New York: Oxford University Press.

Stanfield, B. (Ed.). (2002). *The workshop book.* Canada: ICA.

Building Local Capacity in Eastern Europe

Mariska Kappmeier, Alexander Redlich, and Evgeniya (Gina) Knyazev

Introduction

In June of 1992, Moldova was facing a period of turbulence. During the downfall of the Soviet Union, Moldova embraced independence and positioned itself as a Romanian-speaking state, despite the country's many Russian and Ukraine speakers. This triggered the downfall of the stable relationship between the right bank (Moldova) of the Dniester River and the left bank (Transdniestria[1]), which felt close loyalty with Russia and its Russian identity. Transdniestria declared itself independent, unrecognized by the international community and Moldova. This declaration led to accumulating tensions, which climaxed in a civil war. At the Dniester River, neighbors were shooting each other, resulting in 2,000 deaths. The Russian 14th Army, which was and continues to be based in Transdniestria, intervened. As of July 21st, 1992, there has been a formal peace agreement in place between Russia and Moldova. However, the regional situation more closely resembles a cease fire since all attempts to reconcile the right and left bank have failed. Transdniestria[2] is now a de facto state, with its own government and currency but without international recognition (Fig. 6.1).

Moldova's and Transdniestria's civil sectors reveal this lack of political peace. The absence of concrete agreements and contracts between the two banks is tainting the relationship between these two societies. The relationship is further worsened by political power plays from the two sides. Through case studies of conflicts between citizens of this region, we will illustrate what is at stake for those involved in this conflict as well as what themes of conflict exist. We will then show how the ARIA approach can be used to strengthen the civil societies and equip them with the necessary skills to engage in large-group conflict resolution even when political will is lacking.

[1] In Russian, Transdniestria is called Pridnestrovie. In its English translation numerous spellings forms exist. For ease of reading it is often spelled as Transnistria. In our article we use the form Transdniestria, as an appropriate hybrid between the Romanian and Russian spelling of the Latin form. It is also the term being used in numerous international publications. This term is chosen without any political reason. For an extended explanation of the problems in translating the word Pridnestrovie from Russian to English, see Stefan Troebst (2003).

M. Kappmeier • A. Redlich • E.G. Knyazev
e-mail: mariska_kappmeier@yahoo.de;
redlich@uni-hamburg.de

Background: The Moldova-Transdniestria Conflict

Ion is 12 years old and lives in the border region between Moldova and Transdniestria. For Ion, today is a normal day: after school he spends the

[2] The explicit mention of Transdniestria is done for reasons of clarification and without any political intent for recognition or unification of the two banks.

J. Rothman (ed.), *From Identity-Based Conflict to Identity-Based Cooperation: The ARIA Approach in Theory and Practice*, Peace Psychology Book Series, DOI 10.1007/978-1-4614-3679-9_6,
© Springer Science+Business Media New York 2012

Fig. 6.1 A map of the Moldova-Transdniestrian region

afternoon helping his parents fetch water, and he completes chores for his household and his village. But tomorrow is a special day: tomorrow half the village is going over to the Transdniestrian side where the village still has a field of apple trees. This field is separated from the village by the unofficial border of Transdniestria. Tomorrow the villagers will harvest the ripe apples from their fields, which they have not done for three years, ever since the last official agreement between the local authorities on the Moldovan and Transdniestrian sides came to an end. For three years there have been no official contracts regulating how the villagers can access their fields. All attempts to re-negotiate the terms had failed, until a team of trained conflict specialists, consisting of Moldovans and Transdniestrians, approached the parties on both sides. Through pre-talks and reassurance, these conflict specialists were able to initiate unofficial dialogue-workshops in which local authorities and villages from Moldova and Transdniestria came together. The objective of these workshops was to empower all of the parties to effectively communicate with each other in order to lessen the tensions – created by an over-arching and unresolved political conflict – that had arisen over the past years. In the workshops, fears and hopes were explored and parties were empowered to invent ways to constructively address the local conflict outside of the greater political framework. The ongoing conflict work ended in

a creative solution that enabled the villagers jointly to harvest their fields.[3]

What preparation took place for these dialogue-workshops? What took place that set the stage for the workshops and enabled the local conflict specialists to carry them out?

We will answer these questions in steps, explaining how such a network of conflict specialists can be built and trained for dealing with long-term conflict engagement in such an intangible conflict as the Moldovan-Transdniestrian conflict.

Before we go into detail about the practical aspects of the establishment and training of the conflict specialists, we will focus on the bigger picture and explain our aspirations for our engagement in Moldova-Transdniestria, which the training and the aforementioned conflict work is a part of.

What? Aspiration: Capacity-Building for Conflict Engagement in Regions with Political Tension

In the past, there have been societies that have maintained peace for more than a hundred years, both within that society as well as with their neighbors (Fry et al. 2007). In scientific and political realms, in communities and societies, the vision of a peaceful world without wars appears to be increasingly achievable, which encourages us to strive toward this vision. An expression of this movement is the United Nation's resolution to create a culture of peace, which was adopted in 1999 (De Rivera 2007; UNESCO 2002). This declaration creates awareness that the vision of peaceful coexistence can become a reality for all nations.

It is our goal to develop cultures that undertake peaceful conflict engagement in the political arena, in places where political tensions and open hostilities exist between large-groups (Redlich 2011). In our approach, we support and foster the establishment of a network of competent conflict specialists who are able to facilitate meetings between parties involved in a conflict, if those parties are open to dialoguing.

---

[3]This is a fictional case and included for illustration purpose.

This approach is applicable to communal and organizational conflicts that are triggered or influenced by political tension. These interventions will address the communal and organizational conflicts while helping to establish a culture of peaceful conflict engagement between antagonistic groups and populations.

In more specific terms, this involves fostering the social competence to understand the perspective of the other side – without having to adopt it. This ideal can be summarized as "to understand doesn't mean to agree." For the adversaries this means that they shall understand the perspective of the other party without the pressure to agree with that perspective. To understand the members of another group is already quite difficult if they merely think and act differently, such as members of a different religion, culture, nation, or social class. But developing this understanding when the others are adversaries in a political, economic, communal, organizational or international conflict is an extremely demanding task. The quick stereotyping and simplification of "Us-versus-Them" must be abandoned in favor of the more complex and deliberate perception of "Us-and-Them" (Tajfel and Turner 1986).

The development of local groups with the capacity to engage in conflict (such as private, public, political, organizational or community-based) is part of constructive civil development. Our understanding of building local capacity is informed by the United Nations' definition of capacity-building:

> Specifically, capacity-building encompasses the country's human, scientific, technological, organizational, institutional, and resource capabilities. A fundamental goal of capacity-building is to enhance the ability to evaluate and address the crucial questions related to policy choices and modes of implementation among development options, based on an understanding of environment potentials and limits and of needs perceived by the people of the country concerned (United Nations 1992).

Our approach to local capacity-building exceeds the definition of the United Nations' since we focus on the self-efficacy and self-determination of the population. Therefore, capacity-building in the area of conflict resolution starts at the individual level. Its foundation is to convey competency in individual conflict situations to as many individuals as possible, so they can use it to engage daily conflicts, so that they can be solved without third party intervention. To engage in deeper protracted conflicts, professional conflict specialists should be trained to engage conflicts as a third party. The conflict specialists should at least initially, in building a local culture of creative conflict engagement, be ethnically representative of the range of stakeholder groups in the society. This gives them a deeper understanding of the conflict dynamics and helps them gain the confidence of the local population. Having members of the conflicted parties working side by side also functions as an example of constructive conflict engagement. As we will report later on, specific dynamics of the overarching conflict between Moldova and Transdniestria also manifested in our ARIA-training group and had to be worked through by the participants and trainers. Furthermore, having 'mixed' teams nurtures border-crossing trainings and aids in establishing links to other institutions for conflict resolution on both sides of the conflict, such as courts, trade unions, political parties etc.

This task is difficult and can also endanger the facilitators and participating representatives. Volkan (2011, p. 30) reports a case in which a representative was killed after participating in a dialogue workshop with representatives of the other conflict party. It is hypothesized that he was most likely killed by members of his own large-group, because of his participation in a peace dialogue workshop. Because of such risks, dialogue workshops and networks should be placed under the protection of universities. Universities, being obliged to research and education, hold a special degree of political independence within the framework of political power relations. This kind of university protection was initially utilized in 1970 by Herbert Kelman at Harvard University for dialogue groups between Israelis and Palestinians that took place at a time when members of both sides were legally prohibited by their own groups to have contact with each other (Kappmeier 2008). We strive to follow Dr. Kelman's example.

Why? Resonance Between Humans: The Story Behind Our Engagement

There are three tracks for possible peace intervention in the area of political conflict engagement (see Fig. 6.2):

- Track I: Official diplomatic contact between the politicians representing the involved parties in the conflict, e.g. the peace negotiation of 1979 in Camp David between Egypt and Israel under the moderation of US president Jimmy Carter. These talks led to concrete and binding contracts between the main groups under international law.
- Track II: A workshop is hosted between influential members of the conflict groups, such as members of the economic or union sector, journalists, religious authorities, retired military and politicians, business elite, or academics. These members from all of the involved conflict parties come together to analyze and reframe the conflict. They should develop alternative ways for a possible conflict engagement in an open and creative atmosphere without the pressure to reach binding agreements or to protect any political role, given that they are outside the arena of elected officials. The involved members can also use their influential position within their own society to impact the political decisions regarding the conflict.
- Track III: This track focuses on civil contact between leaders and activists at the grassroots level of the antagonistic groups. This includes leadership and participation in exchange programs, ecumenical meetings or mutual sporting events.

Whenever the political arena is frozen and the government elites are antagonistic towards each other, there exists a very real threat that the populations will be alienated and become hostile towards each other. History contains many examples of this, from the early Egyptian-Assyrian battles over the European religious wars to the national, long-lasting enmities between nations. The recent clashes between the so-called Western and Arabic worlds are also an excellent example of this. For conflict engagement these conflicts cannot only be addressed on the political level (Track I). Dialogue Workshops should also be located on Track II and III.

As a further differentiation, Nan (2005) introduced the concept of a "Track 2.5," which describes dialogue workshops engaging communal and organizational conflict in regions with tension. It is in-between tracks two and three, because not only do members at the grassroots level participate, but so do the 'classical' participants of Track II, such as influential, but informal, representatives from the political and economic sector.

Our work takes place at the 2.5 level, and for this track we use the ARIA approach as a tool of conflict engagement to moderate dialogue workshops. We prefer the term moderation instead of facilitation because the Latin root of facilitation means "make something easy" while moderation means "temper the process" (Redlich 2009). Moderation stresses that the professional moderator is responsible for the process, especially for the modulation of group dynamics like risk shift (Rothwell 1986), polarization (Moscovici and Zavalloni 1969), and group think (Janis 1972). The participants are responsible for the content. In this terminology, conflict moderation means

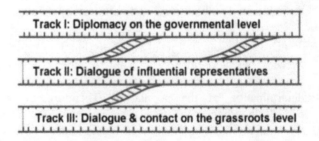

Fig. 6.2 Tracks of official and unofficial diplomacy

facilitating the group work and also mediating upcoming conflicts between the participants.

Dialogue workshops take place in small group settings, where individuals encounter members of the other group. Each person brings his or her own personal needs, feelings, and habits to the table. The task of the moderator is to see that the conflict at hand will not only be negotiated on a political level but also that the psychological and human aspects of the conflict will be surfaced and addressed. In such interventions we find that the third party teams should consist of individuals with knowledge and skill-sets drawn from different sources, especially from political science and psychology.

The training of local moderators in conflict moderation helps preserve and extend the potential of peaceful conflict engagement within the population. The training fosters a greater capacity for handling political tension in large group conflicts. It is accompanied by the hope that the conflict moderators will also set an example and will become multipliers for promoting a culture of peaceful conflict engagement in their society. Results from relevant research have demonstrated that in a stalemate conflict, like the situation in the Moldovan region where the governmental elites do not engage in peace interventions, conflict engagement can be initiated and broadened through the strengthening of the civil population (Kotchikian 2006, 2008). This can be done through such trainings and interventions. Through moderated dialogues on the civil society level, bridges can be built between the conflicted parties. Ideally the population will be encouraged to participate actively in their region on communal, regional, and national projects, and through this engagement they can also reshape the political process.

How? Peace Intervention Through ARIA

Back to the area of tension in Moldova-Transdniestria. Through in-depth interviews, Kappmeier (2012) examined a representative sample of influential and invested members of both Moldova and Transdniestria, ranging from scholars, lawyers, journalists, businessmen and politicians. The results show that the interviewees see the political elite as the cause of the conflict, and not the relations between the populations. A number of respondents felt that the problem in Moldova-Transdniestria should not be defined as an identity-based conflict, because the conflict is not rooted in each group's sense of threat or frustration to their collective identity. For example, some participants expressed the opinion that "This is not an ethnic conflict" or "We are the same [kind of people]." However, the interviews also revealed that the long duration of the conflict is taking its toll and the relationship between the two populations on the Dniester is deteriorating. Even if the situation began as mostly as a political conflict, linguistic and historical aspects have evolved so the conflict now shares many properties of identity-based conflicts (see Rothman in Chap. 1). This is especially prominent in the region of the (officially unrecognized) border where a considerable number of unresolved long-lasting conflicts exist.

What can be done on a civil-societal level to reduce these communal and regional tensions? The majority of the conflict-addressing work on all three tracks is done in "small groups work." In the mid-twentieth century, two approaches were developed for practical work within small groups. One approach that is used by Kelman is called the Interactive Problem-Solving Workshop (Kelman 1986, 2004). In this approach, which is based on work done by Burton (1969), social science knowledge is applied to support the development of constructive and shared political goals between adversaries. This is combined with individual and group processes to solve political conflicts on the Track II level, with the goal of positively impacting Track I policymaking to reach the goal of peace (for case studies see Fisher 2005).

In the other approach, western educational institutions, commercial enterprises, and civil-societal organizations have developed methods for practicing participatory moderation in small groups for consensus-building, project-planning, and cooperation (Klebert et al. 2002; Kaner et al. 2007; Institute of Cultural Affairs 2008).

Both of these approaches prove to be compatible with each other, and are often combined in practice. Currently, there are several working theories about the moderation of privately organized political dialogue groups, which can be used to deal with communal tension in the Dniester region. Which approaches are especially useful for moderating small groups, with the objective of finding a systematic and long-lasting solution in communities and regions affected by political conflict such as Moldova-Transdniestria? The concepts should incorporate the well-recognized criteria of mediation: participation, empowerment, reframing, impartiality, comprehensibility, structure, transparency, cultural sensitivity, adaptability to different (sub)cultures, and no preferred outcome. This excludes approaches in which the third party influences the outcome through political, military or economic power, or through arbitration (e.g. Watson and Rosegrant 2001). However there are plenty of concepts in the realm of political mediation that fulfill the required criteria (Galtung 2004; Kelman 2004; Lederach 2003; Rosenberg 2003; Rothman 1997; Sounders 2005; Susskind, McKearnan & Thomas-Larmer 1999; Volkan 2006).

While in Moldova and Transdniestria numerous attempts were undertaken in the mid-90s to foster Track II dialogue groups (e.g. Hall 1999), these attempts are less frequent in the region nowadays and are largely unknown outside of the classic circles of peace activism. Additionally, in Moldova and Transdniestria there is a lack of experienced *local* moderators who could apply the conflict engagement skills to the region's struggles (Kappmeier 2012). Therefore, it is necessary to build a network of local conflict moderators who can maintain conflict moderation workshops for small groups of representatives from the antagonistic parties, so that they can engage in open dialogue with each other. The establishment of such a network is called capacity-building. Members of the network who are particularly capable and highly experienced could also provide their services for Track II workshops with influential members of both sides. They can also engage in Track III conflict moderation, for communities which experience local conflict triggered by an overarching political conflict.

From our perspective, the ARIA approach developed by Rothman (1997) is especially well-suited for this purpose. We will explore why below.

Why ARIA?

The ARIA approach addresses both the political and psychological aspects of conflict. It surfaces the dynamics of how the conflict affects the intrapersonal relationships of those involved in the conflict, and regulates them in the background of the political conflict. It brings the conflicted parties together so that they can mutually plan concrete actions to address the conflict. ARIA provides a clear structure and hosts a broad repertoire of different methods to support the process (e.g. Passion Word, Story Telling, Solo, Small Group Exercises, etc. See also Chaps. 1 and 3).

For the dissemination of ARIA, Rothman developed a training program that combines a theoretical foundation with practical demonstration, self-reflection, and concrete experiences. It also considers the cultural specifics in which the training and moderation take place. The main characteristics of ARIA include the broad spectrum of values it addresses, its explicit emotion management techniques, and its inclusion of Action Research, which makes it useful as a link between theory and practice. ARIA has been successful in highly complex settings (e.g. the ARIA group 2002) and also incorporates its own evaluation system. It has been used in many contexts from interpersonal, to organizational, to communal and international conflicts.

Broad Spectrum of Value Orientation

ARIA aims to solve concrete resource and goal conflicts while transforming dysfunctional and overwhelmed relationship systems into ones that can engage conflict constructively. Thus it focuses not only on the problem-solving facet of conflict management and resolution, but also on relationship transformation (i.e. conflict transformation).

This dual approach sets ARIA apart from other mediation concepts which often choose exclusively one focus. Often, mediation concepts position themselves as either problem-solving oriented or transformative and have a strong bias toward the chosen orientation.

For example, the "getting to yes" approach spends a tremendous amount of time on negotiating concrete conflict solutions through fostering joint interests and mutual gains (Fisher et al. 1991). That also holds true for the socio-psychological conflict research (e.g. Rubin et al. 1994) which focuses on applicability, the impact of creativity-enhancing strategies, and integrative solutions. These should invite parties to think outside the box and find new ways of how resources could be divided or interests could be handled in order to settle the conflict. Such strategies include the expansion of resources, which can be negotiated, and compensation for concession or logrolling, when one party makes concessions on issues that are not as important for them. These approaches are called problem-solving approaches (Bush and Folger 1994). They can be helpful in tangible conflicts, but tend to neglect the relationship systems between the parties, which are often troubled in intangible conflicts. In these approaches, the formation and transformation of normative acceptable relationships within the conflict system and the authenticity of the intrapersonal experiences are secondary.

In contrast, the transformative approaches focus on the issue of how to transform intrapersonal experiences and how to transform and improve the interpersonal communication within the conflict system (e.g. Bush and Folger 1994; Thomann 2003). ARIA combines the transformative approach (roughly expressed by the words antagonism and resonance) with the problem-solving method (represented by the words invention and action planning). Depending on the nature of each specific conflict, ARIA devotes more time to the former or the latter. Overall, ARIA avoids the bias of being either too transformative or too problem-solving oriented. Instead, it explores each conflict in a participatory manner, gauging where the main need for involvement lies. It does not impose its own orientation on the conflict; rather it looks at the specific needs of the conflict and adapting to them.

Antagonism: Resonance

Another aspect in which ARIA differentiates itself from other approaches is its ability to combine the internal experiences of the conflicted parties with the regulation of their social relationship. ARIA guides parties in a dialogue about personal experiences, which holds importance for the parties and is relevant to the conflict. The parties describe, in a safe setting, their personal experiences and illuminate their needs, fears, disappointments, hopes, motives, and values, which are threatened by the conflict or underlie specific actions in the conflict. This dialogue leads to clarification for the parties that translates into a deeper understanding of the conflict dynamics through the individual narratives the parties share about their experiences, hopes and hurts. They also gain understanding of their own experiences and stereotypes that were developed through the conflict dynamics. This important step allows the conflicted parties to transform their relationship. According to ARIA, the exchange over the intrapersonal experiences also creates mutual resonance in which the parties are able to resonate with the stories shared with each other. In addition to the resonance, the parties develop an understanding of the differences between each other.

It is the aim of ARIA to provide a deeper understanding of what holds the parties in conflict as well as where the sides are coming from. However, as mentioned above, a deeper understanding does not equal agreeing with the other side's perceptions.

This deeper understanding will not be developed solely in harmonic settings. The aforementioned exchange between the internal experiences and the regulation of social relationships is also applicable to separations and dissonant processes that are called Antagonism within the ARIA framework. ARIA gives the dissonant part of the conflict (Antagonism) as much room and importance as the harmony orientated part (Resonance), and the applied problem solving part (Invention/Action). To our knowledge, ARIA is one of few published concepts of conflict work that has included in a systematic manner the antagonistic side of conflict and its emotional aspects, while theoretically justifying this step. Rothman puts it with the term Antagonism (Greek "anti agein:" to act against someone or something) as the first step of ARIA. It deals with the opposing aspects of the conflict that are often a main presence in the daily lives of humans in conflict settings. This part of the conflict is marked by emotional communication, such as hectic, loud voices, anger, expressions of dislike, mutual polarization, generalization and degrading attributions. It is perceived by most people as unpleasant and is mainly avoided in their daily lives (although it is commonly expressed in conflictual exchanges). Antagonistic communication consists of blaming, attributing, us versus them polarization, and projection. These means of antagonism are transformed by the ARIA process into the communication of resonance: respective responsibility instead of blaming, analytic empathy instead of attributing, "we" instead of "us versus them," and taking responsibility instead of projecting (Rothman 1997, Chap. 6). Many approaches of conflict mediation and negotiation try to handle the aspects of confrontation as quickly as possible in order to avoid escalation. They do this by swiftly moving on to the communication patterns of mutual understanding. This also holds true for conflict research and scientifically grounded conflict resolution. Many methods and researchers in fact, tend to avoid or downplay the parties' differences and emotional reactions in an effort to pursue and promote common ground. ARIA suggests that in a deep conflict, this avoidance will be counterproductive and may actually foster the antagonism that is so strongly avoided.

The ROI-ARIA contingency model (see Chap. 1) assumes that in identity-based conflicts, blaming, attribution of negative characteristics, and moments that escalate conflict, such as anger and antipathy between the conflict parties, exist and have to be surfaced in order to achievement a deep understanding in the resonance stage. These unpleasant and polarizing aspects of the conflict arise because parties threaten and attack each other's identities. By smoothing over or ignoring this real conflict and the fear that it engenders, an authentic and deep understanding will not occur. But by carefully surfacing the antagonism and by turning it around from blaming the other side to exploring it, steps are taken towards building resonance.

An important step which Rothman takes is carefully preparing the parties in identity-based conflicts for the entire process before they agree to participate in it. He asks them to agree upfront, that if they engage in an ARIA process that requires Antagonism, the parties have to stay until the end of the Resonance phase. In the above-mentioned points, ARIA corresponds with the Hamburg approach of Communication Psychology and is therefore suitable for cooperation in the Moldova project (Schulz von Thun 1981).

The Hamburger approach also values and incorporates the clarification of emotions (Thomann 2004). Both approaches work with methods focusing on the individual first, the Solo and Duet in ARIA, the Hamburger approach using the metaphor of the Inner Team (Redlich 2009, p. 114). It focuses on process that moves from the identification of opposite perceptions to a deeper inter-individual understanding (Schulz von Thun 1998).

Action Research

ARIA is scientifically grounded and also praxis oriented (Ross and Rothman 1999; Rothman and Redlich 2007). In his action evaluation approach, Rothman gathers the goals and objectives of the conflicted parties in a qualitative manner. This allows third parties and organizations to identify in advance possible conflicts between the goals of the ARIA intervention's outcome. These conflicts can be used for a participatory and mutual conflict analysis, a procedure that also provides research data. One of the criteria of action research is that the participants are systematically involved in the assessment and evaluation, and therefore can influence the research, the interpretation of the results, and how they are applied.

Tried and Tested in Many Fields

ARIA has proven successful in (inter-)national realms as well as communal and organizational conflicts (Rothman 1997). It is also well-suited for participatory work with large groups (The ARIA Group 2002). ARIA can be employed for the engagement of identity conflicts at many levels, from interpersonal to political. It can engage a wide spectrum of conflicts, ranging from conflict coaching with individuals ("Solo"), to counseling a two-person conflict ("Duet"), to facilitating intra- and intergroup conflict ("Conducting"). It can also be used to help groups reach common goals and visions for their future. ARIA tools, attitudes, and principles are fundamental for training and capacity-building as well as for conflict work. These are important foundations on which we are going to build the base of our conflict engagement in Moldova-Transdniestria. Therefore, ARIA is a good tool for capacity-building, that is, for developing a sustainable network of local conflict moderators.

Conflict Moderation Capacity-Building in Moldova: Transdniestria

We previously mentioned that in the long run we want to establish a network of local conflict specialists who can moderate local conflicts (see section "What? Aspiration: Capacity-Building for Conflict Engagement in Regions with Political Tension"). To reach this objective we are following the steps illustrated in Fig. 6.3, below. We have begun with an extensive conflict analysis to assess what interventions are needed and wanted by the civil society in Moldova and Transdniestria (Kappmeier 2012). So far we have achieved the second step, the initial training of local conflict moderators. The scenario at the beginning of the chapter takes place during step Three, when actual conflict moderation takes place. For the rest of the chapter, we are focusing on the training, which occurs in step Two:

For the current project, local practitioners on the right and left bank of the Dniester are trained

in the ARIA-Concept and conflict moderation skills. Trainings that provide competency in conflict moderation in regions of political tension differ in one aspect from trainings in regions without tension. In regions with political tension, the training group should consist of members from the two (or more) large groups involved in the political conflict. This way, the participants are not only being trained in conflict moderation but are also members of large-group conflict parties. The overarching conflict is mirrored in a milder form in the training group's dynamics.

Regardless of the presence of political tension, individual participants are interested in exchanges with the other side and are often also open to peaceful conflict resolution, since otherwise they would not have applied to participate in the training. The tensions and conflicts between their societies are mirrored within the workshop as well. One conflict issue in the Moldovan-Transdniestrian conflict is the dominance of either the Romanian[4] or Russian language. Both languages are spoken on both sides. However, while almost every Romanian speaker also speaks Russian, the majority of Russian speakers don't speak Romanian. In order to not endanger the mutual cooperation with arguments about linguistic conflicts and competition, close attention is paid to maintaining a balanced approach. For example we offer our workshops in two translations: English to Russian and English to Romanian. Furthermore we try to treat both sides equally in all aspects, even though it is not always possible due to different levels of experience and education. We will return to these issues and how they can manifest in the field later on.

Working in a region of political tension, it has been our intention from the project inception to build a stable foundation of a network of conflict moderators, capable of addressing different

---

[4]There is an ongoing political discourse if the Moldovan language exists or if it's Romanian written in Cyrillic letters with Russian terms incorporated. By now this discourse is hijacked by political ideology. For ease of reading we refer to it as the Romanian language, since this is the terminology used by our participants and also by the majority of international publications. This decision was made without any political reason or intention.

Moderating dialogue of
influential representatives by
experienced local
conflict specialists

Moderation of
community conflicts
by local specialists

Training of local
conflict moderators

Conflict analysis

Fig. 6.3 Steps to build a network of local conflict moderators

manifestations of the political conflict on the civic level. To combine these two notions, we are teaching ARIA as well as starting the formation of a group that can be sustained over the duration of the workshop through using the ARIA Action Evaluation process of collaborative goal setting and planning (see Chap. 7). By guiding the group through the ARIA-AE process, the participants are experiencing a process that corresponds structurally with an ARIA conflict moderation process; only the phase of Antagonism is replaced by Aspiration (see Chaps. 1, 2, and 3). In the Aspiration step, the participants and the trainer identify their individual goals for the workshop. They also compare and discuss in depth their interests motivating these goals, as well as their personal wishes and needs, which leads them over to the Resonance stage. Going through the ARIA-AE process prepares the participants for self-reflection and is also their first experience with the ARIA method in its goal-setting variant. To complete and combine the two objectives, the project is divided into four sections:

1. Pre-Interviews (May/June 2010)
2. First introductory workshop (July 2010)
3. Participatory Skype meeting to set the agenda for the second workshop (July 2010)
4. Second in-depth workshop (August 2010)

In the following section we describe the four components of the project, with an emphasis on how the ARIA conflict engagement process is taught.

Pre-interviews: Conflict Assessment

The pre-interviews are the first step in establishing contact with the local practitioners. We consider this an important step, since it serves the following three purposes:

1. Getting to know each other and establishing personal connections.
2. Getting to know the expectations of the participants and familiarizing them with the outline of the training increases the likelihood of a good fit.
3. Obtaining personal recommendations for finding other potential participants.

The pre-interviews are an important step for the success of the training and the objective of building a sustainable network of conflict moderators. Participants are able to develop a feeling for the organizer and establish accurate expectations of what the training would deliver. Going through the pre-interview also increases the commitment of participants to the project and prepares everyone for the project's heavy time investment.

It also helps us as organizers to develop an understanding of what participants expect from the training, as well as why they are participating. Coming into the system as outsiders, this is an important step in building the relationship between us and the prospective participants. Furthermore, it helps us find practitioners we had not yet heard of through personal recommendations. This step is our foundation for building a sustainable network of conflict facilitators.

How to Teach ARIA

Our two objectives – (1) teaching ARIA Conflict Moderation and (2) local capacity-building through the establishment of a sustainable conflict moderator network – require different teaching approaches. In the following example, we explain how we teach ARIA, and then how we focus on capacity-building. To teach ARIA, we used the following case study, which was presented by a participant in the training:

Nicolai and Katharina met and got married when both of them were already considered "older," he was 40 years old, she was 36. They were married for 15 years. But the marriage was not a happy one and they separated when both of them were already past their prime. They lived separately for 15 years, and during that time neither of them found a new partner. Growing older and living alone was difficult, particularly for Nicolai. His children and other family members were worried. Nicolai wanted to move in with Katharina again; in his view things between them were not that bad. Katharina was also unhappy living alone, but she coped better with it than Nicolai did and did not really want to reunite with Nicolai. However, due to the pressure of the family and also because of her loneliness, Katharina allowed Nicolai to move in with her again. That was 10 years ago. Today Nicolai is 80 years old, Katharina is 76. But the living situation has not been going well; shortly after moving in together, the couple started fighting and quarreling again. Today they do not even eat meals together, and they hold negative attitudes about each other's friends. Their attitudes and habits annoy each other; for example, Nicolai's wish to listen to the radio triggers Katharina's headache. Her style of house decoration is too cluttered for him. He blames her for taking away his initiative and argues that she doesn't give him room to express himself. She blames him for the fact that she has lived her life for him.

What can be done in this situation?

This is an example of a two-person conflict, and was provided by a participant during the training. We used this case to teach our participants the ARIA concept. This case is especially well suited for our purposes, since (a) it is a two-person conflict, which is easier to handle than a group conflict, where the group dynamics also complicate the conflict moderation process, and (b) it contains aspects that can be transferred from a training situation and applied to the real-life situation of the participants. In a metaphorical way, it mirrors the political relations between Moldova and Transdniestrian: the Moldovans and Transdniestrians are also living in the "same house" together (living in a close proximity to each other) but they do not eat together (i.e. share normal life and relations), and both are living separately in their own part of the house (i.e. divided by the Dniester river). They also have their own "friends," as the Moldovans are better "friends" with the EU, and the Transdniestrians with Russia. They also maintain strained relationships with each other's friends. And last but not least, just as the case with Nicolai and Katharina, it is unclear which direction they are moving towards – divorce or re-unification? This is a metaphor that is often used by the Transdniestrian and Moldovans to describe their complicated relationship (Kappmeier 2012).

More accessible and applicable in the context of our training, the relationship between men and women also mirrors some dynamics of classic gender stereotypes. This made it easier for the participants to relate to either one partner or the other, and that partner's perspective. We separated our participants into a group of men, who took on the role and perspective of Nicolai, and into a group of women, who took on the role and perspective of Katharina. We also separated our training team, which coincidently consisted of a male and female trainer. Hence we created an "all-men" and "all-women" group. Since one of the authors of this chapter facilitated the process of the women's group, we will share more details on the dynamics of this subgroup than of the men's subgroup.

Antagonism

Just like in real-life conflict moderation, we started off by having pre-talks with each group. Each participant filled out a Solo in which he or she took on the role of Nicolai or Katharina (see Chap. 3 and http://www.ariagroup.com/?page_id=3). After being separated, the men and women started to explore their respective roles. The trainers opened the session by explaining that the next step was to prepare the conflict moderation, when Nicolai and Katharina would come together. The participants were instructed that by the end of the pre-talk, two of them would be the role players for the moderation. Then the antagonistic frame was introduced; the participants were invited not only to share what they blamed the other side for, but also to connect this with a personal story from their own real-life experiences. This is part of the ARIA process, and in the context of the training, it also gave more authenticity and depth to the case and role plays. A lot of resonance was created in the women's group with the concerns and dilemmas of Katharina. The case received a very sympathetic response from the women in the group. Katharina's concerns and experiences deeply resonated with them and created closeness between them, despite the fact that they came from different parts of Moldova and Transdniestria, as well as from different age groups and backgrounds. Almost every woman could share a personal story from her relationship that mirrored the situation of Katharina, and each story resonated deeply with the other women.

After this exercise, which was conducted in the men's group as well, we gathered the ways that each character blamed the other. Table 6.1 shows the results of each group's exploration of the Antagonism process, as gathered from the participants.

The third conflict issue regarding the children ("You never did and you never take care of our children [you are a bad parent]") especially created a lot of emotions within the women's group. Moldova and Transdniestria are still marked by strong gender-based role models, in which the men are not very involved in the household and in the raising of the children despite the fact that the majority of women are also part of the work force. In our role play it was difficult to make the women focus on the fact that Katharina and Nicolai are in their 70s, and that their children are grown up by now. On the other hand, this was the point in which the role-play and the exploration of the Antagonistic phase became "real," and was moved by the women into the "here-and-now." It ceased being merely a role-play as the women's group experienced their own personal emotions. Since this was such an important issue for the women's group, we spent the majority of our time on it, and the women kept coming back to this issue.

Just as in real-life moderation, the pre-meetings create a focus and gather data for the conflict parties to work with in the first encounter when all of the parties will come together. Using ARIA in both real-life moderation and the training for situations of deep, identity-based conflicts, creates a strong focus on the Antagonism stage. We thus prepared our role players for taking on the role of Katharina and Nicolai in an authentic manner, and for connecting some of their own

Table 6.1 Antagonism of Katharina and Nicolai

Katharina/women	Nicolai/men
1. You ruined my life	1. You are a bad housekeeper
2. You are to blame for our divorce	2. You complain all the time
3. You never did and you never take care of our children (you are a bad parent)	3. You don't respect me
4. You are selfish	4. You are bossy
5. You spent all of our money	5. You make an elephant out of a fly
6. You don't help me with the housework	6. You offend me and my friends when I am with them
7. You are a loser	7. You want me to change, so that I am exactly the way you want me to be
8. I feel imprisoned by you	8. You accuse/blame me for nonsense
	9. You turned the children against me

antagonistic experiences to the situation of their roles as Katharina or Nicolai.

To show the participants how an Antagonism session is implemented, we ran a simulated session with our trainers serving as conflict moderators. Two of the participants took on the roles of Katharina and Nicolai. It was due to the preparation that the participants were able to take on their roles and dive into antagonistic narratives regarding their relationship. In a sense, they did "method acting" in which they drew from their own real-life experiences to enroll and authentically engage in the simulation (Stanislavski 1924). In our role-play, Katharina mainly blamed Nicolai for his lack of involvement with the children, for taking her for granted, for never giving her any recognition or appreciation for all of the work she does in the household. Nicolai blamed Katharina for overstating the situation with the children, and also for keeping him away from them.

Resonance: From Antagonism to Resonance

One of the biggest challenges of ARIA, besides hosting an Antagonism session, and perhaps its most important contribution to conflict transformation, is the transition from Antagonism to Resonance. How can we lead parties who were just accusing each other, blaming each other, and re-living their past conflicts, to a mindset where they not only share vulnerable and deep emotions with each other, but also listen to each other?

One important practice is the break between the antagonism and resonance sessions. This break can range from hours to days. It is important to (a) remind the parties that they entered a contract before they agreed to the antagonistic session, namely, they agreed to come back for the resonance session, and (b) encourage them not to talk about the ARIA session outside the seminar room. While having contact in-between sessions is often unavoidable, parties should not talk about the antagonistic session without the conflict moderator being present. These are structural mechanisms that help prepare the ground for the move from Antagonism to Resonance.

Another component that helps the parties move from Antagonism to Resonance is the skillfulness of the conflict moderator. The moderator has to prepare the parties for the different objectives of the steps of Antagonism (surfacing and confronting the conflict themes) and of Resonance (exploring why a theme matters to the parties, which hurt feelings and needs are connected to it). Being *transparent and educative* about the expected switch can set the stage. Once parties come together for the resonance session, it is up to the conflict moderator to create a setting in which sharing personal stories is safe. This is done by using reflective communication, in which the conflict moderator takes on an active role while the new culture of communication gets established. In a nutshell, the moderator applies the following four mechanisms:

(a) Transparency: Being transparent about the change from antagonist communication to resonant communication as well as about the objectives of the resonance step helps the parties prepare for the change. Furthermore, being transparent about the ground rules (i.e. confidentiality, etc.) helps create a safer environment, which helps the parties move towards resonance.

(b) Modeling: By being a model and introducing a language that is both reflective and touches upon parties' own perception of the situation, as well as focusing on their own (hurt) interest and needs, the moderator can help them establish the new pattern of communication.

(c) Encouraging: Using reflective language is often unusual for conflict parties, and is often met with some reluctance, since speaking about one's own interests and needs makes parties more vulnerable toward the other side. By encouraging and inviting the use of reflective language, the moderator can again help establish a safe environment for parties to open up and engage in resonance-based communication.

(d) Monitoring: The most challenging and probably most demanding part for the moderator is the close monitoring of the adapted communication style of the parties. The moment the parties slip back into antagonistic communication the moderator interrupts and supports the parties to rephrase their thoughts into resonant statements. Therefore, surprisingly the moderator can be much more directive and intervening than for example in the antagonism stage, at least in the early stages of resonance.

In our training, we then introduced another intra-group session meeting with the women and men. We asked the participants to take another look at their list of antagonistic framing. But instead of asking them "what do you blame the other side for?" we focused on the question of "*why* does it matter so much to you?" Normally it is quite difficult for the conflicted parties to move from an antagonistic mindset towards an open one, in which they acknowledge their vulnerable feelings. In our simulation it helped to separate the participants again along gender lines. Within the women's group we already had a great amount of openness and sharing during the antagonism stage. Starting with the issues of the children, we could easily identify why this is an important issue. To quote one of our participants: "… [of course it is important] they are the children!" But herein lies the challenge in introducing the resonance session: while some conflict themes are obvious in why they matter, the challenge is to lead the participants to a deeper reflection and sharing of the issue. The level of just saying "they are the children" has to be mined so that deeper feelings, especially the ones that are related to the "mothers" can be unearthed. Very quickly the women once again got stuck on simply blaming "Nicolai" for not caring enough and for neglecting the children. And to move on to the questions of "What does it mean *for you*? Why does it hurt *you* so much?" is the real challenge and opportunity. In our case the women were mainly driven by the motive to protect the children and to ensure that no harm comes to them. Since Nicolai's behavior was seen as hurtful for children they quickly slipped back into blaming him. It is the work of the conflict moderator to change the mind-set from blaming to resonance through questioning. What hurts them so much to see the children neglected? What does it do to them as mothers, as caregivers? What feelings does it prompt within them? The intra-group session helped the participants make this switch, since it was a safe environment that enabled them to talk about their fears and wishes. It was remarkable how even though the case-study about Katharina and Nicolai was a simulation, it became quite real for the women, most likely because the relationship conflict was something the participants could easily relate to from their own experiences. The women were quickly able to share heartfelt narratives from their own life experiences (like the social worker who dealt with families in distress, addressing issues such as abuse and neglect).

However, when we brought the groups back together this openness disappeared again, which is very common in real-life ARIA situations. Despite the preparation of the intra-group session, when meeting with their opponents, the parties are not yet ready to move towards resonance. They are not ready to share their vulnerable feelings involving their fears and their dreams. Nor are they ready to listen to each other.

The explanations of the moderator (regarding what this session is about, how it is different from the antagonism session) as well as his (in this case, Rothman), guiding questions helped the parties move towards resonance. We call this process "diving." As the double iceberg model in Fig. 6.4 shows below, we work with the assumption that the positions of the parties are mirror opposites (such as Katharina blaming Nicolai for "imprisoning" her while Nicolai accuses her of "taking away his initiative"). These positions can manifest themselves through defensive emotions, such as aggressive statements, (verbal) attacks or other antagonistic reactions. In our model, these emotions lie right underneath the surface. The defensive emotions were given room and expressed during the Antagonism period of the ARIA process. During the Resonance process, the objective is now to move deeper towards these vulnerable feelings: the fears and sorrows, but also hopes and dreams of the conflicting parties. These are hidden much deeper below the surface. However, usually the parties are very protective of these feelings and, given the shared history of hostility and conflict with each other, protecting these feelings is a form of healthy self-preservation. If the moderator dives too quickly into these

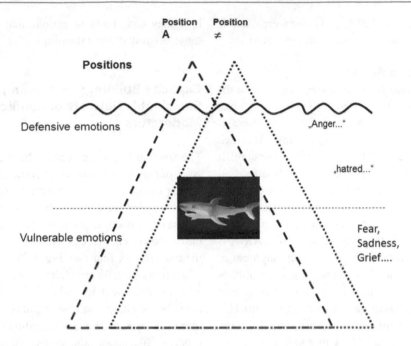

Fig. 6.4   Double iceberg (Redlich 2009, p. 157)

vulnerable feelings before enough trust has been established between the sides, a guardedness can arise, causing the parties to retreat back to Antagonism. In Fig. 6.4 the guardedness is represented by the shark:

In our simulation we also encountered the "shark." Katharina and Nicolai, represented by two role players, were only sharing why the conflict issues mattered to them on a superficial level during the resonance stage. Every attempt to dive into the deeper feelings was met with an artificial narrative or a return to antagonistic statements. Through the conflict moderator's patient redirecting and probing, the communication finally changed when Nicolai opened up and began to share a deep story from his past. He recalled the time when Katharina was pregnant with their first child and was sleeping in their bedroom. She looked so calm and fragile at this point and he felt "a deep connection with her" and "peacefulness in his spirit."

Through this story the dynamic between Katharina and Nicolai was changed: they delved into their past to remember times when their relationship was more harmonious. They started to share what they valued about the times when their

Table 6.2   Passion points of Katharina and Nicolai

Katharina	Nicolai
1. Emotional closeness	1. Comfort
2. Support	2. Calm
3. Renewal	3. Understanding
4. Togetherness	4. Control over my life
	5. Respect
	6. Personal space
	7. Good relationship with children
	8. Love

relationship was still going well, and what they are each yearning for now. It was from this point of understanding that they derived their passion points, which describe what their current relationship is missing and what they desire. These points were collected on a flip chart and are listed in Table 6.2 (above). The passion points are the result of framing through the use of resonance. They provide the basis for the next steps of ARIA – the Invention and Action phase.

The case proved to be quite complex with the differing set of expectations within our two subgroups. However, since we utilized that example in the context of training and mainly to describe and illustrate how ARIA works, we were not able to fully dive into the complexities involved.

Invention and Action

Often these two steps are disregarded due to the fact that time is limited during training, and invention and action are part of the classic brainstorming session and action planning. Although it could be assumed that the work of the conflict moderator has now shifted into purely a facilitation process, we disagree with this notion, since ARIA is not linear and Antagonism can still surface this late in the process. An important feature of this section is the understanding that ARIA is not a linear process and that even though closeness was developed in an earlier session, it does not rule out the possibility that Nicolai and Katharina will leap back into Antagonism. This has happened in almost every small group. Through practicing ARIA in small groups, the participants develop a feeling for the dynamic of the groups, and it gives them an opportunity to practice handling antagonistic emotions in conflict moderation. However, we will not explore this dynamic in depth, since we believe the uniqueness and strength of ARIA, and the focus of this chapter, lies in the engagement of Antagonism and Resonance.

We taught the Antagonism and Resonance phases through observation learning, with the trainer hosting a simulation using role players while the other participants observe. Invention and Action (the last two steps) were taught through small group exercises, after the instructor gave careful advice and theoretical background information on the ARIA concept. We divided our participants into groups of four, with two role players representing Katharina and Nicolai, and two participants as the conflict moderators who lead Katharina and Nicolai through the Invention stage. This stage ideally leads participants to the newfound understanding of where the other side is coming from, along with a deeper understanding of their own purposes and aspirations. It explores the questions of what solutions are possible for both sides, and how they can be administered. The parties now have a fuller picture of what matters to themselves and each other, and why, as well as

how they can create inventions that build upon these newfound understandings.

Capacity-Building: Developing a Sustainable Network of Conflict Moderators

The training has to be seen in the bigger framework of preparing conflict moderation workshops. A year has passed since we administered our first set of training workshops. We have already supported our trainees to guide their first community-based conflicts in the region and therefore reached the third step of four (see Fig. 6.3). The majority of our trained conflict moderators are still involved with us, and we had eight conflict moderators actively working on two independent, self-recruited cases, moderated according to the ARIA process. To support the cases, we organized a four-day workshop, in which the conflict moderators received supervision from us while working on their cases. Participants from last year's workshop also attended, in order to learn from the experiences of their peers and to continue developing their own conflict moderation skills.

When offering a training course on ARIA, one cannot expect nor demand from the participants that they "join" a network afterwards and keep committing their time and effort, and in some cases, risk their safety if members of their own group are or become suspicious of their activities with the "other" (Volkan 2011). This holds especially true for networks that are built in regions of politician tensions, such as the Moldovan and Transdniestrian region, since the participants of the workshop are members of the large-group conflict and they come from both conflict groups. Nevertheless, more than half of our former participants are still very actively involved and many of the others are interested in obtaining further information and continuing to be a part of the network. How was this achieved?

It is our opinion that two aspects are critical in building a sustainable network of conflict moderators: (a) a shared vision between the trainers, and (b) an early start to capacity-building (both educational and empowering) of the participants.

Shared Vision of the Trainers

From the very beginning, starting with the pre-interviews, we clearly communicated our interest in having a long-lasting involvement in the region, if that is something also wanted by the participants. We were clear about our own goals which keep us in the project. Since we had done our own ARIA goal setting and reflection upfront, we followed the ARIA Action Evaluation processes (see sections "Action Research" and "Conflict Moderation Capacity-Building in Moldova: Transdniestria"). and came to the two overarching goals for our work together:

1. Teaching ARIA as a conflict engagement concept
2. Building capacity by developing a sustainable network of skilled conflict moderators.

In the spirit of Aspiration and Resonance of ARIA Action Evaluation, we shared our passions and stories behind our individual goals agreeing that building deep and lasting connections between strangers who share a history and conflict is one of the passions that motivated us in the project. It is one of the core principles underlying our efforts to employ ARIA to build and train an enduring regional conflict moderation team. We also agree that these objectives and purposes are not accomplished through a one-year project, but that they emerge, and perhaps evolve, with a long term commitment from our side to continue the project for an extended period of time. In an effort to model what we taught about making goals clear and collaborative, we structured the workshops to reach our two objectives and communicated these objectives clearly to the participants, starting from the pre-interviews to the end of the final workshops. We also invited the participants to share their objectives and used these to evolve and revise our own as the seminar unfolded.

Capacity-Building and Ownership

Capacity-building is done in a twofold approach. First, we focused on the active involvement of the participants to give them an active voice in how the workshops were structured. To do so, as mentioned above, we used the ARIA-Action Evaluation to help them articulate and reach agreement on their goals. This participatory approach actively involves the participants in co-designing the workshop, and it highlights existing resources within the participants. In the Aspiration step of the AE process we asked participants in small group settings what they want to get out of the workshops. Figure 6.5 depicts some of their goals, and illustrates the tri-lingual approach of the workshop. Table 6.3 lists the same goals in English.

The groups came up with goals such as: "Knowing, practicing, and applying the ARIA concept," and "developing my ability to manage my emotions during mediation." In the Resonance phase we explored why the goals matter to the groups. Participants gave answers such as: "So that we may have the opportunity to develop our knowledge and the abilities to maintain peace" and "If we have enough experience, we can choose the right way to settle the conflict and to live safely." It is noteworthy that these statements were created by participants from both banks of the Dniester and received consensus.

This activity was the foundation for:

(a) Developing inventions for how participants can reach their goals, and for actively building on their resources.

Their resonance statements were also a good base for:

(b) Setting a course for the longer-lasting commitment involved, since becoming a specialist for conflicts in communities of course isn't something that can be achieved through participation in two workshops.

The inventions developed by the participants speak to their active involvement, such as hosting workshop sessions in the second workshop. For sustaining the network, it was important to us to emphasize and share their existing abilities. For example, each morning we had portions of the second set of workshops designed and facilitated by participants themselves, who contributed to the sessions on emotion management, resource allocation, and joint cooperation cases, as well as an example of a family mediation case. Figure 6.6 was taken during the resource allocation case. The high degree of involvement of the participants as well as their abilities allowed us to continue with the project in the way that we did.

Fig. 6.5 Participants' goals
for the workshop

Table 6.3 Extract (English) goals theory and practice of
ARIA

Theory and practice of ARIA
Knowing, practicing and using in practice the ARIA Model
To learn to apply the ARIA method and other methods in order to facilitate conflict through mediation
To get theoretical skills and practical knowledge through the ARIA method

As mentioned above, we engaged in capacity-building through a twofold approach. The second approach was that we ended the second workshop with another Aspiration-based planning process, this time asking the participants where they want to go from here. In this step, we were explicit about our own aspirations: we as convener-facilitators were interested in developing a sustainable network through institutionalizing mediation centers on both sides of the Dniester. This aspiration was shared by the participants. They created ideas for how to develop their own conflict moderation skills with the wish of "staying in touch," and they expressed the need for supervision when participants start

mediating in the third step of the program (see Fig. 6.3). The supervision can be done by the external trainers but also by the participants themselves, which would be an active start to the network.

The competencies of conflict moderation however are not evenly distributed among the participants from the Moldovan and Transdniestrian side. Moldova has a law regarding mediation, as well as certification trainings in mediations. Therefore the majority of Moldovan participants had mediation competencies mainly in the area of court and family mediation. This is missing on the Transdniestrian side. The asymmetry of competencies led to the argument of whether or not participants without former mediation training should be allowed to apply the ARIA approach in practice.

This was mainly directed toward the Transdniestrian participants who, of course, defended themselves against the ostracism. This conflict between the participants from both banks was engaged in a quick version of ARIA: the antagonism was clarified, and the needs and interests behind the positions were illuminated,

Fig. 6.6 Facilitation of a resource allocation case, prepared by the participants

which led to a mutual understanding. This question of competency moved down in importance in the agenda, since the participants developed the consensus that it is more important to work on cases before putting such ostracizing limits in place. Later on, the conflict was solved in a concrete way by the invention of mediation teams consisting of participants from both sides. These mixed teams are now composed of four people: one leading active conflict moderator who has had prior mediation training and experience, a non-certified active co-moderator, and two supporting participants, also from both sides. The supporting team members should be well informed about all aspects of the case which would raise their level of professionalism and colleagueship even though they are not equal in terms of their role as mediators.

Later, a discussion was held about how the members of the network can be further trained and qualified for conflict moderation. We handed the facilitation of this discussion over to the group, and the participants came up with their own, agreed-upon solutions to address the issue that conflict moderation competencies were not evenly distributed between them. They came up with the solution that the trained mediators from Moldova should give a training session in basic

consulting and mediation skills. The training is being organized and held on the Transdniestrian side and is open to new Transdniestrian and Moldovan participants. Through this solution, the group accepted that there are competency differences among them. This is an important indicator that the group has realistic self-perceptions and the capacity to take ownership and create solutions. It gave us a sense that the network is becoming a fairly effective working body.

After a year and a half, it is too early for us to know if we have succeeded in capacity-building that will be sustained over the long-run. One critical point which we will tackle in the next steps of our project is the issue of dissemination. While we are only able to train a limited number of participants so far, we are striving to institutionalize the training facilities within university settings on both sides of the river, to ensure that the trainings will reach more corners of the society.

Evaluation: What Do the Participants Say?

After the workshop was over, we conducted follow-up evaluation interviews. Building on our notions of empowerment and participation, the questions for the interviews were enriched by the input of the participants themselves. They were asked what they would like to know from their peers, and we included their questions in our evaluation interviews. With this information an independent evaluator (Zhygulina-Fahl 2011), who did not participate in the training, conducted phone interviews with 11 participants. We want to highlight the two main points of the evaluation:

1. What do the participants remember about the training after 3–5 months?
2. What is their perception of the network building?

What Is Memorable?

Mainly, the participants remembered the new knowledge they gained and the ARIA approach that was taught in the training, especially the emphasis on the controlled surfacing of antagonistic aspects of conflicts and the shift from antagonism to resonance. They also gained an understanding that while conflict is a negative and straining experience, it also holds potential if engaged in a meaningful way.

The interactions with the trainers and the other participants were remembered as a valuable part of the training. More precisely, the way the trainers interacted with each other and the participants was remembered as being accessible and highly motivating, which overall the participants regarded as a good model. The training was appraised as one of the best that the participants had attended.

One of the participants stated that our training "…was a good atmosphere, based on understanding. [The trainers] were open towards us and wanted to understand [our] need[s], so that they [could] organize their work in a manner that fits with our interests." This perception was shared by other participants, one of whom said about our training:

It is great to interact and be taught by professionals of such high standard. I was also impressed by the human side of all [the] trainers; all of them [are] very intelligent and open human beings… it was a pleasure to talk with them.

A participant said that the ARIA training was superior to other trainings he had undergone because the participants "had the opportunity to develop and conduct parts of the trainings by ourselves, to exchange ideas and receive the information that we needed." The control and autonomy that ARIA gave the participants was highly praised. This praise extended to the ARIA method as a whole, which was perceived as the method that best fit the needs of the participants, despite how demanding it was: "[the trainers] let us work up some sweat during the training with ARIA and Solo. I know that I learned the best method, however demanding it is. I only have good memories."

Building a Sustainable Network

The participants shared the objective of building a sustainable network at the end of the training. We can separate the participants into two groups:

(a) practitioners who want to be involved as conflict moderators, and (b) educators who are interested in sharing the knowledge that they gained in the workshop. The latter (educators) were interested in teaching an alternative conflict engagement style, where conflicts can be engaged through dialogue and mutual activities, instead of using barriers of silence or pushing one's own agenda through a power-grabbing approach.

The structure of hosting two workshops over four days, separated by a month, instead of a single, long workshop created a feeling of durability and supported our objective of building a sustainable network of local providers.

The evaluation also asked participants how we could improve the training, and how to handle three different languages (English, Romanian, Russian) in the workshop. We were not always able to have native speakers translate our material, which was reflected in the quality of our translations. The other points of improvement touched upon the different bases of knowledge and vast differences among participants. While some participants would have preferred a more homogenous group in terms of experience and training, this is not possible due to the different starting points of the two societies.

One of the main points the participants had was that waiting a month between the two workshops was very beneficial in building the network. Another one was that we need an ongoing training for conflict moderators, and concrete conflict cases that our participants can use to apply the new knowledge that they learned in the previous workshops.

Future Prospects

Application in Community Conflicts Under Supervision

Back to the beginning of the chapter: What will come out of this community-based conflict work?

We don't know yet, since this project is still in formation and is unfolding. But we successfully have recruited two teams of independent conflict moderators who worked with us on two community-based conflicts in the border region of Moldova-Transdniestria. Both conflicts are shaped by the ongoing, unresolved, and overarching political conflict. Without the political conflict between both banks of the Dniester River these conflicts would not exist. Of course, the members of this project won't be able to solve this political conflict and should not attempt to solve it. That is a task for Track I negotiators.

Conflict research has shown that the people most affected by political conflict are in the civil society sector (Lederach 1997). The lives of the villagers in the border region are highly impacted in a negative way on the political level, but they do not have much influence to change that. Through this project we attempted to strengthen this civil sector, to introduce an understanding of self-efficacy and that conflict transformation on the community level is possible. This can be done through the mutual experience of communicating with each other, which can also increase understanding and decrease the alienation between the two groups, leading to a stronger, improved relationship between them. Furthermore, we also want to introduce a new culture of conflict engagement: change through dialogue.

In the long run we intend to expand the focus of community conflict work and move up to the Track II level (Fig. 6.2). We intend to have local conflict moderators in mixed teams moderate these mediations. The training and intervention in community based conflicts will be ongoing and help support these new, local conflict moderators.

Expanding the Stage

The Moldova-Transdniestria project sets an example for other regions experiencing tension, especially regions of the former USSR, but also other parts of the world. Analyzing the political context of this conflict from both the views of the Moldovan and Transdniestrian people and from our personal experiences (in our preparation of both workshops and our ongoing work) demonstrates that the Russian Federation and the European Union are powerful players on this small stage. They influence the political elites, the authorities, and people on both sides of the Dniester River. Most of the people we interviewed in the initial conflict assessment research said that the conflict is not resolvable without the cooperation of these actors (Kappmeier 2012; Redlich and Kappmeier 2010). There has to be a common conflict engagement between all parties. Therefore, as this project has unfolded we have initiated collaboration between the Universities of Hamburg (European Union) and St. Petersburg (Russian Federation) in developing cross-border research and training groups for boundary-spanning conflict work.

References

Burton, J. W. (1969). *Conflict and communication: The use of controlled communication for international relations*. London: Macmillan.

Bush, R. B., & Folger, J. P. (1994). *The promise of mediation: Responding to conflict through empowerment and recognition*. San Francisco: Jossey-Bass.

De Rivera, J. (2007). *Handbook on building cultures of peace*. New York: Springer.

Fisher, R. (Ed.). (2005). *Paving the way: Contributions of interactive conflict resolution to peacemaking*. Lanham: Lexington Books.

Fisher, R., Ury, W., & Patton, B. (1991). *Getting to yes*. Boston: Houghton Mifflin.

Fry, D. P., Bonta, B. D., & Baszarkeiwiecz, K. (2007). Learning from extant cultures of peace. In J. De Rivera (Ed.), *Handbook on building cultures of peace* (pp. 11–26). New York: Springer.

Galtung, J. (2004). *Transcend and transform*. Boulder: Paradigm.

Hall, M. (1999). *Conflict resolution: The missing element in the Northern Ireland peace process*. Newtownabbey: Island Pamphlets.

Janis, I. L. (1972). *Victims of groupthink*. Boston: Houghton Mifflin.

Kaner, S., Lind, L., Toldi, C., Fisk, S., & Berger, D. (2007). *Facilitator's guide to participatory decision-making*. Philadelphia: New Society Publishers.

Kappmeier, M. (2008). *Experts interviews on third party intervention and trust*. University of Hamburg. Unpublished work.

Kappmeier, M. (2012). *Where is the Trust?– Conflict and Trust Assessment between Large-Group Conflict Parties for 3rd Parties Conflict Intervention*. (Dissertation) University of Hamburg: Hamburg.

Kelman, H. C. (1986). Interactive problem solving: A social-psychological approach to conflict resolution. In W. Klassen (Ed.), *Dialogue toward interfaith understanding* (pp. 293–314). Tantur/Jerusalem: Ecumenical Institute for Theological Research.

Kelman, H. C. (2004). Continuity and change: My life as a social psychologist. In A. H. Eagly, R. M. Basori, & V. L. Hamilton (Eds.), *The social psychology of group identity and social conflict: Theory, application, and practice* (pp. 233–275). Washington, DC: American Psychological Association.

Klebert, K., Schrader, E., & Straub, W. G. (2002). *Winning group results: Techniques for guiding group thought and decision-making processes with the moderation method*. Hamburg: Windmühle.

Kotchikian, A. (2006). From post-Soviet studies to Armenianology. *Demokratizatsiya, 14*(2), 1–9.

Kotchikian, A. (2008). The impo(r)tence of public opinion: An analysis of public surveys in Armenia. *Armenian Journal of Public Policy: Special Issue*, 330–345.

Lederach, J. P. (1997). *Building peace: Sustainable reconciliations in divided societies*. Washington, DC: United States Institute of Peace Press.

Lederach, J. P. (2003). *The little book of conflict transformation*. Intercourse: Good Books.

Moscovici, S., & Zavalloni, M. (1969). The group as a polarizer of attitudes. *Journal of Personality and Social Psychology, 12*, 125–135.

Nan, S. A. (2005). Track two and a half diplomacy. In R. Fisher (Ed.), *Paving the way* (pp. 161–178). Lanham: Lexington Books.

Redlich, A. (2009). *Konfliktmoderation in Gruppen* (7th ed.). Hamburg: Windmühle.

Redlich, A. (2011). Introduction. In J. Höck, A. Begert, M. Kappmeier, & A. Redlich (Eds.), *Building cultures of peace* (pp. 13–15). Frankfurt: Lang.

Redlich, A., & Kappmeier, M. (2010). Between diplomacy and grassroots: The moderation of constructive dialogues between representatives of antagonistic groups. In S. Rusnac, V. Gonta, N. Sali, & L. Zmuncila (Eds.), *Preocupari contemporane ale stiintelor socioumane* (pp. 163–179). Chisinau: Free International University of Moldova Press.

Rosenberg, M. (2003). *The nonviolent communication: A language of life*. Encinitas: Puddle Dancer Press.

Ross, M. H., & Rothman, J. (Eds.). (1999). *Theory and practice in ethnic conflict management: Theorizing success and failure*. New York: St. Martin's Press.

Rothman, J. (1997). *Resolving identity based conflicts in nations, organizations, and communities*. San Francisco: Jossey Bass.

Rothman, J., & Redlich, A. (2007). Action evaluation und konfliktarbeit. In R. Lange, P. Kaeding, M. Lehmkuhl, & H. Pfingsten-Wismer (Eds.), *Frischer Wind für Mediation* (pp. 37–49). Frankfurt: Bundesverband für Mediation.

Rothwell, D. J. (1986). Risk-taking and polarization in small group communication. *Communication Education, 35*, 172–187.

Rubin, J. Z., Pruitt, D. G., & Kim, S. H. (1994). *Social conflict: Escalation, stalemate, and settlement*. New York: McGraw-Hill.

Schulz von Thun, F. (1981). *Miteinander reden. Störungen und Klärungen*. Reinbek: Rowohlt.

Schulz von Thun, F. (1998). Das innere Team und situationsgerechte Kommunikation. Reinbek bei Hamburg: Rowohlt Taschenbuch Verlag.

Sounders, H. H. (2005). Sustained dialogue in Tajikistan: Transferring learning from the public to the official peace process. In R. Fisher (Ed.), *Paving the way* (pp. 127–142). Lanham: Lexington Books.

Stanislavski, C. (1924). *An actor's handbook: An alphabetical arrangement of concise statements on aspects of acting*. New York: Theatre Arts Books.

Susskind, L., McKearnan, S., & Thomas-Larmer, J. (1999). *The consensus building handbook: A comprehensive guide to reaching agreement*. Thousand Oaks: Sage Publications.

Tajfel, H., & Turner, J. L. (1986). The social identity theory of intergroup behavior. In S. Worchel & W. G. Austin (Eds.), *Psychology of intergroup relations* (pp. 7–24). Chicago: Nelson-Hall.

The ARIA Group (2002). The cincinnati police-community relations collaborative. http://www.socsci.uci.edu/~cpb/istudies/applied/presentations/site/index.html. Accessed 19 Nov 2008.

The Institute of Cultural Affairs (2008). *What is the technology of participation?* http://www.ica-usa.org/?page=whatistop. Accessed 30 Oct 2008.

Thomann, C. (2003). *Klärungshilfe. Konflikte im Beruf*. Reinbek: Rowohlt.

Thomann, C. (2004) Klaerungshilfe 2. Konflikte im Beruf: Methoden und Modelle klaerender Gespraeche. Reinbek bei Hamburg: Rowohlt Taschenbuch Verlag.

Troebst, S. (2003). We are "Transniestrian": Post-Soviet identity management in the Dniester Valley. *Ab Imperio, 1*, 437–466.

United Nations (1992). Agenda 21 [Sect. 37.1]. Conference on Environment and Development (UNCED), held in Rio de Janerio, Brazil, 3–14 June 1992. http://www.un.org/esa/dsd/agenda21/res_agenda21_37.shtml. Accessed 13 Jan 2011.

United Nations Educational, Scientific and Cultural Organization (2002). *Mainstreaming the culture of peace.* Brochure. http://unesdoc.unesco.org/images/0012/001263/126398e.pdf. Accessed 18 Jan 2011.

Volkan, V. (2006). *Killing in the name of identity: A study of bloody conflicts.* Charlottesville: Pitchstone.

Volkan, V. (2011). Vamik Volkan. In J. Höck, A. Begert, M. Kappmeier, & A. Redlich (Eds.), *Building cultures of peace* (pp. 28–42). Frankfurt: Lang.

Watson, M., & Rosegrant, S. (2001). *Breakthrough international negotiation.* San Francisco: Jossey-Bass.

Zhygulina-Fahl, Y. (2011). *How do participants from Moldova and Transdniestria experience a further education workshop in political mediation? A qualitative evaluation study.* Unpublished diploma thesis. Hamburg: Hamburg University, Department of Psychology.

Action Evaluation in Theory and Practice

7

Jay Rothman

Introduction: Origins

As we have sought to establish in the first half of this book, identity-based conflict is the deepest type of conflict requiring its own unique analyses and processes. It seems to us, then, that the same is true of identity-based cooperation; it also requires its own approaches. This chapter introduces one such methodology, which grows directly out of our work in identity-based conflict.

Individually, when I am able to be *resonant* about what I want (e.g. my needs, values, priorities, aspirations) and why these are so important to me, it is the start of my ability to connect and *resonate* with you. If you can do the same, our connection grows even deeper. But even if I have done this work alone and you have not, I can change the dynamic of our interactions. As discussed in the previous section of this book, the deeper the conflict, the more people are called to be clear about why it is important to them: to move away from the blame-game, the attributions and projections and accept ownership and agency over their problems. What is this conflict for? Why has it shown up in my life?

In an age when individuals are increasingly being challenged to cooperate and collaborate

with others, the deeper the cooperation, or the more the need for it, the more people must encounter themselves enroute to the other. To cite my 17 year-old daughter, Liana, paying me the ultimate compliment by quoting me in her slam-poem "Society":

My father once said,
you must look deep inside yourself
in order to see not only yourself clearly
but others as well.

Collectively, it is the same. When groups seek to cooperate with each other across their boundaries, to create a shared "nexus" that is bigger than each of them, going "inward" and working first within their own "boundaries," helps condition and deepen external linkages across boundaries (Ernst and Chrobot-Mason 2011). As in conflict, the more each side does their "solo" work first – who are we as individuals and as a group? what do we seek and why is it important to us? – the more they can join another group of linked individuals in deep cooperation. This step is often resisted. Many times people will say that since they have come to cooperate with the other group, they find the request to first work in their own side uncomfortable. Sometimes we give in. But when we insist and they agree, we find it is worth the effort. While our natural and generally positive inclination is to seek to join others as soon as possible, and to get beyond the barriers and boundaries we find between ourselves and others, in reality, the adage of "going slow to go fast" applies here too (Chap. 1).

7

J. Rothman (✉)
Program on Conflict Resolution and Negotiation,
Bar-Ilan University, Ramat Gan, Israel
e-mail: jrothman@ariagroup.com

J. Rothman (ed.), *From Identity-Based Conflict to Identity-Based Cooperation: The ARIA Approach in Theory and Practice*, Peace Psychology Book Series, DOI 10.1007/978-1-4614-3679-9_7,
© Springer Science+Business Media New York 2012

Groups that seek to cooperate with each other often fail. Commonly, this is not due to intention, but rather to the reality that different groups bring with them different cultures, goals, priorities and values. When these are articulated internally among members of a group and then brought forward to another group, resonance is often close at hand. When this step of developing internal alignment is skipped, all too often groups find themselves at loggerheads with each other. Think of the many experiences you have had in which groups that seem to share the same purposes, are quickly disappointed and enmeshed in disagreements.

This section of the book, growing quite literally out of the work presented in the first half, is about how to "help good people do good work together better" (see www.ariagroup.com). Helping good people work together better has marked my life's work as a facilitator, mediator, action-researcher and consultant. I have worked with too many peace and social justice organizations that are any thing but peaceful internally, or fully live out their ideals of justice in their relationships with each other. As discussed previously (see Chap. 3), this is not due primarily to hypocrisy, though there may be some of that, derived from a lack of self-awareness. Mostly, it is due to a lack of good process by which people can internally and interactively learn to say what they mean and do what they say. As Buber suggests, not connecting words with deeds is the root of conflict (see Chaps. 2 and 3). Gandhi has a similar but more positive formula: "Happiness is when what you think, what you say, and what you do are in harmony."

Unlike in the business world where the bottom line commonly presents a clear focus of collaborative work and shared goals, in the world of human relations, conflicts, aspirations and goals are often fuzzy, egos often cloud vision, and what people care about and why are often buried beneath layers of poor communication, inconsistent purposes and frustrated ideals.

The purpose of the ARIA-Action Evaluation process is to cut through all of this and support people to be clear, with themselves and each other, about what they deeply care about and why, and therefore what priorities and strategies to select.

Overview of Process

Action Evaluation (AE), as we use the term, is an innovative method that uses social and computer technology to define, promote, and assess success in complex social interventions (see http://www.ariagroup.com/?page_id=5 for detailed information about this technology and its use). AE grew out of my work as a theorist and intervener in identity-based conflicts. It was a direct response to recurrent questions that I and other conflict-resolution practitioners, participants, and funders were asking about the efficacy of conflict-resolution interventions, particularly in deep conflicts (see Chap. 1). We asked with increasing urgency, "Does conflict resolution really work? How can we know? What does 'work' mean, who defines it, and how?" And most important, "How can our search for answers about success increase our chances of achieving it?"

Traditional forms of evaluation stand apart from the projects that they evaluate, and illuminate gaps between initial program goals and actual outcomes. In fact, many forms of evaluation exacerbate such gaps by freezing initial project proposals as a game is played to prove to relevant stakeholders (like foundation boards) that projects have accomplished what they initially set out to accomplish. Anyone who has worked in complex social interventions knows they are, by definition, only as good as their ability to be adaptive and agile. In short, project goals must evolve as projects unfold and criteria of success should therefore be dynamic. Action Evaluation joins a project as its ally by helping participants and other key stakeholders define and then formatively redefine success, to forge effective action and make success a self-fulfilling prophecy (Argyris et al. 1985). In traditional forms of evaluation, the criteria of success are usually imposed upon initiatives from the outside, without seeking meaningful and sustained input from the various groups involved in it. Action Evaluation gathers and organizes input and ownership by those involved by assisting them, separately and then together, to create their own criteria for success. Thus, by defining and seeking success in a continuous, adaptive way,

AE is simultaneously an evaluation, planning and intervention tool.

Since the mid-1990s, Action Evaluation has been used to assist thousands of participants, funders, and facilitators in hundreds of conflict-resolution and community and organizational development projects worldwide. These projects have employed AE to help them reach clarity and consensus among stakeholders about *what* they seek to accomplish, *why,* and *how.*

Action Evaluation (AE) fosters passionate participation and ownership. It gathers and organizes essential input for a project, by asking questions about:

- People's goals – What?
- Their values and beliefs – Why? – and
- Suggested action strategies – How?

By asking those most directly involved in an emerging project to individually and then collectively define their goals, articulate core values, and brainstorm action strategies, a project becomes coherent and focused. Participants who might otherwise be at odds with one another about the purposes of their joint effort, can effectively walk in step with one another and reflect together on their practice as they engage in it. As such, action evaluation is a form of collaborative social intervention fostering alignment among key stakeholders as it assists them to define, promote and assess success about their unfolding effort. AE also serves in many situations as a form of conflict intervention in that it brings to the surface any conflicts between participants' goals and strategies, and helps them become more engaged and proactive about addressing them constructively. In summary, by asking stakeholders to collaboratively define their criteria of success, Action Evaluation supports a central principle of all good participatory processes such as conflict resolution and community and organizational development. It is, or should be, almost axiomatic that to effectively engage people in an effort to solve their own problems and pursue their own preferred futures, their deep sense of authentic ownership and participation must be nurtured. Verba called this the "participation effect" showing a causal relationship between participants' sense of own-

ership in a problem and their willingness to stick with a solution-seeking process (Verba 1961; Ross 2001).

Goals, Values and Objectives (or What, Why and How)

In supporting key stakeholders in new initiatives to get on the same page with each other, and *interactively establish criteria for defining, promoting and assessing success*, we invite them to go through a process of individually and collectively articulating responses to an action-inquiry organized around simple What, Why and How questions. First they are invited to describe What they want accomplish in fairly broad and long-term ways (i.e. Goals). Such goals usually represent broad visions. For example to "Promote Community Problem-Oriented Policing" or "To Enhance Race Relations in Our Neighborhood." They then reflect on their goals and share value responses to questions about Why they care deeply, even passionately, about their goals. For example, "I seek community problem-oriented policing so an environment of participation and cooperation is fostered" or "Due to lack of positive contact between different races in our community, I feel fear and distress instead of the kind of connection and comfort I seek where I live." Lastly, given their Goals and Values, participants share their ideas about How to accomplish them most concretely in the near-term. These How ideas define the steps necessary to accomplish goals that have been identified. Unlike more general What Goals, these How ideas are specific, measurable, and ideally establish a realistic timeline for accomplishment. They are specific and outline *the who, what, when and where* of reaching shared goals. For example, "groups of police officers and community members will meet on a bi-weekly basis to assess local problems and determine proactive and cooperative strategies that can be taken to reduce specific instances of crime and violence" or "Black and White youth will gather in the youth-wing of the community center for recreational activities and a meal and participate in carefully structured dialogue about topics of their own choosing on the first of every month."

After individuals answer survey questions built around this What, Why, How formula and adapted to a specific project, they join others from their self-selected or assigned stakeholder group to reach agreement about the Goals they share (after first engaging in a dialogue over their values). Finally, representatives of two or more stakeholder groups convene to reach over-arching consensus on goals and select launching objectives to begin implementing goals in practice.

Action-Evaluation has been designed and used widely by helping professionals, layper-sons, researchers, practitioners, policymakers, grantees, foundation officers and others. We have used it hundreds of times in complex international ethnic conflict resolution initiatives and in a number of U.S. race relations project (see comprehensive AE bibliography). It has been used in higher education and community conflict resolution programs. We have also used it in government agencies as a vehicle for problem framing and dispute system design. It has been used in broad-based and multi-stakeholder community and organizational development efforts as well. In the following chapters, we provide illustrations of its use in such diverse settings as an Israeli classroom with Jewish and Arab nursing students (Chap. 8), in a Mid-Western Medical School (Chap. 9), in an international youth exchange program (Chap. 10), and in Cincinnati, Ohio following Race riots (Chap. 11).

In order to facilitate this very wide range of applications, we have sought to make Action Evaluation as adaptable and accessible as possible. Moreover, it has been built around a user-friendly computer technology made accessible to people with a wide range of professional and academic training and interests, technological proficiency and prior research experience. It is designed so that, with the assistance of a specially trained "action evaluator," various stakeholders in projects or programs will become their own researchers, reflexively studying their own goals and activities as they articulate and enact them.

To date, our 40 or so Action Evaluators have been trained as researcher-consultants who are either already insiders to a specific initiative, or outsiders who can gain trust and legitimacy with project participants while still retaining some analytic detachment. The job of the Action Evaluator is essentially to be a project consultant in promoting reflexive practice by all project stakeholders about their goals, values and action plans as the project unfolds (see Rothman 1997).

Action-Evaluation begins with a systematic and broad-based data collection of the goals of the relevant stakeholders (participants, conveners, interveners, funders, etc.) involved in a new initiative. As summarized above, the Action Evaluation process is launched by asking three broad questions that are customized to each specific initiative – what, why and how:

1. **WHAT?** What internal and external goals do various stakeholders have for this initiative? Another way to think about this question is to pose visions of success against current reality. Various stakeholders (e.g. project funders, conveners and participants) may be asked to

Action evaluation survey	Phase one: ALL INDIVIDUALS	Phase two: EACH STAKEHOLDER GROUP	Phase three: ALL STAKEHOLDER GROUPS
1. WHAT goals	What are my goals for this project?	What are our goals?	What goals are shared between our various group goals?
2. WHY values	Why do I care deeply about these goals?	Why are they important to us?	In what ways do our values overlap, mesh and merge?
3. HOW actions	How do I think these goals can be accomplished most effectively such that the values I hold are fulfilled?	[Specific planning for How to integrate and implement Action Strategies is conducted at the intergroup level during phase three]	How do we best cooperate to fulfill our goals and values?

consider what they hope will change for participants and in the larger social setting due to this intervention and their involvement with it, or how they would define success.

2. **WHY?** Why do the various stakeholders care about their goals so much? What motivations are driving their outcome goals? More conceptually, and directed toward the conveners more than participants or funders, what are the theories of practice and domain assumptions which guide their practice?

3. **HOW?** How will stated goals be met most effectively? Based on the goals and motivations articulated, stakeholders are asked to suggest what kinds of action steps might best contribute to moving from the present to the vision of success they have just articulated.

This data is gathered in one of three ways, or a combination of them: via online questionnaires (respondents go to a password protected website and respond to a customized survey), through face-to-face interviews (which can also be used to supplement data gathered online), or through paper and pencil surveys.

The preferred method to date is through the online computer process since it is highly efficient and makes the questionnaire easily accessible from anywhere in the world where the internet is available. Moreover, thanks to computer technology, the online questionnaire is both user-friendly and self-referential. In addition to narrowing geographic gaps and aiding in data gathering and analysis, the computer-assisted goal setting process is designed to assist respondents in the analysis of their own goals.[1]

After the respondents provide up to three specific answers to the question of "what" are their goals for a specific project, their why and how answers are then in turn each dynamically and self-referentially linked with their own previous responses thanks to the web technology. (For a process description of the action evaluator's steps see http://www.ariagroup.com/?page_id=5).

In many ways the Action Evaluation process and the computer technology developed to assist it, is simply a more efficient, economical and democratic way of doing what we normally do in the field of conflict resolution and development work. It is also deeply scalable. It can be used with as few as two people (sometimes even one can benefit from using the process to clarify his or her own goals, values and action ideas before launching some new initiative – I use it all the time for my own planning work) or with thousands (our largest project to date had 3,500 respondents – see below and Chap. 11).

In contrast to the efficiency of this system of gathering and organizing goal-data, consider how common it is for facilitators to bring people together for a few hours or even a few days in a retreat to determine what they are trying to do (solve problems, improve social conditions, enhance intergroup relations, reduce violence, etc.). Commonly, participants are invited to articulate their goals (and/or problems) and discuss why these goals or problems matter and how they will be accomplished or addressed. As a result of this process, walls are often filled with responses recorded on flipcharts. Or, participants are interviewed and hours of tapes are transcribed and categorized. Often such data represents only small segments of key stakeholders who are able to participate in those meetings or who are willing or able to be interviewed. Moreover, a tremendous amount of time and resources are expended just getting things organized.

The AE process, on the other hand, begins with gathering this kind of data before people meet face to face. It fosters an efficiency that is lacking when people come together to do what we believe is, or should be, largely preparation work of gathering and pre-sorting goal-data. Moreover, gathering data in advance to a meeting through the internet not only helps us prepare for a "hit-the-ground-running" meeting in advance, but we also succeed in getting wide participation in goal-setting which is democratizing because more folks are able to participate. In short, this is a process that can be used to enhance deep and broad participation in program design by assisting in

---

[1] To see how the system works, please try it out by going to www.ariac3.com and putting in the password "practice." Then follow the simple prompts. If you select "return to my email," you can get a copy of your own responses.

setting preliminary criteria of success before programs (or projects, or initiatives, or community development efforts, etc.) are launched.

The data analysis is still somewhat labor-intensive, but there is also tremendous efficiency in moving through qualitative data (based on What, Why and How questions) in a relatively quick and easy way. The Action Evaluators collect the data, enter it into the project website (if it is not entered directly into the system by respondents themselves) and analyze it, with the input and guidance of the project director as needed. Data is analyzed for shared, unique and, sometimes most interestingly, contrasting goals. This analysis is then fed back to the stakeholders when they do gather. This kind of process is familiar to conflict resolution practitioners. The innovation here is not so much in the process itself but the way in which it has been systematized and organized (with the help of a specially developed database system to assist in data analysis, organization, storage and feedback), contributing to both deep encounter and a good use of time and other scarce resources.

Three Stages of Action Evaluation: Baseline, Formative and Summative

The action evaluator works directly with project leaders and key stakeholders to establish a *baseline assessment* for the project, based on the articulation of shared goals among them. Following the baseline assessment, this data is used to design an agenda and action plan that is maximally participatory and has been widely elicited from all key stakeholders. As a project is implemented and gains relative stability in its goals and action strategies, the evolution of its goals can be carefully tracked and monitored, and a new round of what, why and how questions ideally are asked. This *formative assessment* helps determine (and assist) how goals evolve (and we find that they often become more specific and realistic than initial, somewhat abstract goals). Through this entire process, standards for success can be articulated to promote self-evaluation as a project unfolds and to

allow easier external assessment as well. In addition to the many other benefits of this process, it also can help overcome "evaluation aversion" derived from sensitivity to being judged by others about external criteria and static definitions of success. AE makes such criteria internal and dynamic while also fostering an interest in having external evaluators assess participants' success and short-comings in meeting their own evolved goals and strategies. Finally at the conclusion of a project, a *summative assessment* about the goals as they have been articulated and monitored is taken to evaluate their accomplishment.

As summarized in the box below, the three stages in Action Evaluation are: establishing baseline, formative monitoring, and summative evaluation.

Stage 1: Establishing Baseline

Step 1: Articulating Individual Goals

Through the use of an online questionnaire (surveys or interviews), individual participants define what they perceive to be the project's major goals. They articulate *what* these goals are, *why* they care about these goals (or why they are important generally), and *how* they could best be accomplished.

Step 2: Defining Group Goals

Once the individual goals have been defined, the Action Evaluator determines whether each respondent's goal is unique, shared (between two or more respondents), or contrasting with those of other group members. Participants from each group then meet and reach consensus on their own platform of (baseline) goals.

Step 3: Defining System-Level Goals

After determining the shared goals within each identity group, we repeat the same process

Stages in AE

Stage	Action
Establishing a baseline (or undertaking an assessment)	Articulation of definitions of success
	Consensus building of definitions between individual stakeholders within their own groups
	Intergroup consensus building
	Creation of intergroup action plans
Formative monitoring	Implementation of action plans
	Adjustment and monitoring of definitions and actions
Summative evaluation	Questions are asked and measures are taken to see how well an intervention has met its own internally-derived goals
	Definition of criteria for success for next steps or future initiatives

This chart is abstracted from Rothman 2002

across all stakeholder groups. Face-to-face feed-back sessions with self-designated representatives from each stakeholder group assist in this process.

Stage Two: Formative Monitoring

In the baseline stage, stakeholders articulate their goals and motivations in order to arrive at clear and consensual definitions of success. The baseline stage ends with an action plan specifying what needs to be done (as well as by whom, and when) in order to achieve these goals. During the formative stage, participants refine, and sometimes revise, their goals and develop strategies for overcoming obstacles as they begin to implement them.

One of the underlying assumptions of action evaluation is that goal setting is a process that continues throughout the life of a project. No matter how well project participants articulate and agree upon their goals at the baseline, they may discover new goals and opportunities as they go along. In addition, participants frequently need to reconsider goals as they encounter resistance or other obstacles to implementation. Finally, project participants may discover that there is a gap between their espoused goals (what they said they wanted) and the goals implicit in what they are actually doing in their practice (see Argyris 1985; Rothman and Friedman 2002).

The formative stage actually overlaps with the baseline stage because the action plan, which is the main "product" of the baseline stage, becomes important data in the formative stage. It provides project participants with an explicit basis for comparing intentions with what is actually happening in the project. The formative stage, however, is not simply a control mechanism for keeping the project on track. Rather, it uses discoveries, gaps, and contradictions as opportunities for reshaping and fine-tuning a project design. Project stakeholders are asked to function as "reflective practitioners" by standing outside the situation, becoming more aware of their actual goals and strategies for action, and experimenting with new ones (see Schon 1983). Ideally, it encourages an even deeper reflectiveness in fostering "reflexive practitioners" (see Darling 1998).

Stage Three: Summative Evaluation

Finally, there is a summative evaluation stage, or more traditional "evaluation-as-judgment," in which defined criteria of success are used to assess how well an intervention has met its own internally derived and evolved goals. As a project reaches toward its conclusion, participants use their evolved goals to establish criteria for retrospective assessment. Stakeholders will, for example, examine whether they have reached specified goals, and ask themselves, "why?" or "why not?" They will ask themselves how and what they could have done differently or better.

Conclusion

Action Evaluation is a process of goal articulation and data-gathering which is designed to systematize what is normally, though often haphazardly, done as part of the design and implementation of most conflict resolution and community and organizational development interventions. Action Evaluation is a vehicle for systemic reflection, monitoring and mid-course correction as well as overall assessment. This systematization of the intervention process and content is intended to promote reflexive evaluation – defining, promoting and assessing success – among all stakeholders as they move forward in their intervention. Given that a great deal of conflict resolution is about raising awareness and enhancing interactive analysis – specifically about disputants' notions of and approaches to conflict – this process is very consistent with conflict resolution itself. In fact, in some ways Action Evaluation may be viewed as both an adjunct to, as well as a form of, conflict resolution and development practices.

While Action Evaluation is still relatively new, the methodology is evolving-in-use and its application is undergoing further research and development, the need for such an integrated evaluation methodology is clearly an idea – and practice – whose time has come. We look forward to widening the circle of those who are using and improving it.

References

Argyris, C., Putnam, R., & Smith, D. (1985). *Action science: Concepts, methods, and skills for research and intervention*. San Francisco: Jossey-Bass.

Ernst, C., & Chrobot-mason, D. (2011). *Boundary spanning leadership*. New York: McGraw-Hill.

Ross, M. (2001). Action evaluation in theory and practice. *Journal of Peace and Conflict Studies*. pp. 1–15.

Rothman, J. (1997). Action Evaluation and Conflict Resolution in Theory and Practice. *Mediation Quarterly, 15: 2*. Winter.

Rothman, J. (2003). Action evaluation in theory and practice. Beyond Intractability.org. http://www.beyondintractability.org/bi-essay/action-evaluation.

Rothman, J., & Friedman, V. (2002). Action evaluation for conflict management organizations and projects. In J. Davies & E. Kaufman (Eds.), *Second track/citizen's diplomacy: Concepts and techniques for conflict transformation* (pp. 285–298). New York: Rowan and Littlefield.

Rothman, J., & Friedman, V. (2001). Action evaluation for knowledge creation in social-education programs. In S. Sankaran, B. Dick, R. Passfield, & P. Swepson (Eds.), *Effective change management using action learning and action research* (pp. 57–65). Lismore: Southern Cross University Press.

Schon, D. (1983). *The reflective practitioner*. New York: Basic Books.

Verba, S. (1961). *Small groups and political behavior*. Princeton: Princeton University Press.

General Literature on Action Evaluation

Book Chapters

Eck, J., & Rothman, J. (2006). Police community conflict and crime prevention in Cincinnati, Ohio: The collaborative agreement. In J. Bailey (Ed.), *Public security and police reform in the Americas* (pp. 225–244). Pittsburgh: University of Pittsburgh Press.

Rothman, J. (1999). Articulating goals and monitoring progress in a Cyprus conflict resolution training workshop. In M. Ross & J. Rothman (Eds.), *Theory and practice in ethnic conflict management: Theorizing success and failure* (pp. 176–194). London: Macmillan Press.

Rothman, J. (1997). Action: Setting joint agendas. In J. Rothman (Ed.), *Resolving identity-based conflict in nations, organizations and communities* (pp. 71–84). San Francisco: Jossey-Bass.

Journal Articles

Friedman, V., Rothman, J., & Withers, B. (2006). The power of why: Engaging the goal paradox in program evaluation. *American Journal of Evaluation, 27*(2), 1–18.

Rothman, J., & Land, R. (2004). Cincinnati police-community relations collaborative. *Criminal Justice, 18*(4), 35–42.

Rothman, J. (2003). Improving police-community relations in Cincinnati: A collaborative approach. *AC Resolution, 3*(1), 25–27. Fall.

Rothman, J., & Soderquist, C. (2002). From riots to resolution: Engaging conflict for reconciliation. In *The systems thinker*. Pegasus Communications.

Rothman, J. (1997). Action-Evaluation and conflict resolution: In theory and practice. *Mediation Quarterly, 15*(2), 119–131.

Web-Based Publications

Hoffman, M. (2000). Peace and conflict impact assessment methodology: Evolving art form or practical dead end? Berghof research center for constructive conflict management, 2001-10-01. Available at: http://www.berghof-handbook.net/dialogue-series/no.-1-peace-and-conflict-impact-assessment.-critical-views-from-theory-and/.

Darling, I. (1998). Action evaluation and action theory: An assessment of the process and its connection to conflict resolution. Educating as inquiry, a teacher action research site. Available at: http://www.lupinworks.com/ar/Schon/Paper6.html.

Ross, M. H. (2001). Action evaluation in the theory and practice of conflict resolution. George Mason University: Network of Peace and Conflict Studies, 2001-05-01. Available at: http://www.gmu.edu/academic/pcs/Ross81PCS.htm.

Rothman, J. (2001). Action evaluation: A response to Mark Hoffman's comments. Berghoff research center for constructive conflict management. Available at: http://www.berghof-handbook.net/dialogue-series/no.-1-peace-and-conflict-impact-assessment.-critical-views-from-theory-and/.

For multimedia overview of AE methodology in that context see: www.socsci.uci.edu/~pgarb/istudies/applied/presentations/site/index.html.

For interactive summary of AE methodology in that context see: www.socsci.uci.edu/~pgarb/istudies/applied/presentations/site/presentation.html.

Fostering Cooperation While Engaging Conflict: An Inter-communal Case Study

8

Daniella Arieli, Victor J. Friedman,
and Evgeniya (Gina) Knyazev

In divided societies, there are natural "geographies of encounter" (Valentine 2008) in which members of conflicting groups, who normally inhabit separate communities and social spheres, meet and interact regularly over extended periods of time. A space of encounter, as we call it here, is a meeting across a particular divide, which itself is constructed. Natural spaces of encounter can take shape for almost any purpose and can be contrasted to "artificial spaces of encounter," such as intergroup dialogues. The latter are constructed specifically for the purpose of bringing members of different groups together in order to work on a particular conflict to which they are parties. They include intergroup dialogue, conflict resolution workshops, simulations, and the like. Artificial spaces of encounter often provide participants with extremely powerful experiences of relationship building, conflict resolution, and reconciliation – leading to changed attitudes and behavior on the individual level. However, they almost always confront the perplexing problem of lack of transfer of positive outcomes to the so-called "real world."

Natural spaces of encounter, therefore, offer opportunities for "engaging conflicts" within the everyday social frameworks in which groups meet and where they might have a more significant impact (Rothman and Friedman 2001). On the one hand, the relational dynamics of the wider society

may recapitulate themselves within these spaces, such that people experience discrimination, exclusion, polarization, and underlying tension that may erupt into open conflict and greater enmity and violence among groups. On the other hand, the opportunity to meet members of the other group may lead to the building of positive relationships that enhance their ability to live together and cooperate with each other in the shadow of the larger conflict. Positive meetings in natural spaces of encounter may even lead members of different groups to engage in efforts to make changes in social and power relations at the wider, societal level (McCall 2011).

The goal of this study is to inquire into how the ARIA model (Rothman 1997) and the Action Evaluation (AE) method (Arieli et al. 2010; Friedman and Rothman 2001; Rothman and Friedman 2002; Friedman et al. 2006, 2010) can be applied in a natural space of encounter to facilitate constructive conflict engagement. It is based on an intervention conducted with young Jewish and Palestinian Arab[1] students studying

---

[1] The population from which these students come – Arab citizens of Israel – should be distinguished from the Palestinian population living in the Occupied West Bank/ Judea, Samaria, and Gaza – who are not Israeli citizens. There are complex political implications for every term used to name this population of Arab citizens. They are usually referred to in Israel, including in the College, as "Arabs." This term – it can be argued – is a way of negating their national identity as Palestinians. On the other hand, some of our Arab students have told us that they do not consider themselves Palestinian. Therefore, henceforth in this chapter, we have chosen to use the term "Arabs" because it is the "emic" term, that is the term in use.

D. Arieli • V.J. Friedman • E.G. Knyazev
e-mail: daniella.arieli@gmail.com;
victorf@yvc.ac.il; 41knyazev@cardinalmail.cua.edu

J. Rothman (ed.), *From Identity-Based Conflict to Identity-Based Cooperation: The ARIA Approach in Theory and Practice*, Peace Psychology Book Series, DOI 10.1007/978-1-4614-3679-9_8,
© Springer Science+Business Media New York 2012

together in a nursing program at the Max Stern Jezreel Valley College, a public college in Northern Israel. The intervention took place in a natural space of encounter because it involved the entire cohort of first-year nursing students and took place within the context of their academic program rather than as a separate process. The authors of this paper, faculty members at the College, are action researchers who designed and carried out the intervention process and then conducted the process of reflection and inquiry that led to this chapter.

The paper will begin by describing the societal, institutional and organizational contexts of this natural space of encounter. It will describe how the nursing students constructed their particular space of encounter in a way that recapitulated the larger social space in which the College was imbedded. We will then present the story of the conflict that erupted, the intervention using Action Evaluation, and the follow-up. In the discussion section, we more deeply analyze our intervention strategy and the choices we made about implementing, or not implementing, ARIA and Action Evaluation. Finally, we attempt to take a critical look at the intervention and its outcomes relative to our aspirations for conflict engagement in a natural space of encounter. We will address both the intervention method (i.e. the use of ARIA and AE) as well as some of the issues we faced as self-appointed agents of social change within the context of a public institution of higher education.

Natural Spaces of Encounter in a Divided Society

The natural space of encounter that formed among the first-year nursing students at the College was embedded in, and heavily influenced by, a broad social context (the State of Israel as "divided society"), an institutional context (higher education), and an organizational context (the College). Israeli society can be characterized as divided into a national majority of Jewish immigrants and their descendents and a minority of Arabs who are citizens of the State of Israel. The division between Jewish and Arab citizens of Israel has maintained a particularly high intensity and salience due to the intense, protracted and violent conflict between Israelis, Arabs, and neighboring Arab states over competing claims for national self-determination within the same geographic region. Israeli Jews, who are mostly immigrants or the children of immigrants, see themselves as exercising their right of return to their ancient homeland (Zionism). Arab citizens of Israel are the remnants of a larger population that was forced out or fled in 1948 during what Jewish Israelis call their "War of Independence" or Arabs call their "Nakbah," or "disaster." As a divided society, Israel contains deep inter-group schisms than run through the social fabric, with each group having its distinct cultural, religious and political identities (Hargie et al. 2003). While there is considerable ethnic, religious, cultural and economic difference within both groups, Arab citizens of Israel experience inequality and structural discrimination relative to the Jewish majority.

Jewish and Arab citizens of Israel occupy largely separate physical and social spaces and most interactions tend to be temporary, short-term, and instrumental (e.g. giving and/or receiving services). Peaceful everyday relationships among Jewish and Arab citizens often obscure these deep divisions, but there is constant potential for violent conflict. In the wake of street-fighting between Jewish and Arab residents of the northern city of Acre in October 2008, Meir Benvenisti noted in the Israeli daily *Haaretz* on (October 15, 2008):

> The physical space is perceived as a battleground that must be won for 'our side' and defended from invasion by 'the other side.' The government system represents the interests of the ruling national community and discriminates against the minority. Nationalist considerations are used to justify budgetary discrimination, and a sectoral system of incentives oppresses minority communities, which develop feelings of anger that are also fed by the historical memory of national catastrophes and expressed in religious radicalism. External elements, from both sides, enlist to fan the macro-national conflict...The friction between a Jewish population, in which many are new immigrants

from distressed classes, and a population of Arab refugees, most of whom were forced to leave their homes in nearby villages, creates an easily realized potential for violence.

As this case illustrates, spaces of encounter are highly charged with underlying tensions and latent with suspicion and fear. At any moment, these tensions can break out into open hostility and even violence.

The above quotation could be applied to spaces of encounter in institutions of higher education in Israel. Academia is one of the few settings in which Jewish and Arab citizens meet for extended period of time under conditions of close physical proximity, shared activity, and common goals. However, relations between Jewish and Arab students, especially in the universities, have often followed the scenario of polarization and escalation. The Max Stern Jezreel Valley College, on the other hand, has had a history of relatively placid relations between the two groups. It is a public institution of higher education located in Israel's northern "periphery," a region in which 56% of the inhabitants, all Israeli citizens, are Arabs and 44% are Jewish. The student body is approximately 80% Jewish and 20% Arab, though the proportion of Jewish to Arab students varies in each department. There are departments with a majority of Jewish students, departments with a majority of Arab students, and departments, such as Nursing, within which the numbers are almost equal.

According to its English website, the College claims, or at least aspires to be a "model of Arab-Jewish cooperation" (http://www.yvc.ac.il/en/677.html). Indeed, aside from very small, limited incidents, there has been little open conflict between Jewish and Arab students. In fact, the College is highly *un*-politicized, as opposed to the Israeli universities, where student government is often organized along the lines of Israel's political parties.

The lack of open conflict at the College should not be mistaken for cooperation. Although Jewish and Arab students occupy the same physical space over an extended period of time, the social distance between them is large and difficult to traverse. There are clear separations reflected in

terms of who sits besides whom, who helps whom in course work, in the partnerships that form to carry out class projects, and in the social relations that develop during breaks or outside of the College (Arieli and Hirschfeld 2010). The relationship between Jewish and Arab students at the College can best be described by the Hebrew idiom "respect and suspect." Students maintain cordial and businesslike, but superficial, relations while at the same time avoiding discussion or interaction that could bring disagreement or conflict to the surface.

The College is a natural space of encounter, but it is by no means "neutral" in a cultural or political sense. The faculty and administrative staff are overwhelmingly Jewish. The atmosphere in the College reflects Israeli Jewish, and largely secular, culture. For example, all classes are conducted in Hebrew, almost all signs are in Hebrew and English (but not Arabic), and vacations days are scheduled according to Jewish holiday but not on Muslim or Christian holidays (though non-Jewish students are not required to attend class on their holidays). Social activities sponsored by the Student Association cater mainly to the tastes and cultural norms of the Jewish students, resulting in little participation by the Arab students. As with Israeli society in general, Arab students assume the status of a "minority" that must naturally adjust to the dominant, majority culture. There is a special advisor for Arab students, whose job is to provide counseling and workshops that help them with this adjustment.

For the most part, the conflict between Jews and Arabs is openly discussed only in the context of courses in which it is part of the curriculum or in voluntary workshops created specifically for Jewish-Arab dialogue – or what we designate as "artificial spaces of encounter." These workshops often, but not always, succeed in improving relationships among a limited number of students. However, they appear to have little, if any, impact on relationships among Jewish and Arab students in general at the College. As faculty members who speak frequently with both Jewish and Arab students about their relationships with each other, we believed that the College, as a natural space of encounter, offered high potential for transforming relationships. However, we also believed that a process of positive conflict engagement was unlikely to occur naturally and requires conscious intervention.

The Construction of a Natural Spaces of Encounter

A natural space of encounter is a kind of "social" space that is jointly, but usually unintentionally, constructed by individuals who come together and interact over time for some purpose. In this case, the formal boundaries of this social space were delineated by the College for the purpose of providing nursing training. The Department of Nursing at the College was established in 2007 to meet growing demand for nurses and nursing education in a region far from the Israeli universities. As part of an overall effort in Israel to academize nursing, the department aims at providing nurses with both professional training and a bachelors degree as part of their nursing education (Arieli et al. 2009). There is a high demand for nursing education in the northern periphery among both Arabs and Jews. The Jewish and Arab student groups reflect the diversity within their own communities. Both groups include a high percentage of students who are at the lower end of the socio-economic scale and experience social exclusion. Nursing offers vocational opportunities and a means of social mobility for these young people. The majority of student in the nursing program are women, though the number of men in the program is growing.

These formal boundaries to the social space included a specific group of people, delimited time (a certain number of hours together over a four-year period), shared physical spaces (classrooms), a common purpose (achieving an academic nursing degree), a common identity as first-year nursing students, and a set of shared activities-experiences (classes, practical training in the field). Within this formal boundary, a distinct and unique social space took shape as patterned interactions occurred among these individuals. Through these interactions, relationships formed and implicit, shared norms of behavior ("rules of the game") emerged, determining the character of this space.

The fact that this group developed as a natural space of encounter between Arabs and Jews was not a given. Rather, this characteristic of the social space was *constructed*, without conscious intent, out of the "materials" of the situation. By materials we are referring to the highly diverse aspects of identity that the students, as a whole, brought to the relationships that formed. It would be far too simplistic to characterize them simply as Arab and Jewish because there were numerous other differences which could potentially have become salient. For example, students differed in age, gender (women and men), marital status, race (white and black), mother tongue (Hebrew, Arab, Russian, Amharic), religion (Jewish, Muslim, Christian, Druze), birthplace (native born/immigrant), ethnicity/nationality (Jewish, Arab, Palestinian, Sephardic, Ashkenzi, Russian, Kafkazi, Ethiopian, Bedouin), home community (city, village, development town, kibbutz, moshav), and economic status. Nevertheless, the social space evolved such that "Jewish" and "Arab" became the main categories for positioning individuals in relation to each other, dividing them into two groups in dynamic inter-relationship. This division could be observed most explicitly in the seating arrangement, in which the Arab students sat on one side of the room and the Jewish students sat on the other. However, it was reflected in patterns of interaction and common perceptions within each group (Arieli et al. 2012).

In this case, the divide, and the rules of the game that governed relationships with the space, was a reproduction of a larger division in Israeli society between "Jewish" and "minorities" (e.g. Arab). Whether desired or not, students were naturally positioned within one of these groups, from which they encountered the other group across a divide. This division was perceived as something natural or, at least, as something that did not have to be openly discussed or challenged (Arieli and Hirschfeld 2010). The rules of the game called for politeness and cordiality but little, if any, intensive collaboration or open questioning of the status quo.

Action Evaluation and the Outbreak of Conflict

During the early stages of organizing the new nursing department, and before the first students were admitted, Miriam Hirschfeld, the Department chairperson, turned to the first two authors with a request to conduct on-going formative evaluation with the program faculty. The first stage of the research was intended to support the creation of the nursing program through "Action Evaluation" (Friedman et al. 2006). All members of the faculty were asked to respond to a standard action evaluation questionnaire: **What** are you definitions of success for the program? **Why** are they important to you (**Why** do you feel passionate about them?) **How** should we go about achieving those goals?). In-depth interviews were also carried out with selected faculty members from different disciplines. Subsequently, the faculty participated in a "why discussion" and received feedback on the data in the form of a "map" of the nursing program "theory of action." This process led to the formulation of a shared vision for the program as well as the identification of key tensions related to differences among faculty in regard to a number of issues in nursing education (Arieli et al. 2009).

The next stage of the Action Evaluation began in the middle of the first year of the program and involved in-depth interviews with 20 students in order to identify the issues of most importance to them. The key finding was that the relationship between Jewish and Arab students was a central issue of concern. The students described the class as divided into two separate "camps" with practically no social relationships between them. Students also reported a constant state of tension, even if it did not break out into open conflict. They described how students from the two groups seated themselves at opposites sides of the lecture hall, avoided social contact or intimacy during breaks or after class, limited cooperation in relation to their studies (e.g. sharing materials or studying together for tests), and experienced a general feel of suspicion towards the "other side." (Arieli and Hirschfeld 2010).

On the basis of the interview data, the evaluation team decided to distribute a survey questionnaire to all of the students in order to get a more comprehensive picture of the social relations among Jewish and Arab students. The "Social Relations Questionnaire" was developed and distributed during the second half of the second year of the program to all of the first- and second-year students. It included a variety of questions about the degree of social contact and intimacy among students from both groups, the degree of cooperation on academic tasks, and the expectations of students regarding the role of faculty in influencing inter-group relations.

The survey results (Arieli et al. 2010; Arieli et al. 2012) showed that 61% of the Arab students perceived relations between the two groups as unsuccessful and 80% of the Arab students perceived the inter-sectors social relations as a negative factor in terms of their academic success. 75% of the Arab students were also in favor of discussions about the Arab-Jewish conflict and about the relationship between Arab and Jewish students in the program. In addition, they wanted faculty to intervene more actively in shaping these relations. In fact, 73% of the Jewish students and 89% of the Arab students expressed the expectation that faculty would take an active role in providing opportunities for them to work in mixed study teams.

The survey, however, had a powerful unintended impact. It served as a catalyst for openly discussing tensions that had been brewing among the first-year students and were beginning to escalate into open conflict. This escalation began four months earlier with the "Gaza War" ("Operation Poured Lead") in January 2009. During the war, the conflict between Israel and the Arabs was highlighted in the media and became the topic of conversation among Israelis from every walk of life. It was a time of strong feelings and polarization. The vast majority of Israeli Jews strongly supported the military operation as a justified effort to end the missile fire from Gaza into Israel. The vast majority of Arabs identified with the people of Gaza, who they saw as innocent victims of Israeli violence. Tensions between Jewish and Arab students intensified and continued to escalate long after the military operation ended. The students' reaction to the questionnaire indicated that tensions were reaching a point where they could no longer be ignored.

Immediately after the class in which the students were asked to fill out the "Social Relations Questionnaire," there was a meeting of the weekly Interpersonal Communications Workshop, a routine part of the nursing curriculum. However, this time something out the ordinary happened: one of the Arab women students spoke openly for the first time about the deteriorating relations between Arab and Jewish students in the program and the very bad feelings she experienced as a member of the class. Immediately after the class, the workshop facilitator passed this information on to the department chairperson (Miriam), who then asked the Arab student to come speak with her. The student told Miriam that a number of Jewish students had placed a "boycott" on her – very demonstrably avoiding talking to or engaging in any interaction with her. If she addressed them, they ignored her and refused to answer. According to her, the boycott began during the war, when she suggested that the class cancel a holiday celebration in light of the suffering of the people of Gaza. Her suggestion was rejected by the Class Council and the head of the Council, along with some of his friends, began to relate to her with hostility.

In order to clarify the issue, the department chairperson called a meeting of the class and also met privately with some of the students along with the research team. Arab students reported they were suffering from the tension caused by the war, saying that "for us, it's the most difficult. We sit in class and don't speak at all. We try to keep things quiet." Jewish students reported that some of their Jewish friends put pressure on them to cut off relations with the Arab students. They said that "we are friends with everybody and some of the Jewish students take a negative attitude about that ... (and) say that we shouldn't hang around with Arabs." In the course of these meetings, both Arab and Jewish students asked that the faculty "do something" to improve the situation, which they felt was becoming unbearable.

Designing the Intervention: From ARIA to Action Evaluation

The students' suggestion was heard as a call for action on the part of the evaluation team and we felt strongly that we should intervene. Furthermore, the team accepted the students' suggestion of using the "Introduction to Anthropology" course as a forum for addressing the multi-cultural encounter taking place in class and generating a dialogue that might bring the students together. At the same time, we felt that the issue was a potential powder keg and that any action would have to be weighed very carefully. Furthermore, the academic year was only a few weeks away and we would have to act quickly if we wanted to do something while there was still time.

We (Daniella and Victor) made a round of consultations in order to improve our own understanding of the situation and what might be done. We spoke with key faculty members in the Department of Nursing. As luck would have it, prior to these events, we had planned an open meeting with faculty to talk about organizing a "learning community" to look into the issue of Arab-Jewish relations on campus. The meeting was scheduled to take place just as these events with the nursing students were unfolding, so we were able to consult with about 20 faculty members who attended this meeting. In addition, we held an in-depth telephone conversation with a few experts in conflict and intergroup dialogue in the U.S. and Israel. Finally, we met with senior nurses – from the hospital where our students carry out their practical training – who were very involved with the program.

On the basis of these consultations, we began to formulate a plan for intervention based on the ARIA model. In the first stage, we would encourage both sides to separately give voice to the "antagonism" (A) by making their narratives explicit and specifying how they saw the other side and its behavior towards them. At the same time, we would encourage both sides to consider how they themselves were perceived by the other sides. In the second stage we would attempt to effect a transition from antagonism to "resonance"

(R) in which the participants would jointly inquire into the deeper needs that were threatened by the conflict. Furthermore, we intended to carry on the resonance process using art as a media for communication in the Studio for Social Creativity (to be described later). The resonance stage would be followed up by "invention" (I) in which the participants would think together of ways of ensuring that their needs were met in light of the on-going conflict. And finally in the "action" (A) stage the students would translate these inventions into concrete actions.

The majority of people who we consulted about this plan were supportive of it, but others urged us **not** to intervene in this way. These people argued that the right thing to do was simply let matters calm down and allow the daily routine to put relations back in order. They agreed that there were deep tensions, but recommended *leaving these tensions covered up* rather than surfacing them and openly engaging them. They felt that bringing these tensions to the surface would only make matters worse. Members of the staff of the local teaching hospital warned us that any attempt to directly intervene could have a negative effect on our students, seriously upset the system, and lead to "irreparable damage." Some of the Arabs with whom we consulted expressed skepticism about change that does not aim at the institutional level, i.e. the College or the Israeli academic system. They indicated that anything less would be insignificant.

These very stern warnings made us acutely aware of the magnitude of the risk we were taking. Surfacing the narratives and the trauma on both sides might generate an overwhelming wave of negative feelings that would be too powerful to contain, especially given the limited amount of time and resources at our disposal. The thought of creating "irreparable damage" was very sobering. We felt an enormous responsibility. If things went wrong, it might have major negative implications for the students and for ourselves.

Despite these risks, we were not willing to simply to walk away from the conflict. We had little time to think things through about this dilemma, but a way forward presented itself when we re-examined the situation from the students' perspective. The clear message from them was for help in improving the atmosphere in class. Some may have been asking for a deeper Arab-Jewish dialogue, but most of them simply wanted a way of making the current reality more bearable. It seemed to us that we could reduce the risk if we used that desire as the starting point and frame the intervention as "improving the atmosphere in class" rather than engaging the conflict itself. This reframing almost immediately led us to realize that an "action evaluation" (AE) would be an ideal method for carrying out the intervention. Rather than focus on the conflict itself, we would *create a future orientation* and focus the students on what kind of reality they wanted to create together. Such an approach would help us both meet their expressed need and, perhaps, enable us to avoid the worst case scenario. The goal of the intervention was not to restore relations to the "status quo ante" but rather to make those relations discussable so as to create a new and more satisfying situation for both sides. We wanted to create conditions under which the students could both live together and talk openly about the conflict so as to stimulate a process of change.

Implementing the Intervention Design

In order to put this idea into practice we envisioned a four-step process that would be carried out as part of the Introduction to Anthropology course, using six academic hours over a two-week period. The first step was to attempt to "unfreeze" the current situation and make it discussable. "Unfreezing," (Friedman and Lipshitz 1992; Lewin 1951; Schein 1969) is a term used to describe a process of psychologically opening up people and systems to change. In order to provide an unfreezing mechanism for the students, we invited Nazir Majalli, an Arab journalist and peace activist, to give a lecture about relations between Arabs and Jews in Israel. On the basis of previous experience, we knew that Mr. Majalli could speak to Jewish and Arabs students with a wide variety of political views in a way that opened them up to listening and thinking differently.

In his talk, Nazir spoke about the conflict from a personal perspective that displayed an ability to identify with and empathize with fears and deep feelings on both sides. He used the imagery of "walking in the furrow" (the deep cut in the earth made by a plow) to describe the way in which people tend to have a very narrow and limited view and which keeps them hemmed in by walls of hostility. He strongly urged the students to "lift their heads out of the furrow" and look around them. He provided interesting facts that challenged stereotypes and preconceived notions about both sides, clearly illustrating the futility of the conflict as well as the advantages of reconciliation and peace for both sides.

Both Jewish and Arab students reacted positively to Nazir's lecture, which was significant because some of the Jewish students had demanded that we invite someone from the "other side" as well. In the discussion that followed, both Jewish and Arab students expressed many deep feelings. For example, one of the students asked Nazir "if the Arabs were in control, what would you do to the Jews?" adding that "your leaders shot missiles into our cities, which harmed me directly; your leaders are extremists!" The Arab students listened with great interest to the fears expressed by the Jewish students and one of them said, with some empathy that "we all have old prejudices that we all have to change." Both Jewish and Arab students voiced the conviction that, as nurses, they would have to care for different populations and would have to bridge gaps between them in times of crisis that are difficult for everyone.

Immediately after the lecture, we handed out the "Good Atmosphere Questionnaire," based on the standard Action Evaluation questionnaire. It contained the following three questions:

1. *What* is your definition of a good atmosphere in class?
2. *Why* is a good atmosphere in class important to you? Why do you feel passionately about it?
3. *How* would you go about creating a good atmosphere in class?

The students were asked to respond, on the spot, to these questions in writing (either Hebrew or Arabic). After they handed in their questionnaire and took a short break, we divided them into two groups of Jewish students with Jewish facilitators and two groups of Arab students with Arab facilitators. Each group numbered about 15 students. The task of each group was to discuss the question "Why is a good atmosphere important *to you*?" This question was intended to surface the personal feelings and needs that motivated students to desire change. The reason for separate Jewish and Arab groups was to create conditions in which the students felt most comfortable speaking freely and would be able express themselves in their own language.[2]

We asked permission from the students to record the discussion. In two of the groups, the discussion was recorded on a digital tape recorder. In the two other groups it was recorded by hand. A number of themes emerged from these discussions. The theme that was voiced again and again was that the students had no choice but to find a way of living together – not only in the four years of their education together but also in their future work together as nurses. Others said that a good atmosphere in class was important to them because it would contribute to their academic success, improve their grades and other achievements. As one of the Jewish students put it:

> A good atmosphere in class can help us succeed in our studies because when there is a good atmosphere we can help each other with important things. What's more, if we don't know now how to help people who are less comfortable for us to deal with, then we won't be able to do so at work.

There was general consensus among the students in all four groups that it was worth making an effort to generate a good atmosphere in class because it would have important instrumental value.

In one of the Jewish groups, there was a stormy discussion about whether there was a problem at all. For example, one student argued that there was no real problem and that "the problem was created the moment people started talking about it." Another student said that "the class is only about learning and I don't expect that an Arab student will invite me home for dinner," adding

---

[2] Not everyone was able to speak in her or his mother tongue, since Hebrew is a second language for Jewish immigrant students.

that "I guess that are some naïve people in class who want to change the world." Other students described the relationship between the two groups in class as "awful" and that it should not be "swept under the carpet." The bad feelings were expressed in the words of one student who said:

> As far as the Arab students are concerned, I personally feel very threatened and frightened. If (an Arab) student says something I find hurtful, I am afraid to answer him...I can say with almost full assurance that the Arab students don't have that same problem. That's why they...have the confidence to say things I would never dare say."

Some Jewish students pointed out that the interpersonal tensions in class are not necessarily between Jews and Arabs but among the Jews themselves:

> The unpleasant atmosphere is not between Arabs and Jews but between Jews and Jews. I had a run-in with one of the Arab students but my relationships with the other Arab students are just fine. The problem is with the Jews in the class.

This student was referring to the pressure placed by some of the Jewish students on other Jewish students not to develop relations with Arab students.

In the Arab groups there were very few disagreements in the "why" discussion. The general consensus was that it is important to do something to improve the atmosphere in class. The majority of the Arab students said that this goal was important because it impacts their academic success and because creating good relations with the Jews is important in the nursing profession. As one student put it:

> we are in a multi-cultural nation and in our field, we will deal with all cultures. In our field you have to understand and be sensitive to everyone. You can't say 'I don't want to treat the Jews'...we will have to work with Jews in the same departments.

In addition to pragmatic and professional reasons, many of the students said that a good atmosphere is important for them in order to have a pleasant student experience. A few of the students described the pain they feel when relations deteriorated:

> One day I walked into class and said "Good Morning!" and no one answered. That really hurt and set me back.

Among the Arab students, there was no one who claimed that there is no problem or that it is preferable not to discuss the issue.

After the "why" discussions, which lasted just under 90 min, all of the students reassembled in the classroom and we collected all of their completed questionnaires. In order to get a sense of whether we were moving in the right direction (or, perhaps, making things worse), we asked the students how they felt about the process so far and whether they wanted to continue. We wanted to create a situation in which the students felt they had a choice about participating, even if that choice was limited because the intervention was taking place within the framework of a required course. We were prepared to rethink or even stop the intervention if the responses were negative, but all those who spoke up said positive things about the process and expressed a desire to continue. We offered anyone who felt uncomfortable expressing doubts or speaking out publicly to tell us privately. At that point, the class ended and the students were told that we would continue the process the next week.

Right after this first session, we analyzed the questionnaires, especially the first question (What is your definition of a good atmosphere?) and the third question (How should we go about creating this atmosphere?). The answers to both questions were quite similar, so we analyzed them together and grouped all of the students' responses with similar content into single categories. As a result, we came up with the following seven main categories or themes for a good atmosphere in class:

1. Interaction and cooperation among all members of the class.
2. Social activities and creating a sense of togetherness.
3. Creating a separation between the relationships among us and the tensions in our surrounding environment.
4. All students help each other out with their studies.
5. Establishing norms of listening, mutual respect, and politeness.
6. Caring and friendship among all members of the class.
7. Really getting to know each other: to talk, to listen – even to things that are difficult.

Fig. 8.1 The studio for social creativity

Our intention was to present these findings to the students at the next session so that each student could compare his or her vision of a good atmosphere in class with those of others. Furthermore, we intended to use these themes as the basis for proposing specific changes in the students' behavior.

The Studio for Social Creativity

Our intention was to hold the follow-up session in the "Studio for Social Creativity" (see Fig. 8.1), a large fine arts studio in the College where people meet to work on needs, problems, and visions for social change (Friedman and Desivilya 2010). The Studio is an experimental project founded upon the idea that artistic practices can play a useful role in helping people analyze issues, develop new perspectives, engage conflicts, and come up with ideas for social innovation. In recent years, there has been a proliferation of artistic interventions in organizational and community development (e.g. Hjorth 2004; McNiff 2003; Moskin and Jackson 2004). Our belief was that the Studio and the artistic dimension would provide a setting conducive to dialogue, bringing to bear thinking, feeling, and a variety of the senses in the process of creating change in ways that could circumvent highly-charged patterns of discourse.

At that point, it was not yet clear how we would actually go about doing this in the 90-minute Studio session. There were a number of reasons for this open-endedness. First, we did not really know what would happen in the first phase. We needed the information from that phase as well as the students' cooperation before proceeding to the next stage. Second, although the intervention was inspired by Action Evaluation, it was not an "off the shelf" product, but rather a creative process planned under intense time pressure.

In order to design the follow-up, we brought together a team consisting of the first two authors, a woman action researcher from Germany, a Jewish woman painter, two Arab women students from a practicum on social entrepreneurship, one Jewish woman student from the same practicum, and an Arab graduate assistant in the practicum, and an American male drama student who participated in "red nose."[3] This team met in the Studio a few days after the first session and devised a plan for the follow-up.[4]

[3]The "red nose" is one of the most fundamental masks used by actors. In the popular mind, it is often associated with clowning, but the power of the red nose is its ability to enable the mask wearer to see things from a novel perspective and to help others do the same.

[4]This design session was a creative process of interest in itself. However, it goes beyond the scope of this chapter.

Fig. 8.2 The themes

None of the students had ever been in the Studio, which was completely different from their normal classrooms. When the students entered the room, they came into a large open rectangular space with no tables or chairs. On the back wall, there were seven large pieces of flip chart paper, each with one of the themes in Hebrew and Arabic (See Fig. 8.2). Under each theme, there were smaller sheets of paper with the full data (i.e. the theme and all of the responses that were grouped under that them). At the front of the room was a small platform with a wide variety of materials for artwork (e.g. paper, pastels, finger paints, modeling clay). The members of the action research team were waiting for the students in the Studio along with the chair of the department of nursing, who participated as well. The students' anthropology instructor, was the main facilitator. Most of the students were taken aback for a moment when they first entered the Studio. They then began to wander around the space and look at what was posted on the walls. Those who asked what they should do were instructed to read the themes and the data upon which they were based.

After everyone arrived and had a few minutes to explore, the students were asked to sit on the floor in a semi-circle opposite the wall with the themes. The Jewish students grouped themselves at one end of the semi-circle and the Arab students grouped themselves at the other end – as if an invisible line had been drawn between them. The instructor stood opposite them and explained that the themes on the wall were the analysis of the questionnaires to which they had responded a week before. The themes reflected the students' collective vision of a good atmosphere in class. The goal of the session was to give creative expression to these themes and to come up with ideas for putting them into practice.

In our design process, the research-facilitation team came to the conclusion that we did not have time for all of the students to discuss all of the themes and to come to consensus on which ones to adopt, as is normally done in the AE process. Instead, we asked the students to organize themselves into groups of about six, that would include an equal number of Jewish and Arab students, and discuss the themes that were listed and then choose the theme that was most meaningful to them as a group. They should then jointly produce a creative expression of that theme using the art materials, and specify at least one "action item" for putting the theme into actual practice.

For the most part, the students were able to do this and, with a little help from the research-facilitation team, everyone was soon organized and situated on the floor at different locations throughout the studio. As soon as the research-facilitation team began to distribute the art materials, the students enthusiastically went to work – dipping their fingers into the paints, choosing pastels,

Fig. 8.3 Creating

Fig. 8.4 Presenting

playing with the clay, and applying them to the big sheets of paper. The students soon became deeply engaged in the creative activity, talking together and laughing all the time (see Fig. 8.3). Some groups used up the paper they had been allocated and asked for more. The entire time allocated for the creative work was filled with active participation, a sense of play, and a palpable joy of creation. At first the research-facilitation team wandered among the groups, provided additional materials, and interacted with the students. At one point, the team took a sheet of paper and materials and began to draw for itself.

After about 30 minutes, we hung the students' creations on the wall underneath or beside the themes to which they referred. We then asked the students to form a semi-circle opposite the wall. This time they no longer seated themselves automatically in Arab and Jewish groups, but stayed in close proximity to the groups with which they had worked. Each group was asked, one-by-one, to stand together in front of the class beside its chosen theme, to present its creative work, and to explain its meaning to the other students (See Fig. 8.4).

The creative works contained optimistic messages in different languages: Hebrew, Arabic,

English and Russian that expressed messages of peace, hope, fraternity, conciliation, and bridging gaps caused by the conflict and by cultural differences. The pictures contained images such as joined hands in different colors with the word "peace" written in the hand in different languages, a dove with an olive branch in its beak, and a picture of a house, symbolizing the College, at the meeting point of paths coming from different directions (see Fig. 8.4). These symbols all reflected both difference and the place where these differences come together into a single group. The works also contained text such as "the success of one is the success of us all."

At the end of its presentation each group was given an enthusiastic round of applause from the other members of the class. The students posed for pictures taken by other members of the class with their cell phones. By this time, the session had taken on the spirit of a festive event. One group of students suddenly broke out in a birthday song for one of its members. When the members of the research-facilitation team presented their work, it too was received with a round of applause.

When the presentations were finished, one of the students stood up, introduced herself as a member of the Class Council, and thanked the researcher-facilitation team in the name of the students saying "we asked you to intervene and to do something, but we didn't believe that it would happen so fast. It was really wonderful!!" She then added that she hoped that "from now on the students will be able to talk directly with one another about what bothers them." The research-facilitation team concluded the meeting by thanking the students for their cooperation and for the trust they put in us. We also suggested that, during the summer break, they continue to think about ways of continuing to build the positive atmosphere so that they could take concrete action in the coming year.

The students' positive experience was a source of great satisfaction for the research-facilitation team. We were very glad that we had dared to carry out the intervention despite the warnings and the concerns we felt beforehand. We were also happy that we had demonstrated that it was possible to deal with the conflict without exacerbating the division between the sides and in a way that motivated the parties involved to work on the relations between them. Finally, we were happy that the students came away from this experience with a good feeling and we thought it would be right to continue working with this class during the next year.

Following-Up on the Intervention

The second-year nursing curriculum is so overloaded with courses and other activities that there was no room for a formal course or short-term events aimed at building upon the process begun at the end of the first year. Nevertheless, we were able to hold two extra-curricular follow-up meetings with the students in the Studio. Twenty-five of the fifty students attended the first meeting in November 2009 (the semester in Israel begins at the end of October). The goal of the meeting was to pick up the process where it left off the year before and to encourage the students to initiate, individually or as teams, activities that would contribute to realizing the "good atmosphere" as articulated in the various themes. We put up the themes and posters from the previous meeting in order to reconnect with the positive experience and as a reminder of the ideas and action items that were suggested. We sat on the floor facing the posters and the Department Chair asked them about their expectations regarding the coming year(s), what they would like to happen, and what they are willing to actually do.

At the very beginning of the discussion a student who introduced himself as the "Sakhnin Team" (Sakhnin is the name of a large local Arab village), said that he had decided to create an initiative to help and support students in the class who have difficulty with statistics. He explained that statistics are easy for him and one of his friends and that they would like to help others for whom it is more difficult. Then one of the Jewish students asked the Department Chair if it is possible to find a room for the students in which they could meet and work together in small groups. Another suggestion that came up almost at once from one of the Jewish students was a request for Arabic lessons, saying that "I don't know Arabic and also have a problem in communication and understanding customs." An Arab student responded by saying that she would set up a website for the class in which they can learn Arabic words that are important for the nursing profession. Another student proposed celebrating holidays together, which led to many positive responses but also the question of which holidays they would chose and exactly how they would celebrate.

At this point in the discussion, the researcher-facilitators also tried to open up room not just for discussing practical suggestions but also for expressing thoughts and feelings about the Arab-Jewish conflict and its impact on the everyday relationships among the students. The Department Chair stressed that times of crisis can present a special challenge to relations and asked the students whether they have "the ability to maintain relations and their studies at times of distress." One of the Arab students said that "it is difficult to put aside things we see on television." Another claimed that "if there will be another (crisis), it will be just the same as last year" but this same student said that "if we sat together more often things would change." The majority of responses, however, were positive. A number said that they felt that there were significant improvements in the atmosphere in class as a result of the intervention the year before. At that point the discussion took a more personal turn. One of the female Jewish students told how, when she goes home and tells her family that she has Arab friends, they "look at me and tell me that I have changed – as if it's not appropriate." The Arab students who initiated the idea of giving help in statistics said that at first he invited students to his home in Saknin, but they were so reluctant because they were afraid that stones would be thrown at them. He said that this really disturbed him and that they should talk about it. One of the Jewish students said the problem is a lack of dialogue, saying that "there is no dialogue among us and, given the nature of the conflict, things sooner or later explode and then how much can we take or try to understand each other?" A number of students, both Arab and Jewish, spoke about how impor-

tant it is to talk, but that it takes courage and trust to "feel safe and not afraid to say what you feel."

At the end of the meeting, we thanked the students and told them that we think they are really pioneers. Our facilitation team felt that it was highly likely that what they experienced in their class reflects the relationships that take shape in other classes. On the one hand, we felt that the intervention from the year before had born fruit and that the students who participated in the discussion really did care and genuinely wanted to generate change. Nevertheless, we feared that, if there were not some kind of ongoing and structured activity as an integral part of their program, many of the students would not be motivated enough to find the time deal with such a difficult and complex issue. Given the enormous pressure of their academic framework, it is hard for them to find the time and emotional resources for anything else.

Our fears were, in fact, well-founded since even fewer students participated in the next meeting we organized, which was held in January, towards the end of the semester.. This meeting was planned as a workshop in which the students would participate in a role play exercise that would enable them to experience and analyze the processes a group undergoes when in conflict as well as the possible action strategies people can take. We had hoped that about half the class would participate again this time, but only nine students showed up. As a result, we changed plans and devoted the meeting to a discussion about the motivation of the students to participate in activities dealing with the conflict – and what might increase their motivation.

From the discussion it became clear that at least part of the low participation in the meeting could be contributed to the fact that, on this particular day, many classes were cancelled so students went home early. At the same time, the students said that there are people who "don't believe in co-existence and don't connect to these kinds of activities." They added that, if these activities were made compulsory, it would just create more antagonism. On the other hand, the students reported that some of the ideas that were raised in the previous meeting were actually put into practice. A practical Arabic dictionary was put up on a website, a number of holiday parties were held for Jewish, Muslim and Christian students together. The special help in statistics started but did not continue. The students noted that "we did only about 10% of what we wanted to do," but also that the atmosphere in class is "a lot better than it was the year before." When we asked for examples they said, for instance, that now the seating in class is always mixed with no split between the Arab and Jewish students. Another area in which there was considerable improvement was cooperation and mutual help in their studies. As one Jewish student put it, "we help whoever needs help…the barriers have gone down…last year only Jewish students turned to me, this year Arab students ask me for help as well." Another Jewish student said "last year there were a lot of people whom I didn't really know and suddenly I found myself friends with a whole lot of new people from the other group."

Overall the students who participated communicated a positive message, as illustrated by an Arab woman who said:

> I personally came because I think that the meetings we did last year greatly contributed to the atmosphere in our class. I am not saying that it improved things 100% or 90% but at least it passed the 50% mark. For me that's excellent relative to what was before.

Another Arab student added that "last year we didn't even say 'Good morning!' to each other and this year that's changed. I hope it continues." The students pointed out that one of the significant things that made a difference was that this year they are working in mixed teams in their clinical studies and in simulations. They described the situation of working together in the context of their nursing training as what really pushed them to get to know each other and to communicate: "we're together in simulations, we have to talk, to help each other, it really contributes." A few of the students commented that the faculty should try to get the students to work in mixed groups and teams whenever possible. They explained that if students are allowed to organize themselves, they tend to group with people they know, but when "forced" to work with mixed groups it really helps them get to know others and to

engage in dialogue because "there is no choice but to talk with each other."

One of the central questions that came up in the meeting was the question of the voluntary or "coerced" participation in such activities. The students were divided on this issue with Jews and Arabs on both sides. One side held that pressure or requirements that came from the faculty was a good thing. A few said that they probably would not have participated in the meeting in the Studio last year if it had not been required and if they thought attendance would not be taken. Nevertheless, they felt that it gave them a lot and they were very pleased with their participation.

The opposite argument was that under no circumstances should students be required or pressured into dealing with the conflict because such pressure would not help. Rather, it would most likely "strengthen the antagonism" and deepen the reluctance to deal with these issues. Some of the students argued that the issue of conflict should be addressed in the framework of required courses, such as those in the social sciences, since it's a critical issue for their training. Others strongly rejected this idea, arguing that the issue of the conflict should be dealt with as a special course only for those students who expressed an interest and that no student should be forced to participate. This meeting marked the end of the formal intervention at least until this date, which is approximately two years later.

Discussion

The foregoing case study describes an intervention process intended to deal with conflict in a natural space of encounter – that is, a class of nursing students from different groups. Reflecting back on the process reveals the following themes for further analysis: framing the intervention, the right to intervene, circumventing antagonism, unfreezing, customizing Action Evaluation, "transferability" of interventions in natural spaces of encounter, preserving the space while changing it, and intervening in a natural space of encounter.

Framing the intervention. The department chairperson was clearly determined to do something about the situation that had arisen. She was deeply concerned about the emerging tension between Jewish and Arab students and was not willing to tolerate a "boycott" of a student for her perceived political views or any similar behavior. Her initial intention was simply to go into the class and state unequivocally that such behavior was unacceptable and that the students would have to learn how to cooperate and treat each other with mutual respect even if they did not agree or like each other. The idea of "laying down the law" reflected an implicit framing of the problem in disciplinary or moral terms. According to this framing, the situation could have been dealt with at the individual level, identifying and disciplining students whose behavior broke rules of the College or violated generally acceptable codes of conduct.

When the department chairperson asked for our advice on how to deal with this situation, we immediately rejected acting upon this moral or disciplinary framing. Our assumption was that the problem should not be regarded as something personal but rather a reflection of the larger social conflict. In this sense, we imposed a particular political framing onto the situation and this framing had significant implications. We reasoned that personal disciplinary framing would fail to capture the reality. Furthermore, it would most likely be ineffective, if not counterproductive, because using authority and moral reasoning would, at best, only force students to cover up their true feelings. It might push the conflict back under the surface, but then tensions would only increase, making relations between Jewish and Arab students only more difficult and creating conditions for an even more intense outbreak at some later date. On the other hand, we suggested that framing the problem as an *opportunity to engage the underlying conflicts* would make them discussable and potentially create a significant change in the dynamics between the two groups.

Conflict engagement is fundamentally a relationship-building process that enables adversaries to gain a mutual understanding of the structural dynamics of discord, while at the same time facilitating on-going cooperation among them (Rothman 1997; Tjosvold 2006). It draws from an application of the constructivist version of critical theory to inter-group conflict (Foucault 1994; Freire 1997; Hansen 2008) and the identity framing of inter-group relations (Rothman 1997). Critical theory calls for 'problem-posing' processes leading to a 'critical consciousness' of how social ideologies are imposed upon groups by elites and how changes can be made to advance the interests of those oppressed groups. The constructivist version of critical theory addresses how these ideologies become expressed at the individual group and community levels through stereotyping, de-legitimization, ethnocentrism, groupthink, and polarization.

The identity framing of inter-group relations views inter-group conflict as rooted in threats to people's individual and collective purposes, sense of meaning, definitions of self, and fundamental human needs, such as dignity, recognition, safety, control, purpose, and efficacy (Rothman 1997). When parties are at an impasse, identity framing advocates inquiry aimed at exploring why each part holds so tenaciously and passionately on to its position (Rothman 1997). It usually involves articulating individual and group narratives, first within a group and then between conflicting groups. The importance of this process lies in the fact that people's sense of self is often forged in opposition to others. Conflict engagement acknowledges that I am who I am, in part, because of who you are – and vice versa. Most importantly, it creates conditions under which people can jointly and explicitly define the relationship they want even when they cannot solve the overall conflict (Rothman 1997).

The right to intervene. The Department Chair accepted the conflict engagement framing and authorized us to design an intervention accordingly. At the time, we devoted almost no time to openly addressing the question of *whether* to intervene at all and *why* we chose a conflict engagement framing. Once the problem became visible, it seemed obvious that something had to be done. The legitimacy of approaching the situation as an individual, moral or disciplinary problem would hardly have been controversial.

However, the conflict engagement framing, which aimed at changing relationships and dynamics within the class as a whole, clearly stepped beyond the routine, accepted boundaries of our roles as college teachers. Furthermore, intervening within the framework of a required course meant that all the students would have to participate even though none of them enrolled in the nursing program for the purpose of conflict engagement. What, if anything, gave the Nursing Department, and us, the right to impose such a process upon them?

The first two authors and the department chair all shared a personal concern for finding some way to foster open, healthy relations between Israeli Jews and Arabs as members of the same society living in the shadow of an on-going conflict. These concerns were rooted in deeply-held values about people being heard and accepted for who they are, regardless of their views or political orientations. These concerns were also "political" in the sense that they reflected our belief in the importance of pluralism and tolerance as foundations of a democratic society and that Arabs and Jews can find ways of living together. At the same, our perception was that Israeli society is moving in exactly the opposite direction. Thus, we considered it our moral *obligation* to put these beliefs into practice in our workplace, where we might be able to have an impact.

We were committed to fostering a particular kind of relationship that some of the students might have found undesirable or even objectionable. At the same time we were using administrative authority and our power as faculty members over the students to forward this goal. Both Miriam, as the Department Chair, and Daniella, as the students' instructor, held clear and direct positions of power over the students with the ability to reward or punish them. It was not our intention to coerce the students, but as Jewish faculty members we were acting from a position of power and authority that must be acknowledged. Academic administration and faculty have a legitimate right to impose things upon students, but there is a valid question of whether the intervention we were proposing went beyond the accepted academic norms. Finally, we knew we had to be very reflective about our motivations

and constantly examine how our decision to intervene was influenced by our professional agenda, which not only included our intentions to promote social change and generate knowledge but also our desire to publish papers, like this one, which would disseminate this knowledge and contribute to our careers.

One main justification for the intervention was that the students asked the faculty for their help. In meetings with Miriam, both Arab and Jewish students requested that the Department "do something" to improve the atmosphere, though this "something" was never clearly specified. Some members of the class were experiencing significant pain as a result of the situation that had emerged. In addition, the data from our evaluation research indicated that this pain was shared by a majority of the Arab students even if they were not comfortable expressing it openly (Arieli et al. 2012). The existence of pain and dissatisfaction does not necessarily translate into a call for intervention. Furthermore, it cannot be established that those calling for intervention represented a consensus or even a majority of class members. It is possible that the situation would have eventually stabilized and that the students would have found a way of managing together without outside intervention. Nevertheless, we seized upon the fact that some of the students asked for help as sufficient justification for carrying out a conflict engagement intervention with the class as a whole.

A second justification was that the nursing department's vision included a statement which related to the importance of relationships between all members of the department. The intervention was justified on the instrumental grounds that nursing students must learn to work together and to treat all patients with equal care and respect regardless of their identities, political views, or even actions. As the Department Chair put it, "learning to relate to each other in this way is at least as important for nursing students as learning chemistry." This justification was consistent with the stated commitment of the Jezreel Valley College to being a "model of Arab-Jewish cooperation." In other words, we were not simply acting out of personal commitments, but also on behalf of an explicitly stated organizational aspiration or value. Even though the students did not enroll in the program for the purpose of participating in Jewish-Arab dialogue, they chose an institution which has stated that such activities are part of its mandate.

Perhaps the final justification is that **not** intervening would have been implicitly accepting the status quo and might have had consequences as well. We were not outsider interventionists but rather an integral part of the natural space of encounter as faculty members. Every action – or inaction – we took was in some way either strengthening or challenging the status quo. As action evaluators of the nursing program, we already had formal roles as agents of learning and change.

Circumventing antagonism. A key feature of this case is a shift we made in our planned intervention process from one based on the "ARIA" model of conflict engagement to a visioning process based on "Action Evaluation." Initially, the ARIA model (Rothman 1997) was the guiding concept in putting conflict engagement into practice because we were dealing with the issue of identity. The issue of competition over scare resources was hardly evident, at least within the context of the academic program. Nor was there an observable goal conflict among the Jewish and the Arab students. Clearly, the roots of the conflict lay in the construction of two conflicting identities as a key feature of the natural space of encounter. These identities could co-exist as long as each side suppressed those parts of its worldview and needs that the other side found threatening. The outbreak of the Gaza War, however, made expressions of identity by one side unbearable for the other. The physical division of the class into two groups became laden with political meaning making interaction and communication across the boundary extremely difficult.

Given this diagnosis, we believed that the way to engage the conflict was to make these identity conflicts discussable. We envisioned using ARIA to enable both sides to first articulate the Antagonism they experienced and then work towards the development of analytical empathy

and Resonance. Assuming that Resonance occurred, the next step would be Inventing ways of living and working together that would ensure that these needs would be met and then to see that these steps were implemented.

The riskiest, most difficult, and least predictable, part of this strategy was the transition from Antagonism to Resonance. If the Antagonism stage got stuck in the narratives and accusations about past injustices and grievances, we risked placing the students even deeper into the impasse they were currently experiencing. When we stepped back and reconsidered our strategy, we also had to admit to ourselves that none of the students had asked us for this kind of process. Rather they had explicitly asked for our help in doing something to "improve the atmosphere in class."

Given this perspective, it seemed to make the most sense to frame the intervention in *the terms used by the students themselves*, i.e. "improving the atmosphere in class," and to try to give them what they were asking for rather than imposing our framing on them. Framing the intervention in this way meant moving away from a past orientation (i.e. competing narratives) to a future orientation. Furthermore, by focusing on the atmosphere "in class," we were shifting the focus from the wider conflict and from the need to change attitudes and beliefs to a more immediate, realistic and practical goal. Such a framing could include students whose views spanned almost the entire political spectrum, even those who believe that the larger conflict cannot, or even should not, be resolved.

This reframing was very helpful to us. It immediately let us recognize an alternative intervention strategy based on Action Evaluation (AE) rather than ARIA. Action Evaluation (AE) is a method for integrating systematic inquiry into the process of goal setting for social-educational programs and organizations (Friedman and Rothman 2001; Friedman et al. 2006 Rothman 1997, and Chap. 7 in this book). Action Evaluation frames the problem of goal setting involving multiple stakeholders as a process of constructing a shared identity that takes into account people's deepest needs, values, purposes, and definitions of self (Burton 1990). AE is based on the normative position that worthy goals should be clear and understood, freely chosen, and passionately held (Argyris et al. 1985; Friedman et al. 2006). Giving public expression to their deep motivations and the stories that explain them helps people understand and appreciate their own goals as well as those of others, paving the way for productively engaging differences in goal setting (Friedman et al. 2006).

Unfreezing. The revised intervention, as described in the case study, did not begin with the AE questionnaire, but rather with the talk given by the Palestinian journalist Nazir Majalli. The reasoning behind this opening stage was our belief that it would be too abrupt to launch right into the questionnaire without somehow acknowledging the tension in class and its connection to the wider Israeli-Palestinian/Arab conflict (and in fact it was in part through a conversation with Jay Rothman that we decided to proceed on this course). In theoretical terms, our assumption was that the students needed to undergo a process of "unfreezing" before they would be ready for change (Lewin 1951; Schein 1969). Unfreezing is based on the view that the status quo is held in place by an equilibrium of social forces pushing in different directions and that this equilibrium must be upset so that change can occur. Schein (1969) identified three mechanisms of unfreezing: confronting people with information that challenges their perceptions of the situation (including themselves and others), causing people to recognize contradictions between their values or ideals and their own behavior, and creating feelings of psychological safety that mitigate the threat engendered by the first two mechanisms.

Nazir Majalli's talk turned out to be a very effective unfreezing mechanism. For many of the Jewish students, it was the first time they had actually heard an Arab Israeli talk about his experience. By describing himself an Arab and an Israeli who felt comfortable with both identifies, he presented a perspective on the conflict that was very different, and less polarizing, than views commonly expressed by spokespeople or in the media. In doing so, he challenged assumptions and stereotypes of both Jewish and Arab students. He also spoke in ways

that fostered a sense of psychological safety for both sides. On the one hand, he was able to give a frank description of the experience of Arab citizens of Israel, making the Arab students feel heard and legitimized. On the other hand, having participated in an Arab-Jewish delegation to Auschwitz, he was able to speak to and empathize with the fears and aspirations of the Jewish students. In both cases, he did so without blaming or demonizing the other side. However, as mentioned in the case, he also spoke to the gap between students' values and their actions, by challenging them to raise their heads up "out of the furrow" and see a much wider view of reality.

Filling out the AE questionnaire and participating in a "Why?" discussion in separate groups was also part of the unfreezing process. The questionnaire was manipulative (or normative) in the sense that it did not leave maintaining the *status quo* as an option. Rather it assumed the need for change (a better atmosphere in class) and was designed to shift thinking away from the conflict to change. The "Why?" discussion acknowledged the existence of a problem and affirmed the desire for change – views held by most, though not all, of the students. It heightened awareness of the gap between their values or ideals and their current situation. Seeing that others shared similar values and aspirations strengthened the sense of psychological safety.

Customizing Action Evaluation. In designing our intervention, we customized the ideal AE model to the particular circumstances. First, we were not using it for program design but rather to create a new reality within an existing setting. Therefore, rather than define the research question in terms of "definitions of success," we simply defined it as "What is your definition of a 'good atmosphere in class?'" In doing so, we also signaled to the students that the intervention was intended to meet their need as they, or at least some of them, had defined it.

Ideally we would have worked with the Jewish and Arab students separately in order to enable each group to arrive at its definition of a good atmosphere. We would then have been able to compare the definitions of each side, enabling us to determine the extent of agreement on what a good atmosphere would look like, and then work through a process of negotiating a common vision that took into account the views of both sides. However, given the intense time pressure (we had to complete this process in only three 90-minute sessions of the Introduction to Anthropology course), we decided to skip the analytic division into two separate groups and to analyze the data only at the level of the class as a whole.

The methodology was also adapted in our discussion of the "Whats?" and "Hows?" (i.e. "What, in your opinion, is the definition of a good atmosphere in class?"). Rather than conduct discussion about these definitions aimed at arriving at agreement upon them, we treated all of the definitions that emerged from the analysis of the questionnaire as givens and asked the students to give fuller expression to or interpret these aspirations through a combination of discourse and creative (artistic) activity. Defining a vision of a good atmosphere was a goal but it was also a means to create a situation in which Jewish and Arabs students would meet and interact more directly and intensively around a common goal. Thus, after forming mixed groups, we asked them to choose a theme with which they strongly identified and then to create and present the poster together.

We can speculate that the use of creative-artistic practices produced a powerful effect in two ways. It offered an entirely new way for the students to meet each other as well as an immediate outlet for the tensions that had built up. We were surprised by the speed and ease with which the students got into using the artistic materials. In doing so, they were able to express unspoken thoughts and feelings both in what they created and how they created it. They were able to put more of themselves into the interaction – using their bodies in new ways (or perhaps old ways in which these young adults participated in child-like, if serious, play), such as sitting close to each other on the floor and playing with the finger paints and other materials.

Another adaptation of AE was to combine the "What?" discussion with the "How?" discussion. Given the tight time frame, we knew that the 90 minutes in the Studio was all the time that we would have before the end of the semester and the summer

break. On the one hand, we felt strongly that the definitions of a good atmosphere had to be anchored in action if there was to be any effect. On the other hand, it was clear to us that we lacked the time for action planning. Therefore, as part of the poster creation, we asked each group to come up with one concrete "action item" for putting their definition of a good atmosphere into practice. In this respect, we integrated the discussions of "What?" and of "How?" into a single activity.

"Transferability" of interventions in natural spaces of encounter. This case study illustrates how an intervention in a natural space of encounter did overcome the problem of transferability – at least to a certain extent. The short-term results of the intervention were gratifying. The students reported a significant improvement in the atmosphere in class and this improvement appeared to continue into the next school year. The natural space of encounter was somewhat reshaped in the sense that the two groups no longer faced each other across such a deep divide, as evidenced by a much less salient division in seating arrangements. New relationships were formed and students felt more comfortable traversing the boundary between the two groups. A few actions were taken to structure and reinforce the change, but none of them were sustained over time. All of these changes can be seen as responding to the needs that were first uncovered in the evaluation process. There was much less tension and fear about underlying conflicts erupting, but at the same time there was still relatively little direct discussion of these conflicts.

Preserving the space while trying to change it. On the other hand, the outcome of the intervention fell short of our original framing as conflict engagement. The rules of the game within the space of encounter were not significantly changed or made open for discussion. The Arab students were still expected to adjust to the Jewish majority. There did not seem to be any increased openness to discussing potentially sensitive issues such as injustice, inequality, identity. In this respect, the intervention could be criticized as simply palliative or a "band-aid," which actually reinforces the *status quo* rather than challenging or changing it.

We take this self-critique very seriously. One of the difficulties of intervening in a natural space of encounter is the need to preserve the space while trying to change it. Artificial spaces of encounter exist only for the purpose of changing attitudes or behavior – usually at the individual level. These changes can be relatively easily measured by pre – and post-questionnaires, though the accuracy and validity of such changes can be questioned. New relationships and ways of relating may be formed but, once the intervention process is over, the space as a whole dissolves at the end of the intervention. Natural spaces of encounter exist before, during, and hopefully after interventions take place. This feature offers greater opportunities for stimulating long-term change but also the potential for deepening divisions or even destroying the space itself. Furthermore, we do not really possess the tools for evaluating or measuring changes in the space as a whole (i.e. the pattern and quality of relationships as opposed to attitudes).

Artificial spaces are temporary enclaves only loosely connected to the larger institutional structure. Because they are enclosed and dedicated to the process of creating dialogue and the like, they are also more easily controlled and shaped in ways that facilitate successful interventions. Natural spaces of encounter, on the other hand, are more deeply embedded in institutional contexts. Embeddedness offers opportunities for inquiring into and possibly changing features of the context that determine the character of the natural space of encounter and the rules of the game. At the same time, embeddedness means that interventionists are much more exposed and vulnerable to influence and criticism from the institutional context. When there is no consensus among the faculty that this kind of intervention is necessary or even desirable, there is a need for continually building and maintaining the political support that gives it legitimacy.

The combination of both gratification and doubt about the outcomes of the intervention suggest that it might be considered as only one step or stage in a more extensive process of conflict engagement in natural spaces of encounter. Given the very difficulty of making conflict discussable in spaces such as those at the College, this kind of intervention might be seen as a kind of unfreezing process that prepares the ground for more openness and a more fundamental grappling with issues. The foregoing case study, however, illustrates an "opportunistic" intervention in a natural space of encounter. It was designed and implemented in response to conflict that arose under a particular set of circumstances that probably could not be anticipated in advance. We happened to be at the right place at the right time to intervene. Furthermore, the circumstances were such that our ability to follow up and build on the initial intervention were severely limited. This insight led us to consider envisioning a more extensive process that could be built into the curriculum of the nursing program and other academic programs. This process of design and implementation, which has already been done, will provide the basis for future papers on intervention in natural spaces of encounter.

Intervening in a natural space of encounter. In conclusion we wish to return to the questions we raised about our decision, as action researchers, to intervene in natural spaces of encounter, especially given our own role as interested parties. As we stated above, there is probably no neutral position from which to engage in these issues, especially as action researchers. Under these circumstances, it seems to us that the best way to maintain a high ethical standard is through our own reflectiveness and willingness to expose what we do and why we do it to the critical gaze of others, which is what we have endeavored to do in this chapter.

References

Arieli, D., & Hirschfeld, M. (2010). Teaching nursing in a situation of conflict: Encounters between Arab-Israeli and Jewish-Israeli nursing students. *International Nursing Review, 57*(3).

Arieli, D., Friedman, V., & Hirschfeld, M. (2009). The establishment of an academic nursing faculty: Action research in Israel. *International Nursing Review, 56*(3), 299–305.

Arieli, D., Mashiach Eizenberg, M., & Hirschfeld, M. (2010). Social relations, mutual support and satisfaction among Jewish and Arab students of nursing. *Guf-Yeda, 7*, 3–8. in Hebrew.

Arieli, D., Mashiach-Eizenberg, M., Friedman, V., & Hirschfeld, M. (2012). Challenges on the path to cultural safety in nursing education. *International Nursing Review, 59*, pp. 187–193.

Foucault, M. (1994). The subject and power. In P. Rubinow & N. Rose (Eds.), *The essential Foucault*. New York: New Press.

Freire, P. (1997). *Pedagogy of the oppressed*. New York: Continuum.

Friedman, V., & Desivilya, H. (2010). Integrating social entrepreneurship and conflict engagement for regional development in divided societies. *Entrepreneurship and Regional Development, 22*(6), 495–514.

Friedman, V., & Lipshitz, R. (1992). Teaching people to shift cognitive gears: Overcoming resistance on the road to model II. *The Journal of Applied Behavioral Science, 28*(1), 118–137.

Friedman, V., & Rothman, J. (2001). Action evaluation for knowledge production in social-educational programs. In S. Shankaran, B. Dick, R. Passfield, & P. Swepson (Eds.), *Effective change management through action research and action learning: Concepts, frameworks, processes and applications* (pp. 57–65). Lismore: Southern Cross University Press.

Friedman, V., Rothman, J., & Withers, B. (2006). The power of why: Engaging the goal paradox in program evaluation. *American Journal of Evaluation, 27*(2), 1–18.

Friedman, V., Elal-Englert, P., Rothman, J., Friedman, N., & Har Zion-Birnbaum, S. (2010). Action evaluation/C3 in Israel: Concepts and method, In M. Levin-Rozalis & R . Savaya (Eds.) *Issues in Evaluation in Israel* (pp. 137–160) (Hebrew).

Hansen, T. (2008). Critical conflict resolution Theory and practice. *Conflict Resolution Quarterly, 25*, 403–427.

Hargie, O., Dickson, D. & Nelson, S. (2003). Working together in a divided society: A study of intergroup communication in the Northern Ireland Workplace. *Journal of Business and Technical Communication, 17*, 285–318.

Hein, H. (1976). Aesthetic consciousness: The ground of political experience. *The Journal of Aesthetics and Art Criticism, 35*, 143–152.

Hjorth, D. (2004). Organizational entrepreneurship: With de Certeau on creating heterotopias (or spaces for lay). *Journal of Management Inquiry, 14*(4), 386–398.

Lewin, K. (1951). *Field theory in social science: Selected theoretical papers*. New York: Harper & Row. (Republished, 1997, Washington, D.C.: American Psychological Association, pp. 1–152).

McCall, C. (2011). Culture and the Irish border: Spaces for conflict transformation. *Cooperation and Conflict, 46*(2), 201–221.

McNiff, S. (2003). *Creating with others: The practice of imagination in life, art and the workspace*. Boston: Shambhala.

Moskin, B., & Jackson, J (2004). *Warrior angel: The work of Lily Yeh*. Barefoot Artists, http://www.barefoot-artists.org/Lilys_Warrior_Angel_11_2.pdf. Accessed on 14 June 2012.

Rothman, J., & Friedman, V. (2001). Conflict, identity, and organizational learning. In M. Dierkes, A. Berthoin Antal, J. Child, & Y. Nonaka (Eds.), *The handbook of organizational learning and knowledge* (pp. 582–597). Oxford: Oxford University Press.

Rothman, J., & Friedman, V. (2002). Action evaluation for conflict management in organizations and projects. In J. Davies & E. Kaufman (Eds.), *Second track diplomacy: Concepts and techniques for conflict transformation* (pp. 285–298). Boulder: Rowman & Littlefield.

Rothman, J. (1997). *Resolving identity-based conflicts: In nations, organizations and communities*. San Francisco: Jossey Bass.

Schein, E. H. (1969). The mechanisms of change. In W. G. Bennis, K. D. Benne, & R. Chin (Eds.), *The planning of change* (pp. 98–108). New York: Hart, Rinehart & Winston.

Tjosvold, D. (2006). Defining conflict and making choices about its management: Lighting the dark side of organizational life. *International Journal of Conflict Management, 17*, 87–96.

Valentine, G. (2008). Living with difference: Reflections on geographies of encounter. *Progress in Human Geography, 32*(3), 323–337.

Engaging Conflict While Fostering Cooperation: An Organizational Case Study

Michael J. Urick and Vaughn Crandall

Introduction

All seemed calm enough at the Braum University (BU) School of Medicine – it was in a fairly steady state for years and that was the way that everyone seemed to want it. Everything, from the programs to the building that housed the classrooms and offices to the school's logo to the school's involvement with the surrounding community, remained much the same for a decade. It was in this context that Dean Dunlap retired from the school that he had founded to become the university's President, making the way for his protégé, Dr. Harold Pierce, to take his place.

"Everything is going fine," thought Dean Pierce as he took his first steps into his office. The faculty members were all courteous to each other in meetings. They smiled and made idle conversation as they passed each other in the halls, and there was little to suggest a simmering "conflict" between two very distinct faculty identities that existed within the school. Though every meeting Dean Pierce attended was cordial, he increasingly became aware of something festering beneath the pleasant exterior of the School of Medicine. Within his first few days as Dean, he grew to question his initial impression. "Everything might not be as calm as I thought after all..."

During Dean Pierce's first few weeks in his new role, a conflict began to emerge in which identities related to primary and specialty care doctors became salient. To document the conflict and how it was managed, this chapter explores elements of an identity-based conflict that emerged over the course of a strategic planning process for a medical school at a mid-sized public university in the Midwest. The relationship dynamics and conflicts between primary care doctors and specialists in the medical school are the focus of this chapter. The purpose of this chapter is to offer insights into understanding and engaging identity-based conflict within organizations (as opposed to societies, countries, nation states, etc. as has been the focus for much of this book). This case also illustrates the fluidity of the ARIA process as it moved from Action Evaluation (visioning) to Antagonism (conflict engagement) and finally back into Action Evaluation (see Chap. 1 for an overview of the ARIA process). As such, this case highlights the applicability that ARIA has to an organizational context.

This chapter is divided into three parts. The first examines the identity-based conflict within the medical school that was surfaced in the context of a collaborative planning process – the ARIA Group's Action Evaluation (AE) approach (see Chap. 7 for more details on AE). From this process, both primary care and specialist voices became important expressed identities that informed the overall organization's identity as

M.J. Urick • V. Crandall
e-mail: urickmj@mail.uc.edu; vcrandall@jjay.cuny.edu

J. Rothman (ed.), *From Identity-Based Conflict to Identity-Based Cooperation: The ARIA Approach in Theory and Practice*, Peace Psychology Book Series, DOI 10.1007/978-1-4614-3679-9_9,
© Springer Science+Business Media New York 2012

suggested by social identity theory (which states that an individual's self concept is influenced by being a part of a larger group; Turner and Giles 1981; Tajfel and Turner 1985), self-categorization theory (which suggests that people identify or disidentify with others to fulfill the basic human needs of inclusion and differentiation; Brewer and Brown 1998; Hogg and Terry 2000), and theories of organizational identity (in which organizations take upon identities of their own through aspects that are central to the organization, distinct from other organizations, and expected to endure into the future; Albert and Whetten 1985; Whetten 1998). This conflict was then directly addressed through the ARIA conflict engagement process and the overall process was ultimately shifted back into Action Evaluation for working on the strategic planning.

The second portion of this chapter is an analysis and reflection on the case. This section's purpose is to discuss specific results that occurred following the strategic planning process. The most salient tangible changes were in the School of Medicine's goals and mission statement. Following a discussion of these changes, we consider also how the conflict engagement process primed the organization for culture changes. This section concludes by discussing the additional impact of the process 10 years after its conclusion.

The third and final section features reflexive dialogues that the researchers had with Dean Harold Pierce, leader of the medical school, and Jay Rothman, Ph.D., head and founder of the ARIA Group 10 years following the strategic planning at BU. This section examines the most crucial aspects of the process that were either successful or not successful from the point of view of two of the most involved actors during the Braum University process.

In order to examine this case, data collected in 2002 was analyzed and supplemented with a series of interviews of participants in 2011. Note that for this chapter the names of participants and the university have been changed to protect anonymity.

Part One: Process and Conflict Description

A New Leader at the Braum University School of Medicine

In 2002, the Braum University (BU) School of Medicine (SOM) stood at a crossroads. Harold Pierce had recently been appointed as the new Dean as the former Dean transitioned to the role of BU President. Though eager to take on this new role, Pierce understood that leadership changes within an organization often cause the organization itself to evolve. He also knew that such change can be painful to organizational members because it calls into question the identity of the organization and can trigger shifts in the allocation of power, resources, and influence.

Early in his tenure, Pierce became aware of tensions between two groups of physicians: primary care (health care professionals who act as a first point of consultation for all patients–family practitioners for example) and specialist care (physicians with well-developed expertise in very specific areas of practice; neurosurgeons, orthopedists, and oncologists for example). Such tensions were not openly discussed and it seemed to Pierce that the culture of SOM had been one in which such conflict was generally avoided. While formal events and meetings gave Pierce the idea that everything was fine within the school, it was not uncommon for faculty to whisper about their problems and conflicts quietly with those "on their side" where they thought that others who disagreed with their perspectives would not hear. Pierce saw this as something that detracted from the school – SOM needed to have its own unified vision unhampered by divided and gossiping faculty members whose perspectives were not surfaced nor openly addressed.

It is important to note that, in the medical profession, primary care doctors are not regarded as among the most elite medical practitioners. Instead, specialists are generally more highly-regarded by the field and earn higher salaries.

Primary care physicians are often viewed as "generalists" without some of the prestige associated with the "specialists" (Kavilanz 2009). Meanwhile, the school had carved an identity niche for itself in the medical education community as an institution that prided itself on educating excellent primary care doctors attuned to community needs, raising the status of the primary care doctors associated with BU. Nonetheless, many specialist physicians were also associated with the School of Medicine's professors or as affiliates through one of seven teaching hospitals in the region. Therefore, within this culture, primary care physicians held a place of power which did not seem to exist in the broader medical field and they did not want to upset their somewhat unique status quo. Because the importance of generalists within BU contrasted greatly with their place in the broader society, it is possible that the strength and salience of this identity was increased within the SOM (Spears et al. 1999). Pierce had interacted with both primary care physicians and specialists regularly and, though neither had been explicit to mention tensions within SOM, he sensed that the specialist physicians felt as though they were second-class to the primary care physicians.

Dean Pierce thought it necessary to begin a strategic planning process for the school as he was anticipating a decline in state funding and the school needed a new plan incorporating this change. Prior to his appointment, SOM had a culture in which the prior strategic planning processes were very linear and structured. As such, these initiatives often led to outcomes that were predictable and, perhaps, not as innovative as they could have been. The new Dean surmised that SOM needed to have a process that was more open in nature so that it led to ideas that were more "outside the box" and less predictable than previous strategic planning outcomes. In doing so, he felt the process also needed to incorporate the viewpoints of as many perspectives as possible, and that engaging in such a dialogue would be beneficial for the school.

Pierce became resolute to undertake a new kind of "open" strategic planning process. With such a process, it was crucial to select an approach that enabled others to feel secure in speaking their opinions. While he wasn't looking for conflict, he was looking for an opportunity for all voices to be heard, even if it did lead to conflict. He felt like the future vitality of his program depended on selecting an enabling process.

The Action Evaluation Process Begins

Dr. Cameron, the Associate Dean of Academic Affairs of the SOM, had gone to college with Jay Rothman, head of the ARIA Group, and recalled from conversations Rothman's collaborative approach to strategic planning (he also was aware of Rothman's participatory work in Cincinnati, Ohio – see Chap. 11). Dr. Cameron suggested to the group that they call Rothman to see if his approach delivered what Pierce was looking for.

Initial meetings with Rothman and his associate Vaughn Crandall introduced Pierce and the Associate Deans to the Aria Group's Action Evaluation (AE) process in which inclusion and participation are both hallmarks. Sensing that the group was skeptical of the claims, the consultants suggested that the Dean's council meet offsite to avoid any day-to-day interruptions and participate in a sample AE discussion so that they could see firsthand how the process works. The group was fascinated with the deeply participatory nature of the AE approach, citing for example that they were impressed with the insistence in not moving forward with a decision unless all participants were able to express themselves and the group reached meaningful consensus. Dean Pierce and his team viewed the ARIA-facilitated small group process as being promising for SOM at this juncture in its history and, following their AE session, decided to roll it out to the rest of the faculty, staff, and students in the school.

During this initial discussion, Rothman, Pierce, and Crandall explored in a general way whether there might be an underlying conflict that would emerge. At one point in these discussions Rothman informed Pierce that from what he was sensing (and perhaps due to his own professional biases), he felt it was quite possible conflict would emerge and asked the Dean if he was up for that possibility. The Dean said he was.

Pierce sent notices to the SOM community that a new strategic planning process would be undertaken and facilitated by the ARIA Group and that his hope was that all would actively participate in the process thus generating open dialogue, value sharing, ownership, and collaborative implementation of the emerging strategic action plan. The project was broken down into meetings between three different groups, in order to foster new comprehensive goals for SOM. Each group's meeting also indicates one phase of the AE process. The first group, and therefore the first phase was the meeting between Dean Pierce and the Associate Deans, the second group was an Executive Committee consisting of Department Chairs, and lastly the third group was the faculty itself. There was an early hope to involve students as well, but when they showed little enthusiasm for being involved, this was dropped.

With each group, the process began by soliciting input regarding participants' individual goals for SOM in the form of an online questionnaire, which is an integrated component of the ARIA process. Participants were asked *what* their individual goals were for the school. They were then asked *why* these goals matter for them and last *how* they can contribute to achieve their goals. These responses were then analyzed and presented back to participants willing to attend a feedback session. Following the articulation of goals by these three separate groups, representatives were selected to move to an inter-group dialogue session, which produced a platform of consensus goals representing the values of the entire school. While the narrative below describes how these goals were set and how the conflict emerged and was handled within the faculty group, Fig. 9.1 presents a concise reference for the process. Figure 9.1 articulates when the three group phases of the process occurred, who was involved, and how the groups' individual goals lead to the creation of organizational goals. Taken together, Fig. 9.1 and the narrative below will give the reader a solid understanding of how the process at Braum University unfolded.

The first phase lasted from June to September of 2002 when the Dean and Associate Deans articulated their goals, values, and ideas for action through the web-based survey and then discussed and finally refined these at a subsequent group meeting. This resulted in a consensus approved platform of goals representing the Deans' interests, priorities, and values.

The second phase was launched in early Fall 2002, with introductory meetings for the Executive Committee. The Executive Committee members then entered their goals, values, and action ideas online and participated in a similar facilitated feedback session. This process also resulted in a platform of shared Executive Committee goals for the school.

Phase III began with an extensive outreach campaign including emails, phone calls, and personal conversations between Executive Committee members and the faculty. This was to ensure that faculty were aware of the strategic visioning process and understood how they could effectively participate. Eighty faculty members responded to the online questionnaire in late November and early December. As this was the largest group, their responses were the most diverse. Forty faculty members attended a meeting in early December, at which they had small group discussions regarding their goals and underlying values. The consultants, who facilitated this and subsequent meetings (the faculty group had multiple meetings as opposed to the other groups which had one), noted that there were overwhelmingly disproportionate numbers of primary care faculty who attended the first few meetings.

Dr. Vi, a specialist faculty member, noticed a similar thing when she attended her first meeting. Though her schedule was busy and the meeting was inconvenient for her to attend, Dr. Vi heard rumors that very few specialist faculty had attended previous meetings. From her perspective, the specialist voices were still not being heard and the AE process was their best hope to make their opinion count.

A Conflict Emerges

From Dr. Vi's perception, the first meeting she attended seemed to reinforce the perspective of

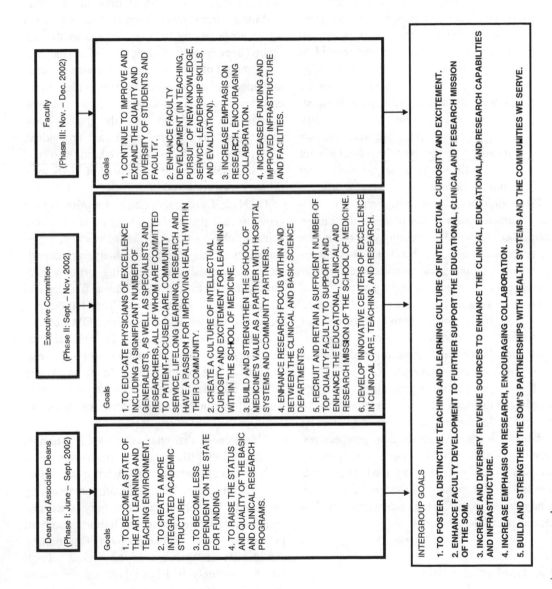

Dean and Associate Deans

(Phase I: June – Sept. 2002)

Goals

1. TO BECOME A STATE OF THE ART LEARNING AND TEACHING ENVIRONMENT.

2. TO CREATE A MORE INTEGRATED ACADEMIC STRUCTURE.

3. TO BECOME LESS DEPENDENT ON THE STATE FOR FUNDING.

4. TO RAISE THE STATUS AND QUALITY OF THE BASIC AND CLINICAL RESEARCH PROGRAMS.

Executive Committee

(Phase II: Sept. – Nov. 2002)

Goals

1. TO EDUCATE PHYSICIANS OF EXCELLENCE INCLUDING A SIGNIFICANT NUMBER OF GENERALISTS, AS WELL AS SPECIALISTS AND RESEARCHERS, ALL OF WHOM ARE COMMITTED TO PATIENT-FOCUSED CARE, COMMUNITY SERVICE, LIFELONG LEARNING, RESEARCH AND HAVE A PASSION FOR IMPROVING HEALTH WITHIN THEIR COMMUNITY.

2. CREATE A CULTURE OF INTELLECTUAL CURIOSITY AND EXCITEMENT FOR LEARNING WITHIN THE SCHOOL OF MEDICINE.

3. BUILD AND STRENGTHEN THE SCHOOL OF MEDICINE'S VALUE AS A PARTNER WITH HOSPITAL SYSTEMS AND COMMUNITY PARTNERS.

4. ENHANCE RESEARCH FOCUS WITHIN AND BETWEEN THE CLINICAL AND BASIC SCIENCE DEPARTMENTS.

5. RECRUIT AND RETAIN A SUFFICIENT NUMBER OF TOP QUALITY FACULTY TO SUPPORT AND ENHANCE THE EDUCATIONAL, CLINICAL, AND RESEARCH MISSION OF THE SCHOOL OF MEDICINE.

6. DEVELOP INNOVATIVE CENTERS OF EXCELLENCE IN CLINICAL CARE, TEACHING, AND RESEARCH.

Faculty

(Phase III: Nov. – Dec. 2002)

Goals

1. CONTINUE TO IMPROVE AND EXPAND THE QUALITY AND DIVERSITY OF STUDENTS AND FACULTY.

2. ENHANCE FACULTY DEVELOPMENT (IN TEACHING, PURSUIT OF NEW KNOWLEDGE, SERVICE, LEADERSHIP SKILLS, AND EVALUATION).

3. INCREASE EMPHASIS ON RESEARCH, ENCOURAGING COLLABORATION.

4. INCREASED FUNDING AND IMPROVED INFRASTRUCTURE AND FACILITIES.

INTERGROUP GOALS

1. TO FOSTER A DISTINCTIVE TEACHING AND LEARNING CULTURE OF INTELLECTUAL CURIOSITY AND EXCITEMENT.

2. ENHANCE FACULTY DEVELOPMENT TO FURTHER SUPPORT THE EDUCATIONAL, CLINICAL, AND RESEARCH MISSION OF THE SOM.

3. INCREASE AND DIVERSIFY REVENUE SOURCES TO ENHANCE THE CLINICAL, EDUCATIONAL, AND RESEARCH CAPABILITIES AND INFRASTRUCTURE.

4. INCREASE EMPHASIS ON RESEARCH, ENCOURAGING COLLABORATION.

5. BUILD AND STRENGTHEN THE SOM'S PARTNERSHIPS WITH HEALTH SYSTEMS AND THE COMMUNITIES WE SERVE.

Fig. 9.1 Three group to intergroup goals

the generalists (primary care physicians and educators). Indeed, Dr. Vi felt greatly outnumbered to the point that she considered herself to be almost alone in the room. Though the process promised that her voice would be heard, she thought that her opinion would be met with much skepticism by the others in the meeting. Still, she did speak up. From her perspective, the goals needed to also reflect the importance of specialists if all faculty were indeed to be treated as being of equal importance. In the first meeting she attended, the primary care physicians met her comments with disproval. From their perspective, the goals needed to reinforce their status. However, the process of AE made sure that any decision regarding the goals of the school did not move forward until all agreed, despite any dissent coming from a minority.

This highlights the strength of one of the primary characteristics of this process: the importance of consensus. By stressing consensus, the AE process ensured that her voice was recognized and her thoughts taken into account in order to represent the specialist groups. The concept of consensus, as applied by AE, stresses that a decision cannot move forward until everyone voices satisfaction with it. Any dissent must be recognized and allowed and somehow addressed in order for the group to move ahead.

This encouraged other specialists, and soon more began to attend meetings. As more specialists joined the conversation, they gained more confidence in speaking up for their perspectives. They felt that, because the emphasis on primary care was so heavy, by the time medical students were introduced to many of the specialties (such as surgery, for example) the students did not view these as plausible career options.

Questioning Identities

Soon, the conversations became more intense as specialists and primary care physicians began to enact openly separate distinct identities which, for the first time, were strongly identified along different and opposing sides in the argument. It became apparent that, in the context of SOM, the physicians defined core aspects of themselves by being part of a particular group (primary vs. specialist) thereby forming in- and out-groups. In these groups, in-group members look upon out-group members as having uniform attributes and perspectives (Hogg and Terry 2001) such as the need for their role to be of importance within SOM thus strengthening their own identities, but also contributing further to biases against the out-group (Brewer 1979; Tsui et al. 1995), which has the potential of causing a greater divide between individuals in the groups. This was evident in the ensuing discussions as some participants became increasingly passionate as the conversation focused not only around what each individual, department, and discipline valued, but also (and most intensely) around the School of Medicine's primary focus or mission.

Dr. Nick, Department Chair of a primary care group, recalls this as the starting point for a very spirited debate. In one particular meeting, representatives of the generalist/primary care departments advocated that producing primary care physicians was the reason SOM was founded and continually funded by the state. They felt that primary care was the arena in which SOM excelled and was nationally recognized. They also emphasized that the School of Medicine served a critical role in the region and state by producing primary care physicians as these physicians play a critical role in the health outcomes of the communities they serve.

This intense dialogue continued for almost two hours with little progress. This issue spurred such a heated debate, and defense by some, because it harkened back to the original founding purpose of the school (a community-based primary care program which was important to both primary and specialist perspectives). Questioning the identity and purpose of the overall school, which seemingly had been built on the sound foundation of providing primary care, now caused SOM employees to question their own individual identities and purpose since individual and organizational identity (including the stability of each) are linked to each other (Hatch and Schultz 2002). Dr. Lisa, Associate Dean of Research, described it as such:

"Primary care people felt threatened. They thought: 'We're changing our mission – we're undervalued by our colleagues and leadership.' There were a lot of personal things going on...primarily fear. The fear of primary care being submerged under other areas." **Associate Dean**

In the middle of the meeting, several people from both "sides" went to try to forge a bridging statement to focus on shared areas of identity, but they failed. Jay Rothman, the meeting's facilitator, told them that the group would try to reach agreement within a certain period of time in order to keep the process moving forward in a positive manner. However, if they failed within the specified time period, Rothman warned them that they would need to stop the visioning process to investigate and address the differences more fully.

A Shift in Focus

The group failed to come to an agreement within the set time period. Seeing this, Rothman concluded the meeting and informed the faculty that they would need to shift the focus of the strategic planning process from visioning (future-oriented and aspirational) to conflict engagement (past-oriented and identity-based), as he felt these issues needed to be studied and engaged further in order for the process to move forward in an effective and productive manner. Volunteers then self-selected to serve on a committee to help explore these identity-based differences further. It was ensured that both groups (primary care and specialist) were evenly represented in the committee. Also working on a volunteer basis guaranteed that the committee members were invested in the process and deeply cared about their own group identity being represented and heard since they were willing to invest their own spare time. There were concerns as well as approval regarding the shift from vision to conflict engagement with a focus on the identity conflict. In favor of the shift, and expressing the need for it one faculty member remarked:

"This is what happens when you suppress fire for ten years and you don't let people talk about the issue." **Faculty Member**

On the other hand, Dr. Dave, a 20-year veteran of the School of Medicine, did not look as favorably on the process as did some others and he angrily stormed out of the meeting when the group moved to conflict engagement. In his own words:

"I've never been through a process that made me angrier. It's because of the changes that were made and how the process was allowed to happen. Because of the process, something that wasn't a big deal became a big deal. Jay took what was a five percent minority and gave it a 50/50 voice. The initial vote was 17-1, but the process gave that one an equal voice and the mission [of SOM] eventually changed based on this idea." **Faculty Member**

Such a statement illustrates three things. First, it highlights the passion that participants had during this planning process. This stems primarily from questions that are raised about identity issues. Second, it showcases the way in which ARIA gives voice to those with minority ideas. Third, it shows how intense the conversation had become over certain issues dealing with how the professors defined their importance within the school. Finally, it illustrates how (through the concept of consensus) one person's voice, which previously might be overlooked, can redirect the process hopefully for the good of the whole.

Rothman, drawing from his own experience, observed that this conflict exhibited characteristics of a "double minority complex" where the visible "majority" (in this case primary care departments and doctors) is actually the numerical "minority" in the larger environment of medical practice. On the other side, the visible "minority" (in this case the specialist departments and doctors) is actually the "majority," at least in terms of power and influence in the larger environment. This creates a dynamic in which both groups operate out of some realistic sense of threatened limitation to their own legitimacy and influence.

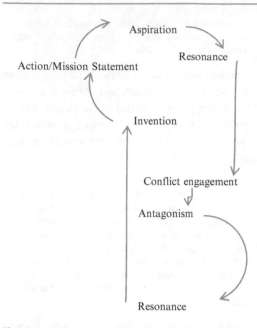

Fig. 9.2 Action evaluation to conflict engagement and back

The ARIA Conflict Engagement Process

As described previously in this book, the ARIA conflict engagement process is dynamic and cyclical and is comprised of four stages that often lead back to earlier stages: Antagonism, Resonance, Invention, and Action (Rothman 1997). The purpose of Antagonism is to surface different identity-based disagreements and perspectives that make them discussable in safe and constructive ways. Resonance, on the other hand, promotes harmony by creating a new focus and direction for the larger group by a more internal focus on each side's needs, values, and narratives. Invention is the process of coming up with options for identifying ways in which a solution might be beneficial to all parties. Lastly, Action creates a specific plan for implementing the solution that the parties have agreed upon.

While ARIA in theory is very linear, in practice it is iterative. Attempting to describe the process at Braum University in terms of each of the four ARIA steps does not do service to the complexity and fluidity of the process. Therefore, in Fig. 9.2 and the narrative below which describes the BU conflict engagement process, the reader is invited to view the four steps in a more dynamic and organic way.

ARIA Within an Organizational Context

Having recognized the double minority complex dynamic, Rothman asked representatives of the generalist and specialty fields to attend the next Steering Committee meeting as temporary representatives of the faculty (as the entire faculty was too large to attend the Steering Committee meeting for the conversation to be productive), in order to help devise a constructive way forward. Without this, he suggested, the conflict situation would, one way or the other continue to be a central issue in the strategic planning process. Looking back on the process, we found three important themes evident in our 2011 interviews of participants:

- The importance of unearthing the conflict and finally speaking about it openly.
- The ability to move forward collectively through discussion.
- The necessity of clarifying the school's identity and collectively what this entity and its members valued.

The antagonism process was characterized by a strict adherence to process guidelines about consensus decision-making that guides Action Evaluation (as described above and in more detail in Chap. 7) in order that all sides might be given a voice and be heard.

By the rules of the ARIA conflict engagement process, the Steering Committee sought to craft a process solution based on the following four criteria:

1. The solution must maintain process momentum.
2. It must be effective and engage the issues fully.
3. It must ensure that the broader constituency (faculty) is brought back in and understands and owns the conflict engagement strategy.
4. It must move the process back into visioning.

During the initial phase of Antagonism and moving into the second phase of Resonance, Dr. Cameron recalls that the most important part of the process was "taking a critical look at who we were." Such a dialogue gave all sides a voice to be clear and direct about the way they negatively framed the conflict with the other side, but also maintained control over this process to not let the conflict get too out of control. Participants reported that the facilitators managed this balance well – they were hands on and encouraged everyone in the room to be respectful to all viewpoints. Engaging in such a dialogue was challenging because it was difficult to not have individuals take things personally. In the process, the great debate became "who and what are we and why is this important?" which has the potential to scare many participants because it may raise questions about the very concepts of how individuals define themselves and their relationship with the organization (Ashforth and Mael 1989).

After the Steering Committee had met, faculty representatives of the Steering Committee devised the following solution (which gets to the heart of the conflict regarding the school's dominant group): "**Re-examine the balance between primary care and the specialties within the School of Medicine**." The rationale behind this possible solution was that a deep and systematic inquiry into the history of the School of Medicine's identity, division of resources, and prestige among departments could be a natural product of the strategic visioning process and would be a necessary step to ensure both parties felt their concerns had been taken seriously. It is important to note that this solution favored neither the specialist nor generalist identity. Because of this, in subsequent meetings this statement created resonance as it moved the faculty from an "us" versus "them" viewpoint into envisioning a future inclusive "we" within SOM. As such, individuals in the SOM managed the boundary between in- and out-groups (Kreiner et al. 2006; Ernst and Chrobot-Mason 2011) so that the common identity and goals of SOM became more important than the smaller group identity of specialist or generalist doctors.

Following the formulation of this solution, the faculty group revisited the goals that they had initially formulated during the AE process. All goals except for those dealing with the generalist versus specialist identity conflict were revised and approved in less than an hour (refer back to Fig. 9.1 for the goals). Debate then returned to the topic of generalist versus specialist emphasis, and eventually it became clear that the creation of

a goal explicitly stating the importance of either the primary or specialist identity would not be consensus-approved. Instead, the faculty collaborated to create goals based solely on shared values (such as quality of education despite the specifics of what would be taught, concern for the community, and personal consideration to students and faculty alike). It was then concluded that the agreed upon goals would be presented at an intergroup goal setting meeting of representatives from all three groups.

Formulating a Mission

In preparation for the meeting, the ARIA Group integrated the goals of the Deans, Executive Committee (department chairs), and Faculty to produce an overarching platform of goals representing an intersection of the interests of all three groups. At the inter-group session, Deans, Department Chairs, and faculty examined summaries of the values and motivations articulated over the course of the strategic visioning process in order to foster understanding and common ground among these members of the School of Medicine. Representatives then used this common ground to craft a platform of shared goals for the School of Medicine. This platform was approved by a consensus vote of all attending participants.

A mission formulated from these goals was also approved by consensus as Deans, Executive Committee members, and Faculty used the lessons learned from the various meetings and the dedicated work of the Steering Committee to create a collaborative statement that included the critical concepts of "patient-focused care, community service, lifelong learning, research, and a passion for improving health in their communities," while also allowing for a continued generalist emphasis balanced with increased attention to specialties and research. The essential philosophy articulated by participants was that a great generalist education must incorporate considerable exposure to and supplementation from good specialists and researchers, and ultimately should produce a physician who can grow in a variety of

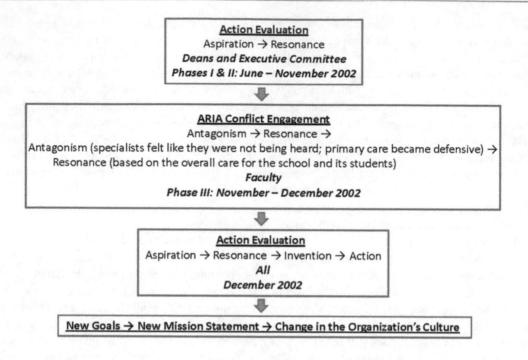

Fig. 9.3 The fluidity of action evaluation at the Braum school of medicine

directions either as a generalist or specialist. The mission developed was:

> To educate culturally diverse students, to become excellent physicians, with a focus on generalist training that is integrated, supported, and strengthened by specialists and researchers, all of whom value patient-focused care, community service, research, and have a passion for improving health in their communities.

Following the articulation of the mission, Action Groups were subsequently created in which members would identify specific steps for accomplishing each of the school's goals. Figure 9.3 concisely summarizes the process described above.

Ultimately, this process led to real and meaningful change within the SOM which is analyzed in the next part.

Part Two: The Analysis

The following section presents an analysis of the Braum University case presented above. In this section, we specifically look at the changes in goals and the mission statement that occurred after the process illustrated in Fig. 9.3. Following this discussion, we specifically examine how changes in the organization's culture were primed. Lastly, this section concludes with a discussion on the impact of the process and its changes 10 years after the ARIA group's facilitation.

Creating Change

It is easiest to understand the change that occurred at Braum State by first examining Kurt Lewin's theory of change. Organizational behaviorist Kurt Lewin proposed a widely accepted model for change that exhibits three stages: unfreezing, transitioning, and refreezing (1947). In this model, unfreezing includes acknowledging the need for change, creating excitement in the organization for change, and planning the change process; transitioning includes implementing the change; and refreezing includes "cementing" the change in such a way that it becomes a part of the organization's assumptions and values. Such a model also suggests a cyclical process whereby once the change refreezes, a new initiative occurs to start the unfreezing process again. Thus, within organizations, Lewin's three-step process is constantly occurring on multiple levels.

For Braum University, engaging internal differences might be considered the unfreezing process. Transitioning can be painful for organizations because this is where the change actually occurs. At Braum University, the goals, mission statement, and ultimately focus were changed during this phase. Pain occurred during these changes because they happened while working through the identity conflict that had been present, but not previously engaged, within the schools' faculty and executives. In order to refreeze, those things that have been changed within the organization become cemented when the change is added to the organization's culture (as will be discussed below). Such organization-wide change is often very difficult as it causes people to rethink their roles, assumptions, and work processes.

For example, individuals at Braum University acknowledged how difficult the change was:

"It was a real challenging process. Any time you go through change, especially when you challenge peoples' thoughts, you see differences in perspectives. It wasn't an easy process, but it needed to happen." **Associate Dean**

Yet, many participants were also aware that a deep change needed to occur as illustrated by Dr. Lisa's comments below:

"Times have changed, politics have changed, students have changed. Change is necessary and people came to that conclusion. People realized that resources got smaller and people would get left out if they didn't change." **Associate Dean**

Reflecting upon the ongoing nature of this change, several commented that the school is a work in progress that will continue to evolve. Indeed, many participants have expressed interest in going through another process similar to the one conducted in 2002 due to changes in the community, students, and national climate (such as changing national policies and recent national reports regarding the shortage of physicians).

Even though change is ongoing, it appears to be somewhat of a paradox that the results of the change also must stick in order to instill confidence in organizational members that the change is actually useful. In terms of this change sticking, Dr. Cameron stated:

"This change will stick. It would have been undone already if it wasn't going to stay. Although revised slightly from 2002, the mission statement we currently have still reflects the themes from ARIA." **Associate Dean**

Three specific tangible changes that we will consider further are goals, the mission statement, and ultimately the organization's culture.

Goals

In the initial process, participants were assigned to groups to help articulate specific goals in regard to the direction of SOM, which were incorporated into the mission statement. Participants reported the goal-setting process to be very transparent. Dr. Nick said that the process of working with others was "fun" and started a much needed "good open academic dialogue." The goals were met with success as they created changes within the school including reallocation of funding.

Dr. Cameron mentioned that this was the first time that the school had ever undertaken a serious, inclusive process in attempting to set and reach organizational goals. Following 2002, the goals were further refined and expanded upon to make them more specific. The revised goals were clearer to organizational members and allowed each department to set goals of their own which support the overall goals of the school. The AE and ARIA processes not only helped create new goals for the organization, but also gave the SOM a model for how to continually revisit and craft new goals in the future.

Mission Statement

As a result of the ARIA process, the School of Medicine crafted a new mission statement based on the goals that they adopted. This mission statement incorporated the importance of both primary care and specialist perspectives. The new mission did not minimize the original focus of the school, but it did move toward including everyone by highlighting the importance of both generalist and specialist disciplines.

This mission statement greatly impacted the culture of the organization. First, it was an observable statement that can be compared with earlier mission statements to see a change in values. Second, it served the purpose of guiding the flow of resources within the school, which ultimately led to the creation of new specialist programs.

Organizational Culture

The culture has indeed changed at Braum University in the years following the ARIA process, as will be examined in this section. Before doing so, however, it is useful to explain that organizational culture can be examined at three levels: (1) the unstated assumptions which lead to (2) values which in turn create (3) observable artifacts and behaviors (Schein 2004). It appears that some important unstated assumptions have not changed within the school (such as the unstated assumption that providing a quality medical education is very important). Neither has the assumption that the School is a community-based program. However, some of the values and artifacts/behaviors have indeed changed.

For example, the stated values have changed in order to emphasize both specialists and generalists. Additionally, the value of increasing research has grown in importance. Observable artifacts and changes in behavior are numerous. Perhaps the most apparent is the change of wording in the mission statement to reflect the importance of specialists. Additional signs of change include different methods for recruiting students, an increased focus on interdisciplinary team-based learning, new specialty courses, increased interaction and collaboration between groups, public acknowledgement of the importance of specialties, the number of students that are choosing to go into specialty fields and the Dean's involvement in support of specialties. Additionally, funding was increased to strengthen the specialist programs in neurology, trauma, clinical research activities, geriatrics, and adult cardiology.

Dr. Cameron sums the change in culture stating:

"Yes, we still do have a lot of primary care students. But that's not the only thing we do and do well...when you think of SOM, you need to think that there's more about us than family medicine." **Associate Dean**

From conversations with participants, it seems as though many individuals feel that the changes in the culture are positive. Dr. Vi, for example, remarked "It's healthier now than it was before." Others suggest that the cultural change at Braum University was discreet. Dr. Nick, for example, mentioned that the organization was founded as primary care focused institution and it still is, though other disciplines have been given more of a voice.

"We enhanced the medical school, but we didn't dramatically change it. It is still an excellent school for primary care. Nobody ever objected to that focus. It just seemed that to some, its focus was to the exclusion of others. And this came out loud and strong during the process. We're a better school. We're bigger and better." **Department Chair**

As Dr. Pat remarked, "Institutions have minds that endure. Even after the individuals have left, the memories survive and are carried on by the culture." This statement is realistic as it reflects the difficulty in creating true organizational cultural change. Yet, it also is optimistic in that it might suggest that the changes to Braum University's culture could endure into the future.

Legacy: 10-Years After

Some interviewees stated that tensions still exist within the school, but that they feel that most of the participants in the ARIA process believe that this is natural and possibly even beneficial for the organization. The most important aspect of these tensions, however, is that they seem to have been manageable. Instead of being unspoken and potentially disruptive as they were in the previous culture, participants noted understanding their colleagues' perspectives better. While it is naïve to think that these tensions can ever be fully eliminated, the nature of the relationships in general is more collaborative and free of major grievances.

Many participants including Dr. Vi and Dr. Nick reported not even considering these tensions strong enough to be labeled a conflict any more.

> *"Within any organization, you're going to have tension. And I'm not talking 'I'm going to punch you in the face' tension. There are always going to be issues you have to manage. This doesn't change when the mission changes. They will always be there. I would never want to be the Dean of a medical school. You have hospital perspectives versus student opinions versus faculty opinions versus what the community wants. How do you manage this? These things change a little bit over time, but I don't think that differences between people are something that will ever go away or change."* **Faculty Member**

> *"There's not really an 'us versus them' anymore. Sure, there are probably people that are still very strongly entrenched in the old way, but there's no movement to change things back."* **Associate Dean**

Interviewees report that only a handful of faculty members have left the organization following the ARIA process. It should be noted that we cannot be sure why such individuals left. However, interviewees suggested that those individuals still upset about the change in the mission statement have either left the organization or have continued to do their jobs well despite disagreeing with the direction. Such turnover is often good for the organization because it allows for those individuals who do not agree with the overall direction of the organization to leave voluntarily (Collins 2001). Perhaps the reason that those who disagreed but stayed continued their affiliation with Braum University is that they continue to support the underlying assumptions of the culture that have not changed (excellent education, commitment to the community, etc.).

Furthermore, interviewees reported feeling more committed to the organization since they were given a voice in the strategic planning process. Such commitment can come from a similarity between the organization's and individual's values (Hackman and Oldham 1976) which have a variety of positive impacts on the organization (Meyer et al. 2002). The match in values is, perhaps, an important reason why very few faculty members have left despite SOM having a cultural

change and others have become more committed. Additionally, there is a sense now that leadership of the school is talking with faculty and not just talking at them. This creates a spirit of inclusion even for those who express a difference of opinion with the majority. Even a major dissenter of the change in the mission statement acknowledges:

> *"The group we have now is the most collegial and engaged I've seen. It has nothing to do with the mission, but with the group of people themselves. I don't see fiefdoms that you can't penetrate. People work together."* **Faculty Member**

While trying to reflect on the ARIA process, several participants reported not remembering much of the details since they have not thought about it for 10 years. In many instances, participants reported the changes made as a result of ARIA are second nature now and not necessarily something they revisit and think about often. This suggests that the changes that occurred were indeed a success and have been properly institutionalized during the "refreezing" phase of cultural change.

Future Challenges

The school still faces challenges, however. Braum University is anticipating painful and dramatic changes in budget. They no longer expect to receive as much funding as they had in the past from the state. Funding through the state had decreased throughout the years and faculty members reported anticipating another cut as a result of the down economy and new legislation. As such, the school recently raised tuition and increased an emphasis on receiving funding for research. Though the process of ARIA helped position Braum University to achieve more funding due to explicitly making research a goal, faculty and leadership are concerned that new funding methods must be considered in the future.

> *"Now we're far more dependent on revenue from clinical operations and grants than we were previously. We had to work to diversify funding streams."* **Faculty Member**

Some faculty members are not as optimistic about the funding situation in which the school finds itself:

> *"Right now we don't have a niche like we used to with the focus on primary care. If the state needs to close a med school, we are in a weak position. And, given the financial status of the state and higher education, who knows what will happen!"* **Faculty Member**

In addition to impending budget cuts, healthcare reform, and an impending shortage of physicians in the US, many participants in the ARIA process suggest that it might be time to go through an Action Evaluation process again in order to help the school plan for the future.

Even considering the potential need for more strategic planning, many participants from the first ARIA Group engagement were very positive and optimistic about what it had done for the organization. Several noted how going through this process created an awareness of why change and growth are important and provided them with a process that they can use in the future to help them with continued growth. Such growth will come from capitalizing on existing strengths while building others.

Part Three: Reflections on BU: Reflexive Dialogues with Two Key Participants

In addition to interviewing participants in the Action Evaluation and ARIA conflict engagement models, researchers also spoke with Dean Harold Pierce and Jay Rothman, PhD, founder of the ARIA Group and developer of the ARIA models. Our conversations were formed as a "reflexive dialogue" in which we interactively discussed who the Dean and Dr. Rothman were (within the context of Braum University engagement), how they viewed their actions, and how they think others viewed their roles and identities (Rothman 1996). This next section presents the reflexive perspectives of Dean Pierce and Dr. Rothman.

Reasons for Choosing ARIA

Dr. Rothman reported having made a connection with Braum University through an Associate Dean in the School of Medicine who had attended the same undergraduate institution he had. Once Dean Pierce commented to his leadership team that the school needed a strategic planning facilitator, this Associate Dean made the connection.

Ultimately, Dr. Rothman considers selecting clients as a two-way approach: "Just as a client hires me, I want to hire my client. There needs to be a fit with the things I value: authenticity, integrity." Dr. Rothman has worked with organizations in which his story-telling approach to conflict engagement was not a good cultural fit. However, he sensed early on that this approach would fit with Braum University's culture. Rothman's idea about his work is that it helps "good people do good work better." He felt that Dean Pierce and his leadership team were "good people" who tried hard to say what they mean and do what they say, being both authentic about their work and intentions and ready for change within their organization.

One thing that made Dr. Rothman sense this was that Dean Pierce and the leadership team invested their own time into the initial Action Evaluation process before rolling it out to the rest of the organization. Similarly, this is how Dean Pierce knew that the ARIA Group was a good fit. After having experienced the Action Evaluation approach, the Dean was impressed by its inclusive nature in developing a strategic vision and plan. "We never had a planning process that was so open-ended with regard to possibilities of outcomes. We needed it because we were a maturing medical school and were witnessing the decline of state funding."

Prior to engaging the ARIA Group in the Action Evaluation process and shortly after accepting his position as Dean, Dean Pierce became mindful of a need for change within the school. "I was beginning to hear rumblings that non-primary care physicians felt like second class citizens. Everyone needs to feel welcomed here." Ultimately, the welcoming inclusive approach of the ARIA Group is what convinced the Dean to roll out the Action Evaluation process to the entire organization. Though he was aware that a conflict could emerge as a result of this process, he did not necessarily expect it. While he knew that Dr. Rothman and his colleagues had extensive experience with conflict engagement, the School of Medicine did not hire the ARIA Group for this reason.

General Recollections/Thoughts on the Process

While many physicians reported that they were surprised at how the conflict emerged in this process, as the leader of the school, Dean Pierce was prepared for it as he had heard rumblings of unrest. The faculty and students were becoming much more diverse and had a variety of different interests and motivations for associating with the school. Dean Pierce was aware that change was coming and was thankful that the ARIA Group helped to make it occur more deliberately. Dr. Rothman agrees: "All of this change was going to happen anyway. This way it happened purposefully."

Going through the process, Dean Pierce was struck by the "unorthodox" collaborative approach of the ARIA Group. In many other strategic planning initiatives, Dean Pierce had witnessed most of the ideas come from the top down. In the ARIA process, rank-and-file faculty members drove the process based on their participation which fit the culture of the organization well.

The process took on a new momentum when Dr. Rothman moved from the Action Evaluation model into ARIA Conflict Engagement. Dr. Rothman recalls how he made the choice to stop the Action Evaluation process and move into Antagonism. In one meeting, there were 80 people in the room having a heated discussion about the goals of the school. At this point, he realized that the process would not move forward unless he diverted the group from its current rut. He realized that he could "overpower" the participants by forcefully guiding them into cooperation. But, this was not his personality or his philosophy. He has built his reputation and that of The ARIA Group on openness and collaboration.

According to Rothman, he recalls one person in particular was extremely excited about the Antagonism process because it uncovered deep conflicts that had been brushed over for quite a long time. Hearing this, and seeing the process going well, Rothman was encouraged as this affirmed his decision to temporarily halt the Action Evaluation and begin Antagonism. Doing so created a space for open discussion.

This is, in fact, one of the most crucial reasons for starting the ARIA Conflict Engagement process. The goal of CE is to create an open dialogue while minimizing hurt. To make sure that people are not hurt, Rothman always looks to see if they're engaged in the process. If they're not, he makes himself available in order to discuss ambivalence or resistance. In discussing the conflict, he also looks for aspects that are new to participants and that might draw them into the dialogue.

Rothman is realistic, however, in acknowledging that someone may resist and be angered by the process. He knew it might even lead to some faculty turn-over if some felt the new direction didn't fit their needs or identity anymore. Such was the case with two of the participants that we interviewed. One mentioned still being deeply hurt and angered by the changes that were made (though he continues to work at Braum University because he agrees with its underlying cultural assumption of having a community-based approach and the collaborative nature of SOM).

Dean Pierce is realistic that not everyone may be happy by the change in the focus of the school. He commented:

"To this day, there are still some [faculty] members who are upset from the process. Sometimes it bubbles up again. But, the bottom line is that we have to make sure that we are responding to the greater community, including internal and external constituents. All I can hope for is that people will play together collaboratively. I'm not here to make sure everybody's happy. People will always disagree, and that's good! I think disagreement is good organizationally as long as it doesn't contribute to warfare. Can they have philosophical disagreements? Absolutely, but we're all working toward something in common." **Dean**

Rothman mentioned that it was interesting to see the identities of primary and specialist care become salient in the process, even if initially through antagonism. He believes that this occurred because they were legitimized by being given a voice. ARIA makes it safe to have a voice and to disagree with the status quo. The "why" process is empowering because it makes people brave by giving them a space to talk.

Successes/Shortcomings

There were several outcomes of the ARIA Group's engagement at the Braum University School of Medicine. Tangibly, faculty and leadership agreed upon a Mission Statement built from the common goals of excellence in education, research, and patient care. Dean Pierce stated that the Medical School, as a result of the process, is different. According to the Dean, the focus is still on generalist medicine, but other things are now important too. He makes the analogy of "widening the tent" to let everyone in instead of being exclusive to only one group.

The Dean has no regrets about the overall process and outcomes. He feels the processes that they utilized positioned them well for the future. Ultimately, he considers it a success because it got them to talk about core issues. This, in turn, allowed the School to grow and change in ways that he thought were very positive. Now specialists feel more at home, resources are growing as a result of new funding streams, and stakeholders view changes as good. Tangible evidence of the growth includes new buildings for research and education, an increase in fundraising, and the completion of the goals that were stated at the end of the ARIA Action Evaluation process.

"We might not be in as good of a place as we are now if we hadn't used ARIA. We've hit some bumps in the road along the way, but we've done very well." **Dean**

The Dean also recognizes and acknowledges the engagement and hard work of faculty and staff:

"The ARIA Group can't take all the credit – that goes to our faculty and staff. But, the process got us moving." **Dean**

Rothman suggests that there were several successes of the process. First and foremost is that the cascading process (within and between the three committees) of rolling out and coordinating the Action Evaluation and ARIA Conflict Engagement methodologies worked well. In addition, he saw passion in the discussions about the school's identity and ownership of the goals.

Both the Dean and Dr. Rothman, however, note that more work can still be done. Dean Pierce is considering bringing in Dr. Rothman and The ARIA Group once again because more changes are on the way as a result of conditions external to the organization.

"The pace of change has been occurring at a blistering rate, and it's not likely to slow down. We started at ground zero during our strategic planning process and it positioned us into a good place, but it may be time to bring in Jay [Rothman] again." **Dean**

In 18 months, the Dean hopes to begin another strategic planning process just as he had done in 2002 and Dr. Rothman already has ideas for how to make this next wave even more beneficial to Braum University. Due to several participants telling the researchers that they would have liked more follow-up from the ARIA Group, Dr. Rothman suggests building in an evaluative piece to do continuous follow-ups on the process. However, he notes that this may not be the optimal solution. Indeed, the most optimal solution would be to help them build a greater capacity to manage the process on their own. He would like to make them more accountable to take ownership of the process so that they may continue to use it for years down the road. This is the true idea of Action Evaluation for Dr. Rothman as he doesn't view it as a consultation tool, but rather as a methodology to help organizations improve themselves.

Conclusion

This chapter examined the experiences of those closely involved with the Braum University Action Evaluation and ARIA Conflict Engagement processes conducted by the ARIA Group in 2002 as an example of the ARIA process in organizations. The most interesting concept here is how the process began using the Action Evaluation model, then moved into Antagonism in the ARIA Conflict Engagement model, and then concluded with a return to the Action Evaluation model in order to identify organization-wide goals and craft a new mission statement. This illustrates both the fluidity of these models as well as their applicability to organizational contexts. This chapter also illustrates the power of giving minority groups a voice and how the Action Evaluation approach allows such voices to have a space of action in which they are heard.

While the process unfolded this way at Braum University, it may not develop in the same manner in other organizations. As Dr. Rothman alluded to in his comments above, each organization's culture is different and the ARIA process might unfold differently depending on the organization being examined. This does not mean that the reader cannot learn from the process at Braum University. Indeed, taken together with the other chapters in this book, the reader can see how flexible the ARIA model is and how useful it can be in a variety of situations. Our hope for this chapter is that the reader considers using the ARIA model not only at the micro or macro levels but also at the meso (in this case, the organizational) level as well. Doing so will help organizations understand and negotiate their identity-based conflicts in a more effective and proactive manner.

References

Albert, S., & Whetten, D. A. (1985). Organizational identity. In L. L. Cummings & M. M. Staw (Eds.), *Research in organizational behavior* (pp, Vol. 7, pp. 263–295). Greenwich, CT: JAI.

Ashforth, B. E., & Mael, F. (1989). Social identity theory and the organization. *Academy of Management Review, 14*, 20–39.

Brewer, M. B. (1979). In-group bias in the minimal intergroup situation: A cognitive-motivational analysis. *Psychological Bulletin, 86*, 307–324.

Brewer, M. B., & Brown, R. (1998). Intergroup relations. In D. Gilbert, S. Fiske, & D. Lindzey (Eds.), *The handbook of social psychology* (4th ed., Vol. 1, pp. 554–594). Boston, MA: McGraw-Hill.

Collins, J. (2001). *Good to great*. New York, NY: HarperCollins.

Ernst, C., & Chrobot-Mason, D. (2011). *Boundary spanning leadership: Six practices for solving problems, driving innovation, and transforming organizations.* Boston, MA: McGraw-Hill.

Hackman, J. R., & Oldham, G. R. (1976). Motivation through the design of work: Test of a theory. *Organizational Behavior and Human Performance, 16*, 250–279.

Hatch, M. J., & Schultz, M. (2002). The dynamics of organizational identity. *Human Relations, 55*, 989–1018.

Hogg, M. A., & Terry, D. J. (2000). Social identity and self-categorization processes in organizational contexts. *Academy of Management Review, 25*, 123–140.

Hogg, M. A., & Terry, D. J. (2001). Social identity theory and organizational processes. In M. A. Hogg & D. J. Terry (Eds.), *Social identity processes in organizational contexts* (pp. 1–12). Ann Arbor, MI: Sheridan Books.

Kavilanz, P. B. (2009). Family doctors: An endangered breed. *CNN money.* http://money.cnn.com/2009/07/16/news/economy/healthcare_doctors_shortage/index.htm. Accessed 30 July 2011.

Kreiner, G. W., Hollensbe, E. C., & Sheep, M. L. (2006). On the edge of identity: Boundary dynamics at the interface of individual and organizational identities. *Human Relations, 59*, 1315–1341.

Lewin, K. (1947). Group decision and social change. In T. M. Newcomb, E. L. Hartley, et al. (Eds.), *Readings in social psychology* (pp. 330–344). New York: Henry Holt.

Meyer, J. P., Stanley, D. J., Herscovitch, L., & Topolyntsky, L. (2002). Affective, continuance, and normative commitment to the organization: A meta-analysis of antecedents, correlates, and consequences. *Journal of Vocational Behavior, 61*, 20–52.

Rothman, J. (1996). Reflexive dialogue as transformation. *Mediation Quarterly, 13*, 345–352.

Rothman, J. (1997). *Resolving identity-based conflict.* San Francisco, CA: Jossey Bass.

Schein, E. H. (2004). *Organizational culture and leadership* (3rd ed.). San Francisco, CA: Jossey Bass.

Spears, R., Doosje, B., & Ellemers, N. (1999). Commitment and the context of social perception. In N. Ellemers, R. Spears, & B. Doosje (Eds.), *Social identity: Context, commitment, content* (pp. 59–83). Oxford: Blackwell.

Tajfel, H., & Turner, J. C. (1985). The social identity theory of intergroup behavior. In S. Worchel & W. G. Austin (Eds.), *Psychology of intergroup relations* (2nd ed., pp. 7–24). Chicago, IL: Nelson-Hall.

Tsui, A. S., Xin, K. R., & Egan, T. D. (1995). Relational demography: The missing link in vertical dyad linkage. In S. E. Jackson (Ed.), *Diversity in work teams: Research paradigms for a changing workplace* (pp. 97–129). Washington, DC: American Psychological Association.

Turner, J. C., & Giles, H. (1981). Introduction: The social psychology of intergroup behaviour. In J. C. Turner & H. Giles (Eds.), *Intergroup behavior* (pp. 1–32). Oxford, UK: Blackwell.

Whetten, D. A. (1998). Preface: Why organizational identity, and why conversations? In D. A. Whetten & P. C. Godfrey (Eds.), *Identity in organizations: Building theory through conversations* (pp. vii–xi). Thousand Oaks, CA: Sage.

Embedding Action Evaluation in an Interfaith Program for Youth

10

Sharon Miller, Jay Rothman, Beth Ciaravolo, and
Sarah Haney

Introduction

Face-to-Face/Faith-to-Faith (abbreviated F2F) is
a multi-faith youth leadership program which
was started in 2001 by Auburn Theological
Seminary in New York City. Working with
Christian, Jewish and Muslim teens from the
Middle East, Northern Ireland, South Africa and
the United States, F2F seeks to develop a new
generation of leaders and to support them in
creatively engaging conflict and cultivating cooperation in a multi-faith global society. In its
first 10 years, more than 500 teens have taken
part in this program (see www.auburnseminary.
org/programdescription).

F2F focuses on inter-religious dialogue, leadership development and building communication
skills. It is built on the premise that religion can
be used as an avenue for peace and that teens can
be taught to value their own religious tradition
and can learn to navigate in a multi-faith world in
order to build understanding and peace.

The goals of the program were established by
the U.S. steering committee and F2F directors
when the program was begun a decade ago. Until

the project described in this chapter, there had
been no further definition of their goals. No one
had asked: How are the goals to be interpreted or
understood by participants and the international
staff? How are they to be actualized or carried out
during the summer intensive and in the participants' home countries? And how will success be
defined and measured?

Moreover, the goals had been determined by
the U.S.-based board without discussion and
input from participants and leaders in the other
regions where F2F works. Ownership of goals is
critical to the success of programs such as this
one, where deep participation is essential. If goals
are perceived to be "imposed" from an external
(and in this case, foreign) organization, they are
less likely to be actualized (see Ross 1999).
Furthermore, if the interpretation of the goals
varies from region to region, there is room for
misunderstandings, and some regions may take
less ownership of the process and thus get less
out of the experience than others.

The conflicts (or as the Northern Irish call
them, the "troubles") each region faces are unique
and thus the frame from which they interpret
these goals is different as well. The Northern
Ireland conflict between Protestants and Catholics,
although "resolved" through the peace process,
continues to simmer just under the surface and
conflict still erupts periodically. Nearly every
Northern Ireland participant of F2F has been
directly or indirectly impacted by arrests, shoot-
ings or bombings of family members or friends.

S. Miller • B. Ciaravolo • S. Haney
e-mail: SMiller@AuburnSeminary.org;
ciaravba@mail.uc.edu; haneysh@gmail.com

J. Rothman (✉)
Program on Conflict Resolution and Negotiation,
Bar-Ilan University, Ramat Gan, Israel
e-mail: jrothman@ariagroup.com

J. Rothman (ed.), *From Identity-Based Conflict to Identity-Based Cooperation: The ARIA Approach in
Theory and Practice*, Peace Psychology Book Series, DOI 10.1007/978-1-4614-3679-9_10,
© Springer Science+Business Media New York 2012

The Israeli group faces the ongoing conflict between Palestinians and Jews as well as between Jews and Muslims, and random and deliberate acts of discrimination and violence happen with some regularity. In South Africa, the conflict is not as visible, but the history of apartheid lingers in the form of segregated communities and limited options of education and employment for blacks and "coloreds." White South Africans are still in a position of privilege, and the groups are still, and often, separated by class and race, so working together across the color divide has sometimes been a challenge for F2F participants.

The U.S. participants have the hardest time identifying with these communal conflicts, as few of them have had firsthand experience with the dynamics of deep ethnic conflict or racial violence. Some of the U.S. participants who are Muslim, African-American, or Hispanic can identify with the discrimination faced by participants in other countries. But in the U.S., where everyone professes to be equal and where discrimination is often denied, it can be hard for U.S. participants to "own" the inequality that exists.

The Structure of F2F

F2F is a year-long program, divided into three phases. Phase One is the selection and preparation of participants, Phase Two, is an intensive two-week summer experience in the U.S., and Phase Three is the follow-up. During Phase One, participants are selected, taking care to maintain a balance between male and female and the various ethnic and religious groups (Muslim, Christian and Jewish) in each region. During the opening months of the program, the students are oriented to the F2F program. Relationships develop, dialogue begins to occur across religious, cultural and ethnic lines, and service projects are planned.

In Phase Two, participants travel to a camp north of New York City for a two-week intensive program where they meet participants from the other regions where F2F operates. They learn active listening skills, they share experiences, and they begin to engage in extensive and intensive activities that surface differences and confront stereotypes and imbedded beliefs about the "Other." They are also challenged to discover the best of their religious or faith tradition (or that of their family) and to dialogue across religious divides.

Often international peace-building programs for teens find that re-entry can be a challenge. It is unfair, some think, to bring youth from troubled countries to a wholesome camp in the U.S., only to send them back home at the conclusion of the program with few resources or support to help with their reintegration. Phase Three of F2F is intended to directly address these re-entry issues and to keep participants connected to the program for at least another six months. The re-entry process has not fully succeeded to date, since the intensive summer experience sets a standard and level of excitement and total commitment that cannot easily be replicated upon returning home. Still, the structure is in place to support this goal. Upon returning home, participants meet regularly with their home group to build on their shared experiences by exercising their new skills to plan service projects and to support each other during re-entry.

Evaluation of F2F

Evaluations of F2F have been conducted since 2001 by one of the authors of this chapter, Dr. Sharon Miller, a sociologist on staff at Auburn Theological Seminary. The evaluation instrument was a standardized survey of questions which measured communication skills, empathy, sense of empowerment within the community, and knowledge of one's own religion and that of others (see Davis 1996). Like most traditional program evaluations, this survey was administered at the beginning and again at the end of the year-long program (see Chavis et al. 1987). Theoretically, one could say that differences between "before" and "after" scores could be at least partially attributed to the individual's involvement in F2F.

However, there are major issues of internal, external, and face validity in drawing conclusions from this survey's results (for a discussion on reliability and validity see Singleton et al. 1988). First, there was clearly a gap between what the instrument measured and the stated goals of the program. Second, because the goals were broad and encompassing, there was no clear or operational definition of success, therefore, it would be difficult to administer a survey that could measure progress towards it. Third, the goals and the criteria for success were defined by only one stakeholder group – the U.S. steering committee and directors – and this had been done only once, at the program's inception. Fourth, the same measure of success was applied to all regions, despite the richness of diversity and the unique circumstances and history represented by each country. Moreover, participants were not being challenged to set goals for themselves or to reflect on what they hoped to get out of the program before, during, or after the summer intensive.

Everyone involved with F2F realized that a better method of evaluation was urgently needed, a method that could better reflect, and involve, shared goals of the program while still being responsive to the needs of its various regions. What was needed was a way for F2F participants to take ownership of their goals, a way to clearly articulate what they hoped to get out of the program and how they would know if they were moving toward meeting those goals.

Action Evaluation and Face-to-Face

F2F's introduction to ARIA and Action Evaluation came at a critical point in the program. As the tenth anniversary of F2F was approaching, the program's supporters and donors wanted more tangible evidence that it was producing results. After nearly a year of exploration and discussion between F2F leadership and ARIA Group staff, the process of Action Evaluation was selected to provide a new way to foster ownership and commitment among the various stakeholders. Action Evaluation was selected, both as an evaluation tool and as a way to address the challenges and opportunities of re-entry. It was hoped that Action Evaluation would help the participants more clearly define their goals and what success looked like to them individually and in groups, and that this would subsequently raise the level of engagement after the students returned to their home countries.

The process of adopting AE, however, was not without hurdles, and thus took a long time. Edgar Schein's classic book *Process Consultation* (1988) suggests that taking time to comprehensively contract between consultants and clients is essential. Any successful consultancy, he suggests, is only as good as the fit between the client's needs and the consultant's expertise and so this fit should be slowly and carefully constructed. Since participants' enthusiasm and trust in the process are key to the success of AE, the Action Evaluators did not want to establish a partnership without first ensuring that the process was clearly understood and was seen as a good fit for a wide array of F2F stakeholders. They sought to ensure understanding of the method and tested the fit through experimentation and adaptation. Optimally, representatives of all key stakeholder groups would have been involved from the start in this contracting process. In the case of F2F, however, the ability to do this was limited by logistics and the structure of the organization. Instead, members of the senior staff took part in the initial conversations and only later was this expanded to include a more representative group of stakeholders.

While it was important for a critical mass of stakeholders to grasp what AE was about, to understand how it worked, and to be convinced that it was suitable for the organization, early in the contracting negotiations there was healthy skepticism about AE. Although there were reports of the success of AE in other contexts, the process seemed confusing, complex and cumbersome to some of the staff and board members. Some of these stakeholders were not fully convinced that it was well suited for F2F. After much exploration and negotiation the senior F2F staff and board members committed to contracting with ARIA to run the process and build capacity for F2F staff to adopt the AE process as its own. A project steering committee, composed of funders and parents of participants and staff from all four regions, was put together to move the process forward. In order to bring everyone on board, an initial AE workshop was held in January 2010 with this steering committee.

Not until this group had actually experienced AE did they fully understand what it was about and the potential it had for F2F. The most convincing part of the experience, according to some (co-author Sharon Miller included), was the chance to hear the personal narratives offered by other participants (see Power of Why Chap. 2). At this point, they realized that the process was not merely about agreeing on goals and objectives and monitoring and assessing them, it was about much more. Each person conveyed the passion he/she brought to F2F, as well as a wealth of experience and a diversity of perspective and background. This was when most of the staff and other stakeholders became convinced that AE was the right choice. Creating collectively agreed-upon goals based upon deeply-held personal beliefs and experiences seemed to many to be ideal for the reflective and developmental needs of F2F at this point in its evolution. This process also had the added benefit of ensuring that the teen participants would have an active role in their own goal-setting. This would give them confidence that F2F would provide them the opportunity to re-establish the organization's goals in a deeply participatory and systematic way, taking into account their own individual needs and values.

However, despite this hands-on introduction, a few of the international staff remained skeptical and unsure if AE was appropriate to their context and worth the demands on their time and energy. From the beginning, for example, one of the home group leaders had been resistant to AE. It wasn't until much later that she finally revealed that even with the trial run in which she participated, she had never felt ownership in the process. In addition, she had been uncomfortable sharing a personal story in a group setting with those she hardly knew. Initial contracting had taken place without her approval or that of the other home group leaders and she did not feel empowered to decline to take part in the process and thus was somewhat resentful of it for quite a long time (though eventually she too found it valuable and a good fit). Ideally, the process would have paused here and further time would have been taken to gain her full understanding and cooperation. Time, however, was limited, and both the F2F senior staff and the AE staff were anxious to get the program off the ground in

time for it to be integrated into the forthcoming summer intensive. Due to these constraints, the home group leader's reticence was minimized and staff and consultants plunged ahead in implementing AE.

Implementation of AE

The entire AE process took participants in F2F one year to complete. As described above, contracting and planning had begun prior to this year, but the process itself began in the summer of 2010 and concluded in the spring of 2011.

Even after the F2F staff had agreed to adopt AE, they still did not realize how much time and effort the process would take. There were challenges in gathering data, in training facilitators, and in conducting meetings since the eighty participants aged 16–19 were located in four countries on four different continents. Although the web-based data gathering instrument that is core to AE facilitated this international collaboration and participatory goal-setting, the geographical spread did present logistical and organizational obstacles.

Phase One – Baseline

The first stage of the AE process begins at the level of the individual. In the spring of 2010 the eighty student participants of F2F were asked to respond to an online questionnaire that asked the following questions: "WHAT do you want to accomplish [through the program]?", "WHY do you want to accomplish this (why do you think it is important)?", and "HOW will you work to reach this goal?" Although each of the participants had no doubt read materials from Auburn about the overall goals for F2F, they were asked about their personal goals for the program. The students were encouraged to be reflexive as they thought about their reasons for joining the program and as they articulated their hopes for the year. Participants' responses ranged from the very personal and specific to the general and impersonal. They were asked to share up to three goals each. Here are some examples from approximately two hundred goals the eighty participants shared:

- To gain confidence and skills in how to be an effective leader.
- I want to learn skills that will enable me to handle conflict effectively.
- To learn more about how religions are compatible…how they can work together and how they aren't always conflicting.
- My goal is to develop the skills and knowledge to help other people in my community. In doing so, I hope to undergo personal growth in the way I think, understand, and observe the world.
- I hope to understand people who are different than me, and to learn about them.
- A third goal I have for this program is to learn more about my own country, religion, and other communities. I want to be able to gain deeper understanding not only of people from other places and backgrounds, but also of my own background.
- My second goal lies in my desire to further extend my knowledge and understanding of my own faith and the faiths of others. I would like to comprehend more deeply how and why my religion appeals to me, to allow me to immerse myself in interfaith and cultural exchanges with others on the programme.
- I hope to achieve the knowledge and skills that I need to learn how to make an impact and difference in this world; trying to bring peace and justice to all religions and ethnic groups.
- Make lifelong friends from around the world.
- My goal is to communicate with youth from other parts of the world despite religious, cultural and ethnic differences on common issues affecting all of us and to be able to understand them and how they think.
- Break down the walls which divide people who come from different religious, ethnic or racial backgrounds.
- Understand others point of view.

Along with each goal, participants were asked WHY that particular goal was important to them. They could do this by telling a story or explaining further their thoughts about that goal. Each par-

ticipant was then asked HOW they could take specific action to achieve the goals that they had listed. These questions began to train participants in reflexive thinking.

As in ARIA Conflict Engagement (see Chaps. 1 and 3), the reflexive process is at the core of AE. This is important to create deep internal and relational understanding. Who am I? What are my priorities and values? Who are you, and what are your goals, priorities, values, and stories? AE invites participants to look deeply within while simultaneously engaging others. The journey inward leads outward and the journey outward leads inward. Participants enter into deep conversations about their beliefs, their stories, their joys, concerns, disappointments, and hopes.

Throughout all stages of Action Evaluation, participants learn and practice reflexive thinking and communication. Ideally, by the process's completion, reflexive thinking will become second nature to participants, thus enabling them to think about and interact with others in a deeply collaborative manner by getting internal clarity about why a goal or issue is personally important to them and learning how to share information about this with others.

The four home groups met in July 2010 at a camp in Holmes, New York. On the first full day, all eighty campers met together for an overview of Action Evaluation and the process they would follow to arrive at shared goals for F2F. A lot of staffing was needed at this point, as regional groups were each divided into three or four smaller groups of five participants each, and groups needed both a facilitator and a scribe (staff had been trained for these roles by the consultants prior to the start of camp). A total of fourteen groups were convened.

Upon arrival, all participants received a copy of their responses to the online questionnaire that they had completed weeks earlier. Based upon their WHY responses, the students chose a single word that would be their "passion point." Each participant shared their word with their small group and told a story about why it was important to them personally. Many of these narratives were deeply personal.

Storytelling fosters resonance within a group by allowing others to understand motives and meaning and to recognize shared core commonalities. Participants could ask for more details until they clearly understood why the story signified the individual's passion point and what was so deeply meaningful about it to the teller. By delving further into the motivations and feelings which lay behind the stated goals, there was a greater likelihood that something shared by the speaker would be understood on a deeply personal level by all the listeners. When enough details had been shared, a common resonance was created among the participants which helped to build and deepen the bonds between them. The personal sharing set the stage for the next step which was more collaborative as they sought to reach common goals.

Here are two stories that illustrate why understanding others and learning more about other religions was important to these participants:

• My father is heavily sectarian and is so bitter about every aspect of the conflict in NI [Northern Ireland] which has been ground in him from an early age. I started to question this a few years ago. His best friend, six days after his wedding, was shot sixteen times in the back due to being in the wrong place at the wrong time. My dad's best friend is paralyzed and in a wheelchair. He is my godfather and when I see him I am always reminded of what was done to him… In the past I didn't feel I could move on but I have been able to. I believe I have the power to change and not have the stereotypes my father did.

• Two years ago I went to an interfaith meeting, I met a Jewish guy, the first I've ever met and I was surprised about what I learned from him. In my family there is prejudice due to my grandmom growing up in Egypt, passed on to my mother and then to me. But it opened my eyes to other people and cultures. He was pretty friendly. He showed us our rooms… My grandmom thought all Israelis/Jews were murderous people, but this changed my views. I was confused, happy, relieved – a very mixed moment. I didn't know what to feel, but it was also exciting. I realized at that moment that I had to expand my horizons.

After a break, during which all the passion words and goal-statements were written on flip charts, the groups reconvened with their home group. The task the home groups had before them was to create common goals for their region from their individual goals. Sentences were constructed and deconstructed, formed and erased, words were argued over and analyzed. Voting on sentences or phrases was a thumbs up (good), thumbs down (don't like it) and thumbs sideways (don't love it, but can live with it). If a person gave a thumbs down, he or she needed to be prepared to offer an alternative word or phrase.

This was the most demanding part of the process, because it required a great deal of negotiation. For example, someone would suggest a change, but another group member would suggest a different change, and the group would have to decide whether to choose between the two or come up with a third option. Since this could occur multiple times within the same goal, and since there were multiple goals, it took what felt like a very long time to reach a final consensus (in actuality it was only a two hour process, which is quite efficient for consensus-building). As one student from the U.S. said, "It was at times both tedious and kind of frustrating. We would finally [reach agreement] on a good sentence and then someone had another proposal. I was getting kind of heated at one time. We put our ideas forward and felt satisfied in the end; it was great to see how in the end everyone was able to work well together." A student from S. Africa remarked, "It helped us think critically. It showed that even though everyone thinks differently, after negotiating for a while we came to agreement about what was important to all of us." A Palestinian participant spoke about how much she appreciated the opportunity "to express ourselves – we spoke about our stories and then we were able to use art" to express our goals (an art project followed that evening, see below). Another from the U.S. commented, "I liked how every single person in the group had something to offer." Participants were using reflexivity, by evaluating their needs and the needs of others, and striving for constructive compromise.

The then-director of F2F, Manar Fawakhry, concluded this stage of AE by telling the participants:

> F2F is ten years old. One of the things we do as an educational program is set goals. Our goals were set ten years ago. We decided we needed to evaluate … what works for you (participants)….We see this as your program, your journey, your experience, and it is our responsibility to revisit our goals that we set and say, "We want to hear your voices." The exact process you are doing, we've done with staff at F2F, with summer staff and with our executive committee. That is, all the different stakeholders who care about this program. And you are right. We have different goals and values and everyone matters. If we think about this program as a tree with different branches - how can this tree have solid ground [in order] to branch and blossom and reach out further? That solid ground is alignment. Despite our differences we are solid in what - we share. To do that, we want - we need - everyone's voices. It's complicated. It takes time, effort and negotiation, but it is essential. And I want to thank you for your commitment and willingness to own the process. I heard someone say yesterday, 'This is really intense, you are asking us to own our voice and vision as opposed to sign up for someone else's.'[1]

Reaching Consensus Goals

Completing these two stages of AE took about three hours. Due to the length of time needed for the last stage (three hours), some staff again began to doubt the value of the process. Was it really worth all the time and effort? Would it pay off? Many of the students were tired and found the goal negotiation process tedious. Nonetheless, everyone persevered. Soon, most began to grasp the purpose of this exercise as they experienced it in its entirety, and they became excited to play an active role in establishing their goals and in their own personal success.

Dinner and a much needed break followed this intense work. The evening session moved away from storytelling and the goal negotiation pro-

cesses to an art workshop in which each participant used colored markers and paper to create a visual image of one or more of their WHY passion words. The artwork was wild and exuberant, simple and complex, as the personalities and passions of each individual emerged.

The next afternoon the participants reconvened and the session began with a "gallery walk." The pictures they had made the night before were placed around the perimeter of the room and everyone had an opportunity to look at each other's artwork. Expressions of delight and engagement were heard as the students saw each other's passion words translated into art. This also reminded the group of the personal values that were foundational to the goals.

The Action Evaluators took the WHATs from each region and grouped them thematically in order to facilitate the group goal consensus. Like the experience at the group level, this stage was demanding on the youths' energy and focus. It was important that every participant's voice was heard and represented since ownership of the goals would foster responsibility in reaching those goals. These WHATs would be the criteria used to guide action planning and self-evaluation during the Formative and Summative Phases.

A fishbowl was set up, with two representatives from each region in the center of the group and their compatriots sitting behind them. The task of the representatives was to meld the consensus goals reached by each of the four groups in the prior activity, to represent each group's hopes and expectations for the program. The representatives were the negotiators who would vote on behalf of their region. Clustered behind each representative were the other members of their home group who gave instructions, comments, and suggestions to be presented in the fishbowl.

This is where things became more challenging (and interesting!). The differences between regions and life experiences became clear as the representatives tried to agree on specific wording for the goals. Words were misinterpreted, challenged, and questioned. Coming up with common language proved to be difficult at points, as words meant something quite different in the different regions. "Collaboration with others" was

---

[1] This, and each of the previous statements from participants, was recorded during an evaluation session that took place at the end of the intergroup feedback session. Holmes, NY, July 6, 2010.

suggested by the U.S. participants as a common goal, to which the Irish and Israeli representatives reacted in horror. "Collaboration" is what gets you killed in their conflicts and means something quite different than "cooperation" or "partnership," which is what the U.S. participants intended. "To train faith-informed leaders," was another phrase that had to be discussed at length. What was meant by "faith-informed?" How would secular Jews in Israel understand this phrase? The Irish representative wanted to know if someone who did not identify with a religion could still participate. What does it mean to "engage" conflict? How would this be understood (or misunderstood) in South Africa?

As before, the negotiations were long and arduous, and at times the noise in the large room becoming deafening. Only after each representative gave a thumbs-up or a thumbs-sideways could a goal be finalized. As each goal was agreed upon, applause broke out.

Throughout this session virtually all the teenagers were actively involved in the process. There were, however, a few individuals at the fringes who seemed disengaged. Some were participants from Israel and Palestine whose English was limited and who likely found it difficult to keep up with the fast pace of the conversation and lost interest in the session. Some found the "fishbowl" format itself to be impersonal and inaccessible.

NORTHERN IRISH	SOUTH AFRICAN	ISRAELI/PALESTINIAN	AMERICAN (U.S.)
1. IMPROVE OUR UNDERSTANDING OF THE FAITH TRADITIONS, CULTURES AND CONFLICTS IN NORTHERN IRELAND 2. DEVELOP UNDERSTANDING AND CO-OPERATION BETWEEN DIFFERENT CULTURES, CONFLICTS AND RELIGIONS AROUND THE WORLD 3. GAIN GREATER SELF AWARENESS, SKILLS, AND LEADERSHIP CAPABILITIES TO RESOLVE CONFLICTS IN OUR OWN COMMUNITIES 4. BUILD AND MAINTAIN NEW FRIENDSHIPS WITH PEOPLE OF DIFFERENT CULTURES, RACES AND RELIGIONS	1. TO DEVELOP AND/OR NURTURE SKILLS WHICH BETTER ENABLE US TO COMMUNICATE AND MAKE A POSITIVE DIFFERENCE IN THE CONFLICTS IN OUR COMMUNITIES 2. TO GAIN A DEEPER UNDERSTANDING OF CULTURES, LIFESTYLES, RELIGIONS, FAITHS, BELIEFS AND PERSPECTIVES 3. TO BROADEN SOCIAL INTERACTION AND BUILD DIVERSE, LIFELONG RELATIONSHIPS 4. TO DISCOVER OR BETTER DEFINE MY IDENTITY	1. CHALLENGE MY IDEAS ABOUT THE OTHER AND GET TO KNOW THEIR PERSPECTIVE 2. LEARN ABOUT MY OWN AND OTHER PEOPLE'S RELIGIONS, CULTURES AND BACKGROUNDS 3. EXPRESS MY AUTHENTIC OPINIONS CONFIDENTLY AND LISTEN TO OTHERS WITH RESPECT 4. USE DIALOGUE TO UNDERSTAND THE CONFLICT BETTER AND TO IMPROVE OUR LIVES 5. DEVELOP MY OPINIONS AND COMMUNICATION SKILLS	1.UNDERSTANDING AND ACCEPTING OTHERS WHO ARE DIFFERENT FROM MYSELF AND GAINING A BETTER UNDERSTANDING OF WHO I AM 2. GAIN KNOWLEDGE AND SKILLS TO BECOME AN EFFECTIVE LEADER AND PROMOTE AWARENESS IN MY COMMUNITY AND BEYOND 3. TO TAKE THE KNOWLEDGE WE'VE GAINED ABOUT OTHER RELIGIONS AND CULTURES IN ORDER TO MAKE A DIFFERENCE 4. BUILD MEANINGFUL RELATIONSHIPS WITH INDIVIDUALS FROM THE UNITED STATES AND THE INTERNATIONAL COMMUNITY

INTERGROUP GOALS

1. TO ACTIVELY AND RESPECTFULLY LISTEN WHEN INTERACTING WITH PEOPLE IN ORDER TO UNDERSTAND THEIR PERSPECTIVE, INCREASING OUR SELF AWARENESS AND MOLDING OUR OWN OPINIONS AND IDENTITIES

2. TO BROADEN SOCIAL INTERACTIONS AND BUILD MEANINGFUL, LIFELONG RELATIONSHIPS WITH INDIVIDUALS OF DIVERSE IDENTITIES.

3. TO EDUCATE OUR PEERS ABOUT OUR OWN EXPERIENCES AND THE SKILLS WE HAVE LEARNED WITH F2F IN ORDER TO PROMOTE PEACE AROUND THE WORLD

4. TO GAIN MORE KNOWLEDGE ABOUT THE CONFLICTS AND OTHER CHALLENGES WE FACE WITHIN AND BETWEEN OUR COMMUNITIES IN ORDER TO DEVELOP SKILLS TO MAKE A POSITIVE DIFFERENCE

5. TO LEARN ABOUT DIFFERENT RELIGIONS, FAITHS, BELIEFS AND CULTURES, AS WELL AS OUR OWN, IN ORDER TO DEVELOP UNDERSTANDING AND ACTIVELY COOPERATE

But the majority hung in there until agreements were reached.

So intense was the process that when the list of goals was finally achieved, the participants broke out into cheers. There was a sense of pride among all members, as they saw how their work had paid off. More importantly, they all felt that they had personally played a role in reaching those consensual goals. In the final goals, they could see some of their words and the spirit of their own personal objectives that had been adapted in the shared intra-group goals and finally evolved into the comprehensive intergroup goals. Here finally were a set of goals they could fully endorse. Here were a set of goals they could own and identify with. Since all participants had struggled with the wording and phrasing the final goals could be understood by all.

The following are the goals reached by each country group, followed by the final goals for the overall program:

The following day, the home group leaders worked with their compatriots to develop from their regional goals specific actions plans for when they returned home. Participants' initial action plans were, however, more aspirational goals than operational. That is, they set ambitious goals for how they hoped to change and grow upon re-entry and during their continued engagement, not specific operational or measurable goals of how to achieve that transformation. Nonetheless these goals were the frame within which specific HOW steps could be planned, monitored and measured. These goals could also be the touchstone to which they could return as they marked their progress throughout the year.

Phase Two: Formative

In the Formative Stage of the Action Evaluation process, which aligned well with Phase Three (re-entry) of F2F, home groups work to implement the baseline goals agreed upon within their group. The Action Planning phase of the project is really about establishing a series of agreed upon HOWs; that is, defined steps that the

participants will undertake in order to achieve the goals that they have created.

The following questions were asked on the Formative questionnaire which participants responded to after some months of returning home and working on the goals their group agreed upon:

- What action steps are you taking to fulfill your specific goals?
- How is it going? Have you made progress towards your goal?
- Looking forward, what next steps are you planning for pursuing your goal?

The purpose of these questions was not to be critical and evaluative. Rather, they were intended to draw a reflexive response that would help students see how much progress they had made towards reaching their goals and what steps they could take to keep themselves on track with (or update and revise) their Action Plans.

As described above, one shared challenge across regions was that of systematic follow-through during Phase Three. The hope was that immediately upon arriving back home, each group would meet to debrief the summer intensive and begin to plan activities and projects they had decided upon in their action plans. But because of logistical complexities, holidays, and schedules, none of the groups were able to meet within a week or two of returning home, and some took more than three months to re-convene. It also took much longer than anticipated for groups to plan projects and activities.

Each region brought its own challenges to this phase of the program as participants ran into obstacles beyond their control. The U.S. home group was spread out geographically and was therefore unable to meet more than two times after the summer intensive, so common service projects were difficult. (This, in part, led to a re-design for the program in which US home group participants will, in the future, be selected from contiguous geographic regions.)

The Israel/Palestine home group also had challenges meeting, since some of the Palestinian teens must cross the border from the West Bank and some Muslim girls were not permitted to travel without an adult escort. In addition, the home group leader remained reticent (though increasingly less so than before) about AE and from a distance it was difficult to know how goals were being implemented.

The South Africa group was also spread throughout Cape Town, but they had been able to build a strong program that included other young people who were not part of the F2F program.

The Northern Ireland group was the best organized and most responsive, due to strong, consistent leadership and the relative geographic proximity of participants. Thus, they were most effective at maintaining their group and implementing the Action Plans they had agreed upon in order to fulfill their goals (i.e. the group WHATs).

Across the four regions there were a variety of projects and events that participants organized and undertook: South African participants, after they had been debriefed from the intensive in the U.S., began preparing for their "summer" program with area youth, a program that they staff and run using many of the same tools and activities they learned at the U.S. intensive. They also volunteered at St. Alban's, a home for HIV positive children. Israeli participants celebrated Iftar with their Palestinian peers (the feast at the end of Ramadan) and they all met together during the Jewish Day of Atonement (Yom Kippur) to discuss "soul searching and reflection." The U.S. group started a U.S. home group blog, planned a video conference dialogue (although they were unable to carry through with their plans), and organized multicultural nights at various schools in the cities where they lived. The Northern Irish group simplified their four goals into four overarching themes of "friendships," "experiential learning of faith and culture," "self-awareness," and "world awareness." They then developed specific programming or activities to work toward meeting each of these goals. The goals and related action plans are listed below to provide specific illustrations of the ideas-to-action process as it unfolded.

Friendships

Date: Friday November 19th
Location: Belfast – perhaps Youth Action venue?

Time: when you can get there from school – 9 pm.
Activity: World Café event – tables, chat, food and music just before Interfaith Week. This will be the flagship event for the participants; they are inviting youth groups from all faith communities to join in table discussions on the interface between faith and youth culture from a NI experience.

They felt this event would fulfil two of their goals as they were taking a leadership role and because of the new friendships they hope that will develop as a result of it! They also want to use the event as a way of promoting F2F in the media, and recruiting new participants from a broad spectrum.

Experiential Learning of Faith and Culture

Date: Saturday February 5th
Location: either Belfast or Derry/Londonderry
Time: all day
Activity: either meeting in Ruth's church and hearing from ex-paramilitaries, tour of Peacewalls and Stormount. OR Tour of Derry/Londonderry – Bloody Sunday theme and Bogside tour.

Self-awareness

Date: Saturday November 6th (hopefully) – will be confirmed in coming weeks!
Location: Portadown
Time: 11.30 am-early evening
Activity: Visit Drumcree Church (site of the major conflict between Orange Men and local RC residents), meeting with Orange Men and ex-paramilitaries. Second part of the day will take place at a Youth Club on Garvaghy Road; this will be for recruitment and to show leadership skills in leading some activities with local youth: eating together and socialising in beautiful Portadown.

World Awareness

Date: Saturday October 9th
Location: Belfast, No. 8 Upper Crescent.
Time: 10.30 am – 5.30 pm
Activity: Film Workshop in morning, Planning for World Café event in afternoon. Also making a wee video for the Peace is Possible event. The aim of the film is that they want to educate their peers about the global consequences of not having peace; they are going to explore this from several angles and include some of their learning from camp – and use other F2F regions as case studies to offset these four invitations.

Responses to the Formative questions from the Northern Ireland group showed substantive progress towards meeting these goals. They also reveal reflexivity as they assess what they have accomplished and what remained to be done:

• I feel that I have gained more self-awareness by being able to recognize when I have prejudices and then being able to stand back and think rationally about the situation.... Also I've become more aware of my surroundings, i.e., the murals (that often depict martyrs from the "troubles," or vilify "the other."), bomb scares, etc., which I honestly didn't think were significant before camp, but now I see how much my environment has shaped me.

• A goal which I feel I have worked on is to gain greater self-awareness, skills and leadership capabilities to resolve conflicts in our own community....I have learned that I am able to work as part of a group and accept other people for who they are, and through this I feel it has allowed me to become more confident in expressing my own personal views.

• Post camp I have been selected as Deputy Head boy in my college, and received the pleasure of captaining my school's rugby squad. All require leadership roles, which I feel very capable of taking due to the skills I have attained through F2F. I feel I have found my voice and have the confidence to lead a group of people, often with conflicting claims. I am constantly trying to develop my leadership

potential. Post camp I have realized the value of time to myself, I do this in different ways and feel it increases my self-awareness greatly. The ability to collect and process my thoughts is one I wish to continually improve.

When asked what they were looking forward to accomplishing, or what the next steps were for them, the following responses were received from this group:

• I plan to gain as much knowledge of Northern Ireland as possible, asking family members, watching the news, reading and researching. As I have said, this will be a lifelong task, but I plan on staying informed and to pass on the history to others. This can make peace possible as awareness and knowledge produce an aspect of sensitivity, which is vital in the peace-making process.

• I am hoping to run an event between my church youth group and the youth group from the mosque in Belfast because of my experience with the interfaith aspect of F2F. I am looking forward to attempting to organize this and I hope it works out!

• I plan on continuing to plant seeds with as many people of different cultures, races and religions as possible. I will do this at any opportunity I receive.... I know that university will be an extremely diverse environment. This fuels my motivation to study and get a place (in university), so I can make as many life-long diverse friendships as possible.

The Formative questionnaire served as a reflexive study for these participants, asking that they take a step back from their activities and assess their individual progress towards meeting their collective goals. Each of the Irish participants expressed that they had made some progress toward meeting their goals, and also acknowledged that much remained to be done.

Phase Three: Summative

Finally, in the Summative phase, actual assessment is made about success or failure in relation to the goals previously set (i.e. the internally developed and evolved criteria of success – or the

HOW ideas for action). Although participants were encouraged throughout the process to engage in reflexive practice, in the Summative phase they are asked to look with a critical eye on what they have accomplished and how well they have done in reaching their individual and shared goals. They are asked to reflect on their goals, values, intentions, successes and failures.

The following five questions were asked in the online Summative questionnaire:

- What are your overall reflections on your experience with Face-to-Face (e.g., what worked well for you and what could be improved for future participants)?
- In reflecting on either your individual goals (before the summer intensive) or your group goals (reached during the intensive), in what ways do you feel you made progress in meeting those goals?
- What has been the most valuable part of the program for you (e.g., what has helped you the most towards meeting your goals)?
- What goals do you feel that you have not fully accomplished?
- Any regrets? Would you do anything differently?

One of the Northern Ireland goals developed during the Baseline phase, was to "gain greater self-awareness, skills, and leadership capabilities to resolve conflicts in their community." The theme of self-awareness emerged as a leitmotif at each stage for all participants (from Baseline to Summative).

Many respondents wrote of their growth in this area:

- My experience with F2F has been extremely life-changing. It has changed my whole outlook on life.
- I developed my understanding of myself and others, my community and other communities which I wouldn't have had the chance to come into contact with. It's helped me in many ways I was surprised at, for example, my individual well-being and confidence level.
- I think I have far surpassed my individual goals from the beginning... I have made better friends and learned so much more than I ever expected! I also wasn't expecting to learn as much about myself as I did about other people.
- I am more open to new cultures, ideas, religions and ways of thinking...definitely made me grow in confidence.
- The most valuable part of the program to me was discovering that my voice will always be heard as there is always someone who is prepared to listen, which has helped me grow stronger and become more confident in speaking out.
- I think that the Summer Intensive was the most valuable part of the program as it helped me to find my voice; however the follow-up program has been equally valuable as it has given me the perfect opportunity to use my voice.

Respondents were reflective, honest and realistic when asked to assess their progress toward meeting their goals. They showed a maturity and perspective that was not generally felt to be present prior to their experiences with F2F.

- The most valuable aspect of the program is that it truly was a year-long effort. Everything was very well organized and I always had something new to do with my home group as part of our follow-up phase. As a result, I was constantly thinking of my goals and all that I had learned in New York, meaning I was able to put this into practice more and more often. This helped me to sustain my new and valuable skills, not allowing me to become complacent.
- I made a colossal amount of progress during the program. I am a wee Protestant lad.... I believe I listen more than ever, maybe due to the onslaught of intentional listening in humidity unheard of in New York. Joking aside, I honestly believe I have changed a lot. And effectively achieved my goals.
- One of my individual goals was to make life-long friends around the world, and I definitely think I have reached this goal and beyond. I think that I have made the most progress towards our group goal about learning more about the conflict in our own area; our follow-up program has been focused primarily on this and I have learnt a lot about the human side of

the conflict as well as the facts. I have also made progress towards our goal about leadership skills and I hope to keep developing in this area.

Several participants eloquently expressed their own process of discovery, goal setting and growth through F2F:

- I have to say that my F2F experience was a life-changing one. It opened my eyes to things that I was blind to all my life. It took me out of my comfort zone and challenged me to question what I thought and why I thought it. The summer intensive was by far the part that worked best for me as it really was like nothing I had ever experienced before. The diversity of people and situations that I experienced in New York was something that could never and will never be simulated in the same way anywhere for the rest of my life. The first and third phase of the course were maybe not as exciting and jam-packed full of fun (as Phase 2) but I always left them feeling like I had learned something; I always felt as though they had made a small change in me. For example when we met the paramilitaries I was proud to be a part of F2F. I was able to see the difference it had made to my life and the change in myself. I could openly question these men and disagree with things they said just as easily as others would agree with them.

- We got to learn from our own experiences, and not have to rely on those of people at home. We made our own minds up, made our own judgments, became our own person. The intensive didn't just help us find aims or goals or hopes, it allowed us to find ourselves. We grew into the people we were meant to be, not the people others wanted to mold us into.

Participants knew that there was, in one sense, no way to actually "meet" their goals fully and finally, but that what they had embarked on was a life-long journey of understanding and acceptance of self and others. This is reflected in the following comments in response to what still remained to be accomplished:

- Today, I still find it hard to speak out against the prejudices that I witness and experience every day. It's a very hard transition going

from being not too worried about what people say about certain stereotypes, to becoming a person that would speak out immediately about an injustice I might happen to overhear. But this is a gradual process that will get easier over time as I build up my experience and confidence in different types of situations.

- I personally feel that I have not accomplished my own goals as I have not been able to fully participate in the third phase. I have not been able to make the difference I promised myself I would make whilst leaving the summer intensive. I know I have made small impacts on people and made friends and family question their views and preconceived ideas, but to me this is not enough. However I also feel that we still have a long way to go…. It is a marathon not a sprint, and I believe that the people in our group will lead in the future, and will stand up in the future, and will change the future. It is not a goal, it is a necessity that we will deliver on.

- I still have my prejudices and the odd stereotype flung about. It's sadly engrained into me - slowly leaving but there for now, which brings a small amount of sadness. However they would probably always be there without Face-to-Face.

- Sometimes I can't help but regret putting all of my heart into the program, especially the summer intensive because then when you come home to 'normality,' everything seems so much worse. And it takes so much more time, effort and energy to adjust than you ever thought possible. However I would not do anything differently. It was going through this experience that has made me the person that I am and I am grateful for it.

Summary and Conclusions

Action Evaluation proved to be central to the programming of F2F in 2010/11 and has laid down solid foundations for what will hopefully be the next successful decade of the organization. It functioned as a frame for the program, and it provided a new structure out of which activities and actions evolved. AE helped participants to think seriously about their personal goals for the program, to work together with others in setting shared goals, and to take ownership of these goals once they had been decided upon. It created a system that required reflection and personal and group assessment and evaluation of what had been learned and accomplished.

The structure of F2F, however, made it difficult for all regions to consistently carry through with AE. A lack of enthusiasm of some individuals within the program contributed to the inability of AE to live up to its full potential in this instance; a lack of buy-in from the beginning from the leadership in one region proved to have a deleterious effect on the overall process there. One of the ways this played out was in the difficulty of getting follow-through on the Formative questionnaire that was e-mailed to participants in that region. In addition, programming there did not grow out of the shared agreed-upon goals, and reflective practices were not built into their overall process. In another region, although there was no resistance to AE from the leaders, their direct use of AE as the frame in which action took place (the HOW) was also somewhat hit or miss. This was likely due to the fact that this program was well-established prior to the adoption of AE, and there was little incentive to shift to the new agenda.

Another impediment to the full realization of AE was its timing within the three phases of F2F. As mentioned earlier, the first phase of the F2F, which takes place prior to the summer intensive, is to be a time of orientation to the program and a time for relationships to develop. Phase One begins in early May, after acceptances have been sent out to participants, and extends to their arrival in the U.S. Phase Two is the U.S. summer intensive in July. Phase Three is the follow-up period after participants return home, which extends from August to the following spring. In our first year, Action Evaluation took place during Phase Two, when all participants were at camp. This meant that goals (WHATs) and values (WHYs) did not inform programming during Phase One and did not become operationalized until Phase Three.

As mentioned previously, the leadership in New York hoped that regional groups would meet within a couple weeks of returning home to plan their activities and actions (HOW) and to begin Phase Three of the program, but his did not happen. Some groups never organized themselves to plan their schedules until late fall. This meant that Phase Three of the program was very truncated and in some cases barely off the ground when it was time for the Formative questionnaire to be distributed. This no doubt decreased the return rate of the Formative survey and limited its usefulness as an instrument for reflection and adaptation.

In response to these two issues, the timing of AE and the slow follow-through by some regions, it was decided that in the current year AE would be introduced to the home groups during Phase One of the program. Each region would engage in the WHAT and WHY for their group prior to attending the summer intensive. This necessitated the training of some new home group leaders in the process of AE, so that they could carry out the Baseline phase before the intensive. When all the regions gathered at camp for Phase Two, they would develop the WHAT for the group as a whole.

This proved to work much better in 2011. The participants once again met in the large activity hall during the intensive to work on their common goals for F2F. The following goals were agreed upon, sometimes after long and protracted discussion. The first goal took over an hour to hammer out, as the differences between faith, belief, and religion were debated and the question of who is included or not in each category was discussed. The word "diversity" was initially part of this goal, but it was dropped because of the objections of the U.S. group, who felt the word held negative connotations.

- To expand our understanding of societies, cultures, faiths, religions, beliefs, and conflicts, and the impact these have on people.
- To use our understanding and experiences to make a difference through social action.
- To build relationships with individuals from different backgrounds.

The previous year, there were five group goals agreed upon. This year, participants arrived at three broader goals for the program as a whole. The same themes of understanding, conflict, action, and friendships are reflected in both years. The evaluation from participants this summer was that the AE process was valuable because it helped to define and articulate the goals for the program and because it provided a structure within which their activities took place. There was some frustration expressed with what was seen as "word-smithing" rather than substantive discussion on the differences between certain words and phrases. Overall, the process of AE has been accepted as integral to F2F and has become the new norm both for regions and for the program as a whole.

There are several challenges to using AE with the F2F program, though none of them is insurmountable. The success and use of AE is dependent to a large extent on the sense of ownership and capacity of home group leaders. The difficulty that arises when this does not take place is evident in the previous narrative. Ideally, all the home group leaders would meet prior to the start of the F2F year, to experience the process of AE for themselves and to be trained to conduct AE with their home group. Since the leadership of F2F is scattered across four continents, this is a costly undertaking (though methods for web-based training are being explored). Another option would be for the director of F2F to travel to each region and, with the help of the local leader, conduct the Baseline phase of AE.

Another obvious challenge for AE is the diversity of F2F participants. Although those taking part must be able to speak English in order to be accepted, their proficiency varies widely. In their home group, language differences may not be much of an issue, but to really take part in the inter-group experience of AE a level of ease with English is needed. Cultural differences, in addition to language, challenge some participants. There are many young women who take leading roles in F2F and in AE, but there are others whose culture creates a reticence for females speaking in the company of males. The geographic dispersal of F2F participants within a region creates its own difficulties as home groups sometimes find it difficult to meet even bimonthly.

Despite the challenges in the first year of AE, the leadership of F2F is committed to the continued use of AE as a framework for creating goals and programming. Although it took more time and effort than anticipated in the first year, the process has helped programming be more focused and nurtured more intentionality on the part of participants. They know from the beginning what goals they are working towards and why they are a part of this program, and they are given the opportunity to reflect on their progress and re-assess their goals throughout their participation.

An unintentional byproduct of F2F adopting AE is the possibility of using AE with other initiatives at Auburn Seminary. The Auburn staff who worked with F2F saw great value in this process and have become strong advocates of its use elsewhere within the institution. AE has proven to be an effective process for goal setting within a group, as a tool that builds metrics for evaluation, and as a way to develop reflection and self-assessment.

References

Chavis, D. M., Florin, P., Rich, R., & Wandersman, A. (1987). *The block booster project*. New York: Ford Foundation.

Davis, M. H. (1996). *Empathy: A social psychological approach*. Boulder: Westview Press.

Ross, M. (1999). Action evaluation in the theory and practice of conflict resolution, George Mason University. http://www.gmu.edu/programs/icar/pcs/Ross81PCS.htm. Accessed 14 Feb 2012.

Schein, E. H. (1988). *Process consultation: Its role in organization development* (2nd ed.), Reading, MA: Addison Wesley.

Singleton, R., Straits, B., Straits, M., & McAllister, R. (1988). *Approaches to social research*. New York: Oxford University Press.

Applying Action Evaluation on a Large Scale: Cincinnati Police-Community Relations Collaborative – Successes, Failures and Lessons Learned

Jay Rothman

Introduction

In Spring 2011, the City of Cincinnati embarked upon a path toward a lofty goal: transforming negative relations between the police and aggrieved members of the community. Thirteen months later, the US Attorney General came to Cincinnati to participate in a signing ceremony and lauded the Cincinnati Police Community Collaborative agreement, as a "national model for fixing the problem, not the blame." Even the Cincinnati chief of police, initially very resistant to the collaborative process said, "the collaborative forged a blue-print around which we significantly reformed policing, policies and practices around use of force and enhanced our relationships with the community. It made the difference."[1]

To achieve a breakthrough in Cincinnati after many years of tense relations, more than 3,500 citizens from all races, faiths, socioeconomic groups, and all walks of life set a new agenda, cooperatively and in dialogue with the police, for lasting change by sharing their hopes and dreams for a brighter future in Cincinnati. Their goals, summarized as "problem solving partnership between police and community," led to a legally binding collaborative settlement forged by lawyers for the police, the community, the city of Cincinnati and the Department of Justice and ratified and monitored by a Federal Court Judge.

What has happened in Cincinnati in the decade following the riots there may serve as a model for other cities and communities who have found themselves enmeshed in deep social conflict. Hopefully, it can also provide guidance for avoiding such unrest. This story is fraught with highs and lows, with successes and failures. Yet, with each success or failure comes a lesson learned, and the lessons learned can serve as vehicles for growth and improvement as Action Evaluation is "scaled up" to transform conflicts in other cities and communities both at home and abroad.

From Haven to Hotbed

A place of refuge. A door to freedom and hope. A haven from the bonds of oppression. All these phrases once described what was also called the "Queen City" for its graciousness and welcome. As multitudes of African-American slaves traversed the underground railroad on their quest for freedom, this is what Cincinnati, Ohio symbolized to them. Women and children crouched in the willows along the Kentucky shore, waiting to cross the over the river from slavery to freedom, from despair to hope. Lanterns were lit in homes along the Cincinnati shore to serve as a nightly beacon. The light promised escape

[1] Personal communication, May 11, 2011.

J. Rothman (✉)
Program on Conflict Resolution and Negotiation,
Bar-Ilan University, Ramat Gan, Israel
e-mail: jrothman@ariagroup.com

J. Rothman (ed.), *From Identity-Based Conflict to Identity-Based Cooperation: The ARIA Approach in Theory and Practice*, Peace Psychology Book Series, DOI 10.1007/978-1-4614-3679-9_11, © Springer Science+Business Media New York 2012

and provided a glimmer of hope for those who had suffered for years at the hands of their oppressors.

Once a point of entry for thousands of slaves using the Underground Railroad, Cincinnati, like so many American cites, had become a place where African-American mothers worry for the well being of their children. They feel fear, distrust, and uncertainty. They worry about their sons becoming victims of violent crime. African American men and women, and other minorities, feel discriminated against in places where they work, drive, walk, shop, or eat. They fear being stopped, harassed, and physically harmed by the very people who are supposed to be protecting them – the police.

What happened to this quintessential Midwestern town on the river? What happened to its innocence and kindness? How did a city whose citizens once risked their own safety to harbor slaves and help them along in their journey to freedom change into a city felt by many of its citizens to be discriminatory, oppressive, and dangerous? Instead of being regarded as a place of freedom, tolerance and racial harmony, the city was thrust into the national and international spotlight as a hotbed of racial tension and strife. In April 2001, rioters took to the streets, hurling bottles and rocks through windows; knocking over street vendors' carts and mailboxes, looting neighborhood stores; shouting obscenities at city officials and police; threatening white motorists; even pulling some from their cars. When did this bastion of freedom and safety turn into a site of fear, violence and oppression?

Cincinnati's racial problems were not unlike those of many other urban American areas. However, they came into the spotlight during that week of the riots, sparked by the killing of an unarmed African American youth. However, both blacks and whites in the city agreed that these problems were not new; they had been brewing for decades. The tensions between the races manifest themselves in the symptoms of economic disparity, workplace discrimination, segregated communities, and actual or perceived racial profiling by police.

In March of 2001, a class-action lawsuit was proposed against the city of Cincinnati alleging years of disparate treatment of African-American citizens by the Cincinnati Police Department, dating back to 1967. The plaintiffs included the Cincinnati Black United Front, the Ohio Chapter of the American Civil Liberties Union, and Bomani Tyehimba – a Cincinnati businessman who said he was handcuffed, roughed up and held at gunpoint during a routine traffic stop. He filed a suit asserting he was unfairly targeted by the police. His case became a cornerstone for a proposed racial profiling lawsuit to overcome what was seen as the 'crime' of "Driving While Black." (See BBC film by that name, 2002.) He and the other plaintiffs claimed that, for more than 30 years, Cincinnati Police stopped, detained, searched and otherwise harassed motorists based on race. They said that the police are at the arm of the white man. Instead of being there for protection, they said that police were seeking them out, harassing them, hurting them, even killing them. Not only was their dignity demeaned, but many feared for their lives.

It was US Federal Court Judge Susan Dlott who decided to search for an alternative dispute resolution process to address this proposed racial profiling lawsuit. As a former domestic relations attorney, Judge Dlott felt that addressing the underlying social issues raised by the perception or reality of racial profiling might be better addressed first outside of her courtroom, though still within its scope. With experience in engaging deeply protracted inter-communal conflicts abroad and in the US, Judge Dlott asked the author to propose an alternative process to resolve the issues and foster social peace in the city. This is where Action Evaluation comes into the story of Cincinnati and its efforts to address a police community conflict many like others around the country and the world. It was to be Action Evaluation's biggest rollout, most trying test and its greatest example to date of how this conflict engagement and collaborative visioning process, could work to establish a shared agenda and positive impact upon public policy.

Background: History of the Cincinnati Police-Community Relations Collaborative

During a 1999 traffic stop, Bomani Tyehima asserted that two police officers had violated his civil rights during a traffic stop by handcuffing him and unjustifiably pointing a gun at his head. Then in November of 2000, an African-American man from Cincinnati was asphyxiated by the police after being arrested in the parking lot of a gas station. These events led to the Ohio's ACLU filing a proposed racial profiling lawsuit against the Cincinnati Police Department in 2001. The ACLU joined forces with the Cincinnati Black United Front (BUF) and Bomani Tyehima to file a class-action lawsuit against the Cincinnati Police Department, alleging more than 30 years of disparate treatment of African American citizens by the Police Department. The lawsuit's goal was to put the Cincinnati police under a court order or consent decree that would force changes in internal investigations and boost data collection on traffic stops and other contacts between police and the African American community.

The federal judge assigned this case, Judge Susan Dlott, did not believe traditional litigation was the answer to the problems of alleged racial profiling. In her view, litigation would only result in further polarizing the parties, and would not solve the underlying issues of social conflict between the police and community. Through Judge Dlott's efforts, all parties eventually agreed to set aside normal litigation efforts and instead pursue an alternative path of collaborative problem-solving and negotiation (see Rothman and Land 2004).

In April, 2001, I was retained as Special Master to the Court to help facilitate the parties along this new path. Along with colleagues from The ARIA Group, we began holding regular meetings with leaders from the three sides (police, city and community).[2] Our original proposal was

to launch an ARIA Conflict Engagement process, suggesting to the parties that without a common definition of a problem – in this case real or perceived racial profiling – it would be hard to imagine how to find a common solution (see Chap. 1). However, this idea was met with substantial resistance from the police leadership. They argued that if the focus were on problems, it would only result in a lot of finger pointing – at them! Moreover, the police (and city attorneys) were unwilling to get engaged in an effort to define a problem ("racial profiling") that they simply did not agree systematically existed within the department other than on rare occasions of bad behavior by a few "bad apples."

In response, to keep the parties together at the table, instead of focusing on problems, we suggested a broad-based visioning process in the form of an Action Evaluation process to be launched by focusing on goals for improving police-community relations (goals being the flip side of problems to resolve). In addition to helping avoid a costly and provocative court battle, the city and the police union (the FOP) found this acceptable because it seemed a constructive process in which members from all parties could work collaboratively to improve police-community relations. For the leadership of The Black United Front, it was promising largely due to the fact that it was to be conducted within a legal framework promising some form of judicial oversight during the process and implementation of its outcomes. The bottom line for all sides was the willingness of the other parties to pursue this collaboratively.

Early in the process we noted a vast difference, however, between acceptance (e.g., "The judge asked us to pursue an alternative and we are willing to do so") and enthusiasm (e.g., "This way makes sense and can work"). Our challenge as outside facilitators was how to motivate everyone equally to take ownership for the process and truly get engaged.

Six weeks after struggling to get traction in the process, on April 7, 2001, three days of civil unrest and rioting broke out in the streets of Cincinnati following the shooting death of Timothy Thomas – an unarmed 18 year-old

---

[2] The ARIA Group, Inc. is a conflict resolution organization based about 60 miles north of Cincinnati. The company's involvement was catalyzed and initially funded by New York-based Andrus Family Fund. The author is the president of ARIA.

black man wanted for misdemeanors and traffic violations. After days of protests and disruption, it became clear to all parties to what became known as the Cincinnati Collaborative that they had a process in place that could truly be both healing and proactive in nature. The Cincinnati community was in crisis, but the Collaborative process presented an opportunity for the community to pull out of the crisis and to make real progress. So began the year-long process that engaged thousands of citizens in Cincinnati in a truly innovative, inclusive and participatory problem-solving process paving the way for a landmark federal court agreement lauded by police experts around the country as a new model.

Utilizing a Broad-Based Participatory Process

The Action Evaluation process used in Cincinnati is defined by large stakeholder participation and contribution to goal-formation and action plans to shape the future. The Cincinnati Collaborative design enabled 3,500 citizens across eight different stakeholder groups to participate (African American citizens, white citizens, business/education/foundation leaders, youth, police and their families, religious and social service leaders, city employees and other minority groups). Community members were invited to share their goals about the future of police community relations through a survey which asked people to respond to the following questions through a website, hard copies or interviews:

- *What* are your goals for future police-community relations in Cincinnati?
- *Why* are those goals important to you? (what experiences, values, beliefs, and feelings influence your goals?), and
- *How* do you think your goals can best be achieved?

Citizens were then invited to participate in feedback sessions with other members of their stakeholder groups to listen to others' responses and to be heard. Participants selected representatives to craft a platform of goals for improving

---

Goals achieved through the collaborative process

1) Police officers and community members will become proactive partners in community problem solving.
2) Build relationships of respect, cooperation, and trust within and between police and communities
3) Improve education, oversight, monitoring, hiring practices, and accountability of the Cincinnati Police Department.
4) Ensure fair, equitable, and courteous treatment for all.
5) Create methods to establish the public's understanding of police polices and procedures and recognition of exceptional service in an effort to foster support for the police.

Fig. 11.1 Goals achieved through the collaborative process

police-community relations – this platform guided negotiators as they worked toward a settlement. The ultimate consensus goals that emerged from nine months of data gathering, dialogue and consensus building, became the cornerstone of the historic Collaborative Settlement Agreement and are shown in Fig. 11.1.

In addition to crafting a platform of goals, participants also had the opportunity within intragroup feedback sessions to dialogue with others and to share their "whys" in a small group setting. People's why stories captured concerns about fairness and respecting differences, needs for safety, and expressions of support for police, their difficult jobs and their being able to perform the duties effectively.

These why discussions were facilitated by four dozen professionals, coming from a diversity of professional backgrounds ranging from psychology and social work to education, mediation and law, who volunteered in this important healing process. They had the desire to utilize their expertise and to take a position of leadership in helping to restore hope within their city. They, too, had a vision of mending the rifts that plagued their community. The following examples summarize the types of "whys" that emerged from the process:

- "I would really like to see people respect each other's values and beliefs, even when they are different. I want all cultures to be treated with respect and fairness…in order for us and our children to feel safe, everyone must be treated fairly, it is the only way."
- "For once in my life I'd like to feel safe…I fear for safety, especially for young people."
- "The media has painted this horrible picture of us police...They're just Monday morning quarterbacks. I'm out there to protect them. I hugged a kid the other day and his mother went off on me. They're teaching their kids to hate us. 'See if you're bad he's going to take you away…' I was proud to wear my uniform two years ago; that has shifted."

The primary role of the volunteers was to facilitate small group discussions during each stakeholding group's feedback session. During small group discussions, facilitators led *why* discussions. These *why* discussions uncovered the hurts and the frustrations that led people to care so much about their goals for a better future in Cincinnati. Their goal was to make sure that everyone in the group had an opportunity to be heard and to express his or her thoughts about why they cared so much about police-community relations in Cincinnati. Each of the volunteers were trained in the ARIA Action Evaluation process, and after the first meeting, the enthusiasm that filled this group was evident. As one facilitator said:

> …I have so much hope that we and all the people we link with and all the projects we connect with can be a catalyst for the transformation of Cincinnati and can also continue the learning that will lead to healing. There is a path, there is a process that will work….

There was a real sense of powerful encounter in the "why" discussions (see Chap. 2). They enabled hundreds of citizens of Cincinnati to experience resonance with one another – to find commonalities between their own and others' fears, hurts, hopes and dreams. This outlet for being heard was what was critical to so many; up until that point, many felt that they were not being listened to and their concerns were not being heard. As stated by a young African-American woman, "When we felt pain, no one from the city came to listen to us. We needed someone to comfort and listen to us." Now people were listening.

Success in Cincinnati

In my analysis, there were five features of the collaborative process that led to its overall success. These include (1) large scale participation in the collaborative (2) the constructive role of the media (3) the collaborative, consensus and court-based process used (4) the use of narratives and dialogue and (5) the institutionalization of the community input and aspirations by the court.

Participation

In her Federal Court Order establishing the collaborative process, Judge Dlott stated its purpose:

> The proposed amended complaint alleges social conflict of great public interest to the community. To the extent possible, the collaborative will include an opportunity to receive the viewpoints of all persons in the Cincinnati community regarding their goals for police-community relations. The participants will state their goals for police-community relations, why these goals are important, and how they would achieve these goals…The collaborative will include an opportunity for dialogue about these responses in structured group sessions… It is anticipated that the openness of this collaborative process and the combination of expert and broad-based community input will provide an opportunity for the parties and the court to create a national and international model for other communities.[3]

Now formally launched and officially legitimized, though with strong and significant opposition (e.g. City Council approved the process and some funding for it in a contentious 5–4 vote), the

---

[3]See http://www.socsci.uci.du/~pgarb/istudies/applied/presentations/site/agreement.htm.

next task for the Collaborative was to gain legitimacy through wide-scale public participation.
As its first act, an Advisory Group which was
established out of the representatives of the parties to the now set-aside proposed lawsuit, determined to invite participation from all citizens of
the city in the goal setting/visioning process.
Based on previous studies of tensions in police-
community relations, the Advisory Group organized the population into eight stakeholding
groups. It then invited, with considerable help
from the news media, everyone who lived or
worked in the city, or was closely associated with
the city (e.g. those in the suburbs), to answer a
questionnaire and participate in feedback groups.
Thirty-five hundred people responded and more
than 700 of those respondents engaged in a total
of nearly 3,000 hours of follow-up dialogue and
agenda-setting.

The views of these participants were summarized in a series of goals (first within each
stakeholder group and then across them).[4] In
addition to establishing principles, the stakeholders also articulated thousands of specific
implementation ideas.

Media

Many conflict resolution professionals will attest
to the fact that media is regularly on the other
side of peacemaking. That is, papers are sold and
the public responds, so the story goes, to conflict.
Good news, news about cooperation, is boring.
However, media coverage of the Collaborative
was almost universally positive and constructive.
Right from the start of the process, with the aid of
a media consultant, the collaborative garnered
tremendous media attention and support, both
from within Cincinnati and beyond. Hundreds of
stories were told in print and radio about the ideals of the collaborative. A campaign was launched
"to get out the voice" about a better future in
police-community relations and the public was

invited through a number of front page stories
and featured news pieces to participate in the
online survey.

One reporter from the Cincinnati Enquirer
was assigned to follow the collaborative and
worked closely with staff to tell the story and be
constructively. The survey data was explicitly
public by order of the court (though names and
identifiers were confidential and protected by the
court). Journalist Kristina Goetz of the Enquirer
asked to see the data regularly and write about it
immediately before dialogue sessions were held
and then afterwards. This served the public and
our process by ensuring timely and full
information.

National Public Radio produced a number of
pieces about the Collaborative and its constructive efforts; the BBC produced a film that also
highlighted strengths of the Collaborative while
also hitting hard about issues of racial profiling in
the city. New York Times writer Francis X. Clines
wrote a very laudatory piece about the
Collaborative that appeared on the front page of
the Sunday paper National News section.[5]

Collaborative, Consensus and Court-Based Process

Judge Dlott had been a domestic relations attorney in the past. She explained that this professional experience made her become wary of
using the court room to address deep interpersonal and social conflicts. The court, she said,
can deal well with issues of guilt, innocence and
remuneration, but not grievances. Determining a
winner and loser in issues of racial profiling
could well just add fuel to the fire (Rothman and
Land 2004).

Al Gerhardstein, a prominent Cincinnati Civil
Rights attorney, was on the team representing
the Plaintiffs (later "the class"), in the proposed
racial profiling case. Known as a gladiator among
gladiators and having sued the police and the
city numerous times, Gerhardstein aspired to a

[4]For a full overview of the process see http://www.socsci.
uci.edu/~pgarb/istudies/applied/presentations/site/index.
html.)

[5]See http://www.ariagroup.com/?page_id=7.

new future, through a path strewn with the legacy of mistrust that characterized police and African American Community relations. As Gerhardstein said in the heady days immediately following the signing of the collaborative agreement in April 2002:

> I like to sue people. That's what I do. I like to cross examine people. I like to go into the court room. It's all very controlled. The lawyer gets to orchestrate it. I put forward the evidence found that I think is most important. It's simple compared to what we are doing here. Because we are not just trying to win. We are really trying to listen, to figure out what everybody's interests are. We are trying to serve those interests while meeting the highest goal which is a safe community where people trust each other. That's hard stuff, not easy to get at.[6]

When the Collaborative Agreement was reached, it was framed by a unique Federal Court document. The overall agreement described in the legal document contains a description of problem oriented policing which frames the overall philosophy and practices at its core. It begins with a "value statement" consistent with Judge Dlott's view about social problems and how to address them:

> Central to a problem solving orientation is that problems are dilemmas to be engaged and learned from and that blame is an obstacle to progress. The overall collaborative effort suggests an alternative to blame: that different groups within the community with different experiences and perspectives share much more in common than not, and can work together on common goals and solve problems together.[7]

In a city known for contentious politics and social divides, a clear success of the Collaborative was the process by which thousands of people participated in a survey about positive visions for the future, and twenty percent of respondents chose to engage in deep deliberation with one another to reach consensus on those visions.

Following small group discussions about Why people cared deeply about their goals, eight representatives were chosen by each stake holder group, totaling around 60, to reach agreement on a platform of goals/visions for the future of police community relations (see Fig. 11.1 above). These five goals and the single text document that was constructed out of them, along with best practices of policing in the U.S. (see Eck and Rothman 2006), formed the basis of the negotiation process that led to what Judge Dlott called "The best policing agreement in America" (Rothman 2006).

Narratives: Why I Care

One of the guiding principles of the collaborative was that even though identity or racial conflicts from the past were not the focus of the process, they were its context. Thus, the process would need to give voice to people's grievances as well as their aspirations. The way it did this was through a story-based process referred to as "The Power of Why" (see Chap 2 and Friedman et. al. 2006). Respondents to the survey about goals for the future of police community relations in Cincinnati were asked to describe What their goals were, Why they cared deeply about those goals, and How those goals could best be accomplished. Here's an example of one person's Why responses:

> ...until we can look at someone who is very different from ourselves and still respect them as a human being with different perspectives and experiences that influence the choices and options open to him/her, we continue to judge each other on the assumptions of economic and racial biases. At heart, all people care about the same basic values of love and work. Unfortunately, some have found doors slammed in their faces while others have had them opened because of where they were born, not what they know. We have to find a way to respect and welcome our differences and cherish our diversity. We have much to learn from each other.

In all, some 3,500 people shared one to three such Why responses via the internet, hard copy surveys or in person interviews. Almost eight

---

[6]See BBC Film, Driving While Black, Product Type: Video; ISBN-13: 9780749232634; Length: 30 min; Publication Date: 2001; Publisher: The Open University/*BBC*.

[7]See http://www.socsci.uci.edu/~pgarb/istudies/applied/presentations/site/agreement.htm.

hundred people then chose to participate in four-hour feedback sessions in which they reached consensus within their own identity group.[8] These participants were given approximately 10 minutes each to share fuller stories based on their written Why responses in. These stories were also recorded. Here's part of another one:

> …Because growing up a white male in affluent settings, I have seen what a difference [understanding] has made in my own attitudes towards African Americans. I have seen especially my own level of fear diminish. If white officers go into black neighborhoods with exaggerated levels of fear, or if they grow to depend too much on use of force to feel safe, we will continue to experience the problems we currently have. I have also learned to be much more discerning. I used to see all - well, many - young African American males, especially those who dressed like gangsters or had dreadlocks, etc. as dangerous and aggressive. Working within the African American community I have increased my ability to recognize the good kids…

The amount of resonance that was generated, and the sense of voice that was nurtured, were clear successes in this project. People felt heard. Connections were made. The platform built by this dialogue also helped, undoubtedly, lead to the successful agreements in every group about high-level principles of practice. That is, each of the eight groups-working with the data we fed back to them in the form of shared ideals and goals synthesized from the data they and their colleagues had shared- reached consensus on a platform of five or six goals that they put forward as their group's vision for the future.

At the conclusion of negotiation process, a number of dialogue group participants were

brought to a focus group to share their reflections on the process and their experience. They received a 40-page text of the Collaborative Agreement reached during negotiations and ratified by the Federal Court. When asked their impression of it, one woman flipped it open to a random page, dramatically put her finger on a random word and proclaimed: "I wrote that!" She of course was speaking symbolically, but her point was poignant. Participants felt ownership.

Even if the sense of ownership and participation were not that long-lived, as will be discussed below, they were at one point a very powerful and visceral experience for many.

Institutionally Mandated and Maintained

While it is fair to say that the core and deep power of the collaborative process lay in people's engagement of their own and each other's Whys, it was a political process designed to lead to constructive and lasting social and structural change in the arena of police-community relations. Two major institutions were fostered out of the collaborative that have made significant contributions to this end. Of the five goals put forward by the stakeholders, the first was the most influential, particularly as it so well aligned with best practices in policing today – "Problem-Oriented Policing." That is the goal of "Police Officers and Community Members Will Become Proactive Partners in Community Problem Solving." Focusing on this goal the collaborative agreement was reached and a five-year plan, which concluded in April 2007, was drawn up along with a several million dollar budget for implementation and monitoring.

The second and perhaps even more important institutionalization of the collaborative was the Community-Police Partnering Center which was established soon after the Collaborative Agreement was reached. In fact, it was central to the agreement itself. Its mission was defined as:

> Partnering with communities and the Cincinnati Police Department, the Community Police Partnering Center will develop and put in place

---

[8]One of the counter-intuitive aspects of the process of building broad intergroup consensus using the Action Evaluation process is that all participants must choose a single stakeholding group, or identity group, to respond from. This can cause dilemmas for people who have many identity aspects that are salient to the issue. For example, a 24 year-old African American Police Officer must choose only one of those three identifiers from which to respond (African American, Police, Youth). Nonetheless, we find this choice and focus is constructive and ultimately when the different groups are brought together to reach overarching consensus forges a powerful, pluralistic, dynamic that moves the process forward.

effective strategies to reduce crime and disorder while facilitating positive interaction and increased trust between the police and neighborhoods.[9]

Lessons Learned

In this section, I will describe what I now see as some key lessons learned and what could have worked better. The first and, to me, the most disappointing element of the project was the lack of ongoing participation by those 3,500 who set the agenda. The second is the way the collaborative process was quickly transformed into an adversarial negotiation once it returned to the courthouse. The third was how the racial conflicts were never actively raised or engaged. The fourth was the lack of buy-in from top leadership and grass-roots activists.

One: Lack of Ongoing Participation

The Cincinnati Police-Community Relations Collaborative brought 3,500 individual voices to the "table" to set an agenda which successfully laid down a foundation upon which the Collaborative Agreement was reached and ratified by the Federal Court. However, this success was, in some ways, over-shadowed by the fact that once the court process and legal negotiation were launched, nine months after the collaborative was initiated and visions established, the people and their voices were sidelined. Instead of moving from new ideals – like improving problem solving relationships between police and community – into sustained efforts to implement these ideals, with the participation of those who stated them, they were "handed-off" as it were to the negotiators.

A basic and well-supported proposition underlying Action Evaluation is the idea that people will be more committed to goals that they articulate and establish themselves. Dubbed the participation hypothesis by Verba (1961), there is a great deal of evidence for the proposition that active

involvement in a process builds commitment. The participation hypothesis suggests initial commitment can first be built by eliciting goals from participants and that additional commitment occurs when participants are asked to join together to reflect upon project goals. One reason is because people become invested psychologically when they spend time on an activity. Another is that participation builds a new social identity that is sustained, at least in part, by working toward common goals. Lederach's (1995, 1997) concept of elicitive conflict resolution has participants define a situation and design their own contextually relevant action program; it clearly builds on the participation hypothesis' emphasis on participants' motivations and commitments.

Action Evaluation's impact, and the participation mechanism, also finds support in the Hawthorn effect; that is, the fact that participants at all levels are asked questions and involved in the process of program design builds support for the program and increases commitment to its goals. While some view this effect as an example of the problems of doing field research, the action researcher sees this finding as an opportunity to direct an outcome in a favorable direction (Argyris et al. 1985). From this point of view, it is not the specific goals which participants identify which becomes crucial in the process as much as the involvement in the process that increases their engagement and their desire to achieve successful outcomes.

One possible reason for this loss of community participation, was that as this project was initiated as a court process, when it returned to the court room, those around the negotiation table were, of necessity, limited in number and focus. In fairly stark contrast to the participatory and collaborative goal setting process, in the court the lawyers reverted to their gladiator roles, seeking to negotiate the most for their respective clients and give up the least.

Whereas in community development types of initiatives goals are regularly translated into plans and actions, and so initially this was the intention for this effort, in this legal process only the public's high-level goals were translated into a legally binding agreement known at the

[9]See http://cagisperm.hamilton-co.org/cpop/.

Collaborative Agreement. This agreement did not articulate any particular path for community involvement that might have built on the literally thousands of action ideas generated from the input – What, Why and How goals – of 3,500 citizens. Instead, and quite positively, several institutions were named and initiated in the agreement: The Friends of the Collaborative and The Community-Police Partnering Center. These were outstanding efforts to build both involvement, and accountability for change among the public. However, neither institution maintained any systematic effort to reach back to the original "framers" of the agreement. This was a significant oversight.

While there were strengths in having an external group, The ARIA Group, facilitate this process, another possible reason for the loss of participation was that when the collaborative was concluded and ARIA completed its assignment to the Court (essentially to organize and run the public collaborative process), there was no real institutional memory or internal ownership of the process. Thus, a major strength of the Collaborative- that it was framed and energized by 3,500 citizens- was all but lost.

When the Community-Police Partnering Center was established, with private funds, to promote the ideals of the collaborative, for better and for worse they essentially started over in their outreach efforts to encourage community participation. By the time the Center sought the names and contact information of the original 3,500 participants, and with the help of the ARIA Group conducted an outreach effort to them, less than a two percent response rate was achieved. This dismal figure was the result, we believe, of the fact that 5 years had passed since the participants shared and reached consensus on their ideals and were essentially at the mercy of the media which had not been much of an advocate of the process since after the early days. Among other things, more than half the email addresses of the 3,500 respondents in the database were inactive. Moreover, the sense of participation and ownership that in some ways was so vital during the collaborative itself was all but extinguished

five years later. In informal conversations with some of the facilitators of the process, the author learned of a great deal of frustration with the outcomes and impatience with continued animosity and antagonism between police and community.

Two: Adversarial Negotiations

Despite the fact that a single-text process was used to narrow gaps between the parties before formal negotiations were launched, and despite the fact that the draft was based on a combination of the goals reached through the participation process and rigorous social scientific research into best policing practices, once negotiations were launched in the Federal Courthouse, in University meeting rooms, even in the Judge's living room, an old attitude of "win, don't lose" prevailed. Each negotiator seemed to revert from being joint members of the collaborative advisory committee[10] to being strict advocates for their respective "clients."

The collaborative process was, for better and worse, built on what is known in diplomatic circles as "constructive ambiguity." That is, when sides cannot agree on the same basis for moving forward, they are allowed to maintain separate mental models about what they are doing and why. An example from the Israeli-Palestinian context might be helpful to illustrate. Immediately following the Oslo Accords establishing a commitment to peace negotiations, the Israeli side stuck to its interpretation that the purpose of this process was to conclude the conflict. The Palestinians on the other hand were equally clear that the purpose of the process was to establish a Palestinian state including East Jerusalem and the Right of Return of refugees. Both of these outcomes were non-starters for the other side.

So in Cincinnati, when as Special Master I invited the parties to the proposed lawsuit on

---

[10] The ideal of an advisory group of collaborative leaders in itself never fully coalesced as hoped – "remember," warned the judge when I complained of continued adversarial attitudes, "they are still gladiators."

racial profiling to consider an alternative path, the City agreed as they believed it would keep them out of court and away from an imposed court order to change: a Consent Decree. On the other hand, some of the key actors in the process, notably the Black United Front and the ACLU were very explicit from the start that the process should end up back in court in order to have the weight and sanction of the court to motivate and, as necessary, enforce implementation of negotiated agreements. As Damon Lynch said in an interview with BBC, "If it were just a soft shoe mediation process, I wouldn't be at the table. If we were just mediating and collaborating and somehow magically we were going to trust each other, I wouldn't be at the table. I like the idea that we will eventually build relationships out of this. Relationship building is key eventually in the long-term. But what keeps me at the table is that there is a Federal Judge, a federal court order that will come out of this".[11]

This "constructive ambiguity," as in the Israeli-Palestinian example, may have been partially responsible for the fact that progress was made at all. It was, however, also partly responsible for continued mistrust and bad blood that re-emerged with a kind of pent-up vigor back in the normal adversarial court setting.

Three: Racial Conflicts Never Addressed

In April 2001 when I was retained by the court to help mediate and guide the parties along this new path, it was based on previous work in community development and experience in addressing "identity-based conflict" in both international and domestic settings (Rothman 1997, 2006). My experience overlapped well with the Judge's view that the "social conflicts" at the root of the controversies over perceived or actual racial profiling needed a broader and deeper process than could be afforded by a win/lose court battle. I began holding regular meetings with leaders from the three sides – The Police Union (FOP),

city and police administration, and the plaintiffs to the suit (the Black United front along with the ACLU). I first proposed a problem-definition process, suggesting to the parties that without a common definition of the problem of racial profiling, they would have difficulties finding a common solution. However, as noted previously, the police leadership strongly resisted this approach.

In response to these concerns, I suggested that the parties undertake a broad-based visioning process focused on improving police-community relations. This was accepted. However, I was immediately concerned about this general acceptance. Not only was a single process being accepted for significantly different and even opposing reasons, but when racial or identity conflicts are strongly present, as they were in this situation, a collaborative, future-oriented process is normally premature (see distinction between identity-based conflict engagement and identity-based cooperation as discussed in the preface and Chap. 1). Nonetheless, I saw my role as being largely responsive and thus when some enthusiasm was generated for an alternative framing – not on racial profiling from the past but improving police-community relations in the future –I threw myself into this purpose.[12]

A few weeks after initial discussions of a collaborative process, when Timothy Thomas was shot, Cincinnati became engulfed in what has been variously described as "riots" "civil unrest" and "rebellion." Despite this, the Cincinnati Black United Front, The American Civil Liberties Union, the Cincinnati City and Police Administration, and the Cincinnati Fraternal Order of Police continued to meet as the Advisory Group to Rothman. The formal establishment of the Collaborative was catalyzed when a New York-based foundation, the Andrus Family Fund, challenged the City to buy in to the court-sponsored exploration of this alternative dispute resolution

---

[11] From BBC Film, "Driving While Black," 2001.

[12] In the conclusion, "lessons learned" I will revisit these choices and suggest how I would make them differently, and do now.

process, by matching its proffered grant of $100,000 and signing on as a formal sponsor and member of the collaborative along with the others named above. At a rancorous City Council meeting on May 2, 2001 the Collaborative, and the city's financial and moral contribution to it, was narrowly approved by a five to four vote, with several amendments regarding transparency of the process.

Thus, the Collaborative moved ahead with a future focus and the "presenting issues" of racial profiling, the legacy of social exclusion of minorities in Cincinnati's history, as well as the more positive past of being the place where river-crossing slaves were freed, were outside the focus and purposes of this process. Had it been anything else, it is likely that the direct route to the court – in a class action suit by the Black United Front against the City of Cincinnati – would have resulted instead.

Four: Lack of Total Buy-In by Leadership and Activists

As noted, the collaborative was agreed to by the Cincinnati City Council on a closely divided vote of 5 to 4. This happened even after the Archbishop of the Cincinnati Archdiocese came to the council meeting where the vote was being taken, and spoke in very strong terms for the need for the Collaborative. In short, the resistance, although also quite politicized due to upcoming elections, was one of political ideology that could be characterized as the difference between notions of representative and participatory democracy. The Collaborative represented the latter (Fung 2006). The resistance from some on City Council represented the former. This divide was never bridged. In fact, it grew worse as instead of gaining participation from political leaders in the process, the process was continually in a push-pull process with that leadership.

This tense relationship was due not only to the original misgivings of a significant portion of Council and the constituents represented by that

contingent, but also due to the fact that the other most significant stakeholder, the Black United Front (BUF), had an ambivalent relationship to the Collaborative as well. This ambivalence was then mutually reinforcing between the BUF and the City. The National Black United Front, of which Cincinnati BUF was then a chapter, was organized in 1980 to promote "Black liberation" and specifically target what they viewed as racial injustices in the US criminal justice system. When the Cincinnati Black United Front filed a proposed racial profiling lawsuit, this confrontation approach was quite consistent with policies of the national movement. Joining city and police leadership in a collaborative process was not. In fact, the leader of the Cincinnati BUF, a prominent minister and community activist Damon Lynch was often caught between his roles as radical activist and city leader. Many times in the life of the Collaborative, questions were raised by City leaders asking how it could be cooperating with an organization that was simultaneously organizing an economic boycott against the city. Of the more than a dozen times when the Collaborative nearly collapsed, the most intense was when a letter accusing the police of "rape and murder" was attributed to Lynch. The letter was made public, somewhat mysteriously, just as negotiations were to begin. Although Lynch remained in a leadership role in the Collaborative, the BUF's actions and approach made others active in the Collaborative wonder about the uneasy partnership and called into question the validity of the whole process.[13] Six months later, on the establishment of the Community-Police Partnering Center (to be discussed below), Lynch and the Cincinnati Black United Front resigned from the Collaborative and were replaced by The NAACP as class representatives when police, city and private leadership laid down an Us-or-Them ultimatum.

---

[13] For more information about this complex dynamic see http://www.enquirer.com/editions/2001/12/04/loc_mayor_boots_rev.html.

Conclusions: Lessons Learned

In this final section I share some professional lessons learned that I have already taken to heart in my own work. The first is the lesson to build capacity instead of intervene in communal conflicts. The second, as alluded to above, is when identity-conflicts are strongly at stake to give them their due before, and during, any future oriented, collaborative process is conducted.

From Parachute Peacemaking to Capacity Building

Perhaps the most important lesson that I have taken from this entire process has been to ensure that such an initiative is wholly owned by local stakeholders. This insight, borne largely from the failure of continued participation, has changed our way of working, in a way that I believe is quite consistent with general changes in the conflict resolution world. In the 1980s and 1990s when the field was very new, a kind of "parachute" approach prevailed in which conflict resolution experts would jump in to the middle of a conflict and provide intervention and some amount of training but rarely much capacity building. The "experts" would then leave, hoping that much of their efforts would pay off and remain in their wake. Increasingly practitioners, funders, and recipients grew wary of this approach and more sustained efforts were launched. However, only fairly recently is the notion of an "elicitive approach" including capacity building for local ownership, adaptation and expertise instead of external expertise, beginning to be emphasized (see Lederach 1995). So too, in our work, we now attempt to work with local leaders and organizations to train, build capacity and help them adapt our approaches and make them their own. Then we move behind the scenes and provide support and coaching as much as needed but as little as possible.

Identity Conflict: First Things First

There is a good chance that had we not shifted from recommending conflict engagement to future-focused visioning, the Collaborative would not have gotten off the ground. Nonetheless, in hindsight I would have been, and am now, much more insistent that conflict framing and engagement must precede visioning when identity conflicts prevail. An example was in my relatively failed attempt to build a truly collaborative group out of the advisory committee. In the future, I would ensure that even if the larger effort itself determined to sidestep the larger social issues (like patterns of racism within Cincinnati itself), those running the collaborative would themselves take on and address, or at least engage, such underlying issues.

While I was advised by many that this was a lost cause – gladiators will be gladiators – I think it depends on what my definition of success would be. For example, if I sought to build deep understanding and resolve long-standing ideological and interpersonal differences, failure would have been relatively assured. However, had I used some of court-provided power and insisted that the advisory group make some of their differences explicit and discussable, I believe that some "working trust" could have been generated and more resilience in the group established. Issues we avoided, in fear that the delicate edifice we were building would tumble down, in fact hit us in the back of the head over and again. The rancor that resulted from the negotiations led from handshake to arm-wrestle as soon as the ink dried on the agreement. However, I don't want this to take away from the many and impressive gains that were made. Nevertheless, they took too long (nearly a decade) and still left much unfinished (see report 10 years later, Osborne 2011).

In short, as an identity-based conflict rooted in issues of race relations, exclusion, perceptions, fear, misunderstanding, history and so forth, it was essential that both the advisory group itself, and, to some degree, the process we launched, engage these issues and make them discussable. The Advisory Group needed to model to the city that it could make its difficult issues explicit and engage in dialogue about them, including its differences about the history and current face of racism, and still work together for a common future. In short, trust needed to be more explicitly built and demonstrated. I relied on a common, but somewhat outmoded, approach to intergroup conflict described as the "contact hypothesis:" allow trust to emerge as an outcome of cooperation to achieve superordinate goals (see Amir 1998; Sherif 1966). For the most part, I still believe in that approach as necessary, but insufficient. Avoiding differences, smoothing over antagonism and focusing wholly on the future and setting grievances of the past on the side, was unrealistic and self-limiting.

While our focus on the future, and for the most part on a no-fault approach to the past, was probably essential to build an inclusive collaborative, we could have partnered more successfully with local initiatives that were engaged in surfacing these deeper issues, as well as articulating that this effort could only be seen as part of the solution since it was only dealing with part of the problem.

Identity-based conflicts are often rooted in a history of social exclusion of social groups, usually racial and ethnic minorities, that generate a bitter legacy of resentment, conflict and often violence. While a new future must be forged to remake that legacy into a more inclusive, collaborative and problem solving set of relationships marked by mutual respect, it can't be done by trying to "wall off" that past and calling for a new future based on some kind of collective amnesia of historical wrongs and grievances. On the other hand, giving vent to such grievances in ways that make people feel guilty, resistant to change and resentful is no more constructive to building a new future. Instead, a third way is to provide ample time and opportunity to surface and engage such issues to build the social and psychological space for people to think together about a new future that will not repeat the mistakes of the past.

Conclusion

In the Cincinnati case, giving the visioning work over to the citizens, while the lawyers for the most part bided their time until they would cross swords in the court room, missed opportunities to do what conflict resolution does best: create carefully structured opportunities for differences in interpretations, experience, perception and analysis to be safely surfaced and engaged in ways that a listening atmosphere is generated and working trust is fostered. This would have stood the collaborative in good stead.

Although the specific events that unfolded in Cincinnati are unique, the general overarching issues of social conflict faced by the city are not. Many cities throughout the US have been struggling with issues of police-community relations and racial tensions for years. Yet, what *was* unique about Cincinnati was the process used to address the conflict. The innovative and powerful partnership that was forged between law, politics and society through the Collaborative set into motion a process of transformation for Cincinnati and all of its citizens.

Although the process itself was imperfect – filled with its share of successes and failures, conflicts and contradictions – it is a process that can serve as a national model for helping to heal rifts and foster cooperation between groups who are entrenched in these types of conflicts, as well as other similarly complex conflicts, domestic and abroad. The truly participatory, bottom-up and consensus-building process that was rooted in dialogue, goal-setting and problem-solving enabled the citizens of Cincinnati to set a powerful agenda and to own it. Not only did the Collaborative process provide a venue for healing by allowing citizens of all backgrounds to share what was on their hearts, but through the mingling of hopes and visions of Cincinnati citizens and officials, it truly helped to set Cincinnati on a path of positive change.

References

Amir, Y. (1998). Contact hypothesis in ethnic relations. In E. Weiner (Ed.), *The handbook of interethnic coexistence* (pp. 162–181). New York: Continuum.

Argyris, C. Putnam, R., & Smith, D. (1985). Action science: Concepts, methods, and skills for research and intervention. San Francisco: Jossey-Bass.

Eck, J., & Rothman, J. (2006). Police community conflict and crime prevention in Cincinnati, Ohio: The collaborative agreement. In J. Bailey (Ed.), *Public security and police reform in the Americas*. Pittsburgh: University of Pittsburgh Press.

Friedman, V., Rothman, J., & Withers, W. (2006). The power of "why": Engaging the goal paradox in program evaluation. *American Journal of Evaluation, 27*(2), 1–18.

Fung, A. (2006). *Empowered participation: Reinventing urban democracy*. Princeton: Princeton University Press.

Lederach, J. (1995). *Preparing for peace: Conflict transformation across cultures*. Syracuse: Syracuse University Press.

Lederach, J. (1997). *Building peace: Sustainable reconciliation in divided societies*. Washington, DC: USIP Press.

Osborne, K. (2011). Reflections on riots & race. A decade later, differing views persist on causes, aftermath. http://www.citybeat.com/cincinnati/article-23047-reflections_on_riots.html. Accessed 6 Apr 2011.

Rothman, J. (1997). Action Evaluation and Conflict Resolution Training: Theory, Method and Case Study. *International Negotiation, 2*, 451–470.

Rothman, J. (2006). Identity and conflict: Collaboratively addressing police-community conflict in Cincinnati, Ohio. *Ohio State Journal on Dispute Resolution, 22*(1), 105–132.

Rothman, J., & Land, R. (2004). Cincinnati police-community relations collaborative. *Criminal Justice, 18*(4), 35–42. Winter.

Sherif, M. (1966). *In common predicament*. Boston: Houghton Miflin Books.

Verba, S. (1961). *Small groups and political behavior*. Princeton: Princeton University Press.

Index

J. Rothman (ed.), *From Identity-Based Conflict to Identity-Based Cooperation: The ARIA Approach in Theory and Practice*, Peace Psychology Book Series, DOI 10.1007/978-1-4614-3679-9,
© Springer Science+Business Media New York 2012

CPSIA information can be obtained
at www.ICGtesting.com
Printed in the USA
LVHW05s2009110818
586694LV00005B/38/P